the BIG BOOK of BLUEGRASS

the BIG BOOK of
BLUEGRASS

Edited by Marilyn Kochman
Foreword by Earl Scruggs

Quill / A Frets Book
New York 1984

GPI Books

Art Director
Dominic Milano

Art Associate
Christina Holt

Graphic Assistant
Mark Medalie

Darkroom
Cheryl Matthews, Paul Haggard

Typesetting
Leslie K. Bartz, Director
 Birgit Byrd, Ellayn M. Evans,
 Frank Fletcher, Pat Gates

Proofreading
Jake Hunter, Jayne Ash, Sandy Rothman

Editor-In-Chief: *Frets* **Magazine**
Roger H. Siminoff

Editor: *Frets* **Magazine**
Jim Hatlo

President/Publisher: GPI Publications
Jim Crockett

Associate Publisher: GPI Publications
Don Menn

Director: GPI Books
Alan Rinzler

Special thanks to Lachlan Throndson for her
expert assistance throughout the development
and production of this book.

Library of Congress Catalog Card Number:
83-60068

ISBN: 0-688-02940-X
ISBN: 0-688-02942-6(pbk)

Printed in the United States of America

2 3 4 5 6 7 8 9 10

CONTENTS

FOREWORD

WHEN I WAS A BOY, bluegrass music —as we know it now — didn't exist. Growing up in North Carolina, all I heard was mostly a lot of country music. It wasn't until after Lester Flatt and I got on WSM Radio in 1953, and later, on the *Grand Ole Opry* in 1955, that our music was able to be brought to the mass audiences. So, the term "bluegrass" wasn't applied to our music until the late 1950s. Actually, I don't think it was until the *Beverly Hillbillies* came along in 1962 — with Lester and I doing the music — that bluegrass music became truly "popular" worldwide. In the late 1950s and early 1960s, rock and roll was becoming so popular that it was questionable as to whether bluegrass would make it or not.

As musicians, so much of what we did was trial and error because we had nothing to follow. So many pickers have asked me, "How could you learn to pick like that with nothing to listen to?" Well, we were just shaping the music style as we went along. Over the years, it took a lot of truly great musicians to develop bluegrass music to where it is accepted and enjoyed today in every corner of the world.

So, when I sit and think back of those experiences, it makes me smile. If you could put yourself back to when I started picking and try to figure out how the banjo, mandolin, acoustic guitar, upright bass, fiddle, and dobro could get along musically, you'd know just what I mean!

My friends and fans always give me the credit for making the 5-string banjo what it is today, but I have to give a lot of credit to the musicians who are taking it further. And the same can be said for the artists who are working on mandolin, dobro, fiddle, bass, and guitar! It is comforting to know the evolution process of our music is still going on.

As we move into the future and find so many new artists, I think it is important that we record what is happening — to make sure that their great work is remembered. And that's why I am pleased to have been asked to take part in this book, *The Big Book of Bluegrass*.

— *Earl Scruggs*

INTRODUCTION

BLUEGRASS IS A WAY of life as much as a kind of music. Its devotees are crazed: They can't get enough of it. Call it ardor, call it mania, call it zeal. Bluegrassitis is easy to catch, and once you've got it, the obsession remains for the rest of your life.

What exactly *is* this music that captivates its fans and practitioners? Strictly speaking, bluegrass is a type of acoustic country music that has evolved from the string bands of the 1920s and 1930s. Fashioned after its founding model, Bill Monroe and his Blue Grass Boys, bluegrass relies on five main instruments: mandolin fiddle, banjo, guitar, and upright bass. Some bands also use the dobro, a steel-string guitar equipped with a metal vibrating disc for acoustic amplification and played with a metal bar in the left hand. Bluegrass is a music whose singing has that "high, lonesome sound." It also has been described as "folk music in overdrive."

Bluegrass is a highly structured music. Each instrument has a specific role, though that role can vary from tune to tune and from band to band. Usually the lead — the central melodic theme — is passed from singer to instrument to singer and back again with lots of creative improvisation and virtuoso technique along the way. At the same time, whoever isn't on the lead is playing backup: an accompaniment providing rich harmonic and melodic contrast with a strong rhythmic foundation.

Bluegrass has distinctive vocal characteristics as well. Most prominent is a high-pitched, tense quality that is often loud and piercing. Songs are sung in two-, three-, and four-part harmonies, and melodies are usually based on the I, IV, and V chords.

Bluegrass is one of many modern forms of traditional country music — a music with roots extending back to the earliest immigrants from the British Isles who settled in the New World in the seventeenth century. They brought with them their own long-standing musical heritage, in which ballads played a central role. These ballads were long tales of love, death, and despair, not usually written down, but transmitted orally from one generation to the next. "Although British ballads and folksongs were perpetuated in all areas of early America, only in the South did they contribute to the creation of a lasting regional music," writes historian Bill Malone, in *Country Music, U.S.A.* . . . . "In their zeal to defend white supremacy and preserve the supposed blessings of a rural society, southerners — through both necessity and choice — committed their region to a course of arrested development in a nation that was rapidly surrendering to the blandishment of urbanism and industrialization." For these reasons, early country music thrived especially in the states of Virginia, North Carolina, Kentucky, and Tennessee.

In addition to ballads the Anglo-Celtic settlers also brought with them their fiddles, which were used for many different purposes: to accompany jigs and reels — popular European dances; to provide music at funerals and weddings; and to stimulate workers at corn-husking and bean-stringing parties.

The banjo first came to America from Africa during the slave trade, sometime between 1619 and 1640. The black slaves made their banjos using hollowed-out gourds, with animal skins stretched over the tops. A stick, which acted as the instrument's neck, was attached at one end. Until the early 1800s, banjos were played solely by slaves on plantations. But in 1823, a white performer, Thomas Dartmouth, used the banjo to accompany his songs in a Jubilee, a type of entertainment developed by plantation slaves and later imitated by whites.

Joel Sweeney, a poor white farm boy from Appomatox, Virginia, is credited with having made many contributions to the banjo: The most important was his introduction of the wooden shell, instead of the gourd, for the banjo's body. Another modification sometimes attributed to Sweeney was the addition, around 1830, of the banjo's fifth string.

The minstrel show, first presented in 1843 by the Virginia Minstrels, consisted of comedy, skits, and banjo and fiddle tunes, performed by white entertainers in

Flatt and Scruggs.

"blackface." This was followed by the traveling medicine show, similar in format to its predecessor, but linked to selling elixirs of questionable value. Vaudeville emerged in the late 1800s — and was also a conglomeration of acts featuring banjo and fiddle music. The Civil War had greatly contributed to the popularity of the banjo in the North, due to the intermingling of soldiers from both sides.

By the beginning of the twentieth century, the guitar and mandolin — originally imported from Europe — were also widely used, as companies like Gibson, Martin, and Sears & Roebuck made them easily accessible to a wide cross-section of musicians.

THE ADVENT of radio did much to foster the growth and development of country music using all these instruments. In the '20s, two programs were of special importance. One was the *National Barndance*, aired from station WLS in Chicago; the other was the *Grand Ole Opry*, from Nashville's WSM. These programs, and hundreds of others broadcast throughout the nation, helped popularize country music, and inspired the formation of countless country bands.

The most significant kinds of ensemble to emerge during this period was the country duo, usually consisting of two brothers, one playing mandolin, the other playing guitar. Groups like the Blue Sky Boys, the Delmore Brothers, and the Bailey Brothers, popular during the '30s and '40s, were the direct predecessors of the bluegrass band. The country duo's music was fairly basic. The guitarist usually played rhythm and sang melody; the mandolinist played melodic instrumental improvisation and sang harmony. In 1927, one country band got together that was a bit different from all the rest. The brothers — Charlie, Birch, and Bill Monroe — called themselves the Monroe Brothers. Listeners hearing the group for the first time were impressed by Bill's dazzling mandolin style, the hard-driving runs of Charlie's guitar, and Birch's bass and fiddle work. Birch eventually left the trio and the remaining brothers developed quite a following.

Determining when "bluegrass" first became a separate musical entity has generated heated debate throughout the years. Some say it was 1938, when Bill Monroe formed his own legendary band: The Blue Grass Boys, named after the nickname of his native state, Kentucky. Others claim it was a year later, when they joined the *Grand Ole Opry*. Some claim there was no such thing as bluegrass until 1945, when the Monroe band included the 3-finger banjo style of Earl Scruggs, as well as Monroe on mandolin, Chubby Wise on fiddle, Lester Flatt on guitar, and Howard Watts on bass. It was a magical combination. Still many others insist that bluegrass was not really bluegrass until the style began to have imitators. According to one noted authority of this school, this happened for the first time in 1948 when the Stanley Brothers recorded "Molly And Tenbrooks," a song they learned at a Bill Monroe concert.

No one, however, disputes the fact that by the early 1950s, Monroe's style, and that of his imitators, was universally referred to as "bluegrass." The name of Monroe's band became a generic term, like aspirin or scotch tape. There were dozens of bands who now played bluegrass. The Stanley Brothers, Ralph and Carter, got their first instruments from a mail-order catalog, and developed some of the most haunting vocal harmonies ever to be heard in a bluegrass band. Jim and Jesse McReynolds enhanced the tradition with Jim's smooth singing and Jesse's innovative mandolin work. The Osborne Brothers became one of the most popular bluegrass ensembles. And then there were Flatt and Scruggs, who had left Monroe's band in 1948 to form the legendary Lester Flatt, Earl Scruggs and the Foggy Mountain Boys.

By 1953 there were more than ten bluegrass groups with major recording contracts. Bill Monroe signed with Decca in 1950 and produced for them such classics as "Uncle Pen." Flatt And Scruggs signed with Columbia in the same year after their Mercury recording of "Foggy Mountain Breakdown," an all-time bluegrass favorite. Another early hit was "Feudin' Banjos" first recorded in 1954 on MGM by Don Reno on banjo and Arthur Smith on tenor banjo.

This early heyday did not last long. In the mid-'50s, Elvis Presley overwhelmed America's music scene, and rock and roll lured many fans away from country music. Most bluegrass musicians, if they got any work at all, were forced to play in sleazy bars and nightclubs — for little money to boot. Radio stations stopped playing bluegrass; and the number of recording contracts dwindled. Even Monroe had trouble keeping his band together. One of the few groups that managed to thrive was Flatt And Scruggs And The Foggy Mountain Boys, which was sponsored on television and radio by the Tennessee-based Martha White Mills flour company.

Thankfully, this period was only temporary. Interest in folk artists like Leadbelly and Woody Guthrie had existed since the '40s. The Weavers were formed in the late '40s. But in the late '50s a new generation of popular folk groups like the Tarriers, the Limeliters, and the Kingston Trio emerged. The Kingston Trio's 1958 recording of "Tom Dooley," an old mountain ballad, is credited with igniting a new era of commercial folk music by the early '60s.

The folk movement of the '60s had tremendous impact on bluegrass. People across the country were exposed to traditional material, and eventually "discovered that there were more legitimate purveyors of folk songs — musicians who grew up with the authentic material," says mandolinist David Grisman, whose own interest in bluegrass was triggered during this period.

According to banjoist Pete Wernick ("Dr. Banjo") of Hot Rize, a contemporary bluegrass group from Colorado, the folk movement made two main contributions to the world of bluegrass. "The folk boom of the '60s marked the emergence of bluegrass as a nationally significant music form — one that was more than a regional style of the Southeast," he says. "It also gave bluegrass a commercial shot in the arm by opening up new markets in the North."

Popular folk artists like Joan Baez and Bob Dylan drew heavily from traditional material. Baez recorded songs of the Carter Family — one of the earliest and most influential groups in country music. The New Lost City Ramblers based their repertoire on recreations of old-time banjo and fiddle songs from the the '30s and, in 1958, the New York-based Greenbriar Boys, who introduced bluegrass to a new generation of folk music enthusiasts. In the '60s, Bill Monroe hired his first non-Southern musicians for the Blue Grass Boys.

On the other hand, many traditional bluegrass groups tailored themselves to the folk boom by including popular folk songs in their repertoire. The Stanley Brothers recorded two albums of folk material called *Hootenanny* and *Folk Concert*. Flatt And Scruggs And The Foggy Mountain Boys recorded a best-selling album of folk material called *Songs Of Our Land*. They also recorded such Bob Dylan tunes as "Like A Rolling Stone," and "Rainy Day Woman."

The folk boom was not the only factor contributing to the growing popularity of bluegrass. The intellectual establishment was paying attention, too. In 1959, folklorist Alan Lomax published a much-acclaimed article about bluegrass in *Esquire* magazine, giving the music a new kind of popular validation. Then, in 1962, CBS launched a television series, *The Beverly Hillbillies*, about a hillbilly family that struck it rich, and moved to Beverly Hills, California. The theme song from the show, "The Ballad Of Jed Clampett," was performed by Earl Scruggs And The Foggy Mountain Boys, along with vocalist Jerry Scoggins, on the show. Lester Flatt did sing the vocals when the song was recorded, however, and the song became a #1 hit in late '62.

There were other signs that bluegrass was gaining wide acceptance. In 1959 the Osborne Brothers were welcomed at Antioch College, paving the way for the performances of myriad bluegrass groups in colleges throughout the country. In the same year, Flatt And Scruggs played at the famed Newport Folk Festival (in Rhode Island), further strengthening the link between bluegrass and folk music. And in 1962, bluegrass reached as far afield as New York's prestigious Carnegie Hall, when Alan Lomax presented Earl Taylor and the Stoney Mountains Boys in concert.

In 1965, promoter/manager Carlton Haney founded the first annual multi-day

Senator Robert S. Byrd plays for Nashville's WSM.

At a bluegrass festival in Japan.

bluegrass festival in Fincastle, Virginia. Though the crowds were thin at first, the spirit caught on; by the end of the decade these musical events began proliferating throughout the country, and there are now hundreds of bluegrass festivals every year.

In 1966 *Bluegrass Unlimited* began publication. In 1967, the movie *Bonnie And Clyde* used as its theme the 1950 recording of "Foggy Mountain Breakdown" by Flatt And Scruggs. A few years later, the movie *Deliverance* used "Dueling Banjos," a remake of the original "Feudin' Banjos," as its theme. This, too, became a Top-40 hit.

In the later '60s, a few bluegrass groups thought they would have greater mass appeal if they adopted more popular elements in their music. In 1966, Jim And Jesse recorded the country song, "Diesel On My Tail," including electric guitar, pedal steel, drums, and piano. In the mid-'60s, the Charles River Valley Boys recorded a well-received album called *Beatle Country*. And in 1969 the Osborne Brothers committed the ultimate sacrilege: They electrically amplified their banjo and mandolin, and at one historic performance were actually booed off the stage. Then what many thought impossible occurred: Flatt and Scruggs disbanded after 21 years. In 1969 Earl Scruggs formed — with his two sons — a country/rock band called the Earl Scruggs Revue. Earl continued playing banjo, Randy Scruggs played acoustic and electric lead guitar, and Gary Scruggs played electric bass. (Lester Flatt continued the original sound with members of the Foggy Mountain Boys, renamed The Nashville Grass.)

Other bands were also moving in new directions, under the bluegrass banner. The Country Gentlemen, formed in 1957, were one of the first groups to use non-bluegrass material in their repertoire on a regular basis. They eliminated the fiddle, but used the other bluegrass instruments. "They had the same kind of harmony singing, but they were consciously going for a different audience," says Peter Wernick. "They were interested in doing folk songs bluegrass style." They also recorded some Beatles songs, like "Yesterday," and the theme song from the movie *Exodus*. They "harmonically modernized folk songs," according to David Grisman.

In the early '70s, the New Grass Revival, headed by mandolinist/fiddler Sam Bush, combined the sounds of rock with bluegrass, formulating a bluegrass spinoff called "Newgrass." Their first album included such songs as Leon Russell's "Prince Of Peace." It also included Jerry Lee Lewis' "Great Balls Of Fire." "This had certain rhythmic aspects that had not been done in bluegrass before," says Wernick. "There is a rhythm riff in the beginning — all the instruments doing the same thing at the same time. This does not occur in bluegrass. Newgrass shows how you can get creative with a form — break the rules — but still use most of the Bill Monroe style:

the banjo rolls, the mandolin playing, and a lot of the same kind of fiddle playing."

EXPERIMENTATION continues — and so does bluegrass. In fact, the music has become so popular all over the country, you can hear it now just by staying at home. Television viewers are familiar with the twangy sound of the Scruggs banjo, the rapid, crisp licks of the mandolin, and the powerful chords of the guitar. Bluegrass is used in commercials to sell everything from trucks to cornflakes.

In recent years the print media has also taken notice of this folk art form. *Country Music, Newsweek,* and *People Magazine* have covered Monroe. *Newsweek* wrote about celebrated mandolin virtuoso and innovator David Grisman. Although no longer considered a bluegrass artist, he is heavily rooted in bluegrass. *People* featured multi-instrumentalist and singer Ricky Skaggs, who also won the Country Music Association Award for Best Vocalist and Best Newcomer of 1982 (despite the fact that he's been playing since he was about five). Skaggs also was the recipient of several *Frets* Reader Poll Awards.

Bluegrass and its related forms has also been acknowledged by leading classical artists. On Yehudi Menuhin's television series, *The Music Of Man,* the world renowned violinist fiddled up a storm in *Bluegrass Concerto* with French-Canadian fiddler Jean Carignan.

Political figures are not exempt from the bluegrass craze. When Senator Robert S. Byrd (West Virginia) is not behind the closed doors of a congressional meeting, he may be at a recording session. Byrd's *Appalachian Fiddle Tunes* is a testament to his fiddling finesse. And there's the group of Capitol Hill journalists who occasionally gather together, not to gossip about the latest political scandal but to pick and sing. They call themselves Informed Sources. Another Washington newgrass aggregation is The Seldom Scene, comprised partly of professional and business people.

Bluegrass is not confined to the United States, either. It's played on practically every continent. Australia, Japan and European countries boast several enthusiastic festivals each year, not to mention numerous bluegrass clubs. And even in Israel, people are pickin' and singing. Topnotch bluegrass bands like Bill Monroe, the McLain Family Band, Jim And Jesse, and the Country Gentlemen tour regularly overseas.

There are several publications that currently cater to bluegrass. In a time when many magazines are folding, bluegrass publications somehow manage to survive. *Bluegrass Unlimited* is devoted solely to the music; and publications like *Frets, Mandolin World News,* and *Banjo Newsletter* regularly feature bluegrass news and artists. Beside magazines, there are many books that offer how-to instruction on playing the various bluegrass instruments (see Recommended Reading List in Chapter V).

Despite the broad acceptance of bluegrass, however, *books* covering its history, its performers, and its music are hard to find. Volumes have been written about the history of country music, but very little has been documented about bluegrass in particular. A handful of obscure publications and assorted magazine articles feature bluegrass-related topics, to be sure, but none of them give the whole picture — until now.

All of the material in this book has been compiled from the pages of *Frets.* Founded in 1979, the publication features a high percentage of bluegrass articles written by musicians who are intimately acquainted with the complexities of the style.

The Big Book Of Bluegrass doesn't tell you everything there is to know about bluegrass. Only a lifetime of listening to the music, playing it, and talking to its greatest practitioners could accomplish that. But this work does provide the *most* information, history, instruction, and lore ever compiled — the broadest, most all-inclusive picture of bluegrass published to date.

We hope it shows why bluegrass is here to stay.

— Marilyn Kochman

Special thanks to David Grisman and Peter Wernick for their perspectives on the evolution of bluegrass.

1.
THE
FOUNDERS

BILL MONROE

BLUEGRASS MUSIC is a relatively recent arrival on the American scene. It was born in the early '40s, predating the advent of rock and roll by only ten or twelve years. The face of bluegrass, unlike that of rock and roll, is the image of one man: its progenitor and main influence, Bill Monroe. Certainly, bluegrass has its roots in the music of the southern Appalachian mountains, and there have been bluegrass innovators since Monroe; but no one can deny that bluegrass music is Bill Monroe's own creation.

There are few non-classical mandolin players alive who do not owe the foundations of their styles to Monroe. While he has inspired the gamut of bluegrass, jazz, and even rock mandolin players, he himself has seldom strayed from tight stylistic parameters of melodic, distinctively rhythmic playing.

The style, form, and themes of Monroe's music are strictly determined. The basic band is always mandolin, guitar, banjo, string bass, and fiddle. The guitar and bass are rarely featured as lead instruments; with the chop chords of the mandolin, their function is to provide the punch rhythm of the band. The chord progressions are simple, usually limited to two or three changes per tune. The lead instruments —mandolin, fiddle, and banjo — generally trade solos with the vocalists. The beauty of the music lies in what is so elegantly stated within these limitations.

Monroe's instrumental compositions express a range of sound and emotion unequaled by any performer in his field. They have come to comprise a primer of songs that every mandolin player must address. "Rawhide," "Kentucky Mandolin," "Bluegrass Stomp," "Bluegrass Breakdown," and "Wheel Hoss" are all challenging bluegrass mandolin classics. Many echo the fiddle tunes Monroe heard as a child; others are intense, fast pieces that communicate his own energetic musical vision. The songs he writes convey a haunting reality, almost always concerning themselves with some aspect of love — love cherished, rejected, fulfilled, or lost. Some songs reflect Monroe's childhood and culture, "Uncle Pen" — an ode to the man who taught him music — probably being the most famous of these. Some songs deal with the lonely existence of life on the road, others are honest expressions of Monroe's religious beliefs. All of Monroe's songs cut straight to the heart with a simple and beautiful poetic quality.

There is little comic or novelty material, because Monroe is a very serious man who cares deeply about his music. For nearly 40 years, he has been striving to bring that music up from his heart and deliver it to his audience.

It all began on a farm in the hills near Rosine, Kentucky, in 1911, when Bill Monroe was born. He was the youngest of eight children. Throughout his childhood he was exposed to hoedown music and to the blues. He mentions a black guitarist and fiddler, Arnold Schultz, as being one of his main influences. Monroe's Uncle Pen Vandiver, a fiddler, further sparked his interest in music, and the fiddle was Monroe's first choice as an instrument. However, his brother Birch had already claimed the family's fiddle. Bill's second choice was the guitar, but his brother Charlie had claimed it. That left only the mandolin.

Monroe did get to play guitar somewhat, initially, and would regularly "second" on the guitar for his Uncle Pen at local house parties and hoedowns. Monroe says that if things had turned out a little differently, he might have been a blues singer. It was the early cross-influence of the blues and hoedown music that led Monroe to his

Bluegrass pioneers Bill Monroe and Lester Flatt perform together again during the '70s. During the '40s their singing and songwriting had created the core of the most influential Monroe band in the history of bluegrass music. This classic group included Earl Scruggs on banjo, Chubby Wise on fiddle, and Cedric Rainwater on bass, providing a stylistic and commercial model for everything that followed.

synthesis of the two styles into bluegrass.

Both of Monroe's parents died before he entered his teens and he went to live with his Uncle Pen. At 17 he left Kentucky to follow Charlie and Birch north in search of work. Jobs were scarce, but eventually he found employment in the East Chicago area, stacking barrels at the Sinclair oil refinery. At times, he was the only one of the three brothers working and he supported the other two on his small salary.

Bill, Charlie, and Birch had continued with their music after the move north and gradually they began to get scattered jobs as a trio. House party dates led to short road trips for WLS radio's *Barn Dance Tour,* with the brothers also doing some exhibition square dancing. For a while Bill continued at Sinclair, taking time off to do the WLS shows, since all three brothers agreed that though music was a more enjoyable way of making a living than refinery work, it was nowhere near as steady. But finally the brothers were performing enough and Bill was able to quit at Sinclair. It must certainly have been a difficult step. The country was in the depths of the Depression, and any job was a good job. Being employed was an incredibly lucky situation that one didn't walk away from. Quitting at Sinclair was a gamble; but luckily for Monroe, it paid off.

After some initial touring with the WLS *Barn Dance,* Birch settled into a steady refinery job and left the group. Charlie and Bill continued as a duo, the Monroe Brothers, and through a series of associations with radio stations they gained a following throughout the South and the rural Midwest. Their recordings sold well, but the brothers had difficulty getting along and after six years the act split up. The Monroe Brothers went in entirely different directions. It is generally accepted that Bill found his position as the younger brother to be unworkable; that he longed to prove himself with his own music, independent of Charlie.

Bill immediately set about putting together his special style of music, something through which he could express himself in an exciting and different way. It was 1939 when the first grouping of the Blue Grass Boys appeared on radio station WSM's *Grand Ole Opry,* and they caused quite a stir. Their music was supercharged, even in its seminal form. Originally a quartet with mandolin, guitar, fiddle, and string bass, the Blue Grass Boys didn't add banjo for two years. That step would finally and completely define the classic bluegrass sound.

Dave "Stringbean" Akeman, who played in the frailing style of Uncle Dave Macon, was Monroe's first banjo player. Also joining the group was an accordionist, Sally Ann Forrester; Monroe later said that he decided to add the accordion because his mother had played the instrument. The accordion was gone from the group by the autumn of 1946, however, as was Akeman's banjo, when Monroe made his first record-

Bill Monroe was joined onstage at a 1982 Kentucky bluegrass festival by mandolinists (L to R): David Grisman and Sam Bush. Monroe has made this kind of invitational jamming a tradition at his personal appearances.

*The proud "Father of Bluegrass Music,"
Monroe plays rhythm mandolin at a 1982
concert in San Francisco.*

concern was the music.

The late '40s were good for Monroe, but times were changing. Lester Flatt and Earl Scruggs left the Blue Grass Boys to form their own bluegrass-style band, and there began a succession of Monroe bands through which passed virtually every great figure in bluegrass music, save its mandolin players. Carter Stanley, Jimmy Martin, Don Reno, Mac Wiseman, and many others were once Blue Grass Boys.

The early '50s saw the start of a difficult period in Monroe's career. Country music in general was having an identity crisis in light of the rock and roll revolution. Though bluegrass had never, since its inception, been widely popular, Monroe had always made a good living. With rock and roll sweeping across the country, and with the advent of television, much of Monroe's economic base was eroded and jobs became harder to secure. Ironically, one of Elvis Presley's early recordings included Monroe's "Blue Moon Of Kentucky" on its B side.

It must have hurt Monroe deeply to see his expanding career suddenly and severely decline. What attention the world did give bluegrass went to Flatt and Scruggs, who had managed to make inroads into other entertainment circles. Monroe did his best to survive musically and financially, withdrawing to his farm when jobs were scarce. He resisted all temptations to revamp his music along more popular lines. Through his intense pride, even his stubbornness, he weathered those lean times. The roots of his perseverance may have gone back to his childhood when, the youngest of the family and troubled by poor vision, he developed a need to excel, to be successful. Through that he forged a single-minded attitude about himself and his music. He drew upon all his experience and strength of will to achieve his goals, realizing that the music was the most important thing in his life. It has never been otherwise. He has always stayed on top of his music, never changing, never faltering.

The folk revival of the early '60s helped Monroe toward a comeback. It also brought him a new audience of northern college students. On the heels of this renewed interest came the popularization of bluegrass festivals, and Monroe was able to found his own at Bean Blossom, Indiana, in 1967. While Monroe had always been regarded as the father of bluegrass music, his achievements at last became more popularly recognized and he was elected to the Country Music Hall of Fame in 1970.

Today, Monroe continually tours the country and still performs regularly with the *Grand Ole Opry*. Any other artist who had made such a monumental contribution to his field might be content to rest on his laurels, but Monroe's drive is as strong as ever. He says simply, "The road life — I like it. I like to travel. I like to see the country."

ing with 22-year-old Earl Scruggs. Scruggs had joined Monroe in December of 1945, and his rapid-fire three-finger banjo picking, unheard of at the time, was the final ingredient in the bluegrass sound. The Blue Grass Boys at that point became the classic Monroe band of Monroe on mandolin, Lester Flatt on guitar, Scruggs on banjo, Chubby Wise on fiddle, and Birch Monroe on bass.

The music was at an incredible peak, having jelled both stylistically and commercially. There was nothing else like it. Monroe and his Blue Grass Boys toured constantly, in many cases with their own tent show (featuring performers like Uncle Dave Macon) and an exhibition baseball team. Each week the band returned to Nashville for the *Grand Ole Opry* broadcast. It was the beginning of a movement, and Monroe had no peer as a composer or as a performer. Others were to follow shortly, but Bill Monroe and the Blue Grass Boys, with their lightning playing and exciting singing, were on top.

Many classic bluegrass pieces came from this era. One of the Blue Grass Boys' early signature tunes was a reworking of Jimmie Rodgers' "Mule Skinner Blues" into Monroe's own style. Monroe's tenor voice was high and clear, and it seemed to express a feeling of deep lonesomeness. His mandolin playing had developed significantly by this time. It emphasized strong melody and a syncopated, driving rhythm that pushed the band. A hard worker, he expected his band members to be the same and he must have been a difficult man to work for at times. But always, his main

BILL MONROE'S music developed steadily from his days with the Monroe Brothers, back in the '30s, on into the mid-'60s. There has always been a great deal of movement within its strict boundaries, especially in Monroe's mandolin playing.

Monroe has always tried, he says, to make music he plays fit with the group he is in, though in his own style. Because of that, Monroe's playing has covered a great range; at times it has been intense, but it has never been flippant or contrived.

To accent his backup playing, Monroe developed a powerful right-hand rhythm chop with an almost drum-like effect. Using a loose, limber wrist motion he gained incredible speed on his solos. He drew on a great deal of blues phrasing and noting and punctuated his leads with an outrageous syncopation of right-hand downstrokes. The result was one of the most distinctive and remarkable mandolin styles of our time.

In the following interview, Bill Monroe talks about his playing, his early musical influences, his songwriting and composing, and his long career as a performer.

OVER THE YEARS, *in talking about when you began playing, you've mentioned a guitar player named Arnold Schultz as an early influence. Could you tell us a little about him?*

Arnold Schultz. He was a black man, you know, and he played guitar and was a woderful guitar man. Played the blues, that was what he played. If he was following a fiddler or somebody with a guitar, he really played a different style. I never heard anybody could play anything the way that Arnold Schultz played it, behind fiddle numbers. He played a wonderful rhythm. He could also play the fiddle, you know, a few fiddle numbers, and he played for some square dances.

Did you learn songs from him?

No, sir. I've always loved the blues played on the guitar, and when he would play them I loved the way he could do it. There's other people that could play blues too; there was people around where I was raised who could sing the blues like that.

Were these black people?

No, they were white people. There were very few colored people that would come around Rosine, Kentucky, where we lived; but Arnold was a fine man and I always loved to hear him play. There's really no

man that you could pinpoint to say that his music is in my music, the way that my music is lined out. It's just like Jimmie Rodgers: I've sung some of his numbers, but they was done bluegrass style, which would override his style. If I was going to do Jimmie Rodgers alone, I would just use the guitar myself and do it the way that he did.

But you never tried to do that, did you?

Back in the early days I could have, you know, but mandolin's been my instrument ever since I was a young boy.

I've never met a bluegrass mandolin player that didn't — at least at first — try to play like you. What is your reaction to everybody trying to copy Bill Monroe?

Well now, I feel good about it; every man has to start somewhere, and if my music helped him get started, why I'm one hundred percent for him to do that. I guess a lot of people learned from that and went on into other kinds of music, and a lot of people still play it the way they learned it.

Does it flatter you?

Well, I like it either way. Of course, if they play my music and play it the way I have it lined out, I think it's fine. I thank a lot of them for doing it.

How did you react in the early '50s when Elvis Presley recorded your song

"Blue Moon Of Kentucky"?

I thought Elvis had a good voice. He apologized to me for the way that he changed "Blue Moon Of Kentucky," there at the *Grand Ole Opry*, when he came there and sung it one Saturday night..The record company told him that he needed a style of his own, and so that's what he was searching for when he recorded "Blue Moon Of Kentucky," and I think he had it right for his new style. So, I told him if it would help him get that then I was one hundred percent for him.

You've said that in the beginning what you were trying to do more than anything was to find your own style on the mandolin.

That's right, and there's a way that I play that had never been played before by anybody. And the way that I use the chords or anything like that in following a lead instrument was never played the way I do it.

The many subtle changes your playing has undergone through the years has always been remarkable. For example, when you played with your brother Charlie you played in a different style. You've said that style was not yet bluegrass.

That's right. It was a style to match his kind of singing and the kind of singing that we'd do in the early days.

Were you concentrating less on the mandolin exclusively then and more on the entire sound?

No, I was searching for things on the mandolin then. But, to fit our kind of singing, what I was playing then was what we needed. The kind of style that I play now wouldn't have matched me and Charlie back in the early days.

It seems that the one person other than Arnold Schultz whom you emphasize as an early influence is your uncle, Pen Vandiver.

Yes, sir, him being the first fiddler that I ever heard, naturally. He was a good fiddler too. He was hard to beat when it came to playing old-time square dance numbers. He had the most perfect time of any fiddler in the world, and he had a wonderful shuffle; you never see anybody today that can play that kind of shuffle.

How old were you when you began listening to him and playing with him?

I would say from around six years old, something like that, on up through to 10 and 12 years old, I listened to him close. Then on up through my teens Uncle Pen and I would play for square dances.

With you on the guitar?

Yes, sir, just where we could make a little extra money, you see. Back then, that was in the Depression when a dollar really meant something. We did a lot of house parties, and some of them had square dances there at the house. The people would all dance and they would donate 15¢ a set.

Another early influence in your music was the church. What were your early church experiences?

I guess, back in the early days, with the Methodists and the Baptist churches, everybody come there to hear the singing and the preaching. They had a Methodist church there at Rosine and a Baptist church. They had a good choir singing there; a good lead singer, and back in them days they had tenor singers and bass singers and alto singers. That was way before baritone singing came around.

Do songs like "Wicked Path Of Sin" come out of that tradition?

I would say it might have touched it in some way, but through the way I was searching for the bluegrass style of singing gospel I wouldn't take a whole lot from Baptist or Methodist. It's a difficult gospel altogether from Methodist and Baptist. I don't believe I ever heard a quartet there in church. Bluegrass gospel, I think, is wonderful.

When you were playing with your brothers, before you played with Charlie as a duo and while you were working for the Sinclair Oil Company, had you played professionally much?

Well, just back to Uncle Pen and me playing for dances and house parties.

Did you think much about future economic opportunities with the oil company when you decided to try being a musician?

It wasn't that I decided to be one or the other. Times was rough back then and musicians didn't have the best chance in the world. Very few radio stations paid anything, you see. It was taking a big chance, leaving a good job and going into music.

When did your music become bluegrass?

When me and Charlie broke up, I went to building around myself to form the music that I wanted. Any man that I hired had to play my style or he didn't belong in my group. It went to building from that, doing the numbers that would help us get started in that kind of music.

What made it "bluegrass"?

The state of Kentucky gave it the name. That's the state I'm from, and I wanted to use some kind of a name from that state so the people would know it was where I was from. So, I took the name "bluegrass." There's not a prettier name in the world than that.

As far as the music goes, though, what were the changes that you made? Is it true that in 1938 you got a band together to play your music and rehearsed for a month?

Well, I went to working on it back in late '38 and on up into '39. You see, it gave whoever was going to play for me a chance to practice and get it right. Maybe if a man was holding down a job or something, he'd like to play and sing but he wasn't ready for a big radio program like the *Grand Ole Opry*. So, I had to rehearse them and get them just the way I wanted them.

There are many stories about your first appearance on the Grand Ole Opry — *that people listening couldn't believe it. Did you expect that?*

I knew I was going to go in there and

Monroe, formerly a professional dancer, demonstrates his Kentucky clog-dance on his birthday, 1982.

give them everything that I had. I had heard the *Grand Ole Opry* for a long time, and I didn't think that they had anything on me in the way of being better than what I was because I wasn't in their class. I wasn't doing old-time country music, singing, or playing old-time mountain fiddle numbers, whatever you want to call it.

Did you have a feeling of bringing a new kind of music to these people?

I had a feeling of bringing it to everybody that I played in front of, whether it was the *Grand Ole Opry* or otherwise. I was going to take that to 'em and they could accept it or not.

Did it matter to you whether they accepted it?

Well, I wanted them to accept it, 'cause I knew I had to have them on my side if I was to really put it over and make money at it.

Over the years you've avoided changing your sound for commercial reasons or any other consideration. How have you been able to keep the Bill Monroe sound so pure?

It's been hard at times. You might have a fiddle player or a banjo player that wants to put his stuff in it, you see. So, it come right down to where he either had to play mine or he had to get him another job. And he couldn't win out, because if I didn't want his music, why, he'd have to play mine. I couldn't sell his style on the *Grand Ole Opry* — it had to be mine. So, I had to watch people like that and be sure that they played what I wanted. Record companies never gave me any trouble. I always done what song I wanted to do. They never told me I had to do anything. I think they knew to start with that I wouldn't do it. Now, if they gave me a song that I thought I could do, and it was a good song, why I would do it; but it would be in bluegrass style.

If you could pick a band that was the greatest Bill Monroe band, which would you pick?

Well, you know, if I told you this — if I said I would take somebody by the name of George over somebody by the name of Frank, and they'd all been Blue Grass Boys, it would hurt 'em, you know. Say if you worked for me three years and it was a wonderful group, then you and the rest of the group left and I brought in a new bunch; well, your days would have been fine, but when they come along with theirs, their days would have been fine. So you couldn't say that any group could have beat different groups down through the years. I've tried to keep good clear singers that could sing with me — a lead singer who played a good guitar. I've tried to keep the right kind of banjo player and the right kind of fiddle player. And a good bass, to help me keep time straightened out. But, I think each man with me has had his chance; and when he was with me, he would have been hard to beat. They was all good in their day, and I give every man credit. And here's another thing: You might have the finest guitar player in the world, but he might be a man

that really wanted beer and whiskey. The next man that come along might not be hardly that good, but still be a good, clean, honest man. You have to figure that out, you see, and see which one would really be the best one for you to work with every day.

How did you work with musicians in whom you saw potential?

I'd give a man all the chance in the world, and if I could give him any advice, I would do that too. But as long as he worked hard at it and I seen he was improving, I wouldn't ever bother him.

I believe it was Don Reno who said you were always fair, that you would work with a man to help him get the music right.

Speaking about Don Reno, when Don Reno come to me and the Blue Grass Boys, he needed Bill Monroe and the Blue Grass Boys to make Don Reno. But Don Reno helped me a lot. He was a good, honest man, a hardworking man. He would drive that banjo hard, and he was a good singer. That's the way that it's gone, down through the years.

You mention drinking and its destructive effect on music. You're a rare person in music in that you don't drink or smoke.

Well, I don't think I could have been a drunkard, a beer hog, and have ever led the Blue Grass Boys to where they are today. If I had been, I'd have done been barred from the *Grand Ole Opry* and I'd have probably had no telling how many fights. I don't think you have to drink any kind of a drink to make you a better musician. If you think you have to do that, you need to think it over, because I don't think your mind's working real good. I think you need to be sober.

Could you tell us about some of your experiences with your tent show back in the '40s, when you had people like Uncle Dave Macon and harmonica player DeFord Bailey on the bill with the Blue Grass Boys?

You talk about the tent show — I had that for years, and that gave us five days of work, Monday through Friday; and then back to the *Grand Ole Opry*, so that made six days. If, say, I went on 15, 20 minutes with me and the Blue Grass Boys, then we'd have some comedy for about 15 minutes, then go back to the bluegrass quartet, then maybe have a good fiddle number, and then DeFord Bailey. So it gave you a fine lineup down through the show.

Was DeFord Bailey a novelty act?

No, sir, no. There was no comedy with DeFord. It was strictly the harmonica the way it should be played: "Pan American Blues," "Lost John," "The Evening Prayer Blues," numbers like that. You couldn't beat him. He was fine.

How about Uncle Dave Macon?

He was a fine showman. Had a good voice and played a good 5-string banjo in his style, and he done a little comedy down through his show. When he was going over fine, he went along just like a clock working. Everything was perfect.

You had comedians with some of your

early bands, but you got away from that later. How did the change come about?

Well, back in the early days the people was trained all over the whole world for so much comedy in a show, so that's why I carried one comedian. Later on, when Stringbean [Dave "Stringbean" Akeman] would work with me, that would give me two comedians. Two working together, they was really powerful, onstage, you know. They could really get the laughs. And that would break the monotony of going from one number to another. It would let the musicians have a little break. Later on there got to be so many numbers like "Blue Moon Of Kentucky," "Mule Skinner Blues," "Footprints In The Snow," and "Uncle Pen," that the people would pay their money and want to hear; and they would want to hear fiddle numbers, banjo numbers, the quartet. So, by the time you get to all that, you don't have much time for comedy. And I think comedy takes away from a good bluegrass show. Bluegrass is way further up in the world than a lot of people give it credit for being. It tells the truth. A lot of songs are true songs. It gives me a good feeling to hear good bluegrass. And I know that a man, if he's a hard worker in it, is doing his best because he wants to hear it that way and he hopes it'll touch you the same way. That's the way I am with my music; I like to play for myself, and I hope that it's really getting next to the people who listen, too.

A lot of the songs you've written are songs about being on the road. Is the road a difficult part of your life?

Well, I raised two children, James and Melissa, and they knew that if I went out and worked five days and made what money I could, that I was coming home to them. They knew that I'd be back there, and that I would want to see them just as much as they would want to see me. And they allowed for all that, you know, so that's the way it went for a long time. The road life, I like it. I like to travel, I like to see different country.

But you must have seen it a dozen times!

I have. I've been down a lot of the road so many, many times. But I still like to travel. That's the way it's been for me. Trips have been hard, but you know a promoter, a booker, he has to do the best he can do. If you're putting on a show in San Francisco, they'll take the best nights that they can get out of the week for the show. That's the same way all over the whole country —Friday, Saturday, and Sunday is good.

Do you ever get bored on the road?

Oh, not too much. If you go out and stay a week or so, or three weeks, you're glad to get home. But then if you work around home maybe a couple weeks, or months, you like to get back on the road again.

How do you go about writing songs — say, "Kentucky Mandolin"?

If I'm writing a number like "Kentucky Mandolin" and I've got it started to where I enjoy the first notes, I search for the notes to tie on to that, to keep it going on the way I want it to where it still sounds good to me. Of course, there's breaks in any number where you might not be crazy about where you're going to take it right then, say, whether you can get to another position in another key. "Kentucky Mandolin" was a number that I was writing when I was in California years and years ago. Doc Watson was playing it with me and I didn't have a title, so he give it the title "Kentucky Mandolin."

Do you change songs any after you get the basic form down?

No, I stay as close as I can to the way that I write a song. That's the trouble with a lot of musicians; they want to do it their way, and their way ain't the right way. They ought to think about the man that writes the song and try to do it right, try to do it his way. It would be much better for them, because they don't know where they're going with it — a lot of them don't. They're jazzing a song up, putting a lot of wild notes in it to show off more than anything else.

Are there any mandolin players you particularly like?

There's a lot of good mandolin players, I guess. Take people like Jim and Jesse [McReynolds]. I always thought Jesse had a good style for their singing and everything; it's different, and I think he really plays a good mandolin.

What kind of music do you listen to when you relax?

I like different kinds of music. Of course, bluegrass is number one. I like blues, or I like jazz, if it's not too wild. I like beautiful gospel singing. I like symphony. I've heard some rock and roll that I like. I sure have always liked Elvis Presley's singing, because he done a lot of gospel songs and had a good quartet behind him. So, there's a lot of good music. I like good fiddle music, but I don't like to see a man that plays a good fiddle let some other kind of style override him and get him into that.

Was Kenny Baker sort of a swing fiddler before he came to you?

I think so. But I think Kenny does a wonderful job of playing my music.

Are there any new mandolins being made that you like?

They make some mandolins over in Japan that have got wonderful fretboards and play good. They're new, you know; they haven't had a chance really to get the tone in them. I think a mandolin has to be played a lot to get the tone.

In a mandolin, do you look for a sound like the sound of the mandolin you have now?

I hope that any mandolin will have a good sound. A lot's in the man that plays the mandolin. I think you have to be really careful and search for the tone. And, when you get the tone right, everything that the mandolin will stand or take, don't ever ride it, keep it right there.

Is your mandolin the Bill Monroe mandolin? Is that the one that matches your style?

Yes, sir, it's been a good mandolin down through the years.

Are you particular about the picks you use?

Bill Monroe sings with Jack Cooke and Ralph Stanley of the Clinch Mountain Boys in 1981.

I like a heavy pick. I don't like a real light, thin pick because I don't think you can get a tone out of the mandolin with a thin pick. I let the point wear off, because if it's too sharp, why, you don't get the tone. I've tried tortoiseshell and it's pretty good. I use Gibson bronze strings.

You sometimes use a different tuning — on "Get Up John," for instance. Are there others that you haven't recorded yet?

Yes, but it's been so long [*laughs*] I can't remember how I tune them.

How do you feel about amplifying the mandolin, either by using an electric instrument or by attaching a pickup to an acoustic one? You've never done that yourself.

No, sir. I've played other people's mandolins a little bit that was electrified. I guess it's alright, according to what kind of music you're playing, what you're trying to do with it. I think it'd be good to play for dances like that, probably.

Do you still practice a lot?

We do. We sing and practice some. We play as we ride the bus, you know. If you're working every night, you get a lot of work right there, and a lot of times you can come up with something new right from the stage that will help your music.

Does new material come to you when you're up on the stage?

Sometimes it does, yes sir. I listen for music or where it could go to; where you could start from one note and go into something that would really help a number.

Do you play set solos? In "Bluegrass Breakdown," for example, you might play the melody in one solo. Are you trying to create new things in that way onstage?

If it's the "Bluegrass Breakdown," I do the best that I can do with it. I try to play my break as good as I can do it. I don't think it should be changed. It should stay the way it was wrote. With numbers like "Arkansas Traveler," "Katy Hill," I don't think you need to make it do something and ruin the number; and that's what you would do if you tried to put other kinds of music in it. They're for square dancing. You know what timing a number should be and if you get out there and make it to where it's a hundred miles an hour, you've lost your mind. It could never be right; no way in the world it could be right. It's just like a waltz number. If you go out there and play it so fast nobody could waltz — who wins there? And who loses? The musician does. The dancer, he can't do it, because you've ruined it. Any musician ought to learn timing. Now, that's the main thing in music — and there's a lot of different timings. Any young musician ought to be sure to learn it the right way. There's numbers like the "Orange Blossom Special" where you know it's a show-off number, a selling number just like "Rawhide" or "Black Mountain Rag" or something like that. But you just got a few of them numbers, so get back to the real thing. If you're going to play the "Watson Blues," why, it's an old southern-style of blues and you don't need to put

hot notes in it. You need to learn where a hot note should go, and not let it override the number to where it's going to hurt it. If you're going to play jazz or if you're going to play round dance music then you can throw every hot note in there that you want. Wouldn't hurt a thing.

Is the same thing true of singing?

Well, it works sort of the same way. If you've got a voice that can handle the song right, you stay on the note and follow your melody, your voice will have a good chance and will help that song. The people out there will hear what you're doing. When you go to putting extra stuff in it, they know it don't go that way so you're only kidding yourself. If you're going to sing "Blue Moon Of Kentucky," you better hold close to the way it was wrote. Or "Kentucky Waltz," or "Uncle Pen" — that's a true song so you wouldn't want to make a show-off song out of it; you want to let the people hear the fiddle music and every word the way the story goes.

Of all your songs, are there any you sing better than others?

I wouldn't think so. On any song I would do my best. I don't ever go out onstage and piddle around with it. I give my throat and my voice a chance. By doing that, you've done your best right there and put some power behind it. That's all you need to do with it.

Do you enjoy having the audience sing along with you?

Oh, I love that. That's a great part of our shows today.

You once said that you thought of bluegrass as a type of competition between band members. Is that the way you view it today?

I think that's the way it is. You know you've got competition in bluegrass music. If you play a banjo number the best you can play it, the next man that's out there, he's going to play it hard. You've got people up there like Earl Scruggs and Don Reno to face, and you better come with the best that you've got or you're not going to sell. It's the same thing with the singer. He'd better do it good, because there's another man they're going to introduce who's going to come out and sing his best. Same thing about the mandolin, or a quartet, or anything. It's a challenge. It's music that needs a lot of practice. You need to practice every time you get a chance.

— *Dix Bruce*

A SELECTED MONROE DISCOGRAPHY

Solo Albums (on MCA): *Bean Blossom*, 2-8002; *Best Of Bill Monroe*, 2-4090; *Bluegrass Instrumentals*, 104; *Bluegrass Memories*, 2315; *Bluegrass Ramble*, 88; *Bluegrass Special*, 97; *Bluegrass Time*, 116; *High, Lonesome Sound Of Bill Monroe*, 110; *I Saw The Light*, 527; *I'll Meet You In Church Sunday Morning*, 226; *Kentucky Blue Grass*, 136; *Mr. Bluegrass*, 82; *Bill Monroe, Country Music Hall Of Fame*, 140; *Bill Monroe's Greatest Hits*, 17; *Bill Monroe Sings Bluegrass, Body And Soul*, 2251; *Road Of Life*, 426; *Uncle Pen*, 500; *Voice From On High*, 131; *Weary Traveler*, 2173. (on Victor Records): *Lester Flatt Live Bluegrass Festival*, APLI-0588; *Stars Of The Grand Ole Opry, 1926-1974*, 2-0466. (on Columbia Records): *Bill Monroe And His Blue Grass Boys*, CS-1065. (on Coral Records, 100 Universal City Plaza, Universal City, CA 91608): *Bluegrass Style*, 20077; *Bill Monroe Sings Country Songs*, 20099; **Singles:** *Footprints In The Snow*, MCA, 60074; *In The Pines*, MCA, 60074. **With James Monroe:** *Father And Son*, MCA, 310; *Together Again*, MCA, 2367. **With the Monroe Brothers** (on Camden Records, 7500 Excelsior Blvd., Minneapolis, MN 55426): *50 Years Of Country Music*, ADL2-0782; *Smokey Mountain Ballads*, ACL-7022; *Sound Of Bluegrass*, ACLI-0535; *Feast Here Tonight*, Victor Records, AXM2-5510; *Bill And Charlie Monroe*, MCA, 124.

MONROE'S MANDOLIN

*G*IBSON'S ORIGINAL F-5 mandolins, manufactured from 1922 to the end of 1924, are considered by many to be the creme de la creme of acoustic fretted instruments. The F-5 series was developed jointly by Lewis A. Williams, one of the founders and major stockholders of the company, and Gibson general manager Guy Hart. In late 1919, the company invited a well-known concert mandolinist, Lloyd A. Loar, to join the staff as an advisor, demonstrator, and later, acoustic engineer. Loar was asked to work closely with the engineering department on new developments in the line and to tour the country to promote the instruments. He was prominent enough as a performer to make his endorsement a valuable asset for Gibson, and he personally signed the instruments categorized as the Model 5, or "Master Model," editions. These included the Master Model F-5 mandolin, the Master Model H-5 mandola, the Master Model L-5 guitar, and a few Master Model K5 mandocellos. Approximately 170 Loar-signed F-5 mandolins were produced between the F-5's introduction in 1922 and Loar's departure from the company in December, 1924. These mandolins were designed and built as classical instruments. Their celebrated association with the bluegrass idiom can be attributed to the Father of Bluegrass, Bill Monroe. No story about Bill Monroe would be complete without a discussion of his famous F-5, so Nashville writer Ingrid Fowler has provided us with a close-up look at this historic instrument.

* * * *

Bill Monroe's Gibson F-5 mandolin bears the serial number 73987. It was signed and dated by Lloyd Loar on July 9, 1923. Bill bought the instrument in 1941 after seeing it in the window of a barbershop in Miami, Florida. Bill remembers that he was just walking around town when it caught his eye: "Maybe I'd had breakfast someplace and was just out window-shopping," he recalls, "and I seen this mandolin in this barbershop, and I stopped and went in."

He was playing an F-7 then and simply wanted something better. The mandolin in the barbershop window had everything that he was seeking. In his own words today: ". . . a wonderful fretboard, and a neck that is really small. It's got a lot of volume and is a wonderful rhythm mandolin." The barbershop transaction cost Bill $150.

About 25 years ago the instrument either fell or was dropped, Bill doesn't remember which, but the upshot was that the carved scroll on the peghead broke off. Although he intended to have the broken piece replaced he never got around to it. He carried the broken scroll with him for a long time, but eventually it was lost. The odd-looking peghead with its missing scroll has become a Monroe trademark and a symbol of bluegrass music.

There's another trademark feature about the peghead, too. The peghead inlay originally read "The Gibson," but where the word "Gibson" used to be there is only a gouged-out area in the wood. The story behind that dates back to an accident — somebody dropped the mandolin — which broke off the instrument's neck. Bill decided to send the damaged mandolin back to the factory for repairs. "I had four or five more things I wanted done to it," he told us. "It needed frets and tuning keys, and I wanted to have it refinished because it had gotten pretty scratched up, so I sent it to Gibson. This was around 1951. They kept it four months, and when they sent it back all they'd done was put the neck back on. That's all they did! I got kind of aggravated."

Bill declines to talk further about the incident, having long since put his aggravation behind him, but we've heard that the factory did perform the refinishing. In any case, at the time Bill was so unhappy with what had — and hadn't — been done to his mandolin that he took a pocket knife, gouged the company's name out of the peghead, and then scraped off whatever finish had been applied.

Bill doesn't use a pickguard on his F-5. "It's better for me for it to be off," he explains. "I think it makes the mandolin sound better. It vibrates better with it off. It might take care of the mandolin better with it on there, but it's better for me with it off."

There seems to be little about the instrument that's important to Bill beyond what it can do. He's certainly more music-directed and, to him, it's a tool. When asked about the mandolin he doesn't reply in terms of its style or its design. Instead, he says, "It's got a sound that no other mandolin's got. You can separate the notes on it and every note will ring. It's got a quality that I don't hear in anything else." Although he has used other mandolins on occasion, and though he owns a couple of others, he has no interest in being onstage with anything else but F-5 No. 73987. Since he never gives it a rest, it gets a lot of handling and a lot of work, so it needs a lot of repairing.

Some of the repairs on Bill's mandolin have been performed by Randy Wood, one of the country's most respected instrument craftsmen (and the former owner of the Pickin' Parlor in Nashville). Randy has replaced the fretboard, and at one time he replaced the old pearl nut — only to have Bill bring the mandolin back a few days later to get the original nut re-installed. Bill said that the mandolin sounded better with the old one. Monroe's concern for the instrument was such that he requested that Randy take the mandolin home with him each night, rather than leave it in the shop.

Bill and Randy once discussed resetting the neck because the action was getting so bad, but Bill decided against having the work done because he thought it might change the sound of the instrument.

The physical characteristics of Bill's instruments may not inspire him to eloquence; but there's no question that the musical qualities of that magic mandolin have inspired Bill Monroe to unsurpassed musical eloquence, just as he has inspired the thousands of devoted followers of his music who play in his shadow.

— *Ingrid Fowler*

Bill Monroe without Gibson F-5 mandolin #73987 is like George Burns without his cigar, Tom Landry without his hat, or the Lone Ranger without his mask. It's safe to say that no single instrument has been so closely identified with a particular performer, and with a particular musical style, as Monroe's venerable Lloyd Loar F-5. With it, Monroe wrote the book on bluegrass. Generations of bluegrass fans came to recognize it as a symbol of their music; and recently, many of them were surprised when some of its most distinctive battle scars were eliminated by skillful cosmetic surgery at the Gibson plant.

"It's as if," complained one bemused *Frets* reader, "they fixed the crack in the Liberty Bell!"

There was ample cause for surprise. The restoration not only beautified features of the mandolin that had become as identifiable as Bob Hope's nose, it also signalled the end of a well-known grudge that Monroe had held against Gibson for nearly 30 years.

The story really begins in 1951. Monroe, who had bought the mandolin for $150 ten years before at a Miami, Florida barbershop decided to send the instrument back to the factory to have a broken neck repaired. "I had four or five more things I wanted done to it," he recalls. "It needed frets and tuning keys, and I wanted to have it refinished because it had gotten pretty scratched up. Gibson kept it four months, and when they sent it back all they'd done was put the neck back on. That's all! I got kind of aggravated."

So aggravated, in fact, that Monroe pulled out a pocket knife and gouged the "Gibson" inlay out of the instrument's peghead. Thereafter, he turned a cold shoulder to the Kalamazoo, Michigan, company. And so things remained until early last fall.

A few years later, a fall knocked the scroll off the end of #73987's peghead. Monroe carried the broken piece around for a long time, intending to have it glued back on; but the work was never done, and eventually the broken scroll was lost. By that time, the battered peghead was as well known in bluegrass circles as the face of its owner. There was no mistaking Monroe's mandolin.

Time heals a lot of things. Gibson, grateful for the exposure Monroe had given the style F-5 instrument, sought to make amends for the 1951 misunderstanding. They were aided by the good offices of Nashville, Tennessee, radio personality Billy Grammer. Early last year, Product Development Manager Rendal Wall and Artist Relations Director Pat Aldworth went to Nashville, Tennessee, bearing an olive branch in the form of a new Gibson F-5L mandolin. They presented Monroe with the instrument in recognition of his extraordinary achievements as an instrumentalist, and offered to make any repairs he wished to F-5 #73987.

Monroe accepted the offer, and on September 1, #73987 came home to Kalamazoo to get a new peghead scroll, new peghead veneer and inlay, and a new fretboard. A team of Gibson experts, headed by master mandolin luthier Dick Doan, carried out the restoration.

The old peghead veneer was carefully separated from the peghead. A new scroll, made from matching curly maple, was fitted where the old one had broken off, and a new veneer was shaped to the peghead's outline. Doan decided to bind and inlay the veneer separately from the instrument, both to minimize handling of #73987 and to give him the opportunity to easily redo the veneer in the event the first attempt failed. The finished and bound veneer was affixed to the peghead and the edges carefully finished so that its junction with the old binding would be undetectable. The old tuners were replaced with new ones, a new fretboard was installed, and the instrument was re-assembled. Nothing else — not the bare spot on the soundboard where years of playing have nearly worn through (Monroe isn't partial to finger-rests), nor any other part of the body — was touched.

The mandolin and its owner were reunited in early October. Wall made the presentation, as flashbulbs popped. "It's wonderful to have it back," a beaming Monroe told Nashville reporters who were documenting the historic moment. "This is one of the greatest days of my life."

Monroe said that he and Gibson had "made up and forgiven each other." Then he couldn't resist giving an impromptu recital, putting #73987 through its paces. "Listen to how it rings, and keeps on ringing," he said. "I've been offered $40,000 for this mandolin, but I don't think I would sell it even if they went up to $500,000. It's meant so much to me and what I wanted to do."

— *Jim Hatlo*

Bill Monroe is still going strong. In March of 1983, President Reagan honored Monroe at the White House as "the only living American who created a style of music." From this year on, June 30 will be declared Bill Monroe Day in the state of Tennessee.

Aside from Bill, current band members include Kenny Baker on fiddle, Wayne Lewis on guitar, Mark Hembree on bass, and Blake Williams on banjo. Since this article originally was published in 1979, the following Bill Monroe albums have been released on MCA: *Bill Monroe Sings Bluegrass, Body And Soul,* MCA 708; *Bean Blossom '79,* MCA 765; *Bluegrass Memories,* MCA 2315; *Bill Monroe And Friends,* MCA 5435.

RALPH STANLEY

IN DECEMBER 1946, two young men, Carter and Ralph Stanley, stepped up to a microphone at radio station WCYB in Bristol, Tennessee/Virginia, and launched a new "wake-up" show, *Farm And Fun Time*. At dawn that cold day, people throughout rural Virginia and Tennessee heard a special duet as the two brothers exchanged leads, sliding into the half-tones, blending their voices gently with simplicity and conviction.

Listening to early Stanley Brothers recordings today you can hear faint echoes of Mainer Mountaineers, the Monroe Brothers, the Carter Family, the Blue Sky Boys, the Sons Of The Pioneers, a little Grayson and Whitter, Johnny and Jack, and lots of Beauregard; but it is unmistakably Stanley.

Unabashed simplicity, in singing and in picking, has been the hallmark of the Stanley sound Ralph Stanley has perpetuated and refined since Carter's death in December, 1966. Today Ralph Stanley is one of the patriarchs of bluegrass, and his sky-reaching tenor voice and the simple, bright clarity of his banjo are sounds dear to the ears of thousands of loyal fans.

In his long career, Stanley has put together some of the finest bluegrass bands ever, with some of the finest lead singers: Larry Sparks, Roy Lee Centers, and Keith Whitley. The current version of his Clinch Mountain Boys includes veterans Curly Ray Cline on fiddle and Jack Cooke on upright bass, with young newcomers Charlie Sizemore singing lead and Junior Blankenship playing lead guitar.

In May 1976, at his annual Carter Stanley Memorial Festival, Ralph Stanley was awarded an honorary Doctor of Arts degree from Lincoln Memorial University, a small, liberal arts college near Cumberland Gap, Tennessee, not too many miles from the "rollin' hills of ol' Virginia" where Carter (b. 1925) and Ralph (b. 1927) were raised. Faithful to his origins, he still lives in McClure, Virginia, not far from his birthplace.

Ralph Stanley is known as a man of few words, but when you can get him talking, typically, he will tell a story or two and then end with a quiet chuckle, a sound as identifiably Stanley as any you are likely to hear. Speaking of his well-known "Clinch Mountain Backstep," he once said, "All the tunes I write are real simple. They are so simple a good musician can't play them." And then he chuckled.

*　　*　　*　　*

YOU'VE BEEN PLAYING *professionally now for more than 30 years. What have been some of the most memorable moments of your career?*

Carter and me moved to Bristol from station WNVA in Norton, Virginia, and started this program, *Farm And Fun Time*. I believe we started there on a Saturday, and had an hour program. I know two weeks from the time we started, with Carter singing lead, me on the banjo, Pee Wee Lambert on the mandolin, and Leslie Keith on the fiddle, we played this place in Belfast, Virginia. It was a school, this first date, and it was a pretty good-sized school. We had two packed houses. Now that was one happy time, because that began to show us that maybe if we had it that night, we might have it on and on and on. We started playing five, six, seven nights a week. And everywhere we'd go we'd pack 'em one or two times. I know for

Today, Ralph Stanley is one of the patriarchs of bluegrass, and his sky-reaching tenor voice and the simple, bright clarity of his banjo are sounds dear to the ears of thousands of loyal fans.

a time in '47 we was booked as high as 90 days ahead. We'd get dates in the mail and a lot of them we couldn't answer, and we just had to throw 'em in the wastebasket. Those were some real happy days. Leslie Keith had been in the business for several years, and we didn't know much about it. Well, he had him a little folder, just a two-page something that had his picture and his family's picture and had a history of the "Black Mountain Blues" on it. Well, he sold this on the radio, on our daily program. And in six weeks' time he sold something like 5,000 copies. So we had a little songbook made, just a little bigger, and started selling it, and in six weeks we sold over 20,000 copies at 50¢ apiece. That was money at that time. When that started coming in, those were some happy days.

What would you say were some of the most difficult moments?

About 1955 up to 1958 were some of the lean years. This rock and roll trend, with Elvis Presley, changed everything around. Flatt and Scruggs, Don Reno and Red Smiley, Bill Monroe, and the Stanley Brothers were the only bands I know who survived that. Now, I've seen times when you didn't make it. There was a year or two in Bristol we roomed at the YMCA, for four dollars a week. And I've seen many a week I couldn't pay that rent. But you had to stay with it. We wasn't makin' a livin' at it then, but we survived.

Many new bands are struggling to survive in a crowded business. What kind of advice would you give to a young musician who was just starting out?

Well, for a banjo player, I think maybe he might have a favorite [banjoist] he could get some licks from. Then — a lot of people might say it's impossible to do this now, but it's not — do your best to get a sound of your own. Then get your own licks, if you can. If you want to get some of my licks and Don Reno's licks or somebody else's, get them. But use them the way you feel it. I've heard fellows say, "This fellow over here, you can't tell him from Earl Scruggs." Well, that might be true; but Earl Scruggs has done made it on that lick. So you're not doing a thing but helping Earl Scruggs. If people want to hear "Foggy Mountain Breakdown," why 99 percent want to hear Earl play it. I've heard players play it just as good or better than him; it's not the same.

Would you encourage young musicians to try to make a career of music?

Yeah, I'd say so — if you can get something that people would like and take to, and get something of your own. That's the main thing in this business. Now, ninety percent of the bluegrass bands today at one of these bluegrass festivals, unless you're watching them on the stage, you can't tell who it is. Now, when Bill Monroe comes on, you can tell who it is. You can tell who Jimmy Martin is. You can tell who Ralph Stanley is. There's just a very few you can tell without looking at them. You'll find a lot of groups will go out on the stage and will go

over with a bang, but they're not making a living at it. They're not getting paid for that. They're not selling any records. That's the importance of it — our record sales, and the demand for the places, and what you get paid when you go there.

You've recorded over 70 albums now. What are some of the songs you take the most pride in?

I'd say "Rank Stranger," "White Dove," "Man Of Constant Sorrow," "The Fields Have Turned Brown," "Two Coats," "Clinch Mountain Backstep," and "Hard Times."

Since you mentioned those banjo tunes, could you tell us a little about your first banjo and how you learned to play?

Of course, our mother did play the 5-string banjo. She played it the old-time style, what I call clawhammer. Some people might call it drop-thumb. She would tell us about how, back when she was a little girl, she had 11 brothers and sisters and every one of them played the banjo some; and she would tell about going to the old-time dances. At that time they just played maybe the banjo by itself, or sometimes with a fiddle. They didn't have guitars around there then. She said she would play the banjo many a time until daylight, all night, and then walk about five miles and hoe corn all day. She must have liked music real well to do that. Carter and me finally got our mother and daddy in the notion to get us an instrument apiece. I know my aunt, Roxie Smith, my mother's sister, lived about a mile from us; and she'd raise pigs. My aunt also had a banjo. I wanted a pig so I could raise me some hogs. I remember my mother told me I could have a choice; she told me I could have either one I wanted. My aunt wanted five dollars each for the pig and the banjo. I took the banjo, and I'm glad I did, 'cause it's done more for me than a pig would have done. I couldn't have took the pig where I took the banjo.

What style did you play then?

Well, I played the old-time way, claw-hammer. And I don't think that banjo had any name on it. Back then they judged the banjo on how many brackets it had, and if it had 39 brackets, why then it was a good banjo. And this one did.

What happened to that banjo? Do you still have it?

No, I don't have that old banjo — but I guess I've found 25 people that [say they] have!

What year did you start playing

About 1938 or '39, I guess. I had never heard any three-finger [picking] at that time. I didn't start playing three-finger style until about 1946 or '47.

Who influence your picking style?

Well, mother started me off. She had a real smooth hand. Never missed a lick. I didn't hear too much picking on the radio. Me and Carter originally got interested in old-time music because our daddy bought a radio, a battery Philco radio. Especially on a Saturday night when something special

was on, why, the house would be full of neighbors. They'd walk for two or three miles just to hear the radio. And we heard people playin' music. I remember that Wade Mainer, of Mainer's Mountaineers, played banjo. He used one finger and thumb in his style. And I took up that style and played it a while. Maybe I might have heard Buster Moore, too. In 1947 I recorded "Little Maggie" on our second Rich-R-Tone session, two-finger style. I believe the first man I ever heard playing with three fingers was Snuffy Jenkins, if I'm not mistaken.

When did you get your first good instrument?

After I played the old one I was telling you about for maybe a couple or three years, why, I found a banjo in a Spiegel's catalog that I thought was the prettiest thing I ever saw, and I ordered that. I forget what it cost, maybe $23 or $24. But anyway, one of my uncles has a credit account with Spiegel's. I didn't have that $23 or $24, so I ordered it in his name. I paid — seems like it was three dollars a month. And I cut minin' timbers. Back in our country there's a lot of coal mines, and at that time you'd cut timbers. That's the way I bought my second banjo. Back then the mailman carried mail to our house on a horse, and I remember he had the banjo across in front of him. When he brought it from the post office, I was waiting at the mailbox. I didn't play that banjo too long before I bought an old Gibson from a coal miner in Tom's Creek, Virginia. I gave him $50 for it. I played it a while, and then I heard about the [Gibson] Mastertone banjo. I heard about one for sale in North Carolina. An old banjo player who played with three fingers had it; I believe his name was Mack Crowe. Leslie Keith, he knew of the Mastertone. I went down one day and bought it — paid $175 for it. In all, I guess I've owned 50 banjos.

Where did you get the arch-top Gibson you now play most of the time?

I got it in Sacramento, California. We worked a college out there, and this old man about 70 years old was at the concert. He was from Mountain City, Tennessee. He told me he had an old banjo that he never did play very much, and said he might trade it to me. He said, "Just anything I can get to thump on a bit [is all right]. I don't care whether it's any good or not." So I went home with him, and he dragged it out from under the bed, and I traded banjos with him. It had dust on it about a quarter of an inch thick. It's just a Gibson Granada Deluxe, about a 1926 or '27 model.

You play a Stelling Gospel from time to time. What made you decide to play the Stelling?

I wouldn't say the sound is any better; maybe it's not as good as my Gibson. But it's good enough to record some of the songs with. Geoff Stelling wanted me to use that banjo and demonstrate it. As far as I'm concerned, if you wanted to buy a new banjo, I don't think you could beat the Stell-

ing. If I didn't like the sound and believe in it, I wouldn't play it. But I wouldn't put it ahead of the old one.

You once said that Bill Keith told you that part of his idea for chromatic banjo had come from listening to your playing of "Clinch Mountain Backstep." Can you recall that conversation?

We were talking somewhere about it, and he wanted me to play the "Clinch Mountain Backstep." It sets sort of a trip on the bottom string. I don't know what you call his type of playing. Mine don't sound like his, but it gives you an idea of how to get the sounds on the other strings.

Do you have any particular strings you like to use?

I just use one thing, then another —just anything I can get hold of. I might have a string on the banjo that's been there a year. When I break one, I replace it.

How would you describe the sound that you're looking for in your banjo, and the sound you want to hear as you put the whole band together?

Well, I always like to play the banjo as close as I can to exactly the way you say the words. In other words, if you put a slur in a word, you put it in that instrument, if you can — make it sound just as much as the way the song goes. That's the way I do [it with] every one of the fellows that works with me. Curly Cline is a number-one fiddle player, but when we go to record I show Curly on just about every session how to play the fiddle on my records. He does it the way he sees it.

When you and Carter did your now-classic Mercury recordings in the early '50s in Nashville at the Owen Bradley Studios, did you have any idea you were leaving a permanent mark, a standard that would be there for a long time to come?

Not at that time, no. I think every person and every band has a highlight in life, when you're really on the ball and maybe the songs are coming to you. I don't care how good a songwriter you are; if it don't hit you just right, you can't write. There's a certain time in your life when things come to you. And that was the time for us.

— *Douglas Gordon*

Since publication of this article in Nov. '79, Ralph Stanley has cut six more albums on the Rebel label (Box 191, Floyd, VA 24091).

Ralph Stanley and the Clinch Mountain Boys in the early '70s. (L to R): Curly Ray Cline, Ricky Lee, Stanley, Keith Whitley, and Jack Cooke. Following his brother Carter's passing in 1966, Ralph has continued the Stanley Brothers' mountain style of bluegrass up to the present.

A SELECTED STANLEY DISCOGRAPHY

Solo Albums: *A Man And His Music* (Box 191, Floyd, VA 24091), Rebel, SLP 1530; *Hills Of Home,* King (220 Boscobel St., Nashville, TN 37213), 1069. **With the Clinch Mountain Boys:** *Cry From The Cross,* Rebel, 1499. **With the Stanley Brothers:** *The Best Of The Stanley Brothers,* Starday (220 Boscobel St., Nashville, TN 37213), SLP 953; *The Legendary Stanley Brothers — Recorded Live, Vol. 1,* Rebel, SLP 1487; *The Legendary Stanley Brothers — Recorded Live, Vol. 2,* Rebel, SLP 1495; *The Stanley Brothers' Sixteen Greatest Hits,* Starday, SD-3003; *The Stanley Brothers Together For The Last Time,* Rebel, SLP 1512. **The Stanley Brothers & The Clinch Mountain Boys:** *Mountain Boys,* King, 615; *Mountain Song Favorites,* Nashville (20 Music Sq., Nashville, TN 37203), NLP 2014.

EARL SCRUGGS

MANY ARTISTS STAND OUT IN the history of music as important innovators in technique, style, or instrument design. But few musicians have so wholly helped to establish the foundation of the bluegrass musical idiom as Earl Scruggs, who almost single-handedly created and shaped the sound of an instrument: the magical, tantalizing, twangy, syncopated voice of his 5-string banjo.

Although the 5-string banjo had been popular in the nineteenth century in minstrel shows and as a parlor instrument, it had come back into the limelight during the '20s and '30s in the hands of frailing-style entertainer Uncle Dave Macon. It wasn't, however, until the '40s that it found its greatest advocate: Earl Scruggs. Scruggs turned it into a major lead instrument, thrilling the ears of thousands of listeners, and starting a stampede of 5-string banjo enthusiasts that carried to every corner of the world.

I remember meeting a Czechoslovakian band at the *Grand Ole Opry* several years ago. Onstage they could mimic the lyrics of any bluegrass tune, but offstage they had to communicate through an interpreter. The banjo player knew only one English word, but it spoke in volumes: "Scruggs."

Scruggs. The word conjures up sounds, techniques, and images of a special type of banjo, a picture so complete in the minds of most string musicians that any definition would be redundant. Non-musicians know the word too, whether they associate it with *Bonnie And Clyde, The Beverly Hillbillies,* or Flatt And Scruggs. The banjo man from North Carolina's western hills has become more than a part of American music; he has become an integral part of American life.

Earl Eugene Scruggs was born on Jan. 6, 1924, in Shelby, North Carolina, in an area known as the Flint Hill community. His father, George Elam Scruggs, was said to have played some banjo and fiddle; but Earl's memories of his dad are vague. George Scruggs died when Earl was only four years old. Earl's mother, Lula Ruppe Scruggs, was an important factor in Earl's musical development. Her encouragement allowed him the freedom to leave home and pursue a life in music.

Earl's mother and his younger sister, Venie Mae, were not musically inclined; but his brothers, Junie and Horace, and his older sisters, Eula Mae and Ruby, all played banjo and guitar. By the time Earl was six years old Junie had done enough experimenting with the banjo to spark Earl's interest. However, the major influence, as Earl remembers, came from a relative named Smith Hammett. Hammett played banjo with a form of three-finger picking, and he had a small banjo — which he generously gave to his young admirer. Earl began to emulate Hammett in a childhood game that acquired more importance when Scruggs learned that "local folks really loved it, they'd just stand around and listen."

Before long, the child prodigy had become a local star. By the time Scruggs entered his teens, he was playing at some nearby square dances. His desire to increase the exposure of his new-found musical gifts was curtailed by his obligation, as he says, "to be the breadwinner" after his brothers and sisters married and left home. The responsibility of providing for his mother, and their household, was his.

The music business was an unknown quantity for him then, and looking into it was like "looking into a dark room," remembers Earl. He played with a few local bands, and was "forced to weigh carefully whether it would be stable or not." At the

age of 15, Earl got a job playing with Wiley and Zeke Morris, who billed themselves as the Morris Brothers. Zeke played mandolin, and Wiley played the guitar. At that time, their style came under the heading of "country" music.

Earl's distinctive three-finger picking technique was beginning to take shape. Still, he felt it needed refinement — but he wasn't quite sure what that would take. "I wasn't happy about what I was doing, but I didn't know what to do about it," he says. Since he was breaking new ground, there were no other musicians with whom he could trade licks and ideas.

At the end of World War II, Earl's mother encouraged him to pursue music as a career. In 1945, at age 21, Earl had the opportunity to meet Bill Monroe, and it wasn't long before Scruggs was invited to come aboard Monroe's band, the Blue Grass Boys. In addition to Earl on banjo, the band consisted of Howard Watts ("Cedric Rainwater") on bass, Chubby Wise on fiddle, Monroe on mandolin — and a guitarist named Lester Flatt. That group played together for three seminal years, firmly establishing the foundation of the music style that was to become recognized as "bluegrass," a term coined from the band's name.

In early 1948, discouraged with the music business, Scruggs left Monroe to move back to North Carolina. A few weeks later, Lester Flatt also resigned. Scruggs and Flatt then decided to organize a band to work in the Carolinas/Virginia area. The new group featured Howard Watts on bass, Jim Shumate on fiddle, Lester Flatt on guitar, Mac Wiseman on guitar, and Earl on banjo.

The band's theme song was a Carter Family tune called "Foggy Mountain Top," and from that song the band derived its name, Lester Flatt, Earl Scruggs, and the Foggy Mountain Boys. In the summer of 1948, about six months after the band was formed, it recorded its first series of songs: "God Loves His Children," "I'm Going To Make Heaven My Home," "We'll Meet Again Sweetheart," and "Cabin In Caroline." During the following two years the band recorded twenty-nine 78-rpm sides for the Mercury label. In the fall of 1950, the group signed for its first recording session with Columbia.

The band was very active during the early '50s, playing show dates in most of the southeastern states. On one trip. Scruggs was approached by a salesman from the Martha White Mills flour company and was asked if the band would be interested in working on the company's radio shows. The program aired six days a week on WSM, out of Nashville. The musicians agreed, and made their first appearance for Martha White Mills in June 1953.

By 1955, the Martha White radio promotions had developed so much interest that the company increased Flatt And Scruggs' exposure to a series of 30-minute TV shows, aired in six different cities. In addition, the band was put on the *Grand Ole Opry,* with Martha White as the sponsor. The band taped the morning radio shows and then traveled 2,500 miles each week by car to Columbus, Georgia, on Monday; Atlanta on Tuesday; Florence, South Carolina, on Wednesday; Huntington, West Virginia, on Thursday; Jackson, Tennessee, on Friday; and back to Nashville for WSM-TV on Saturday. In 1960, the Foggy Mountain Boys appeared on a national TV show entitled *Folk Sound USA.* Soon afterward, the band was invited to perform at the Newport Folk Festival. The Foggy Mountain Boys had a sound that was enjoyed by musicians, bluegrass devotees, and general audiences alike.

The '60s saw the music of Earl's banjo carried onto virtually every airwave in the nation. The band's "The Ballad Of Jed Clampett," the theme song of the TV show *The Beverly Hillbillies,* became a #1 single in late 1962. Later in the decade, Earl's classic "Foggy Mountain Breakdown" topped the charts as the hit theme of the film *Bonnie And Clyde.* The '60s also saw Earl's three sons enter musical maturity, and family jam sessions were common in the Scruggs household. Earl soon realized that the three young gentlemen, who had become part of his musical tradition, might very well be destined to play an active part in his musical future. The home jams took on more intensity, and after 40 years of banjo playing, Earl discovered a new, and even more exciting challenge.

In 1969, Earl was ready to make the most dramatic change in his entire career: the formation of a band featuring Gary, Randy, and Steve Scruggs, performing with Earl under the banner of the Earl Scruggs Revue. He separated from Lester Flatt. In the heat of much controversy sparked by bluegrass die-hards, Earl moved to another plateau, creating new sounds with his 5-string banjo. Many of the tunes he plays today have the

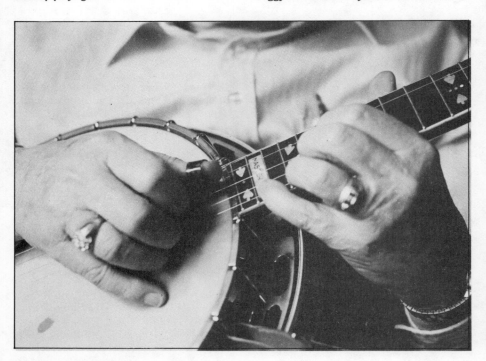

Close-up of Earl Scruggs playing high on the neck of his Gibson Mastertone banjo. Scruggs, pioneer of the 3-finger five-string banjo in a bluegrass setting, moves his picking hand far from the bridge to achieve a softer tone for back-up playing.

same titles as those originated and performed with strictly acoustic musicians. Now the backup is a combination of acoustic and electric — and the sound is eclectic. It's "Foggy Mountain Breakdown" and "Earl's Breakdown" in another time and place, yet still coming from the hands of their creator, Earl Scruggs.

The gifts Scruggs has given to the world of 5-string banjo are priceless, and the future holds even more in store. Scruggs is one of a kind. Although many banjoists have emulated his style, none have surpassed his solid, syncopated licks. While some banjoists have run chromatic circles around "Shucking The Corn," none have ever laid it down like Earl.

During the following interview, Earl and I sat in his Madison, Tennessee, home — occasionally looking out the window at the tour buses that stopped to let passengers take pictures of the Scruggs house. When I asked him what he thought when he found his three-finger picking style taking hold, he said, "It really made me wonder what would happen if I had the exposure." Earl Scruggs doesn't wonder any more.

AFTER YOUR FORTY years of banjo playing, did you go through a relearning process when you got into the music of the Revue?

Quite a bit. Like, many chords I already know — but had never exercised or activated. The rhythm patterns for much of the Revue material were different from what I had done for so long. But Gary and Randy had been playing a lot of the current material at home, and I was sitting in on a lot of jam sessions with them, and friends would drop by; so really it didn't jump out at me all that much. It has been a refreshing, happy, and rewarding challenge.

Have you found situations with the Revue where you can't get what you want from the banjo?

There are definitely tunes that I don't think the banjo should be part of. I've found that true in all forms of music.

Do you have trouble maintaining your volume level with the other members of the band? Do you find that you have to play harder, or that they have to hold themselves down?

No. I use an amp onstage strictly as a monitor. If somebody's too loud, the engineer on the board will cut him back. We only run into amp volume level problems when we are in a small auditorium, and find that the acoustics are extremely good. Our main mix always comes from the board.

Do you bring along your own sound equipment?

We use primarily rental equipment, and the only things we take along are our instruments and amps. I have a bus, and we carry our own stage equipment with us.

Are there any new mechanical developments for the banjo, like the Scruggs tuners

[*pegs that allow controlled d-tuning of a string*], *that you see in the offing for your current style of music?*

I would like to add one more bass string — a fifth/fourth string [*laughs*], if you know what I mean — to get a low note for some tunes. I've tried a Keith tuner [a single peg with controlled stops] on the fourth string, but the problem is that the winding doesn't let the string slide all the way on the nut accurately enough. I've got an idea I'm working on that should give me a way around the problem. If it works, it should be much more accurate.

Do you use the Scruggs tuners much today?

Yes, I still do "Earl's Breakdown" and "Flint Hill Special" using the tuners. Those still go over well onstage; they are good picking tunes for me and they come off well. I've played some of those tunes so much that I wouldn't sit down and play them for my own amusement. But I'm out there to entertain, and I like to see a good smile from the audience and watch them get into the rhythm.

What was the first banjo that you used professionally?

I had a Gibson, but it wasn't a Mastertone and it didn't have a metal tone ring in it. It was real shiny and it was blue. They called it a model RB-II, and the one I had was an original 5-string. The fretboard was made to look like pearl and the back of the resonator had a large, colorful design on it.

Don Reno once told me that he traded banjos with you. Can you tell us what happened?

Well, Don traded me his banjo and a guitar for my banjo. I liked the sound of his banjo, and he liked mine. I didn't do it to get the guitar; I just liked the tone of his banjo.

Have you tried other banjos that are available today?

I'm trying the OME banjo now. I've been trying one out on the road now, just to see what they can build. I find it to be pretty good.

What are your feelings regarding flat-top tone chambers versus arch-top tone chambers?

I prefer the flat-top. The main thing I have noticed in the sound of the flat-top, as opposed to the arch-top, is that the flat-top has more depth in most banjos. You might say it's like a 10-inch speaker compared to a

12-inch one. I prefer a deep, mellow tone; however, you will notice variations in either type of tone chamber.

Do you find that one records better than the other?

I wouldn't say one records *better* than the other, but I've been able to get a more mellow result from the flathead.

When you're in the studio, do you look for a different quality of banjo sound than you do when performing onstage?

No. I try to get the same sound in the studio as I get any place else. It takes a little time to EQ the board and find a mike that will do the job. I've searched very hard to get exactly the sound that I like when I get on stage. Your engineer helps too. Most of the time I work very closely with him to get what I want whether I'm on the stage, in the auditorium, or in the studio.

You are using a pickup now, aren't you?

Yes, I'm using a Barcus-Berry. I have the pickup positioned underneath the head, about an inch back from the bridge. I've found that if you get too close to the bridge, you're going to start muting the tone of the banjo. The position I use seems to eliminate losing any volume or quality; and if I want to go acoustic I can just leave the pickup in there. It doesn't affect any type of work I want to do. I do use an equalizer most of the time, and on concerts I just go straight through the board.

Do you also work into a microphone?

Well, I used to work just into the mike on our concerts. I get basically the same tone with the pickup — not *quite* the same, but it gives me the freedom to maneuver around onstage.

When you were working into the mike, where did you position it in relation to the banjo head?

I placed it in front of my hand, in the lower section of the head.

Did you experience any right-hand technique problems when you began using a pickup?

No. I get most of my tone variation with my right hand. I don't get quite as much depth with the Barcus-Berry as I do with the mike; I lose a little bit there. But I still move away from the bridge when I play backup to mellow the tone as much as possible.

Is there anything you do in the studio to improve or enhance the recording characteristics of the banjo?

I like the sound of the banjo, as I hear it, to come through as much as possible. Sometimes we will switch around with mikes to get what I want. In the last two or three studio sessions we have done, I used the mikes and no pickups.

Have you tried many different kinds of heads?

With my banjo I have to use the heaviest of everything, both bridge and head. Otherwise my banjo seems to be tinnier. I've tried to thin the bridge down and stuff like that. I've tried the Five-Star [Stewart MacDon-

ald] head and found that it is the best-constructed head that I have run into; but it seems to be just a little bit thinner than the Remo Weather King, so I do use a Weather King head on my banjo.

Do you prefer plastic heads over the skin heads?

Well, if the humidity was very low, and everything was right for the skin head, a head like the Roger's Three-Star [a famous brand of skin heads, no longer available] was superior to anything that I have used since. But 85 percent of my working time, the humidity was at a point where the tone would be dull — just not there. The only way to compensate for that was to tighten the head, or dry it out, and fool with it every day. And, if you forgot to loosen it, and the humidity went down, you'd burst the head. So, I never knew when I got to a performance whether I had a head on my banjo or not. The plastic head solved that problem, but I think I lost a little bit of tone quality there. If I look back over the years on a day-by-day basis of reliability, I've gained a lot. What I've lost is tone, but I've gained in reliability.

What kind of strings are you using?

I've been trying several different brands. I use a medium-gauge. I've tried Stelling, Vega, and so on. Actually, I like a .010" high *D*, a .012" *B*, a .014" *G*, a .016" low *D*, and a .010" fifth string.

At what height do you prefer the tailpiece?

I just bring it down enough to have the proper amount of tension so that the bridge won't slide. I have also found that if the tailpiece is too long, and gets too close to the bridge, it will start muting the tone.

Do you try to play everything open, or do you use a capo?

I use a capo a lot. I don't use a sliding capo for the fifth string, I use the little L-head spikes [in the fretboard] instead.

Have you developed any new tunings for the Revue music?

I've just been using the standard *C* and *G* tunings, and going to *D* tuning for songs like "Reuben's Train."

Who do you use for repair work?

I've been using Henry Buck in Hampton, Georgia. He's the best that I've found. He does necks, inlays and all kinds of building. I've had him do some refinishing work and refretting, and he really does some fine work.

What are some of the most important things that up-and-coming banjoists need to concentrate on?

Speed is one thing that I never put emphasis on. You must keep the syncopation and tempo so you can handle the tune. Try to play as clean as you can. Years ago, I was picking a boogie thing, just playing it by myself. I was going over and over it. It had no special tune to it, just a boogie style. My mother heard it, and she said "Earl, if you're going to play, play something that has a tune to it!" And the reason she said that was because there wasn't a guitar

player with me to follow the chords. I figured that if she couldn't figure out what I was playing, certainly somebody that didn't hear me every day couldn't tell what I was playing, either. That's when I became a firm believer that you should stick to the tune as much as possible. The other thing is that I *was* trying for speed, and found that it was better to slow down and be clear. What I concentrate on is playing the tune. In that I include pick-up notes — that is, going into a line. And when you get through with a line, finish it clean. Play as much of the tune itself as possible, and let the other things like rolls [right-hand fill patterns] be just icings and goodies, because they will only work if the tune is being played clear. Also, concentrate on learning good backup if you're picking with others, and on *when* to do fill-ins — not just *how* to do them. Your rolls and other goodies should be secondary. But intros to a tune, and coming out of a line, are so important. In other words, phrase what you're trying to say. That's my theory.

— Roger H. Siminoff

EARL SCRUGGS initiated one of the most important accessory developments in the history of the 5-string banjo when, in the late 1940s, he devised a method of quickly untuning the *G* and *D* strings a controlled distance and then, just as quickly, retuning them to their previous pitches. These pegs became known as "Scruggs pegs," and are often called d-tuners — either because they de-tune the string, or because they adjust the strings into an open *D* tuning.

The use of these tuners is highlighted in many of Earl's tunes. The most prominent of them is "Earl's Breakdown," in which the *B* string is d-tuned during a pause in the instrumental. When Scruggs first recorded "Earl's Breakdown," he played it by simply untuning the regular *B*-string tuning peg; but he had trouble bringing the string back up to pitch precisely.

Scruggs designed an extra peg that would rub against the *B* string and "choke" it, forcing it to raise in pitch through contact with a special bumper on the additional peg. For a few years, he used only one "Scruggs peg" on his banjo. Later he decided to add a second one for choking the *G* string. The first designs, he recalls, utilized a "4:1 ratio regular geared Grover peg." Scruggs fitted a machine screw into the hole in the string post so that the screw would "work like a cam against the string." A screw was then fitted to the peghead so that the peg could turn no further when in the closed position. An additional screw was positioned to contact the peg's cam when it moved in the opposite direction, but this one was adjustable — allowing an adjustment of tuning for the peg's two positions.

The two pegs were fitted into a plate that was clamped to the face of the peghead. The

The Foggy Mountain Boys onstage at the Opry in the mid-50s. (L to R): Paul Warren, Earl Scruggs, Buck "Uncle Josh" Graves (hidden), Curly Sechler, and Lester Flatt.

entire tuner assembly was then covered with a box-like coverplate of thin metal.

Many people thought Scruggs was being secretive about his invention, but he was perfectly willing to remove the coverplate and show how the system worked. The coverplate was there for another reason.

"When I made it," Earl recalls, "I drilled into the peghead — and you should have seen those pieces of inlay fly! I made the cover to hide the mess."

Each peg had an adjustable string-bumper that would bend the string sideways and raise the pitch. Stops were affixed to the pegs and the plate to assure positive stopping and starting points. The strings were first tuned in the open D position, with the third string at F# and the second string at A. Then the tuners were tuned to the closed position, where the third-string bumper would "choke" the third string up a half-tone to G while the second-string bumper would choke the second string up to B.

Many variations of d-tuners have since been produced. These tuners were made up of a set of straight pegs, some small brass hinge parts, a few thumb screws, two carburetor idle-adjusting screws, and two special brass shafts.

Once of the most prominent changes in this accessory was developed by Dan Bump of the Beacon Banjo Company in Putney, Vermont, and banjoist Bill Keith. Their interest developed out of a desire to make "a better tuning peg." The Keith tuners have internal cams with adjustable stops so that the peg can first be used to tighten the string to playing pitch, and then be set up as a d-tuner. To assure that each knob will turn an approximately similar distance, the machines are provided with two different string post diameters. The one with the larger barrel is used on the third string, and the one with the smaller barrel is used on the second string. The different diameters release proportionally different amounts of string. Today, Earl is using the Keith pegs on his banjo.

WHEN YOU FIRST began playing with Bill Monroe, how did you know what kind of technique to use, or what kind of runs to play?

I just played my own style. I had two tunes down pretty well then: "Sally Goodin" and "Dear Old Dixie." "Sally Goodin" I thought he could relate to, and "Dear Old Dixie" — I didn't know how to try that on him. But I did those two tunes deliberately because they were so different. At that time "Dear Old Dixie" wasn't being played at all, but I thought I'd give him both tunes.

How did you know that your music would fit, and that he would want you to stay?

Oh, I knew in my mind that it would work. I thought it was right because of his catalog of songs and the material he had. We got down to the *Opry* and we played all the way through. His closing show was at 10:00. The last bus out of Nashville was at 10:00, or 10:05, or something like that. Bill still hadn't said anything about whether he wanted me to go to work with him or not. So I just picked up my banjo and said, "That's it, I've got to catch this bus." He looked at me and said, "We'll leave at 10:00 Monday," just like that. I said, "I can't." At the time I had a touch of the flu; and for another thing, my clothes were in Knoxville. So I told him, "I've got to go to Carolina for a few days," and he said "Well, be back next Saturday," and that's how I began working with him. He never did say,

"You can have the job."

At the time when you joined Bill Monroe, who else was in the Blue Grass Boys?

He had his brother Birch playing bass, Sally Forrester [wife of fiddler Howdy Forrester] playing accordion, Jim Andrews playing tenor banjo and doing comedy, Lester on the guitar, Jim Shumate with the fiddle, and him with the mandolin. That was the band.

You said that when you came into Monroe's band there was an accordion and a tenor banjo. How do you feel today when you hear all the talk about changing the instruments in a bluegrass band?

The banjo, in itself, was a *real* change. The Solemn Ol' Judge [George Dewey Hay, the *Grand Ole Opry* emcee from 1927 to 1951], when he used to put me on the stage, he'd say, "Here's Bill and Earl with his fancy 5-string banjo." He never referred to it as just "his banjo"; he'd always add the word "fancy." The banjo was almost as much a part of making the band sound different as putting an electric instrument into the band.

How about the dobro? When did you introduce it into the Foggy Mountain Boys?

Josh Graves came on in — I think it was 1955. We actually hired Josh to play bass. We needed a bass player and we needed a comedian. Josh was working with Mac Wiseman over at WRVA in Richmond, Virginia. So he came over and was playing bass, and we thought it [the dobro] was so good that we'd try a few tunes with him. The audiences just loved it. As soon as everything sort of settled, we hired a bass player — Jake Tullock — and put Josh on dobro full time. There wasn't any bounce-back from anyone that I recall, saying, "This is not the way it should be."

Why do you think today's audiences

Earl Scruggs in the mid-70s.

have more difficulty accepting a change, such as adding a drummer to a bluegrass band?

To me, I think they should at least give it a listening chance. Now, there are a lot of bad drummers that should be criticized, just as well as pickers. But I think a good, tasteful drummer is a great asset to the group. Before we even had the acoustic upright bass, a bluegrass band was just the guitar, the fiddle, the mandolin, and the banjo. Even the doghouse [upright] bass was quite a bit of a "no-no" as far as a lot of people were concerned. But it turned out that it was a great asset, with a lot of bottom that helped to fill in the sound. If drums are played tastefully, it sure sounds better than a bunch of musicians stomping their feet on the floor to get a beat.

Do the drums provide a different kind of rhythm than the bass?

Yes, they do. They give the bass more of a chance to do what the bass is supposed to do. When Jake used to play bass with us, he had the fourth string running down real loose and he would slap it against the fingerboard, and that was nothing except a substitute for the drum. I think if drumming is done tastefully, it's an asset; and I believe that it will be accepted by everybody, in time. I must tell you that I even looked down my nose at the drums — before I began to play with them.

Could you tell us more about your relationship with Lester Flatt?

Lester and I were almost like brothers. In fact, we used to talk once in a while about how he and I were closer than we were with our own brothers. During the years, we had eaten every meal together, ridden in cars thousands of miles together, and our thinking and discussions were pretty much the same way about music and everything. It just was a good, real close relationship. The reason for the breakup came, I guess, mainly because I wanted to try something different. Actually, before the breakup, we had signed a contract with Columbia Records — it was an attractive contract — and in the deal we had to start taking some advice from the record people as far as what they thought was commercial, as opposed to some of the stuff we were cutting. Our stuff just was not selling. *Now* those tunes are selling. If they had been selling *then* as well as they are selling now, the record people would have been happy. But it didn't work that way. Another situation was that [Earl's sons] Randy and Gary were coming along musically. Some of their music, and some of their buddies who dropped in, sounded so good that I just wanted to try something else. It wasn't a bad feeling toward each other [between him and Lester] as much as it was that I felt I was depriving myself of some things. By that, I mean that I *love* bluegrass music, and I still like to play it; but I do like to mix in some other music for my own personal satisfaction, because if I don't, I can get a little bogged down and a little depressed.

You can just get a little tired of playing the same thing over and over.

Do you ever get tired of playing "Foggy Mountain Breakdown," or "Earl's Breakdown"?

I do, until I see the reaction coming back from the audience. When I go into the tune, I am out to entertain. If I start a show, and the audience is the least bit relaxed, I'll leave the tune off for a while. Once I see their expression and that they're enjoying it, that turns me on to it again.

We talk so much about bluegrass music. How would you define it?

Well, I was just thinking about an article I read the other day. You know Bill [Monroe] has the credit for being the "Father of Bluegrass." That article said that the banjo was the only indispensable instrument in bluegrass music. Now, I don't want to take credit for it, but I do think you've got to have the style of banjo in there. Then to make it complete, you need the fiddle, mandolin, guitar, and bass. The dobro is a real asset because it gives you a wider range of material you can do, since it can fill in so many empty spots.

Does bluegrass have to be strictly acoustic?

[Pause] No. To make it back in the '40s and '50s and '60s, it would've had to have been acoustic. If you get a balance with the drums, and whatever the song is calling for — if it's calling for sustaining notes — I don't see any reason why some electrical instruments couldn't be added. Anything to make the song sound a little better, is my way of looking at it.

Was there one period in which you felt most prolific with your instrumentals?

I got into trying to write tunes when I worked with Bill. We used to do a lot of rehearsing. By that I mean, Bill had a four-seat, stretched-out 1941 Chevrolet limousine, and he and I would sit in the back seat while traveling and go over some of the old songs Bill knew but didn't use in his show, like "Molly And Tenbrooks," and "Little Joe," and some of those songs. We'd ride a lot of nights after a show, going to another gig, and sit back there and pick. He was writing some new songs, Lester was writing some new songs, and I was helping. I never wrote any [instrumentals or lyrics] that I got credit for while I was with Bill. After Lester and I organized the Foggy Mountain Boys in 1948, I started putting some ideas that I had all along into tunes. The first one was "Foggy Mountain Breakdown." As far as my writing is concerned, sometimes I might write a couple in three or four months and then it might be two or three years before another one would come around that I felt strong enough about to record.

During what time span were the greater portion of your instrumentals created?

"Foggy Mountain Breakdown" was in 1948 and "Earl's Breakdown" came in '51. I think it was less than a year after that, that "Flint Hill Special" came. That's when I put the other tuner on the banjo and used two tuners. [*Ed. Note: Earl first began using one "Scruggs tuner" on the D string, and later added a second tuner for the G string.*] I just don't remember what years it was that I did tunes like "Ground Speed," or "Shuckin' The Corn," or "Randy Lynn Rag," or those types of tunes.

It seems that the chromatic picking style has become quite popular. Have you spent any time trying to adapt it to your picking technique?

No, for some reason, I just haven't. I don't know whether it's the lack of talent or the lack of interest; I just haven't got interested far enough in that style of playing to want to work it out.

Do you feel it's not important to your music?

Not as important as what I'm doing. I'm a full believer in carrying the rhythm section along, and it just seems to me that when you get into that, you separate from the rhythm part. It sounds good — like Bobby Thompson on the *Hee Haw* show, that theme is out of sight the way he does it. I think chromatic picking is strictly for a tune like that.

Do you plan to continue using the flat-head [tone chamber design] banjo with the new music?

I will continue using that same banjo. The sound is just right for me, and it works with everything.

The design styles of bluegrass instruments have gotten to be quite a status-symbol thing. Have you had a preference for the design style of your banjos, such as inlay patterns, wood finish, or plating?

No, I never have. In fact, Louise [Earl's wife] has told me a lot of times that I have the worst-looking banjo of anybody in the business. Really, the sound is what I'm looking for. I keep my banjo up as far as frets and other adjustments are concerned, but if the varnish gets looking worn, that doesn't upset me that much. I've recently had my banjo re-done, but it wasn't just for beautification; it was just because it really needed it, and I had the time off to go and have it done. Years ago, when I sent the banjo back to the [Gibson] factory, they

put those inlays in there [*pointing to a painting showing his banjo with a "bowtie" inlay pattern*]. A little later, that began to bug me a bit and I thought it needed a change. I hadn't thought that much about it until somebody told me they could replace the original inlay. I do like for it to look as original as possible.

Several people have said, "If Earl Scruggs had played a Paramount banjo, it would have been the bluegrass banjo, and the Gibson banjo would have been unpopular." How did you get into the Gibson banjos?

My first banjo was a mail-order banjo. I thought it came from Sears Roebuck, but my brother said it came from Montgomery Ward. But it looked like a Kay banjo. It didn't have any name on it — it was just a cheap banjo. When I was growing up, I was only exposed to a couple of good banjos, and they just happened to be Gibsons. That turned me on to looking for one, and I ran across mine in a pawn shop. That's how I got into it. I've never played a Paramount. I do think that most of the people who were using Paramounts were tenor banjo players, especially in the Carolinas. The Gibson was too hollow-sounding for a straight pick, and needed a mute or something.

You once told me that you like to set the tailpiece just tight enough so that the bridge won't slide. What height bridge do you use?

I've always used a five-eighths [5/8" high] bridge, and I'm real used to that height.

Do you thin the bridges down or re-work them in some way?

No. I just use them standard. But for my banjo, I look for the heaviest ones I can find. Sometimes you find them thinner than normal. I like to have a full-cut three-leg bridge for my banjo.

Have you changed your string selection during the past year?

I'm still using the same gauges [.010" high *D*, .012" *B*, .014" *G*, .016" low *D*, and .010" high *G*] except I think I told you before that the fourth string was a sixteen [.016"] and I believe that it is actually a twenty-two [.022"]. I have switched from

the Vega strings, and I am just using the Stelling strings now.

When you tighten the banjo head, how do you determine how tight it should be?

Just by feel. For my banjo it seems that if I get it really tight and back off just a slight amount, it works just right. I take it almost to the bursting point and then back off about a quarter turn, or something like that.

Have you ever used a metal thumbpick?

Yes, I have; but I get a very metallic sound. I've found that I should use as heavy a thumbpick as I can get, with not too long a point. It's unbelievable the difference in sound you can get between a good, heavy thumbpick, and a thin one. I guess it's because I play with a hard stroke, I get more depth with a heavy pick.

The Vega Banjo Company once had an Earl Scruggs Model banjo. How did that come about?

Well, I had worked with Bill Nelson — he was the president of the company. Nelson made up a bluegrass banjo and showed it to me. I gave him my ideas and that's how it started. After he sold the company to Martin [C.F. Martin Organisation], they didn't want to operate under the same terms, so we dissolved the agreement.

When you were performing with the Earl Scruggs Revue, there was a lot of distance onstage between performers. In your bluegrass band, you worked a lot closer together. Which do you prefer?

I would rather work close. Lester and I used to work with one mike. It seemed that working into one mike would give you that living-room type of playing together. I get a better feel for the music working close than I do just getting a feedback from the monitor — you know, just hearing the parts from the monitor and not from someone standing next to you.

Does using a pickup mean that you won't have to work close to other musicians in the future?

No, I think we will be working shoulder to shoulder, but we just won't have to swarm into one mike for the instrumentals. I think it also looks a little more uniform and gives a better appearance.

— **Roger H. Siminoff**

A SELECTED SCRUGGS DISCOGRAPHY

With The Earl Scruggs Revue (on Columbia): *Country Chart Busters, Vols. 1 & 2*, C-32618, C-32720; *Family Portrait*, PC-34336; *Earl Scruggs Revue*, KC-32426; *Today And Forever*, JC-36084. **With Lester Flatt:** *Flatt And Scruggs With The Foggy Mountain Boys*, Mercury/Phonogram, MG-020542 (re-released as Pickwick JS-6093); *Flatt & Scruggs At Carnegie Hall*, Columbia, CS-8845; *Flatt & Scruggs Greatest Hits*, Columbia, CS-9370; *Story Of Bonnie And Clyde*, Columbia, CS-8751; *World Of Flatt & Scruggs*, Columbia, CG-31964. **Singles:** *Blue Moon Of Kentucky*, 1-11176; *Drive To The Country*, 3-10992; *Give Me A Sign*, 1-11176; *I Could Sure Use The Feeling*, 3-10992; *Play Me No Sad Songs*, 1-11106; (on Mercury/Phonogram, 1 IBM Plaza, Chicago, IL 60611): *Back To The Cross*, 7063; *Cora Is Gone*, 7059; *Pain In The Heart*, 7061; *Take Me In Your Loveboat*, 7067; *Till The Dew Drops Fall Upon*, 7068. **Out of print:** *Foggy Mountain Banjo*, Columbia, CL-1364; *Folk Songs Of Our Land*, Columbia, CL-1830; *Hear The Whistles Blow*, Columbia, CL-2686; *Flatt & Scruggs Foggy Mountain Chimes*, Harmony Club (Box 925, Hollywood, CA 90068), HS-11401; *Flatt & Scruggs With The Foggy Mountain Boys*, Columbia, HL-7250; *Nashville Airplane*, Columbia, CS-9741.

LESTER FLATT

E ARLY IN THE morning on May 11,1979, Lester Flatt entered the cardiac care unit at Baptist Hospital in Nashville, Tennessee, suffering from severe chest pains. Not quite eight hours later he died of heart failure, succumbing at last to the string of major illnesses with which he struggled valiantly over the past few years. So ended the life of one of the three most influential men in the evolution of bluegrass music.

Lester Raymond Flatt was born June 19, 1914, in Overton County, near Sparta, Tennessee. He was one of nine children of a sharecropping farmer and fiddler. Married at 17, Lester went to work in a mill in Covington, Virginia, where he formed a band called the Harmonizers. He made his radio debut when the group played over a station — WDJB — in Roanoke, Virginia. He later went to work with the Happy-Go-Lucky Boys before an opportunity came to play full time with Charlie Monroe and his Kentucky Pardners.

Although by that point the Monroe brothers, Charlie and Bill, had been separated for a couple of years, Charlie still felt that a mandolin was an essential part of the Kentucky Pardners' sound. Lester was hired as a mandolinist and tenor singer. His wife Gladys was hired as a singer and guitarist, using the stage name of Bobbie Jean. Flatt later claimed that after leaving Charlie he never picked up the mandolin; but he did a creditable job on the instrument. His mandolin playing is preserved on *Charlie Monroe On The Noonday Jamboree — 1944* (County Records [Box 191, Floyd, VA 24091], 538).

Later in 1944, Lester quit the Kentucky Pardners and returned to Sparta, getting into the timber business for a few months. Then he received a telegram from Bill Monroe, at that point one of the hottest and most exciting acts on the *Grand Ole Opry*. Lester did not hesitate to accept a job as rhythm guitarist for Monroe's Blue Grass Boys.

He was then 30 years old, and during his four years with Monroe he blossomed into a superb singer, guitarist, and songwriter, virtually defining all those roles in the style of music that has come to be called bluegrass. His singing was high, though unstrained, and distinctive; his guitar playing was economical and straight to the point. It was punctuated by the ascending lick that came to be called "the Flatt run" in his honor. It would become one of the hallmarks of bluegrass. His songwriting — much of it done in collaboration with Monroe — displayed a flair, perhaps even a genius, for evocative simplicity. Some of the many classics coming from that era were "Sweetheart You Done Me Wrong," "Little Cabin Home On The Hill," and "Will You Be Loving Another Man."

In 1945, Earl Scruggs brought his unique and exciting banjo style to the Blue Grass Boys, and Bill Monroe suddenly found himself heading the most dynamic band in country music: Monroe and Scruggs, the premier instrumentalists of their time; Chubby Wise, a superb fiddler; and Lester Flatt, playing solid rhythm, singing true and with feeling, and writing more and better material all the time.

It was too good to last forever. Weary of the constant grind of the road, Scruggs quit in 1948. Two weeks later so did Flatt; and as he was working out his notice, so did Cedric Rainwater, the bass player. Rainwater was actually the man who made the suggestion that he, Flatt, and Scruggs form a band of their own. That they did within weeks, adding singer/guitarist Mac Wiseman (himself now a bluegrass legend) and fiddler Jim Shumate to a group they called Lester Flatt, Earl Scruggs,

And The Foggy Mountain Boys.

As with the Blue Grass Boys of 1945-48, the Foggy Mountain Boys of 1948-53 were a band marked by tremendous creative energy. Scruggs, only 19 when he joined Monroe, was still bringing his faultlessly tasteful banjo style to perfection, while Flatt continued to write song after song — such classics as "If I Should Wander Back Tonight," "Little Girl Of Mine In Tennessee," "I'll Never Shed Another Tear," "Cabin On The Hill," "Blue Ridge Cabin Home," "Cabin In Caroline," and many others.

In 1953 Flatt and Scruggs signed with longtime sponsor Martha White Mills. The theme song for their product (flour) became better-known nationwide than the product itself; Flatt and Scruggs moved to Nashville and became *Opry* members in 1955.

Their music took a mellower turn in the years that followed, but their reputation continued to grow. They became darlings of the folk revival of the '60s, which took them to every corner of the country. At the same time, through radio — and later, tele-vision —shows, and through hit records like *The Ballad Of Jed Clampett* (the first bluegrass record to go to #1 on the *Billboard* charts), they strengthened their appeal to their bread-and-butter country audience while gaining national attention as well.

The partnership of Flatt and Scruggs came to an unhappy end in 1969, with each wishing to do different things in music. Scruggs and his sons continued with the progressive bluegrass that they pursue to this day. Flatt returned to a traditional sound. It was a sound without the earlier fire and intensity, but it was warm and endearing. With his band — which he called the Nashville Grass — he spent another decade on the road, on the *Opry*, and on radio and television.

Though the Nashville Grass had fluctuating personnel, it was a consistently fine band. The last four or five years were somewhat difficult for Lester Flatt. His body began to give out, though his desire to perform remained. He had suffered heart problems as early as the mid-'60s, and he underwent five hours of open-heart surgery in Nashville in July, 1975. With admirable determination, he kept his band together and continued to appear; but he became increasingly more frail. Pneumonia and flu hospitalized him for three weeks early in 1978. Late that year he suffered a cerebral hemorrhage, and though for some months he appeared well on the road to recovery, the cardiac seizure he suffered in May was more than his weakened body could stand.

Some 250 mourners attended his funeral in Hendersonville, Tennessee, including John Hartford, Roy Acuff, Grandpa and Ramona Jones, and Ernest Tubb, among others. On May 14, he was buried in the Tennessee hills near Sparta.

An extremely influential performer in bluegrass, country, and, indeed, all of American music, he nevertheless remained modest about his success and his fame. But history will not overlook his contributions as a pioneer of bluegrass music, and his imprint on the music itself will endure for as long as it is played.

— *Douglas B. Green*

A SELECTED FLATT DISCOGRAPHY

Solo Albums (on Victor): *Best Of Lester Flatt*, APL1-0578; *Lester Flatt, Live Bluegrass Festival*, APL1-0588; *Foggy Mountain Breakdown*, ANL1-1202; *Nashville's Greatest Instrumentalists*, ANL1-2181; *Stars Of The Grand Ole Opry, 1926-1974*, CPL2-0466. **Others:** *Flatt Gospel*, Canaan (4800 W. Waco Dr., Waco, TX 76703), 9775; *Lester Raymond Flatt*, Flying Fish, 015; *Tennessee Jubilee*, Flying Fish, 012.
With Earl Scruggs (on Columbia): *Changin' Times*, CS-9596; *Country's Greatest Hits*, Vol. 1, CG-9; *Fabulous Sound Of Flatt & Scruggs*, CS-9055; *Flatt & Scruggs*, CG-30; **Flatt & Scruggs At Carnegie Hall**, CS-8845; *Flatt & Scruggs Greatest Hits*, CS-9370; *Hard Travelin'*, CS-8751. **Others:** *Greatest Folksingers Of The Sixties*, Victor, VSD-17/18.

DON RENO

THIRTY YEARS AGO, a successful, lightning-fingered banjo player with Bill Monroe And The Blue Grass Boys decided to venture out on his own. Today, many performances, many recordings, and many, many miles of touring later, Don Reno has become almost as fundamental a part of the bluegrass tradition as Monroe himself. First with the late Red Smiley, then with Bill Harrell, and now with a band that includes two of his sons, Reno has built a reputation for faultless playing and innovative stylings. He attracted attention in the '50s by adapting older standards and jazz-tinged pop songs to his formidable three-finger technique, and he also created a tune with guitarist/banjoist/mandolinist Arthur Smith — "Feudin' Banjos" — that later became one of the classic all-time banjo instrumentals. Renamed "Dueling Banjos" and recorded by Eric Weissberg and Steve Mandel, the tune was the hit theme of the movie *Deliverance*.

Reno has delivered his own brand of banjo music to awed listeners since he was in grade school. Born February 21, 1927, in Spartanburg, South Carolina, he seemed to take to the instrument through sheer instinct. "It was kind of born in me; the first time I picked one up I just started playing," he recalls. "It like to scared me to death."

He was performing on radio before he was in his teens, and he had his own band when he was 22. Reno and guitarist Red Smiley established their group, the Tennessee Cut-Ups, as one of the best in the business. The band has never lost that distinction. After Smiley's death in 1972, Bill Harrell joined Reno to keep the Cut-Ups lively style in front of audiences around the country. Today the Cut-Ups draw heavily on some home-grown talent: Reno's oldest son, Ronny, who now performs with his own group when not working with country star Merle Haggard.

Offstage Don Reno is soft-spoken, with a southern drawl so slow that it is next to impossible to have anything other than a relaxed conversation with him. Onstage, however, he comes alive with an infectious energy that crackles in his flashy banjo licks and pulses in his high tenor singing. He still spends much of the year on the road, and he shows no signs of slowing down.

* * * *

*L*IKE SOME OTHER *top bluegrass artists, you broke into the mainstream with Bill Monroe and the Blue Grass Boys; but when did your professional career* begin?

The first group I was with was the Morris Brothers — Wiley, Zeke, and George. I was only 12 years old when I started working with them. I was playing both guitar and banjo then, but they wanted me to play banjo. We played on WWNC in Asheville, North Carolina, and then we moved to WSPN in Spartanburg, South Carolina. I worked with them about a year, I guess, and then went to work with Arthur Smith. I worked with him for three years, and then the service started breaking the group up. I formed a band called the Carolina Hillbillies with Hank Garland, Pee Wee Boyd, John Palmer, Merilyn Morris, Howard Thompson, and myself and we worked until I joined the service. I was in the Army a little over two years. When I first come out in '46, me and my brother opened a grocery store,

Don Reno and his five-string banjo. An alumnus of the Bill Monroe band, Reno performed with Red Smiley and the Tennessee Cut-Ups until Smiley's passing. He continues the Cut-Ups today, joined by his three talented sons. Onstage today, his flashy banjo licks and high tenor singing still crackle with infectious energy.

and I piddled around with that for about six months. Then I started another group locally and worked with it until I joined Bill Monroe in '48. I went with Monroe about a year and a half, I guess. I left Bill in '49 and organized the Tennessee Cut-Ups.

Did you leave him or did he leave you?

I left him. I just wanted to start my own group. I never had any trouble or anything with Bill. In fact, I never got fired from a job in my life. We had a great time together.

Who was in that first group of Cut-Ups?

John Palmer, my nephew Verlon Reno, Bill Haney, Chuck Haney, and Jimmy Pruett.

When did you meet Red Smiley?

December 27, 1949, in Roanoke, Virginia, through Tommy Magness, an old-time friend of mine. I wasn't doing too well in South Carolina. Tommy and I had kind of decided, back when I was with Bill and he was with Roy Acuff, that we was goin' out and start a group. So he finally called me and said he had left Roy and was ready to start things up in Roanoke. I had a show in Greenville, South Carolina, and I told him I'd like to bring Bill Haney, who was my cousin, and Verlon, my nephew, with me if I came up there. Tommy said, "Well, I've got a guy by the name of Red Smiley and a guy by the name of Al Lancaster." Me and Verlon was doing duets at that time. We all met at the radio station in Roanoke on December 27, 1949, and did our first radio show unrehearsed. Then, when Verlon got drowned in June of 1950, me and Red started singing together all the time.

You were with Red right up until the time he died?

Yeah — that was January 2, 1972. There was a lapse, though. I left Roanoke at the end of '64. Red's health was awful bad, and I knew he shouldn't be traveling on the road. We had an established morning television show in Roanoke, an hour and a half every morning. I left him with the television show and went back and got Chuck Haney, Doug Alston, and Ronny — my oldest son. But Red went back with us in '69 and worked until he died.

And then you and Bill Harrell got together?

Well, me and Bill *was* together. Actually, the first time I worked with him was when Red and I hired Bill as a mandolin player in 1955. Then he went in the service, and Benny Williams played mandolin with us for a while. When my son Ronny learned mandolin, he started playing mandolin with us. Me and Bill started working together in December '66, and we were together almost 10 years.

What happened to your partnership with Bill?

I wanted to go back to Virginia, so I bought a home in Lynchburg, and it was quite a gap of traveling distance between us. Bill had this bad car accident that laid him up at his home in Maryland for a long time. The only work around the Washington area is in cheap-paying clubs, and I don't care for that, so me running back and forth from Lynchburg to Washington actually wasn't even feasible. I kept Bill on the payroll until he was able to go back to playing some stuff that he usually played around there.

Of all the groups you've had or been part of in your many years of playing, which one do you think was musically the best?

Me and Red Smiley, when we was together. We had a good, tight group; the same group stayed together for 10 years. Mac Magaha (fiddle), John Palmer (bass), Red (guitar), and myself were who reorganized the Tennessee Cut-Ups back in '55. You see, we had disbanded, and I worked for a period with Arthur Smith — from '52 till May of '55. But me and Red was getting calls for recording dates and engagements when we was separated. Our records was being played heavy back then.

Was there one point where you really came along, where you felt that you were developing fast?

Seems like in '53 we started recording some different stuff. I decided I wanted to put the banjo in a perspective where I could get more listeners for it. I was after the bigger markets like New York City and Chicago, places like that. And I recorded some of the old pop tunes that finally did catch new listeners for the banjo. I was very inventive for a period of about 10 years.

What do you think stimulated that inventiveness?

I don't know where it came from. It was just something inside of me that kept pushing.

Was there any particular banjo player or style or something that you heard that influenced you?

No. I was just after something different, something that nobody else was doing or had done. I started taking stuff from the guitar neck, steel guitar neck, fiddle neck, and mandolin neck and applied it to a banjo.

A lot of your technique on many of your pieces seems to be closely related to flat-picking technique, even though you're using fingerpicks. Do you think that you could play some of the pieces as easily with a flatpick if you didn't have fingerpicks on?

I probably could, but there's places in some of the flatpicking where you want to get a roll, and you can't get a roll with a straight pick.

How about a piece like "Follow The Leader"? Can you play the run in that tune as easily with a flatpick, and do you think of it as a flatpick run?

I think of it as a flatpick run, yes; but on the banjo, when I got the lick perfected, I used a down-and-up stroke, down with the thumb and up with the front finger with split-second timing in between it. It's actually easier now — I guess because I've done it so much — with a thumb and fingerpick. I can get more tone out of it with the thumb and fingerpick than I can with a straight pick, but I can do the same thing with a straight pick.

Do you think of the things that you're doing with fingerpicks as being rolls, or are you always thinking and working a note at a time?

On what you call straight picking, it's notes. I know where to tie them in, and then there will come a place where maybe a roll will fit better.

Are these rolls techniques that you developed on your own, or are they things that you picked up from somebody else who was playing at the time?

Actually, I didn't pick them up from anybody. I just did them.

Did you ever play a different banjo in the studio than you did on stage?

No, I played the same banjo for years — an old Gibson RB-4 Mastertone. Now I'm playing a Stelling, and I'm recording with the Stelling, too.

What does it have that the Gibson doesn't have?

Well, it seems like it's a little easier to play than my Gibson, which is dead with old age. I've gotten used to the Stelling. The action is a little lower than it was on the Gibson, for one thing. Of course, when I was playing the Gibson, I was used to the action being a little high; but after playing the Stelling, when I pick up something with the action higher, it doesn't seem to be as easy to play.

Are you particular about the kind of strings you use?

I like a light-gauge string. Joe Morrell's got a light-gauge string that I seem to like better than anyone else's. He's from Bristol, Virginia. I used to like the Black Diamond set when they had the bronze fourth, but they quit making it. You may have trouble when you put a new fourth on — when you thump it, it scrapes. But it don't do that on Joe Morrell's fourth. That's one reason why I like it so well. You don't have to play the string a week before you get rid of that scraping sound, where I belt out rhythm and pick on it.

Do you change strings often — just to get "new strings" sound, for instance?

No. I never perspire while playing, and if nobody else don't pick my banjo up, I wouldn't rust a set of strings out in a year.

So you only change them when they break?

Yeah, as a general rule — unless somebody comes around and wants to play my banjo, which I'm always glad for them to do. After a few playings like that, if I get some rust on, I'll change.

Have you done anything at all to customize your Stelling?

No, just tightened the head. Cox Head has come out with a head that has a hole in it, and I found out that this gives me a better sound. But the only thing that I've done to the banjo itself is made sure the head's tight. I've been thinking about experimenting with different bridges — I used to do that all the time. I drove myself crazy.

Don Reno and Bill Harrell in the early 70s. Harrell was Red Smiley's first replacement as Reno's singing partner.

How has being a bluegrass performer changed for you in the last 30 years?

I try to keep up with the changes — watch people, find out what they're liking, what they don't like, talk with people. I think that our audience is real great right at the present. We're getting a lot of the young children. I notice five- and six-year-olds are coming around, asking for autographs like they used to. There was a period when they didn't, so this is encouraging. The college circuit, a crowd of young people, is very interested in the origin of our music. These things, I think, will push it forward and keep it alive. There was a slack period in the business when nobody seemed to be much interested; I remember when there was somebody interviewing you all the time, and then there was a period when that didn't happen. Now that's coming back again. All these different things are what makes it. Each person that says one word or does one thing for it helps it in some direction.

Do you have any desire to be part of the progressive "newgrass" movement?

No, not really. It's probably good — I'm not kicking it. But they're leaving the trail, and some of them are going into orbit with it, to where it's going to take three years to figure out what they're doing. I think at one period in my career, I stepped in a little too deep several times. Like maybe, for in-

stance, "Little Rock Getaway." I don't know if the people was ready for that when I did it or not — about '57, '58, somewhere around there, when I was having pretty good success with a lot of the old standard popular stuff from the '20s and '30s. Actually, I only recorded that because somebody told me that it couldn't be played on the banjo — which was a poor business reason, as far as I'm concerned [*laughs*].

Are you still developing new things, and if so, are you doing it because you want to, or because you think you have to?

Well, I *am* developing new things, and I'm thinking of it in these terms: You want to play something so that somebody has got an inklin' of what you're playing. Most everybody around the country can whistle a few bars of this tune or that tune, and if they hear it, they recognize the tune. Because I was brought up to like all types of music, I never did put a clamp down and say, "Well, I'm not going to do this or do that or do the other." I'm going to try to do what people want me to do. And you'd be surprised at the tunes that some people will ask for in different places.

Does your long-time fiddler, Buck Ryan, help you with new players, getting them to be part of the band's profile?

Oh yeah, in a quiet way. We kind of lead them in the direction we want to go. Actually, you get better music this way, faster and quicker. You don't leave no hard feelings. You've always got to have that spark, that spirit in a band. A man don't want to feel like he's a dud. In the first place, I'm not going to hire a man until I'm sure I can pretty well tell what his scope is when I get him.

Who are the two new musicians that you've added on?

Steve Wilson and Bonny Beverly. They both switch off on different instruments. Bonny mainly plays guitar and Steve fiddles along with Buck. Steve's working dobro most of the time now and he plays the bass. When my younger son, Don Wayne, is out of school and working with us, he plays bass and Steve plays dobro. Of course, Steve also does singing and Don Wayne plays banjo. So I'm actually using six in the group. Don Wayne's 16 now. I've been lucky. I never tried to force it on any of my children, but they all made musicians.

Are you doing now what you really feel is the most rewarding thing for you?

Yes, I am.

How do you do that for 35 years?

Well, you see, like Dale and Don Wayne, they're progressing beautifully as young musicians and they've got an awful lot of energy. At home, in their room, they've got tape recorders and stereos and this, that, and the other thing. They're listening all the time. They listen a while, and pick up their instruments and play a while, and this is kind of like not having to tell the kid, "You got to do your homework." You *hear* them doing it, and you hear them progressing. And Ronny is in Nashville, working with Merle Haggard.

Well, all that puts a spark back in me — makes me know that I've got to get somewhere and do my homework every once in a while!

Let's say that the other two boys really wanted to go off into a different area of music. Would you go with them if they changed, if they decided to do something electric?

No, I wouldn't do that. I didn't do it for Ronny, and I wouldn't do it for Dale. Now, Ronny is more oriented toward wanting to come back to the music he started with than toward what he's doing today. But I figure it like this: I'm too old to change. If I did change, I'd be facing a whole new audience that didn't know me.

Somehow, the standard bluegrass group has become primarily a mandolin, a fiddle, a guitar, sometimes a dobro, a banjo player and an upright bass player. Is there anything else that you've ever thought should be added to that, or maybe taken away from it?

I have oftentimes thought, and started to do it several times, that — well, I think that if the xylophone was played tasteful behind a bluegrass group, it would add to it.

That's wild!

Yeah, it's wild. I'm not talking about "Cumberland Gap," and stuff like that, but about using it on some of your slow stuff, if it was played tasteful. I've never tried it; but I remember when I was a kid, I heard Jack Shook And The Missouri Mountaineers working on the *Opry*. They had a xylophone in their group, and it blended with the guitars, fiddle, and bass. The xylophone always seemed to sound so pretty behind

them. I can still hear it ringing in my head.

How did your new album with Arthur Smith [Feudin' Again, CMH, 6234] come about?

Me and Arthur had talked about it for several years, and finally he called me and said, "Let's do that album we've been talking about." I said, "All right. What do you want to do?" He said, "Well, I'll select some numbers and you select some," and I said, "OK." He sent me some of his tunes that he wanted to do, and I told him, "It's been so long since I've played some of them, you're going to have to send me the sheet music on this stuff and let me run over it [laughs]!" I wanted to be sure I got the right chords and the right tune!

How do you feel when you look back on more than three decades as a bluegrass performer?

I think I've seen some of the most dedicated fans that any type of musician has ever had, and I'd like to thank them all for the support that they've given me. I talk with a lot of people, and a lot of people call me on the phone and write me letters, and I answer them back. I try to stay in touch with them. They've been wonderful to me, that's all I can say. I'm very thankful to every one of them.

— Roger H. Siminoff

This interview originally appeared in *Frets* in August '79. Band members of the Tennessee Cut-Ups remain the same — with the exception of fiddler Buck Ryan, who died in 1982.

A SELECTED RENO DISCOGRAPHY

Solo Albums: *Fastest Five Strings Alive*, KGO (King Records, c/o Gusto Records, 220 Boscobel St., Nashville, TN 37213), 1065. **With Red Smiley** (on KGO): *Country Singing & Instrumentals*, 776; *Country Songs*, 701; *Hymns, Sacred Gospel Songs*, 693; *World's Best Five String Banjo*, 861; *World's 15 Greatest Hits*, 853. *Best Of Don Reno And Red Smiley*, STR (Starday Records, c/o Gusto Records, 220 Boscobel St., Nashville, TN 37213), 961; *Heavy Haulers*, PPK (Powerpak Records, c/o Gusto Records, 220 Boscobel St., Nashville, TN 37213), 290; *Fiddling Buck Ryan*, RRR (Rural Rhythm Records, Box A.T., Arcadia, CA 91006), 244; *16 Greatest Hits*, STR, 3001.

JESSIE
McREYNOLDS

MANDOLINIST Jesse McReynolds always has had the desire to "do something different, to be original," and he has consistently worked toward that end. When he and his brother, guitarist Jim McReynolds, were just learning to play, Jesse was tireless. Jim would rest when he got tired, do something else, and return when he was refreshed. But Jesse never stopped picking. No matter when Jim would resume, there would be Jesse — still playing with as much zest as when he began. That dedication paid off. Jesse has developed into a master mandolin player, equally at home playing bluegrass, rock, western swing, or country.

Throughout the years Jesse has proved to be not only a brilliant player, but an innovator as well. In the late '40s he developed a unique style of mandolin playing, known as crosspicking. Inspired by banjoist Earl Scruggs' three-finger style, Jesse recognized that the technique could be applied to mandolin playing as well — using a straight pick instead of fingers. He then worked to perfect that concept.

A few years later, Jesse developed the style known as split-string playing. With his fingernail fretting just one string of a string pair, or both strings at different frets, he was able to introduce additional harmonies into the music he played. Through these innovations, Jesse McReynolds tremendously expanded the capabilities of the mandolin by adding new dimensions to its sound.

Jesse's musical versatility is not limited to the mandolin. He also plays fiddle, and several years ago recorded an album of fiddle music (*Me And My Fiddles*). His most recent album, *Jesse's Guitar Pickin' Showcase,* features him playing mostly original tunes on guitar.

Jesse McReynolds was born in Coeburn, Virginia, in 1929 to a musical family. His father, Claude McReynolds, played banjo and fiddle, and hosted square dances on Saturday evenings. Jesse's brother-in-law, Oakley Greear, was an excellent fiddler who gave Jesse his first fiddle instruction. Of course, Jesse's brother, Jim —two years older — also demonstrated musical talent at an early age. It is ironic that Jesse first learned to play guitar, and Jim first learned to play mandolin. When neither brother got too proficient on his respective instrument, they switched, and made rapid progress.

Most of the music the two boys played as youngsters was "whatever we happened to hear on the radio," says Jesse. They listened to the popular groups of the day: the Delmore Brothers, the Monroe Brothers, the Bailes Brothers, and the Blue Sky Boys.

In the tradition of the then-popular brother duet groups, young Jim and Jesse formed their own band in the mid-'40s, calling themselves The McReynolds Brothers And The Cumberland Mountain Boys. One of their early professional ventures was playing on a mid-day radio show on WNVA in Norton, Virginia. In 1949 they went to Augusta, Georgia, and along with multi-instrumentalist Curly Seckler and banjoist Hoke Jenkins, they formed a bluegrass band. It was here that Jesse developed the rudiments of his famous crosspicking style. Hoke played a version of Scruggs' three-finger style, and Jesse began experimenting with an adaptation for the mandolin. Jenkins and Scruggs executed their techniques using the thumb and first two fingers, but Jesse used only a flatpick.

In 1950 the brothers left the South, where bluegrass was flourishing, and settled

in Wichita, Kansas, where they worked on radio station KFBI. Instead of playing bluegrass, the brothers played the polished western music of the Sons Of The Pioneers. Songs such as "Cool Water" and "Home On The Range" became part of their repertoire. But the next year, Jim and Jesse left the accordion and steel guitar players behind, and moved to southern Ohio, where they played yet another type of music. Along with singer/guitarist Larry Roll, they formed the Virginia Trio, singing predominantly gospel tunes. It was with this group that Jim and Jesse made their first recordings — which featured Jesse's crosspicking technique.

Jim and Jesse always have been known for their outstanding bands. In 1952 they received a recording contract from Capitol Records and gathered a fine group of sidemen: Tommy Jackson and Sonny James on fiddle, Hoke Jenkins on banjo, and Curly Seckler on guitar. The group did not play western or gospel music, but rather bluegrass, producing such classics as "Are You Missing Me" and "Too Many Tears" [20 Great Songs By Jim And Jesse]. In "Just Wondering Why," on the same album, Jesse introduced his second innovative technique: split-string playing.

Under the Capitol contract, the brothers established their current name: Jim and Jesse and the Virginia Boys. Capitol's management felt it would have more commercial appeal than the name they had been using, The McReynolds Brothers.

The brothers' success with Capitol was interrupted when Jesse was drafted in 1952 to serve in the Korean War. Even adversity can have its benefits. Jesse met Charlie Louvin, singer/guitarist with the Louvin Brothers, and Don McHan, who would later join Jim and Jesse's band. When Jesse was discharged from the Army in 1954, he and Jim moved to Wheeling, West Virginia, where they played on radio station WWVA's Jamboree. They and many other bluegrass artists received their first widespread recognition through that program.

When Jim and Jesse moved to Live Oak, Florida, in 1955, they continued to play bluegrass with the Swanee River Jamboree, a local Saturday night hillbilly music revue, and they also played on a live radio show over station WNER. By the end of the decade the brothers had begun to perform on various television stations throughout the South. The Ford Tractor Company sponsored their programs in two Georgia cities: Savannah and Albany. The Mariana and Crestview mobile home companies sponsored the brothers' television shows in Florida and Alabama. Jim and Jesse's band now included fiddler Vassar Clements, banjoist Bobby Thompson, guitarist Don McHan, and bassist and comedian Chick Stripling.

Finally, in 1959, Jim and Jesse signed a contract with the Martha White Flour Company, whose success in sponsoring Lester Flatt, Earl Scruggs, And The Foggy Mountain Boys made the company anxious to sponsor another bluegrass group. Under this contract, Jim and Jesse continued their travels throughout the South. They also won numerous engagements on radio station WSM's Grand Ole Opry.

By the late '50s — at the height of Elvis Presley's popularity — it was clear that rock and roll, not country music, had captivated record buyers. Fortunately, there was one record company, based in Nashville, that still believed in the commercial viability of country music. That company was Don Pierce's Starday label, and in 1958 Jim and Jesse signed a recording contract with them. Their songs cut on this label, such as "Border Ride" (Country Express) and "Let Me Whisper" (Bluegrass Hall Of Fame) have become classics.

The '60s were years of major importance to Jim and Jesse. They got a recording contract with Columbia, and two of their songs, "Flame Of Love," and "Gosh I Miss You All The Time" were made into a single (Columbia 4-41938) and were included in the Top 50 on the Cashbox charts. This was followed by more frequent appearances on WSM's Grand Ole Opry. In 1962 they were assigned to Columbia's new country label, Epic, and played with yet another top-notch band. Included were Jimmy Buchanan on fiddle, Allen Shelton on banjo, and Don McHan on guitar and vocals. Their all-time favorite bluegrass albums, Bluegrass Special and Bluegrass Classics, widened Jim And Jesse's exposure even more. In 1963 they performed at the Newport Folk Festival in Newport, Rhode Island. Then, in 1964, they received an honor that was "like a dream come true." They were invited to become regular members of the Grand Ole Opry.

Despite these successes, national enthusiasm for bluegrass music, which was brought about by the folk revival of the early '60s, was beginning to decrease. It was no longer economically feasible for Jim and Jesse to pursue bluegrass. They decided to capitalize on rock and produced Berry Pickin' In The Country, an album of adaptations of some of Chuck Berry's tunes, such as "Johnny B. Goode" and "Maybelline." Another change of approach followed shortly afterward when they decided to turn more to mainstream country music. Their first venture in this style, the single "Diesel On My Tail," became an immediate hit and made it to Billboard's Top 10. This was followed by an album of the same name, which was a best-seller for 18 weeks.

In the early '70s Jim and Jesse signed with the Opryland record label, producing another hit single, "Paradise" (out of print). They also started their own record label, Old Dominion.

By the mid-'70s, bluegrass festivals had multiplied to the point where it was possible for Jim and Jesse to return to a predominantly bluegrass style. Their current band consists of banjoist Tim Ellis, electric bass player Keith McReynolds (Jesse's son), and fiddler Blaine Sprouse, who has played with Bill and James Monroe, Jimmy Martin, and Charles Louvin.

WHAT, OR WHO, WERE your most significant musical influences?

Bill Monroe, the Blue Sky Boys, and Red Rector. Red and I were coming up at the same time, but I listened to him a lot. I also listened to the Morris Brothers, Mainer's Mountaineers, and Paul Buskirk. The main person who influenced me was Earl Scruggs. I thought his banjo style would work for mandolin. I learned everybody's stuff, but at the same time I tried to be different.

How would you describe crosspicking?

Crosspicking is a backwards roll, like the technique used in banjo playing. I learned how to do this on the mandolin, using a pick. I have always wanted to do something different, no matter what kind of instrument I played. In the back of my mind I always wanted to be original.

What is the basic picking pattern for crosspicking?

The pattern is down one, up two. The stroke has the same rotations as the 5-string banjo roll. I pick the third string with a down-stroke, the first string with an up-stroke, and the second string with an up-stroke. I usually play the first string open, like the thumb string on the banjo. I get a lot of extra fill-in notes by hitting one string open all of the time. When you hit an open string, it gives you more of a full roll. If I am playing the fourth, second, and third strings, I play the second string open.

When crosspicking, do you hold the pick differently than when you are rhythm picking, and do you use mostly wrist action?

The way I hold the pick when crosspicking is basically the same as when I'm rhythm picking. I do use mostly wrist action.

On what kinds of tunes do you apply crosspicking?

On medium-fast tunes like "Dill Pickle Rag" and "Snowbird" [*Mandolin Workshop*]. There's a limit to how fast you can play tunes using that technique. On the banjo you can play tunes like "Foggy Mountain Breakdown" faster than you can on the mandolin, using the crosspicking technique.

How long did it take you to perfect this technique?

I'm still working on it. It comes and it goes. It's hard to keep the speed up if I don't practice long enough. Sometimes I walk onstage and it doesn't work out well. I'll be real stiff and will miss a lot of notes. I have not reached the point where I can just relax and do it.

Earl Scruggs' banjo style influenced you to develop crosspicking for the mandolin. Did you have any particular influence in developing the split-string style of playing?

No. I have always played around with the mandolin a lot, trying different tunings and things like that. I developed the split-string style by accident — by fooling around and experimenting with different kinds of things. I like not having to use a special tuning to get the sound I want.

How would you describe the basic split-string technique?

I fret the outer string of a set with my left pinky nail, and then pick both strings of that set together. The fretted first string creates a harmony to the other string in the set.

What kind of tunes do you use this technique on?

Most are slow tunes like "Help Me Make It Through The Night" and "Green Green Grass Of Home" [*Mandolin Workshop*]. You can't use this technique on fast tunes.

Does your pinky nail wear down fast? Do you ever put any nail polish on it to help it out?

It does wear down fast, but I have never used any nail polish on it. I have to watch the nail so that I don't overdo it. You can wear down the nail to the point where you can't get anything but a rattle. I sometimes threaten to get an artificial nail that's real tough.

What was your audience reaction when you began to use these techniques?

It wasn't much different — except from the musicians, who understood what I was doing. I get more compliments from musicians than from other people.

Do you do any particular exercises to maintain your techniques?

I practice runs. If I lay off the mandolin for a while, my playing gets rough and doesn't come out smooth. I practice a lot on the road. I must keep up my speed.

How many hours a day do you practice?

On the average I practice a few hours every day. But I don't practice mandolin all the time. I practice guitar or fiddle to keep my fingers limber. If I played mandolin all the time I'd probably get bored with it. I play guitar a lot and try different styles. I sometimes do fingerpicking on the guitar just to have a variety of things to occupy myself with.

In backup playing, do you use full chord positions, or just two-note chords?

Mostly two notes. When I sing I chord very little. A lot of people can sing and play at the same time. Maybe I have a one-track mind because it's hard for me to do that. If Jim is singing lead, I play backup, but as long as I'm singing, all I have ever been able to do is play simple chords — and sometimes I get off beat doing that.

Do you do a lot of chording up the neck?

Yes. In crosspicking I have to play a lot in the higher positions, since the first string is usually played open. You have to get all the high notes on the second string back in the upper position to keep the first string ringing open. I do a lot of noting in the upper positions.

When you are not playing crosspicking style, do you still chord up the neck?

I play whatever fits the occasion. Sometimes I play low on the strings; sometimes I play high on the strings. It depends on how I feel. I play by ear. I don't have a particular way of doing it.

What was the first mandolin you ever played?

It was a Gibson A-50. Jim owned it first, and he gave it to me.

What kind of mandolins have you used?

I basically use a Gibson. I originally got a 1924 Gibson F-4, and I had it converted to an F-5 in the mid-'60s. They took the back and side of the old one and built a new top.

Jim and Jesse McReynolds and the Virginia Boys in their classic formation of the mid-60s. (L to R): Jim Buchanan, Dave "Joe Binglehead" Southerland, Jesse, Don McHan, Jim, Allen Shelton.

It's basically a new mandolin. I also play mandolins built by Lou Stiver of Akron, Ohio; John Wynn of Ozark, Missouri; and [Charles] Jean Horner of Rockwood, Tennessee.

Which is the best you ever used?

The Gibson, the converted F-4. I just like the sound of it. It's like no other mandolin I've ever heard. It doesn't have a bass bar in it.

Do you set up your mandolins yourself?

Yes. I set them up my own way. I adjust the width of the strings on the bridge. I set mine a little wider apart than the average mandolinist does. When I get a mandolin that has already been set up, I usually cut the bridge down, reset the gaps in it, and spread the strings apart more.

How far apart do you like the two strings of a set to be?

I'm not exactly sure what the distance is between them. I'd say it's about 1/8". The wider distance helps me with split-string playing.

How high do you like to set the mandolin bridge?

I just lower it and raise it until it feels fine. Sometimes, when I am in certain climates, the top of the mandolin will give a little bit, and I'll have to raise the bridge. Sometimes it will seem a little tight and I will lay it back down.

Do you ever use any special tunings?

No. I tried to a few years ago on several tunes, but found it limiting.

What kind of action do you prefer at the nut?

I like a low action near the nut because I like to play a lot of fast tunes like "El Cumbanchero" [*Mandolin Workshop*] and "Border Ride" [*The Jim And Jesse Story*]. To get fast notes you have to have a low

action. You have to get a pretty touch on it. If you have to mash the strings, it will slow you down a lot. It becomes like walking in the mud or running in the water. You have to put more tension on your finger.

Are there any types of strings that you prefer to use?

I usually use medium-gauge Gibsons, whatever composition I can get. I usually buy a dozen first strings, a dozen second strings, and a dozen third strings. The fourths don't break as often. I find it hard to get the third strings in bronze. I've also used GHS strings and Sho-Bud Guitar strings. I usually don't change strings until I break them. I very seldom put a whole set of strings on at once. Some other strings sound better when they are new, but they die quicker.

Do you ever break strings during performance?

I usually break a couple of strings in every show.

What kind of picks do you use and how do you hold them?

I use standard Fender mediums. I put rosin on my fingers and rub them together, which helps me in holding the picks lightly.

Where do you like to position the microphone on the mandolin?

I like the mike to face the lower f-hole. If the mike picks up real well, I'll focus it in the middle of the mandolin. But if the mike is very directional, I'll put it near one of the f-holes.

How far away do you stand from the mike?

It depends on how good the mike is. If it's real sensitive, I stand six or eight inches away, but if it's a directional mike, I have to get as close as I can when I play instrumental breaks. For rhythm playing I may stand two or three feet away.

What kind of mike to you prefer?

I don't prefer any particular brand. I just need one that picks up a good distance away.

Have you ever used an electric pickup on your mandolin?

I haven't used a pickup in about seven or eight years, but I used to use a DeArmond. I didn't use it as it came. I stripped it down. I took the metal off of it, and just used the basic parts mounted on my own little board on the pickguard, so it wouldn't touch the mandolin.

Have you ever owned one of the vintage Gibson F-5 mandolins signed by Lloyd Loar?

No. I never did. I would have liked to have one when they were at a reasonable price. I've found that a lot of people can make copies of the mandolin that to me sound just as good as the original Lloyd Loars. I'm happy with playing my Stiver, which is a copy of a Gibson. I also like my Gibson — the converted F-4.

How do you and Jim develop arrangements?

I do most of the arranging. Jim has to approve it. We work on whatever arrangement best fits the song, and that way we get the best harmony. I work more on trying to get different sounds on songs than Jim does. Sometimes he goes along with my arrangement; sometimes he doesn't. But if I come up with an arrangement on a song that he doesn't like, rather than have any problem with it, I drop the idea and say, "We'll do it however it feels natural to you." We compromise a lot with each other. When two people get together to do an arrangement, someone has to give somewhere. It's easier for one leader of a band to work at things than for two.

What current mandolinists do you admire?

Jethro Burns. He doesn't play strictly bluegrass. He plays it all and is very accurate. Doyle Lawson is also very good and important today.

What do you think of some of the contemporary musical trends, such as "newgrass" and mandolinist David Grisman's "Dawg" music?

Newgrass doesn't suit me, but it's good to have differences. I think Grisman is good. He's a musical genius. He takes a melody and puts it where nobody else has been before. We recently discussed the possibility of doing an album together someday.

What advice do you have for an aspiring mandolinist?

Somebody who wants to learn to play mandolin should get one of the books available. There are so many good ones on the market today. And of course, it is necessary to listen to as many other mandolin players as possible. And, most important, *practice!*

— **Marilyn Kochman**

Since this article appeared in November '80 several personnel changes have occurred: Besides the McReynolds brothers, the band's lineup today includes Mike Scott on banjo, Steve Thomas on fiddle, and Keith McReynolds on bass. Recent releases include *Jim And Jesse Today* (CMH 6250), and *Homeland Harmony* (Double J Productions [Box 27, Gallatin, TN 37066] DJ 1002).

A SELECTED McREYNOLDS DISCOGRAPHY

Solo Albums: *Jesse McReyonolds: Me And My Fiddles,* Atteiram (Box 606, Marietta, GA 30061), API 1030; *Jesse's Guitar Pickin' Showcase,* Double J Productions (Box 27, Gallatin, TN 37066), DJ 1001. **Jim And Jesse:** (on Epic, dist. by CBS): *All-Time Great Country Instrumentals,* BN-26394; *Berry Pickin' In The Country,* LN-24176 and BN-26176; *Bluegrass Classics,* LN-24074 and BN-26074; *Bluegrass Special,* LN-24031 and BN-26031; *Diesel On My Tail,* LN-24314 and BN-26314; *Old Country Church,* LN-24107 and BN-26107; *Saluting The Louvin Brothers,* BN-26465; *We Like Trains,* E-26513; *Y'All Come! Bluegrass Humor With Jim And Jesse And The Virginia Boys,* LN-24144 and BN-26144; *20 Great Songs By Jim And Jesse,* Capitol, DDTBB 264; *Country Music And Bluegrass At Newport,* Vanguard, VRS-9146 and VSD-79146; *Mandolin Workshop Hilltop* (Box 23262, Nashville, TN 37202), HS 202; *Sacred Songs Of The Virginia Trio,* Ultra-Sonic (available from Double J Productions); *The Jim And Jesse Story,* CMH (Box 39439, Los Angeles, CA),9022; *Country Express,* Starday (c/o Gusto Records, 220 Boscobel St., Nashville, TN 37213), SLP 109.

SONNY OSBORNE

SONNY OSBORNE is in a class by himself among bluegrass banjo players. As the driving instrumental force behind the Osborne Brothers, he has been a leader in every aspect of his profession — playing, singing, writing, arranging, and producing. He has developed a unique banjo style, combining the discipline of bluegrass with an uncanny ability to improvise and a compulsive desire to innovate. As a result, his playing has expanded the commercial frontiers of the banjo into the pop and country fields, and has earned him countless awards from fans and peers alike. Since Sonny joined Bill Monroe 30 years ago, making his professional debut at age 14, he has proved to be a precocious and prodigious artist.

* * * *

*C*OULD YOU DESCRIBE *your earliest influences on the banjo? Was there a particular player who inspired you to take up the instrument?*

There was no [major] influence behind it. I had seen Larry Richardson play up close when he was playing with my brother Bobby. They used to practice at our house in Dayton, Ohio, around 1947. When I saw Larry play — I don't know why — but I just seemed to think I could do that, too. It looked relatively easy. There was a teacher from Haur's Music Store in Dayton, who was offering lessons on how to play the banjo. He would give you a certain number of lessons if you bought a banjo from that store. I bought a Kay, for about $100. I just jumped right in there. I went home and told my dad, and he gave me $20 for the down payment. We had a lot of bluegrass records at that time. It seemed so easy. I was listening to the Stanley Brothers' recording of "We'll Be Sweethearts In Heaven" [*The Stanley Brothers, Vol. 1,* Roundtree, RSS-09] and I thought, "I believe I know how to play that," even though I had never even held a banjo in my hands.

You mean you could hear all the different things Ralph Stanley was doing?

Banjo music has always been like a picture in my mind. I can actually see the notes; there are forms to it. It's not a sound, I hardly hear the sound. It's just the picture I paint in my mind. I would sit in school and figure out how the thing would go. I didn't have to learn, I already knew how to do it. I think the first day I got the banjo I played "We'll Be Sweethearts In Heaven." One day I didn't have a banjo and I couldn't play and the next day I had one and I could. I'm thankful to God it was like that; there are times now when I really need that ability, because I don't practice as I should.

How much did you practice when you were learning?

I used to play more than eight hours a day. We lived on a farm and my dad worked for the National Cash Register Company in Dayton, and we'd have to keep up the farm. I started playing in the winter of 1948, and that spring and summer when work had to be done outside, I would do the chores until I knew my dad would be in bed. Then I'd quit, get off the tractor, and bring the banjo out on the back porch and sometimes play till 4:30 or 5:00 in the morning, using only my fingers, no picks. My dad always got up at 5:15. When I finished playing, I'd hop into bed real quick and pretend to be asleep. He'd always open the door and look at me to make sure I was in bed. I had such a tremendous drive to play. It wasn't the type

Sonny and Bob, the Osborne Brothers, at a California bluegrass festival in the late '70s.

hand was all about, I copied Earl as closely as I possibly could, and I set out to learn everything he had ever played. I literally wore his records out. Those 78s used to turn white if you played them a lot, and on ours you could see the white bands wherever his banjo breaks were.

When Snuffy Jenkins played, did he just use the forward roll?

I don't believe Snuffy actually played the backwards roll. Earl's sense of timing was so great that he had the ability to reverse what he was doing to make it come out right. You see, if you only use a forward roll your notes won't come out evenly. You'll have a note that takes too long to get to and you'll also have notes that you play too soon, and you can't get around that without breaking up some kind of timing. But with the backward roll you can be going forward and then reverse it, and you can get to that note a whole beat faster. Or you can decide not to get to it as quickly, whichever you need to make the line come out smooth.

When did you start evolving your own style?

In 1957, Flatt And Scruggs released "Randy Lynn Rag" [*Golden Era*, Rounder, 05], which was the first time Earl got his right hand tangled up and they let it go through. He had made some mistakes on earlier records but they were all left-hand mistakes. When I heard that, it dawned on me suddenly that I had to start learning my own style, because all I ever played or listened to was Scruggs, and if he went downhill he'd take me right with him. So, I just completely turned off my old style and started out immediately on something new. After 1957, I didn't listen to any other banjo players. I never even bought a banjo record. I started to listen to steel guitar and saxophone and piano. I tried to duplicate drum rhythm patterns with the picks on the banjo. I listened to every instrument you could imagine, and tried to transpose that music to the banjo. I wanted anything that was different.

That sounds pretty radical. Didn't you worry about alienating your fans?

At that time we started changing a lot of things to develop our own style — our harmonies, the mandolin style — and I didn't worry about restricting myself. We were right in the middle of the rock and roll boom and nobody was listening to bluegrass, anyway. So there was no great popularity at stake. I played "Indian Love Call." I did a rock and roll break on "Don't Be Cruel." I played a saxophone break on "Blue Monday." I even got into jazz a little bit, which really helped my left hand. I learned how to improvise new chords and progressions.

Watching you improvise onstage is fascinating. It's like watching someone think on his feet. Every lick seems so spontaneous. Where do all those ideas come from?

Everything I play is improvised. It has always been like that. Since the very beginning I've had the ability to hear something

of thing I felt I *ought* to do. It was something I *had* to do.

Your dad was a banjo player too, wasn't he?

He played clawhammer style and he showed me tunes like "Cripple Creek," "Cumberland Gap," and "Sally Ann." And I had all the new songs, every record I could get. My brother Bobby also played the banjo. He could have been a great banjo player, if he had wanted to be. About the middle of 1949, Bobby saw Scruggs play in Bluefield, West Virginia. I had never seen Earl play. I had only heard him play a couple of times. I was doing one roll, the thing that Earl used to start off his theme song. Lester Flatt would play the guitar, and then Earl would play a real fast roll on the banjo. I was doing that, but I wasn't doing it right and I didn't know it. Records in those days were 78s and our player didn't have all those speeds on it. Bobby finally showed me how to do it [the fast roll] right. It involved a forward roll and then a backward roll too. From that point on, everything really fell into place. I was able to incorporate that pattern into everything I had been doing wrong. I was having a timing problem before that but the backward roll really solved it. That's what made Scruggs so great. He was the first to do that.

How long did you consciously copy Earl Scruggs' technique?

From the very beginning, and I'm still doing so today. I can play every break and every background note that he played on record up until about 1963. Earl was the first person to really understand how to play the banjo right and, to my mind, nobody has improved on what he did since. His right hand is absolutely the best. His timing is superb. His tone is perfect, and his rhythm playing is absolutely superior to anything before or since. From 1952 on, when I finally understood what the right once and then repeat it. I might not use it 'til years later, but I don't forget it. One time in the studio we were recording "Love's Gonna Live Here" [Decca, out-of-print], the old Buck Owens song, and a lick popped out that I heard on a Chuck Berry record about five years before. It just came to me and it worked perfectly. I didn't need to try it out or practice it.

Your style also is characterized by a soft touch, especially for a bluegrass player. It seems like you're barely hitting the strings.

There's no need to play that hard. Your instrument will sound better if you play it easy. That's one of the most important things I learned from playing with Bill Monroe. If you play hard you will play rough most of the time, because you can't really judge how hard you're hitting each string. You have to concentrate more on keeping your timing smooth. When I used to play with Jimmy Martin in the early '50s, I played very, very hard just to be heard. But that was before I had nerve enough to say, "Don't play so damned hard." It's just normal for me to play that way.

Do you find that you sacrifice drive if you play too lightly?

No. That part is not in your hand itself. It's in your mind. Drive is how you hear something, how you phrase. It's a matter of timing, and playing easy gives me much more control. It's the same thing as a guy singing and he puts a little soul into it. You have to put a little of yourself into it. I emphasize by playing softer in some places and harder in others. But I never get to the point where I'm really playing hard. You don't need to.

It's amazing to think that you were only 14 when you went to work with Monroe. Most kids that age would have trouble enough asking him for an autograph, let alone a job.

Actually, I never said a single word to Monroe before I got hired. Jimmy Martin and I went to see him together, and Jimmy did all the talking. He had worked for Monroe once before. He quit about 1950, about the same time Bobby and Larry Richardson parted company. Then Bobby and Jimmy started playing together. They'd practice at the house and I used to get to play with them. I wasn't very good back then, but of course, I thought I was the best there was. Nobody could touch me. Bobby went into the service in 1952. Jimmy started working in Middletown, Ohio, at a radio station; but he'd still come over to our house and we'd sit and play and talk a lot. Then around July, Jimmy heard that Monroe was going to be at Bean Blossom [Indiana] and he asked me if I wanted to go and see him. I asked my dad, and he said okay. When we got there, [fiddler] Charlie Cline was the only man Bill had with him, so Jimmy asked him if he'd like the two of us to join the group.

Just like that? What happened then?

Bill said all right. That's all there was to it. I never even got introduced to Bill. The first playing I ever did for Monroe was at a recording session the day I got to Nashville. They had a recording studio set up on the second floor of our hotel. Jimmy just called my room and told me to come down and play. The following Saturday night we played the *Grand Ole Opry*. The first song we did was "Rawhide" [*Blue Grass Instrumentals*] and I was scared to death, I mean literally. My knees were shaking. I must have passed somehow, I guess. I didn't know how I got through my break. Bill is the kind of guy who wants to know immediately whether you're strong enough to play with him. He did some other things I didn't appreciate too much, but now when I look back, I can see that it really made a man out of me in a hurry. I'd be at the microphone playing and Bill would get right up behind me and play every off-timing lick he could think of, just to see if I could concentrate. I will say one thing: When Bill wanted to play straight, he had the best timing on the mandolin of anyone. He could really make you play. If you had anything in you, he could bring it out.

When you left Monroe, did you hook up again with Jimmy?

Bobby got out of the service in 1954, and he and Jimmy and I started a group, and we moved to Detroit in August of 1954. We worked with [fiddler] Casey Clark over at the Union Hall on Mack Avenue, and they broadcast it live every Saturday night on WJR radio. We also did a Friday TV show on station CKLW. We really got hot in Detroit and we got an RCA Victor contract and recorded *20-20 Vision* and *Save It, Save It* [both out-of-print]. Bobby and Jimmy had the best duet I ever heard. You just couldn't get any better.

How long were you based in Detroit?

We stayed there from August 1954 to August 1955. By then Jimmy Martin's personality and my personality just could not get along. Several things happened that I really didn't like. One time a guy in Nashville named Troy Martin called Jimmy and asked us all to go to Nashville to do a radio show. He said that we'd each get paid $60. Jimmy held out for $75, and Troy said, "They won't pay it, Jimmy, but the far-reaching effects of this show are absolutely unreal. You really need to do this." Jimmy said, "We need $75 a week apiece," and Troy said, "They won't do it." They hired Flatt And Scruggs instead. It was the *Martha White Show*! Not many people know about that. I was sitting right there when he turned it down and it absolutely killed me, because I wanted to go to Nashville. I'm not saying we could have done what Flatt And Scruggs did, but there were thirteen or fourteen million dollars involved in that deal.

Within two years, though, you had a new lead singer, Red Allen, and you had a recording contract with MGM, which was one of the biggest labels in the country. And this was when every other bluegrass group was getting swallowed up by the rock and roll boom.

Bluegrass music took a nosedive out of this world in those days. Monroe was working for $150, $200, and $300 a day, just like everybody else. You took whatever you could get. It really became evident that rock and roll was going to be a big part of music around 1956 or 1957, and we were lucky enough in '56 to get with MGM. They had Conway Twitty and Connie Francis, who were the two biggest stars in the country, and all the rest of us were just way below them. I didn't like it at the time, but I realize now it was a godsend, because we were being used as a tax write-off. The good thing about it was that every three months we had a single record released, right on the money. It didn't matter what it sold.

Did that give you freedom to develop in new ways?

We got a lot of music recorded right then. We got a lot of our ideas; the high lead trio was started back then. We pretty much had carte blanche to experiment in the studio, 'cause nobody was buying bluegrass records, anyway. We were mad that we didn't progress with MGM, didn't move ahead commercially. But the thing we didn't realize was that they were really laying a good foundation for what we did in the mid-'60s. When we finally got a hold of "Rocky Top" [*Best Of The Osborne Brothers*] the foundation was already there, and the very instant it was released everybody said, "That's what they've been looking for." And it was.

"Rocky Top" sounds more like a country song that was written to sound like a bluegrass song.

The song was originally written with a slow shuffle beat and we changed it. We did the same thing with "Roll Muddy River" [*Best Of The Osborne Brothers*]. Another hit we had, "Up This Hill And Down" [*Up This Hill And Down,* Decca, out-of-print] was a blues song, and I had to figure out some way to take the banjo and play blues on it. So I tuned it down to another key. It had a very different sound and people were jumping up and down saying, "Wow, man, that is really great." But it was done by necessity. When we decided to do "The Kind Of Woman I Got" [*Modern Sounds Of Bluegrass,* Decca, out-of-print], there was absolutely no way to play it, but I was convinced it was a hit song and I had to do something on it. So I tuned the banjo down four frets to *E,* which is very, very low and did a Don Rich guitar break.

How did you keep the strings from rattling?

I had a banjo specially put together for that occasion. We could only do that song in *E.* We couldn't sing it in any other key. So I asked the Vega Banjo Company if they would build me a wide-body banjo, with a real deep body. This was when I was endorsing Vega banjos, and they had a Sonny Osborne model on the market. So they sent me this thing that I call the "Fat Banjo."

It was huge — probably two or three inches deeper than normal — and boy, was it hideous looking. It had an old top-tension tone ring. The first time Bobby saw it, he just laughed. But when we got to the song, it worked. It had a deeper sound and I put heavier strings on it; it sounded really nice.

You have used some other strange banjos, like the 6-string. What was the motivation behind that?

From about 1962 I really started getting sick of the idea that a *D* was the lowest note you could play on the banjo. If you got to a song with anything lower than that, you had to go to another place on the instrument to play it, which changes the whole outlook of the song. So I had C.E. Ward in Charlotte, North Carolina, build me a neck that was a little bit wider, with the same exact inlays as my Vega 5-string neck. That way if it didn't work out nobody would ever know I'd changed. I got the neck on a Monday and on Tuesday we went in and recorded. I had myself so psyched up that I never missed a note.

How did you tune the low string?

It was tuned to a *G,* an octave lower than the third string, so I had three *G*s, in octaves, to work with. I used an .025" gauge string on the low *G.* That banjo had a real effect. Of course, playing fast has never really bothered me, but now I physically can't play fast because of that banjo. It was about a half-inch wider and it spread my hand out. When I went back to the small neck, I wasn't able to have the speed. I played it exclusively for four or five years. I tried to get people like [banjoists] Bill Emerson and Eddie Adcock interested in it, but nobody was willing to take a chance. I played everything I knew on it and I just finally decided it was an idea that people weren't ready for. So I put it aside in 1975.

Didn't you also try a dobro banjo?

Yes. I was the first guy to play one of those things, too. Josh Graves called me one day and he said, "I have got an instrument for you!" I said, "Great!" See, I didn't realize Josh had gotten suckered in on this thing, and he just wanted to put it off on somebody. So I bought it for $150. It had a dobro body and a 5-string neck, but it was made really bad. Later on I asked the Dobro company to build one for me and they said they weren't building them anymore.

How did it sound?

The notes would sustain real long. I had a field day. I even started playing through an amplifier, and I contemplated giving up the banjo for a while and playing that thing all the way; but fortunately Bobby talked me out of it. It had no volume at all, and no penetration. But God, what a pretty sound on ballads. As loud as you could play, a normal conversation would drown it out. Some old boy finally offered me $350 for it and I sold it. Actually I saw another one recently that I really liked and I'm thinking of buying it. Curtis McPeake, of Mt. Juliet, Tennessee, is building one that's round like a banjo. It's got a spider core.

Sonny Osborne, known for his onstage antics, at a Delaware bluegrass festival in 1981.

You said you "see" tunes on the banjo. Is it also true that you always think out your parts and make up whole arrangements in your head without ever touching the instrument?

Yes, that's true. I can sit and think of breaks and how they're supposed to go and it works in my mind. We did a thing called "Blue Moon Of Kentucky" [*Up To Date And Down To Earth*] on an album a number of years ago. We were on the road and I was driving that night, and in about three hours I had worked out the whole timing thing on the banjo instrumental and the mandolin instrumental parts, and outlined everything. When everybody else got up the next day I said, "I want to play 'Blue Moon Of Kentucky' this way," and it worked out really nice and smooth.

You know, with all your recording, there is still no definitive Sonny Osborne banjo album. Do you have any plans to record one in the near future?

I have an idea for a new album that I hope to get to sometime this year. I'm thinking of calling it *The All-American Five*. I'm going to put as many different kinds of music on it as possible. You know, like old bluegrass, maybe some blues or jazz. I've asked Bela Fleck and Carl Jackson to work on it with me, and write some original tunes that would incorporate all three of our styles. Carl is one of the best chromatic players, and Bela does some jazz things that are unreal. The songs on it would be longer, four or five minutes, and we would have a section of our own. And we'd play together, too. I don't think anything like that has been tried before.

It seems like you have always prided yourself on trying new things. It's nice to

see the juices flowing as strong as ever after all these years.

I think my best playing is still ahead of me. I just hope that when all is said and done, I can put back into the banjo as much as it has given to me.

SONNY OSBORNE is known for dispensing advice freely, particularly on the subject of banjo playing. We talked about his practice methods and what he recommends for beginner and professional alike.

Have you maintained a consistent practice regimen through the years?

In the last ten years, practicing is something I have not done enough of. It's ironic how all this is set up. When you first start out and nobody cares what you sound like, you have all the time in the world to sit and play. Then when you get well-known and everybody really expects a lot from you, you don't have the time to practice. It seems backwards to me. The hardest thing, of course, is the picks. If you can stay used to the picks on your fingers, it's much easier to play. Even if you don't physically practice, I find that if you put the picks on and leave them on for an hour or two it helps, because it keeps that contact. It's really a delicate thing. In your mind there can't be any space between the pick and the finger. They must be one. I have sometimes gone a week or ten days without ever touching the banjo, and it shows. I have this saying: "If you don't know the banjo during the week, it won't know you on the weekend!" If I can get the banjo out and physically play it, I'll try to play for an hour a day.

What kinds of things do you play?

I play anything and everything that comes to my mind. I just want to keep my left-hand fingers on the strings and keep them well adjusted to the fretboard, and move my right hand. Sometimes I'll watch television and practice and do nothing but keep my fingers moving for a length of time. That way when I get onstage my rolls are still there and my muscles are still intact.

What practice methods would you recommend for aspiring young players?

First of all, I would tell anyone who wants to learn how to play the banjo to get everything he could from Earl Scruggs between 1947 and 1960. *Foggy Mountain Banjo* [Columbia, CL-1364] is the supreme album to have. Get a record player or a tape player with a variable speed control. I would put all this music onto tapes and I would categorize it, like "fast music," "slow music," "background music," and so on. I would get as good a banjo as I could after I found out that I was really interested in it. You may later find that you need a teacher to straighten you out on finger rolls and things like that, or you may need a book like the one that I wrote. If I were a parent buying a kid an instrument I would get him the cheapest thing I could find. If that drive is there, it will come out. After you find out that the kid really wants to play, I would get the best instrument I could afford, because you can only go as far as an instrument will let you.

You mentioned a book you wrote. When was that?

I started in 1957 and Mel Bay published it around 1963 [*Mel Bay's New Bluegrass Banjo*, by Sonny Osborne, Mel Bay Publications, Pacific, MO 63069]. It was the first book ever written on Scruggs-style banjo. I wrote the whole thing, music and all. It has all the basic rolls and how they go together, forwards and backwards. I would either get a book like that or find somebody to straighten your hands out. If you run into me on the road, I'll do it myself. If I've got the time, I'll sit right there and show you anything you want to know. Then if you want to be an excellent banjo player you have to practice anywhere from two to ten hours a day. You should practice everything you can — scales, left-hand notes, and anything that comes to your mind. You never can practice too much. It also helps if you can find someone else to play with because timing is so important to banjo players.

Can you define the role of each hand in banjo playing?

To me the right hand is the most important because that's what controls your timing. If you've got a good right hand, the left hand will come naturally. The right hand should develop "staying power." You should be able to play and not get tired. I also think that if you play easy, you'll play smoother, and I think the smooth sound is what you should be looking for.

What methods would you recommend for building up the right hand stylistically?

I think you need the basic Scruggs style to begin with, because once you get the Scruggs style down, your fingers will do anything and you can go on to other things, like chromatics. After that, it's strictly a matter of personal taste as to what you practice. I'm assuming, of course, that you already know the different chords and positions on the neck. Just find whatever style you really like and concentrate on practicing that particular right hand. Eventually, I'd like to have a school where a professional player could come and get specialized instruction on any aspect of banjo playing. The instructors would be people like myself or people like J.D. Crowe and other great players. The school would be a place where they could just come and stay while they learned.

Could you reveal the secret for getting the full volume and tone out of the instrument?

Every banjo sounds best at a certain place. It is usually from the bridge forward — about three inches. You can find that spot if you play the thumb string, the first string, and then move your hand forward on the banjo head, starting from the bridge. You'll hear the tone change and you'll find out exactly where that banjo sounds the best. Then you can take a pencil and mark where your fingers are supposed to go, and keep them there until you get used to that feel. And the volume will come naturally as long as you play at that spot; wherever the tone is the best, the volume is the best, too.

SONNY'S NEW SOUND

BANJO ENTHUSIASTS have noticed a marked improvement in Sonny Osborne's playing over the past five or six years, and much of the credit is due to the Gibson Granada flathead banjo that Sonny bought in 1975. That 1934-vintage instrument has rejuvenated Sonny's playing and has enriched his music.

As Sonny tells the story, it was practically love at first sound.

What made you switch to the Granada at a time when you'd already solidly established your career on other banjos?

There was something amazing about the whole thing because I didn't want a banjo at all. I had been playing a Gibson RB-4 flathead for years, and I thought it was one of the best banjos in the country. Bobby and I were playing a show in Asheville, North Carolina, and Tom McKinney invited us over for dinner afterwards. I had heard that Tom had some nice instruments and he brought out this Granada. I played it some, but I really didn't like it and I gave it back to him. We went in to eat, and then about halfway through the meal something struck me, and I excused myself and went back in and started playing it again. The difference was like daylight and dark. I could not put it down. I sat there and played that thing until four o'clock in the morning. That was the sweetest sound I ever heard in my life. As soon as I picked it up that second time I knew it was home, right there.

What was it about the sound that you liked?

It's clean and it's clear and every note sounds just like bells ringing, no matter how hard or soft you play it. The style of banjo I play comes from steel guitar; it comes from electric guitar, piano, and saxophone; and the Granada accepts those things well. The RB-4 didn't have that sustain.

The banjo has never really been known as a sustaining instrument.

But this one does. That banjo has made a new player out of me. I've got a completely different outlook on the whole thing now. In the beginning I wasn't playing anything I hadn't played before; but for the first time I could hear, and make everybody else hear, what I was doing. I've been playing the same style stuff since 1964, but with the

RB-4 I couldn't get it out. And I couldn't expand on those ideas because I was having a hard enough time just getting them across. Now that I know every note will be heard, I can add an extra note or a new phrase and build off my old ideas. Having this instrument has upgraded my playing probably sixty percent. Another thing about the Granada, it came along just exactly at the right time. We had realized everything we'd wanted to realize, and I was just about ready to hang it up. I'd gotten to the point where I didn't really want to play anymore. We'd won every award that we could possibly win, we'd had hit records, been at the White House, I mean we had really taken our music as far as we could go with it. There was just not much fun in it. So I thought, well this would be a good time now to maybe learn something else to settle in on for the rest of my life. But that instrument has added ten extra years to my playing career.

GEAR FOR THE GIGS

SUPERIOR PERFORMERS choose superior equipment, and Sonny Osborne is no exception. His choices in instruments and accessories, however, reflect the same strong, unabashed individualism that characterizes his music.

What is your main performance banjo?
My 1934 Gibson Granada which is an original 5-string. [*Ed. Note: Many of the vintage Granadas in circulation today were built as 4-strings, and were later converted by replacing the original necks with 5-string necks after bluegrass became popular. An original 5-string is indeed a rarity.*] I've also got a new Stelling Sonflower that I use when I have to travel by plane.

Are there certain characteristics that you look for when selecting a new banjo?
It's kind of hard to define. I like a banjo made out of curly maple. Maple has a crisper, ringier sound than mahogany. The size of the neck is very important. The neck has to be heavy and big because you've got to have something to hold onto. I would also insist on gold plating because I'm convinced that the gold on the tone ring has a lot to do with the sound. It gives it a softer, warmer sound. The size of the frets is also important. The new, wider fret will give you more sustain, and your notes will be cleaner and easier to play. I also like a pearl nut. Pearl is harder than bone; it is almost like stone. It really wakes up the sound.

How do you set up your banjos? Do you keep the action real low?
I fix the strings to the height where there is no buzzing, and then I raise them a little bit higher than that. For bridges, I like the

3/4" bridge that Snuffy Smith, from Springdale, Arkansas, builds. They're very, very good. I like a high bridge because I find that it gives me a cleaner, fuller sound. It's also easier for me to play. To get the best tone out of a banjo you've got to get the pick just a little under the string and pull up on it, instead of hitting it from the top. The higher bridge gives you room to do that comfortably.

How much do you tighten the tailpiece?
I don't. I leave it at just about the angle you would get if you put a string from the top of the bridge back to the tension hoop. The tailpiece actually slants upward. In the old days you would crank the tailpiece down to the point of almost touching the head to kill some of the hollow sound of the skin head. But nowadays you don't have that hollow sound, so you just put it on there to where it's tight enough to stay on.

And how much do you tighten the head?
I make sure it's tight enough and level. The tension hoop has got to be level, because otherwise it warps real easy. The head has just a little bit of give when I press it. The secret of making a banjo sound good is to have all the parts tight, and then to adjust the head a little bit at a time. When I get the sound I want, then I don't mess with it 'til it breaks.

When you started playing, skin heads were the only available heads. The new plastic ones must be easier to work with.
Banjo playing is so different than what it was in the early '50s. Sometimes you'd buy the heads unmounted. You'd take the old head off and you'd just have the tone ring. You would take that piece of skin and put it in water and soak it, and it became very, very limber. Then you draped it over the tone ring and put the stretcher band down over that. You'd wait for it to dry a little bit and then take a razor blade and cut around that stretcher band. Then tighten it down somewhat and the composition of that skin just glues itself together. Then you can finish tightening it down. I've put many of them on like that. Sometimes they'd last a month, sometimes three months. Banjo players nowadays don't know what all of us older guys went through in order to play. All you have to do now is put a head on it and that's it. Back in the old days, you had to work on your banjo almost daily if you were playing all the time. It was highly irregular if you would go three days without having to do something to it. That's why I admire Earl Scruggs so much, because his banjo always sounded good — he had to be a genius at setting it up. You had to take the bridges and thin the ebony part down 'til it was very, very thin and keep the tailpiece almost down on the head. If you didn't do that it sounded real tubby. The heads back in those days had to be extremely tight, just as tight as you could get it. Don Reno said one time that the secret of setting up a banjo was to get it a quarter of a turn from breaking.

With the plastic heads isn't it a lot easier to get a consistent sound from day to day?

Sure. I would have to sit on the bus with a hair dryer to try to keep the head dry. Once in Oklahoma it was raining terribly, and I got about three quarters of the way through the show and it [the banjo] just gave out. Everything I hit on it just went doomp, doomp, really nothing. And Robby, Bobby's son, looked over at me and said, "That's the worst sounding banjo I ever heard in my life." You had to love it in those days to play it. It was a challenge. You had to beat the instruments and you had to beat the elements too.

What kind of strings do you use?

I use my own strings. They're made through the Marlin Steel Guitar Company in Reidsville, North Carolina. I use an .011" gauge for the first, second, and fifth strings; .013" for the third string; and .020" for the fourth. I've been using these strings for ten or twelve years now. I like them because they don't break easily and they really sustain well.

Are there any particular types of picks that you prefer?

I use two National metal fingerpicks; for thumbpicks, I use a cheap, multi-colored one that has as wide a striking surface as possible. It's got a full sound, and it more closely matches the sound of the National fingerpicks.

When you find it necessary to use a capo, which type do you prefer?

I use the capo made by Tom McKinney, from Asheville, North Carolina. It remains on the banjo. I just slide it back over the nut when I am not using it. I don't ever capo in C. I think when you get past B, you really start losing tone quickly. This capo is built specifically for that. It just goes up to the 4th fret. The capo is made out of stainless steel, and it's small and out of the way. You don't ever have to worry about digging in your case for a capo. It's always right there. They cost about $25 and will last a lifetime.

There is a wide variety of microphones on the market today. Have you found one that works best for you?

I use a Neumann U-87 microphone, and I will not play without one. I put the flat side of the U-87 between the top center of the head and the area where the neck joins the body. I put it about six to eight inches above the banjo, and I aim it down at where the flange and resonator join. It seems like the banjo sound goes upwards and to the left when it comes out of the pot. This position also keeps the pick noise from carrying.

Do you play differently in the studio than you do onstage?

I play as easy as I possibly can. I play lightly anyway, but in the studio I cut my volume in half. It gives me the best tone and it keeps me out of everyone else's micro-phone. I set the board as close to a mid-range as I can. You can get a much more natural sound without those extreme highs and lows. Then when I remix, I add a little echo. A lot of echo gets muddy, but a little really makes it sound loose.

— *Herschel Freeman*

BOBBY OSBORNE

MOST BLUEGRASS musicians — if described in the same terms used to classify major-league baseball players — would be labeled "good field, no hit." In other words, their playing is hot, but their singing leaves something to be desired. Bobby Osborne, on the other hand, would be in a category unto himself. His peerless tenor singing has all but obscured his revolutionary contributions to modern mandolin technique.

Unlike the majority of bluegrass mandolinists, who base their playing on tremolo or repeated notes, Osborne relies heavily on single-line melodies. As the first melodic mandolin soloist in bluegrass, Osborne is widely imitated among today's musicians. Few, however, could guess the origin of his style.

Born in Hyden, Kentucky, on Dec. 7, 1931, Bobby began playing acoustic guitar, electric guitar, and fiddle at an early age. His electric guitar was the springboard for a way of playing that ultimately gave bluegrass mandolin a whole new musical vocabulary.

"What really helped me with the mandolin," he says, "was that on electric guitar I learned the notes to the fiddle tunes I'd always been interested in. I got to listening to fiddle tunes like 'Billy In The Low Ground,' 'Katy Hill,' and 'Old Joe Clark.' When I got with the mandolin, I could hit a lot of open strings, and the positions were a lot closer together; it was much easier to play the fiddle tunes on the mandolin than it was to do it on the guitar. So I related the two together. Of course, the first time I ever tried to play a fiddle tune was on a fiddle, but the mandolin was as close to it as I could get.

For the past 30 years, Bobby's unique style has been an integral part of the sound of the Osborne Brothers — a band that also features his brother Sonny, on banjo. But it wasn't until the release of his recent instrumental album *Bobby And His Mandolin* that his instrumental talents got their share of the spotlight. The album focused new attention on this important aspect of Bobby's music, and brought him well-deserved recognition as one of the instrumental pioneers of bluegrass.

*   *   *   *

ISN'T IT TRUE THAT COUNTRY *star Ernest Tubb was among your earliest musical influences?*

Yes. Ernest Tubb got me started listening to country music. Our dad used to listen to the *Grand Ole Opry* on Saturday nights, and I got to hear Ernest. At the time I was under 16 and my voice was low like his. I loved to sing his songs, and I learned to play electric guitar, too. I had a Regal acoustic guitar with a DeArmond pickup on it, and my dad bought me one of those big old Epiphone amps. I thought I was rich then. We were living in Dayton, Ohio, and I played lead for a while with a group that included guitarist Chuck Swain and a little guy named Shorty Hobbs, who played electric mandolin. That was in the late '40s.

How did your interest in fiddle and mandolin evolve?

About the time I was playing the guitar, my daddy had an old fiddle and I got to fooling with it. I always did like the fiddle. I got familiar with the fingering positions, so it wasn't much of a problem to transfer them to the mandolin later on. I'd listen to

Hank Garland, "Sugarfoot Rag," and things like that. So I related that straight to the mandolin in no time at all. When I got to doing that, that's where my style started. In 1951, I was playing the guitar with the Lonesome Pine Fiddlers. When Jimmy Martin joined the group, he played the guitar and I switched to the mandolin.

It seems like your roots are in country music. How did you get involved with bluegrass?

The guy that got me into bluegrass was Earl Scruggs. I listened to the *Opry* one Saturday night, and he played "Cumberland Gap." At that time I never knew who Bill Monroe was. This was around 1946 or 1947. I wanted to see Earl, but I didn't even know who he played with. All I listened for was Scruggs on the banjo. I heard on the *Opry* that they were coming to Memorial Auditorium in Dayton, and I got a chance to see Flatt and Scruggs with Bill Monroe. Ernest Tubb was the first guy I ever saw live onstage, and Bill Monroe was the second.

When you saw Monroe, were you still playing electric guitar and singing Ernest Tubb songs?

Yes. When I turned 16 my voice changed up to where it's at now, but Ernest Tubb songs were the only things I knew. So on something like "Walking The Floor Over You," I'd sing it in the same key, C, but I'd move it up an octave to where I sing it now. But then I got interested in bluegrass through Earl Scruggs, and I let Ernest go by. When the Blue Grass Boys came to Memorial Hall, I learned that Bill Monroe was the head of the group and Earl and Flatt played with him, and Chubby Wise played fiddle.

Did Monroe inspire you to start playing the mandolin?

No, I was still mainly interested in the guitar. I always wanted to imitate Flatt's voice. I bought a songbook from them that night, and I saw that Flatt was playing the guitar with a thumbpick and a fingerpick. So I laid the electric guitar down and got me a thumbpick and a fingerpick and started rehearsing with the acoustic guitar.

Did you give up the electric guitar?

Not immediately. I was still playing electric with Chuck Swain at WPFB in Middletown, Ohio. They had a little jamboree there, and a boy named Larry Richardson came through that picked the banjo and sang. He was a guest on the radio show, and afterwards I got out an acoustic guitar and me and him sang a few songs together. I later decided to quit this other group because I was more interested in bluegrass. I'd already seen Monroe, and my voice had changed, and I'd started singing some of his songs. I learned "Molly And Tenbrooks" and some songs like that. Larry and me got to singing together, and I just laid the electric guitar down and was never interested in it again.

Didn't you and Larry join the Lonesome Pine Fiddlers together?

We joined up with Ezra Cline and a fiddle player named Ray Morgan in late 1948 or early 1949. We worked schools and square dances on Saturday night until about 1951. Then Larry left the group and Charlie Cline replaced him on the banjo. Jimmy Martin came to work with us right after that, and that's when I switched over to the mandolin. By then, it was a known thing that the tenor singer was supposed to play the mandolin. So I went over to North Carolina and bought me a little old mandolin for $15. It was a A-50 Gibson, with f-holes. It noted easy, and I just wanted to see if I could learn how to play one.

When you started out, did you play Monroe-style breaks?

At that time, I'd never heard of mandolin players like Red Rector or Pee Wee Lambert or anybody else. Bill Monroe was the only one. I used to play "Rawhide" and "Bluegrass Breakdown," but I never tried to imitate Monroe. You can't beat a guy at his own game.

When did you first use your melodic style in public?

Around 1953, when I got out of the Marines. I got into the style on songs like "Auld Lang Syne" and "Silver Rainbow" from my brother's Gateway instrumental recordings. "My Aching Heart" was the first song on a major label that I got to put my style on. That was on the *Country Picking And Hillside Singing* album on MGM in 1955 [out of print]. I stuck to the melody as much as possible; but I added some notes here and yonder. That's the way I'm doing it right today. I don't like to hear guys get completely away from the melody and just play a bunch of notes. Anybody can play a lot of notes; but I think the melody is important, too, and if you stick to the melody and just put in a few extra notes that makes it a little different that way.

Your breaks always have a nice, smooth rhythm to them. Does that also come from your fiddle playing?

I've always related the mandolin to the fiddle. It fits in real easy with what I do. Even the breaks on songs like "Little Cabin Home On The Hill," it's just like a fiddle tune. I relate all the breaks just like a guy would take his bow and keep a good flow of notes going all the time. Every once in a while, from one line to another, I'll do a little tremolo part just to break the monotony.

You get a strong treble out of your mandolin. Is that something you do on purpose?

That's just where my hand feels comfortable. I like a lot of treble. That's why I don't like the Gibson round-hole mandolins. You have to play them too close to the bridge to get any sound out of them. The best place to play an instrument is where it sounds the best, regardless if it's got a strong bass or a strong treble. I guess my style always had a lot of treble. Also, the pick I use gives the tone I like. I've always used a real hard pick, even when I've played electric guitar.

I heard your picks are custom-made?

I use my own brand of picks. They're made up by Leonard Stadler of the Marlin Steel Guitar Company in Reidsville, North Carolina. They're shaped like old Gibson teardrop picks, small and white.

What determines how hard you hit the strings?

I believe I play the mandolin just like I sing. If I'm in a good mood and my voice is good and I can put a lot more power into a note than I normally would, I do. If it don't feel like it will do it, I slack off and take the short cuts. I think a guy does that in his playing too, whatever mood he's in. If he's not in a good mood to sing, he can't sing, and if he's not in a good mood to pick, he can't pick.

Do you have to play with a hard picking stroke to get the tone you want?

No. If you've got a good instrument, it'll take care of that. You can take a good instrument and hit it too hard, and, you'll lose the tone. It's better to play one soft and get a better tone out of it. There's also a certain place, somewhere between the end of the fretboard and the bridge, where the tone is the best.

How do you find that spot?

If the place where you'd normally hit the strings doesn't have a good tone, then you should reach your arm forward or backward — about an inch either way — to where you can find the best tone. I think that comes more naturally to a guy than to have someone like me say, "You've got to play it right there," because every arrangement is different.

What position is comfortable for you? Where do you rest your arm?

My forearm rides on the tailpiece. My wrist or fingers don't ever touch the body of the mandolin, or the top of the bridge. Sometimes I'll lay my wrist down on top of the bridge just for comfort; sometimes I place my wrist in that position when I'm playing a slow song. Sometime my wrist ain't working just right, and that'll be one of the short cuts I'll take to make it sound the same. My pick hits right at the end of the fretboard, and I keep the pick level with [perpendicular to] the strings and go straight up and down to get the best stroke. If you play with the pick at an angle, you'll lose tone and volume.

What kind of strings do you use?

I've got my own strings, made by GHS. Their gauges are [from first to fourth]: .011", .016", .024", and .038". I used to use a .040" fourth string, but it was so big it didn't fit normal down in the groove of the bridge. You can get the same volume out of a .038", and you get more speed.

How did you settle on those gauges?

When I used to buy Gibson strings, their first string used to be about .009"; the second was an .011" or .012". All of them were thinner than mine and they broke a lot quicker. I came up with the gauges on the strings I use now, and Leonard Stadler said he would put them out with my name and

The Osborne Brothers publicity photo in the 70s. Sonny is pictured with his Vega "Sonny Osborne Model" banjo, and Bob with his vintage Gibson F-5 mandolin. Together with fellow Kentuckian Red Allen, the Osborne Brothers developed a new style of three-part harmony singing.

Bob Osborne
concentrates on a
mandolin tune,
with Dale Sledd on guitar,
at a Pennsylvania show
in 1974.

picture on them. We call them Bobby Osborne Marlin Mandolin Strings, but they're made by GHS. The Gibson strings had a good tone but they had a thin sound because the gauge wasn't heavy enough, and I wanted that good, loud, heavy sound. I didn't know it at the time, but the heavier the gauge, the longer they'll play without breaking.

How high do you set your bridge?

I used to keep it real high. You get a lot more volume when you keep your action high, but it's harder to play and I don't think you get as good a tone out of it. The bridge should be at the height where you can get the best tone out of your instrument. Mine's set up now to just exactly where it won't rattle. I can hit it as hard as I want to, but it's a lot easier to play. Because I play the fiddle, I've got the mandolin down to where I can note it [with the left hand] and use my fingers on it just like I do on a fiddle.

Why did you remove the pickguard from your mandolin?

Anything that you've got on an instrument is going to hold the volume back. The pickguard covered up almost all of the lower f-hole and cut the volume down.

Did you make any other adjustments?

I put a little piece of felt under the tailpiece. Without that little felt on there, you can hit your mandolin, and immediately after you let your [left-hand] fingers up, you'll hear an extra ring. With that little piece of felt right under the tailpiece, when you hit the strings and remove your fingers, there's no extra ring. No ring, nothing.

What is your main performance instrument?

The one I play onstage is a 1924 Gibson F-5 Lloyd Loar model. I bought it in November 1980 from a guy named John Nance in Hyden, Kentucky. He just called me up one night and asked me if I could help sell it for him. When I played it, it was so nice that I decided to buy it for myself. I really wasn't looking for another mandolin. I've also been playing a 1926 Gibson Fern model F-5 for about 30 years, and it's a great instrument. But I prefer the neck of the Loar. It has such a nice feeling. It's got a pure dreamboat neck on it, like the neck on Monroe's mandolin.

What's the difference in tone between the Fern and the Loar?

The Fern has the best bass strings I've ever heard on a mandolin. The two high strings have a tinny sound. It may be in the bridge or in the frets, which have been on there since 1964. They're the big frets, and all I've done is file them down.

Did it come with big frets?

No, I put them in there myself. The little frets just kept wearing out. They'd last about six months with the amount we were playing. Of course, I played a lot more at home then than I do now. I didn't know this at the time, but with the big frets your strings are easier to press down and get a clear note from. You don't have to press down half as hard. They're guitar fret wire, that's what they are. That's the first thing I did to this Loar when I got it. This Loar has got two first strings that are out of this world. I'd rather pick the Loar, on account of the neck being so small. It's given me a little more heart to do more playing on it than I would on the Fern.

Which instrument did you use on your recent recording, Bobby And His Mandolin?

I used both. The album was my brother Sonny's idea. He said there wasn't another mandolin LP out like it, so he suggested I pick out a dozen or so of my favorite fiddle tunes and record them. Six of the songs I wrote myself, so naturally I wanted to include those. They are "Springtime," "Gatlinburg," "Topeka," "Sandy Ridge," and a couple of others. The rest I learned from other fiddle players. I got "High Level Hornpipe" from Howdy Forrester, and Buddy Spicher showed me "Limerock." Curly Ray Cline is the first guy I ever heard play "Old Sledge." He tunes his first string to *D* and leaves the others the same. I changed the tuning to get all the open strings. It was a little bit different and I never heard anyone play it on the mandolin. I'm just crazy about cross-tuning things anyway.

When you use cross-tuning, is the mandolin tuned to an open chord?

On "Old Sledge," it's tuned *D-A-D-A*. That gives you a sound like Monroe gets on "Get Up John." I used the same tuning on "Sally Ann." I hit my fourth string open all the time to get that drone effect. On "Gatlinburg," it's more or less a "Black Mountain Rag" tuning, with the only difference that on the fiddle your first string comes down to a *C♯*. It's tuned *C♯-A-E-A*. On the mandolin, I split the tuning on the first pair of strings. The first is *E* and the other is *C♯*. Then the other pairs are *A-E-A*. So when I note the top string it comes out in harmony.

Are there any particular types of fiddle tunes that you prefer to play?

I like the hornpipes, because that separates the men from the boys right there. Anybody can play a regular "Bile Them Cabbage Down" or something like that on the mandolin. A hornpipe has prettier notes and it's a hundred times harder than something like "Sally Goodin." If you've got a fast wrist you can play "Sally Goodin" and "Fire On The Mountain" real fast, and it sounds like you're getting right into it, and that you're better than you really are. I played the tunes on my album at just the tempo where they felt comfortable. They're not so fast that you're skipping over notes. It should be real easy for people to learn those tunes if they want.

What makes hornpipes more difficult to play?

There's more melody notes to them, and they're in harder keys, like *B♭* and *E♭*. I take the notes and put them into the breaks of other songs. They're fancier notes and they change the sound of the breaks.

Your solos come out so clean and clear. What's behind that crispness?

I believe that the limber wrist I use helps. The rhythm of my wrist goes right into the flow with my left hand, and everything fits together. I don't think you could play my style with a stiff wrist. Most of my melody notes are fretted, unless I'm playing in an open key like *A* or *G* or *D*. You get a better tone out of a note if you fret it. You have more control over it. I also try to use downstrokes for all the notes I want to emphasize. You get more volume out of them. You don't get any volume or tone when you're stroking up. But I think the main thing is my finger movement. I take advantage of every finger I've got. You've got these two-finger and three-finger guys that slide into notes rather than hitting them head on. A lot of guys don't ever use that little finger there. All four fingers, they'll just fit right in place on a mandolin or a fiddle, and I just use them exactly as they fall naturally.

Do you sing better if you don't have to concentrate as much on playing?

Yes. A lot of the songs are hard to sing, you know — so many words. I've always had to think more about my singing than my playing. If I'm paying attention to my mandolin playing 50%, I'm only giving 50% to my voice. And the people out there, the first thing they're listening to is the voice, so the mandolin is not that important. Nobody ever wanted to hear me play mandolin. I could go onstage and just stand there and sing, and nobody would mind.

For somebody that's been as influential instrumentally as you have, that must be a disappointment. Would you like to be playing more onstage?

Years ago I would've loved to have been more of an instrumentalist than I am now; but now it doesn't make any difference. My singing is what's got me where I'm at, anyway. I never considered myself to be a great mandolin player, but a lot of guys have told me they like what I do. I know that I've got a good style of playing and what I do fits exactly where it's supposed to. For me, that's enough.

— Herschel Freeman

A SELECTED OSBORNE BROTHERS DISCOGRAPHY

On CMH (Box 39439, Los Angeles, CA 90039): *The Osborne Brothers,* CMH 9011; *The Essential Bluegrass Album: The Osborne Brothers and Mac Wiseman,* CMH 9016; *The Osborne Brothers In A Bluegrass Concerto,* CMH 6231, *From Rocky Top To Muddy Bottom,* CMH 9008; *I Can Hear Kentucky Calling Me,* CMH 6244; on MCA: *Modern Sounds Of Bluegrass Music,* MCA 117; *Yesterday, Today, And The Osborne Brothers,* MCA 119; *Voices In Bluegrass,* MCA 105; *Fastest Grass Alive,* MCA 374; *Rubeeeeeee,* MCA 135; *Country Roads,* MCA 141; *Up To Date And Down To Earth,* MCA 129; *Best Of The Osbornes,* MCA 2-4086; *Bluegrass Instrumentals,* MCA 104. **Solo:** *Bobby And His Mandolin,* CMH-6256; *Bluegrass Concerto,* CMH-6231.

JIMMY MARTIN

WHEN THE NITTY GRITTY DIRT BAND'S landmark album *Will The Circle Be Unbroken* was released in 1972, featuring such guest artists as Mother Maybelle Carter and Merle Travis, music critics hailed the Dirt Band for bringing long overdue recognition to classic country artists. To many, however, the real "sleeper" of the album was bluegrass stalwart Jimmy Martin. His stirring singing and powerful guitar playing on "Sunny Side Of The Mountain," "You Don't Know My Mind," and on other songs he transformed into bluegrass standards, brought Jimmy's talents full force to a whole new generation of acoustic listeners, many of whom were not yet born when Jimmy first came to prominence with Bill Monroe And The Blue Grass Boys in 1949.

Over the past 30 years, Jimmy Martin's "Good 'N Country" style has become instantly recognizable to bluegrass audiences — a combination of booming guitar runs, heartfelt singing, and an aggressive rhythm. It is an approach shaped as much by Jimmy's brassy artistic temperament as by his prodigious talents, and it has brought out the best in a long line of playing partners. His vocal trios with the Osborne Brothers in the early '50s have yet to be equaled for their beauty and precision, and his recordings with his own group, the Sunny Mountain Boys, rank among the finest examples of hard-driving bluegrass ensemble playing.

His most famous songs include "Uncle Pen" with Bill Monroe, "20-20 Vision" with the Osborne Brothers, and a string of classics with the Sunny Mountain Boys, including "Ocean Of Diamonds," "Sophronie," "Free Born Man," "Mr. Engineer," and "Widow Maker." His recording career culminated with the gold album he shared for *Will The Circle Be Unbroken.*

Today, Jimmy continues to play a full schedule of festivals and concerts, and his love for bluegrass and his intensity onstage continue unabated.

* * * *

COMPARED WITH THE *playing of other traditional bluegrass players, your guitar style has a lot of runs, and you really push the beat. How did you* develop that?

The timing was always natural to me, ever since I used to sing under the apple trees on Sundays with all the other kids. It came from playing with a feeling, and just patting my foot in time. I learned the basic chords from an old hillbilly named Reuben Gibson, who lived in the hills around Sneedville, and I taught myself how to play. I heard Lester Flatt and Charlie Monroe both play runs, but I didn't try to top them. I mostly just developed them how I felt, when it came natural for a song. Like the "Uncle Pen" run I did with Bill Monroe. That was my ideal [*Ed. Note: idea*] for putting a run in.

When did you decide to audition for Bill?

In the summer of 1949; I was 22 years old. He had Mac Wiseman singing lead with him then, and Flatt and Scruggs had moved on to WCYB in Bristol, Tennessee, where I could listen to them every day. When Lester and Earl had been with Bill, along with Chubby Wise and Cedric Rainwater, that was my favorite group. He didn't do a song wrong when they were together. I was working in a little band over in Morristown, Tennessee, and I told some of the boys, "Mac's voice

don't blend as good with Bill, and I know all the songs that Lester and them used to sing with him, so I think I'll go to Nashville and just sing one with Bill." I told the fiddle player that if he'd go with me to the *Grand Ole Opry* I'd pay his bus ticket down there and back. I remember watching Bill from the balcony, and afterward I went backstage and got to sing one with him and one by myself, and he asked me if I wanted to go on the road with him. He said it would be hard traveling, and I said, "Bill, it can't be no harder than plowing corn or digging a ditch or pulling a crosscut saw." I think that's why we got along so well. We were both country boys, raised tough. We understood each other.

The chemistry was certainly there musically. You stayed with Bill a long time and recorded a lot of great songs. Was the work taxing?

We worked hard, but the music was always good and I really enjoyed it. The only time we got off a year was the week after Christmas. A typical day was to do a 5:30-5:45 a.m. radio show, then catch a few hours sleep before heading out to play a schoolhouse in Tennessee or Kentucky. Sometimes they'd have a microphone, sometimes we'd just stand up against the blackboard and sing without one. We learned to play the music so you could still hear the singer, and it taught us how to play the background to suit the voice. If Bill sang loud, I played the guitar loud and he played the mandolin loud. If Bill sang soft, I softened up.

I imagine this attention to the singer helped in the recording studio.

That also made it a lot easier to record. You set one microphone in the middle, and the quartet sang at the same loudness, and everyone knew when to move in or out with their instruments. Bill used to write a lot of songs on the bus, and by the time he finished a new song we'd heard it so much we already knew it. We'd play it two or three times onstage to polish it, and then we'd go into the studio. Usually within a couple tries, we'd have it hooked. I liked "Little Georgia Rose" and "On And On," "I'm Blue, I'm Lonesome," and we did some good gospel quartet numbers, like "Wicked Path Of Sin" and "Walking In Jerusalem Just Like John."

It seems as though the discipline you got through your work with Monroe was carried over into your own recordings with the Sunny Mountain Boys. The arrangements always sound so tight and clean, and are well matched to the vocals.

The secret is trying to fit in with what everybody else is doing. If Bill made a run on his mandolin, I'd try my best to back up his run. I wouldn't try to just do something that I wanted to do. I'd try to do what made *him* sound good. "Memories Of Mother And Dad," it was naturally a sad song, so I'd put a break in my voice and Bill would say, "Jimmy, can you do a little bit more of that? It would sure sound good, and I'll put mine

right there." Me and Bill would sit on the bus and pick the guitar and mandolin, and the little licks he'd do on the mandolin I'd match on the guitar, and he liked it, you know. If he'd kinda backhand the mandolin, come up backwards, I'd come up backwards on the guitar and it fit.

So it's more a matter of timing than tempo?

I didn't keep the same pace all the time. I play the guitar to whoever I'm playing with. If I'm playing with a good banjo player who's got a good roll, I try to roll my pick in rhythm just like he's doing to make it sound good. Drive it more, in other words. I tried to get my band to play with the same feeling that I was singing. That makes me sound better and it makes the music sound better, because they're right in timing with me. Timing is not only on your instruments, it's in your singing, too. I always try to blend my voice so that it fits in with the other voices, and not say the words every which way. You've got to know how to tone your voice to sing with a guy like Bill Monroe, then turn around and sing lead and sound good with a fellow like Bob Osborne. There's as much difference in their singing as there is between daylight and dark.

Wasn't singing a much more important part of your musical education than playing an instrument?

Gospel quartets were all we sang around my hometown, Sneedville, Tennessee. We used to sing at funerals, and in church, and that way we learned to sing all the parts —the lead, the baritone, the tenor, and the bass. That way I could always find someone to sing with, no matter what part was needed. I used to tell my mother, "One day, I'm going to go to Nashville and sing in Bill Monroe's quartet." That's what really attracted me to Bill.

You played with Monroe on two separate occasions. When you left the first time, wasn't it to join forces with Bobby Osborne?

Actually, I left to play with Larry Richardson, a banjo picker who was playing with Bob at the time. We arranged to meet in Bluefield, West Virginia, but when I showed up Bob was the only one there, so we decided to team together instead. I really enjoyed singing with him. I remember Bob's daddy saying, "Jesus! You couldn't get cornbread and butter no closer harmony than you and Bobby gets on that." We worked with the Lonesome Pine Fiddlers, and it was tough making a living, but we did get to record four songs for King Records in Cincinnati. Me and Bob and Charlie Cline and Curly Ray Cline. We did "She's Just A Cute Thing," "Blue Eyed Darling," "You'll Never Be The Same," and "Lonely Heart." Then when Bob got drafted into the Marines, I went back to Middletown, Ohio, to work with Smokey Ward on WPFB.

Was this when you first started playing with Sonny Osborne?

Yeah. Sonny was thirteen years old by this time, and he had gotten pretty good on

Jimmy Martin and his son Ray on mandolin sing a trio with guest banjoist J.D. Crowe in Gettysburg, Pennsylvania, 1974.

the banjo. We used to use him on the Saturday night shows. Then I got a call from Bill Monroe, saying he'd like for me to come and record with him in Nashville. I set it up that if Sonny could show Bill he was good enough to record with us, he could become a regular member of the Blue Grass Boys. I wanted Sonny to have a job that would work him hard because we were talking about going back together as Jimmy Martin and the Osborne Brothers when Bob got back out of the Marines, and Sonny was good enough on his baritone and his banjo playing. We stayed with Bill a year and a half, and then in 1954 me and Sonny and Bob moved up to Detroit to play with [fiddler] Casey Clark.

That was really the first time you started to have any success on your own?

When I was working with Bill for the first time, I had an offer from Steve Sholes of RCA to record solo, but I couldn't travel with Bill and sing my own songs, too. Now that I finally had the voices to work with, we signed a four-song contract, and that's when we cut "20-20 Vision." That song was written by some fellow down in Nashville, who showed it to us when we went in there to record. It had been recorded once before by Gene Autry! Real slow and smooth. When Bob and Sonny heard it, they said, "Don't tell me we're gonna record that!" But it was a Number One record for us, and it established our style. We played every Saturday night on the *Big Barn Frolic* in Detroit, which was kinda like the *Opry.* They held it in a large union hall, and broadcast it live on KCLW radio.

Were you paid well for that gig?

Casey used to pay us $225, plus all we could make off selling our pictures. That was good, steady money back in those days, plus we didn't have to travel much at all. During that time, they called us from Wheeling, West Virginia, and asked us if we'd like to be regulars on the *Wheeling Jamboree,* which was a really popular show. But when I asked them how much did they pay, they said $10 a man per night, so we figured we were pretty well off where we were.

When did you first form your own group, the Sunny Mountain Boys?

Right after me and the Osborne Brothers split up. I liked to sing with Bob so much and I liked Sonny, and wanted to make a real good go of it. Since we couldn't get along I said, "Well Jimmy, there's no use trying to work with anybody else." So I hired me two musicians from Baltimore, Earl Taylor on mandolin, and Sam Hutchins on the banjo, and I formed the Sunny Mountain Boys. That's when I went over to Decca Records, where we cut some good songs like "Hit Parade Of Love" and "You'll Be A Lost Ball." Then I hired Paul Williams to play the mandolin and J.D. Crowe on the banjo, and things started really going good. I'd have to say that lineup brought my records out and got me on my feet more than any other musicians I've had in the

Sunny Mountain Boys.

Over the years you've had a lot of great musicians in your group, including Doyle Lawson, Alan Munde, and Bill Emerson. What do you look for in a musician?

I try to find players with a professional attitude. Those people who hate to make a mistake. If J.D. or Bill Emerson made a mistake, down in the dressing room you'd hear them nearly break their banjo putting it in the case. You never have to get on a pro musician about messing up your song, because he'll stand there and feel guilty himself. They were pros from start to finish. I never did get my ribs punched out by the banjo neck. They never did knock my hat off, nothing like that onstage. I've had to pick my hat up off a lot of musicians off the stage. If you ever want to get nervous, you be there and start to talk, and then have your hat lying down on the floor. It's just another one of those sad experiences.

Musically, what is the most important to you — volume, tone, or timing?

It's a combination of all those things. I used to tell J.D., "Play as strong as you can, but look for the good tone." It's timing, number one. Next is good notes, clear notes, and getting good tone out of the instrument. If you play with a guy long enough and look for that sound, you'll get the tone that fits right in with his voice. It comes from where you hit the strings, how you note it, and the sort of pull that you pull out of it. It all goes back to the timing, and the feeling that you put into it.

Your guitar comes across so strong on record and in person. How do you get that lively, popping sound?

I've always liked to play loud and sing loud. I like to ring the guitar right up with my voice. I use a medium-hard pick, and I hold it real close to the tip so I can get a better crack on it. I also keep my action high. You can't keep it low and play hard, it'll buzz every time. I've always used Martin, Gibson, or Mapes strings, but now there's a guy [Joe Morrell] from Bristol, Tennesee, who packages "Jimmy Martin" guitar strings. Each pack has my picture on it. The strings are between medium and heavy gauge.

On your album covers, I see you posing with your Martin Herringbone D-28, but it seems that on each succeeding album the guitar has more cracks in it. Do you keep playing it because the tone is so good?

Actually, I've got two Herringbones and one's pretty clean. The one you're talking about I paid $75 for back in Detroit when J.D. and Paul were with me. We used to have a guy come into the clubs, and in club singing you get hoarse, all the smoke in there. This guy would come over, and he'd get up and sing a couple of sets for me. He'd bring this guitar and his woman would come to the club, peep in, call him names, and raise all kinds of cain with him. He'd go home and they'd argue, fuss, and feud. So one night he went home around two o'clock and when that started, he just took

Jimmy Martin and the Sunny Mountain Boys onstage at the Grand Ole Opry in the early 1970s. (L to R): Alan Munde, Vernon Derrick, Martin, and Gloria Belle (partially hidden).

that guitar, he said, and whopped it right over her head. That's how the cracks got in the guitar! So after that I bought the guitar, and I had all the pieces put back in it and fixed it up. It's a good-sounding guitar.

Being included on the Will The Circle Be Unbroken *album must have seemed like a reward for all the years you devoted to bluegrass. It certainly brought your songs to a much wider listening audience. What kind of reaction did you have when they first approached you?*

Bill McEuen [the Dirt Band's manager and producer] called me one day and he said, "Jimmy, would you consider recording an album with the Nitty Gritty Dirt Band?" I said, "Well, what do they do? Who are they?" I didn't know that they'd had a hit song called "Bojangles." So, I said I wouldn't mind it after he told me they'd had a Number One hit song. He picked out the songs he wanted me to do. He especially wanted the "Grand Ole Opry Song," "Sunny Side Of The Mountain," and "You Don't Know My Mind." I picked out "Losing You Might Be The Best Thing Yet," and "My Walking Shoes Don't Fit Me Anymore." Anyway, when my kids got home from school I said, "Guess who I'm going to

make an album with? The Nitty Gritty Dirt Band." All the kids started hollering, "Golly, Daddy, they're popular. Everybody over at school's got their albums. That'll be really good for you!"

What was it like doing the actual recording?

I really enjoyed those sessions because they were good people to work with. They played all my songs with me. We didn't have any rehearsals beforehand. We just went right in, like we were a-picking. In fact, Vassar Clements fiddled "Patricia On The Turnpike" and we were just fooling around, and they got that one. We didn't know they were recording it and they said, "That's a good one right there. I think we'll just keep that." Them boys [The Dirt Band] picked day and night. They didn't want to sleep at all. It was great getting to be in the studio with Doc Watson and Merle Travis and Mother Maybelle and Earl Scruggs, all at the same time. I was real proud to receive a gold record for that album.

What kind of advice would you give to young musicians who want to get into bands?

If you want to play bluegrass, you have to concentrate on that one kind of music,

and really love it. It takes a good musician to play it and play it right, and you have to practice a lot to perfect your licks instead of hitting a note any which way just to get it out. You need to know where to put the note, and play with the timing that fits the singer. That way you can play with any band, whether it's Jimmy Martin or the Seldom Scene, and make them sound better. You need a good instrument, you need to know how to get the tone out of it, and you've got to know when to put a lick in and how to make it fit. It's the same thing with singing. You've got to get the tone, and have the right feeling. It takes a long time for groups to stay together to get tight.

You are one of only a handful of bluegrass musicians who has led his own band for more than 25 years. Despite all the changes in personnel, you seem as committed today to your original style as you've ever been. What keeps you going?

I love bluegrass. It's the only kind of music I ever will love. When I sing those songs it hits me deep, and when I'm at the microphone I give it all I've got. I want to see bluegrass stay up so bad, and do something for it however I can.

— *Herschel Freeman*

A SELECTED MARTIN DISCOGRAPHY

Sunny Side Of The Mountain, MCA 79; *Jimmy Martin And The Sunny Mountain Boys Sing,* MCA 101; *Good 'N Country,* MCA 81; *Country Music Time,* MCA 91; *This World Is Not My Home,* MCA 96; *Big And Country Instrumentals,* MCA 115; *Singing All Day And Dinner On The Ground,* MCA 137. **With Others:** *Will The Circle Be Unbroken,* United Artists, 9801; *Mr. Good And Country Music,* Decca, DL 47-69.

2.
KEY
BAND
MEMBERS

KENNY BAKER

P LAYING WITH Bill Monroe and the Blue Grass Boys is like being in the
starting lineup for the New York Yankees. You're a part of one of the most
powerful and respected organizations in your field, and sooner or later just
about everybody connected with it knows who you are. A lot of famous
names have come out of the Blue Grass Boys, musicians who made — and are
making — big-league reputations in bluegrass. But none has worn the characteristic Blue Grass Boy white hat as long and as nobly as fiddler Kenny Baker.

It was 1958 when Baker first tucked his fiddle under his chin as a Blue Grass
Boy, with the solemn expression that has become his trademark. Though it was ten
years before he became a truly permanent fixture in the band, he has now become
so closely identified with it that imagining Monroe without Baker is like imagining
Holmes without Watson. With his long tenure in the fiddle chair of the world's most
prominent bluegrass band, Kenny's playing has had a tremendous influence on a
whole generation of fiddlers. No history of twentieth-century American fiddling
would be complete without a chapter on Kenny Baker.

Surprisingly, Baker wouldn't have become a fiddler at all if it hadn't been for a
series of musical "battlefield commissions" during World War II — a long way from
the bluegrass fields of Kentucky and the pine woods of the Appalachians.

Though he came from a musical family, he had never taken a serious interest in
fiddling. "My daddy played old-time fiddle," Kenny recalls. "There was one lying
around home all the time. I was maybe seven or eight years old when I got to
kicking around with it, but my daddy didn't know if he wanted to teach me to play.
He didn't seem to think I had a good ear then, so I didn't bother with it any more
until after I got in the service."

Barely 16 when he enlisted in the Navy, Kenny took his boot camp training at
Great Lakes, Illinois. "They assigned me to this engineering school in Philadelphia,
and after three or four months I was sent to Norfolk, Virginia to go out on this
destroyer escort."

With a guitar stowed in his locker, Kenny shipped out for the South Pacific —
where the seeds of his future career were to be sown. Ironically, it was in New
Guinea that he first heard the Texas swing fiddling of Bob Wills, and the jazz violin
stylings of France's Stephane Grappelli. "I'd heard mountain-style fiddling all my
life," Kenny says. "Really, I'd been *stuck* with it. I'll be honest with you, it didn't
excite me at all. But when I was in New Guinea I heard the music of Bob Wills And
The Texas Playboys, and somebody had this recording of [The Quintet Of] The
Hot Club Of France [with Grappelli], and I realized there was stuff happening on
the fiddle that I'd never even known about. And that's when I started *liking* fiddle."

Still, nothing might have come of it if some of Kenny's shipmates hadn't
volunteered him for unexpected shore duty. "We were having a beach party in
New Guinea with this USO troupe," he recalled, "and they were asking if anyone
wanted to play. Some of the boys on my ship knew I had a guitar, so they went up
and talked to somebody, and the first thing I knew I was up there playing."

Kenny didn't realize it, but the surprise gig probably was the most important
audition of his life. His musicianship caught the ear of the troupe's bandleader. "He
asked me, 'If I can get you a release from your ship, will you come and travel with
us?'" Kenny recalls. "I looked at him and said, 'Yeah,' but I was thinking, 'Big deal.' I

just knew there was no way he could swing it. So I went back aboard ship. About 9:30 that night — I had already turned in — here they came! We loaded my gear and I was ready to go."

Reassigned to USO duty, Kenny spent 33 months entertaining servicemen and backing visiting celebrities, such as Hollywood screen star Carole Lombard — who was later killed on a USO tour. He wound up in Okinawa. And there his career as a fiddler began.

"It was in 1945, and I was still affiliated with the same outfit," he says. "The Army Red Cross nurses wanted to put on this big country square dance — except nobody knew how to play country fiddle. I told the bandleader, 'Well, if you'll get me a fiddle I'll play the doggone thing. It won't be great, but I'll hack it out for you.' So the Navy got me a fiddle. It was a fine fiddle, although of course it was set up for a violinist, and I had to jack the bridge down a little bit. But I played two numbers maybe four hours straight, and from that night on I never had a guitar in my hands again."

When Kenny mustered out a couple of months later, the bandleader sent the fiddle home with him. But Kenny didn't have any inkling that he'd ever play music professionally stateside. "I was eager to get married, and what have you," he says. "You know how young boys are. I never had no thoughts about professional music, none whatsoever. It had just been a sideline."

He went to work for a coal company. "They'd have a few get-togethers now and then," he says. "They'd put on something at the local Lions Club like a comedy show, near Christmas, to make money for the needy. And I got to play there with a group of boys. From that, we started playing four nights a week — and still working in the mines!"

In 1952 Baker left mining to join the band of country artist Don Gibson, and he was on his way. But he didn't connect with Monroe until three years later. "It was in Knoxville, Tennessee," Kenny recalls. "I was with Don Gibson, and I met Monroe there. Bobby Hicks was playing fiddle for him. Monroe told me if I ever wanted a job, ever wanted to travel with him, to just call him. I heard him play 'Roanoke' and 'Cheyenne,' and that really sold me on that kind of music. So I started paying more attention to Monroe's music, and started to play it. It took me a while — I nearly quit a couple of times. But two years later I called him."

When Baker joined Monroe in 1957, bluegrass — like country music in general — still was reeling from the commercial shock-waves of rock and roll. But Monroe was at peak form. His first long-playing record, *Knee Deep In Blue Grass,* was released in the spring of 1958. In February of that year Kenny went into the studio with the Blue Grass Boys to cut Monroe's second album, *I Saw The Light,* playing and singing on such tracks — now classics — as the title cut, "Life's Railway To Heaven,"

Kenny Baker onstage with Bill Monroe And His Bluegrass Boys.

"Wayfaring Stranger," and "Precious Memories."

It was the beginning of a career that found Kenny in the studio for the recording of a lot of Monroe's most famous numbers, including "Scotland," "Pike County Breakdown," "Crossing The Cumberlands," and "Shenandoah Breakdown," as well as songs he co-authored with Monroe, like 'Big Sandy River" and "Baker's Breakdown." (Almost as active at writing as he is at playing, Kenny estimates he has written around 80 tunes on his own, such as "Festival Waltz," "First Day In Town," "Long Cold Winter," and "Bluegrass In The Backwoods.")

Kenny came and went a few times between 1958 and 1968, but he is now solidly entrenched as the elder statesman of the Blue Grass Boys. Many great artists have passed through the group during Kenny's association with Monroe, from Bill Keith to Butch Robins, but only Baker has become a symbol of the band who is as recognizable as Monroe himself. Unques-

tionably, he is the dean of the Blue Grass Boys; and, as such, the dean of bluegrass fiddlers.

WHAT KEPT YOU from joining Bill Monroe for good when you signed on in 1958? How many hitches have you served with the Blue Grass Boys?

This year [1982] is the fourth time I've worked with Bill; '68 was when I came back. You see, I had two youngsters coming up, and times wasn't too good back in them days, money-wise. I had a good job there at home coal-mining in east Kentucky — Bethlehem Steel Corporation and Consolidated Coal Company. I didn't have to go looking for work. They asked me if I wanted to go to work. I had those boys, they were about six and eight, and boys need a man around, you know. So that's why I left.

What made you finally decide to get out of coal mining and stay with bluegrass?

My youngest boy got out of school; and I wanted to play, didn't want to be humped over in the mines up there. I felt if I was ever going to play any more, right then and there was the time. I called Bill — he had Benny Williams working with him — one morning. He said, "Well, let me call Benny." And about five minutes later he called me back and said, "Come on down on Thursday."

You've been performing with Bill for so many years — how do you keep making the next show fresh and interesting? Can you keep it fresh?

I think each and every show is different in some respect, even though you may be doing practically the same numbers. There's always a new audience. You can keep it fresh to a certain extent. Now, if you've got a lot of mileage on you on one trip, you may go out and act like you're feeling good, but it will show up in your music.

As far as music goes, you have two main roles with Monroe — lead and accompaniment. When the fiddle doesn't have the lead, what should the fiddler be doing?

Ever since I've worked with Bill, he's told me to pick up the slack, you know. Maybe sometimes the banjo's not playing backup up to standard, so I'll fill in there. Same with Bill — he's doing more backup now than he's done in years.

Do you have any particular warm-up routine that you follow before a performance?

Most of the time I'll work on a B♭ scale. When you're able to get that working properly you can pretty well maneuver wherever you want to go. I usually play it in first position. I play some stuff in second and third position, but not a whole lot.

I've noticed that you hold the frog of the bow kind of sideways in your hand. Did you learn that from your father?

No, that came from having a bow that had very few hairs in it, and I just adjusted that way. It's very improper to hold a bow the way I hold it, I realize that, but I'm com-fortable with it now. I've even tried to break myself of doing it like that, but I can't get away from it.

Do you use much vibrato in your playing, even though that's really not an old-time fiddling technique?

It comes from what you hear. I get a bang out of listening to a lot of different violinists. I hate a flat, dry sound. When you're playing waltzes and stuff, if you play it straight with no vibrato then you've got nothing on it to start with. Same thing with a lot of singers, you know.

You're noted for your crescendos; do you do that with the bow, or do you do that with the mike?

Just with the bow. It's just the way you feel it. I'll tell you what, I've tried to explain a lot of bow movements and things to people, but there's no way to relate it to them. It's just how you feel it, how you hear it.

Do you do a lot of double-stops?

Oh yeah. Quite a bit. Stuff I've just learned on the fiddle, mostly. I learned a lot of that from listening to Bob Wills when they were using two or three fiddles, and you get a fuller sound by playing double-stops.

How do you view jazz violinists like Stephane Grappelli and Jean-Luc Ponty? Do they influence you at all?

Yes, they do. Grappelli's my man. I find that music very easy to listen to, but it would be hard for me to take some of their music and apply it to Monroe's music. I guess everybody gets their ideas from somewhere, and without a doubt, Grappelli has influenced several fiddle numbers of mine. I'll tell you what, I can get carried away from any type of music if it's *played* well. Me, I'm a Fritz Kreisler [violinist, 1875-1962] fan; I love listening to that guy's records. There are some classical players I really get a bang out of. Then in jazz, I enjoy Stuff Smith, Eddie South; but you know, playing with Monroe you don't try a lot of that stuff.

A lot of young fiddlers would give their eye teeth to play with Monroe. A lot of the people who read this probably are wondering how they can get where you are. What would be your advice to a young fiddler coming up today?

My advice to 'em would be to put in all the time on it that they can. I'd say they've got to know in their mind what they want to accomplish, and they shouldn't stop 'till they can make the fiddle sound like what they're hearing in their head. I think any beginning fiddle player should play mostly slower numbers. That way they get more usage of their bow, with a longer stroke. Of course, not everybody plays with a long bow, but me — I think I can play about as fast and as accurate with a long bow as a lot of people can by chopping it up with a lot of short strokes.

Of course, you're one of the most popular fiddlers in the world, and you're playing with the most famous bluegrass band in the world. Do you think somebody who's fiddling with a regular band can at least make a decent living?

No. Not unless he's moonlighting. See, I make a fair amount on my records. And of course, I've been with Bill a long time.

What's the most satisfying thing about that involvement with Monroe and bluegrass? How does it feel to be Kenny Baker?

Well, I get a bang out of it. I'm just me and that's it, like everybody else. I know a great number of musicians who play much better than I play. I know a lot of young boys coming up who are real accurate. Blaine Sprouse is one. James Bryan. Jim Campbell from around Detroit, Michigan — he's about 16, and he's got a good ear. But these young guys are what I really get a bang out of — 'cause I helped to teach a bunch of 'em.

— Roger H. Siminoff

A SELECTED BAKER DISCOGRAPHY

Solo Album: *Farmyard Swing*, County (Main St., Floyd, VA 24091), 775. **With Bill Monroe And The Blue Grass Boys** (On Decca/MCA): *I Saw The Light*, DL 8769; *All-Time Country & Western, Vol. 3*, DL 4134; *Blue Grass Special*, DL 4382; *I'll Meet You In Church Sunday Morning*, DL 4537; *Bluegrass Instrumentals*, DL 4601; *Blue Grass Time*, DL 4896; *Kentucky Blue Grass*, DL 75213; *Bill Monroe's Country Music Hall Of Fame*, DL 75281; *Bill Monroe's Uncle Pen*, DL 75348; *Bill Monroe And James Monroe*, MCA 310; *Bean Blossom*, MCA 2-8002; *Bean Blossom '79*, MCA 3209; *Master Of Bluegrass*, MCA 5214.

MIKE AULDRIDGE

SEVERAL YEARS AGO, at a festival in Berryville, Virginia, Mike Auldridge walked over to jam with a group of dobro players. Several of them promptly put their instruments away and left. One remaining player leaned over to Mike and whispered, "And the legend grows." From those who overheard the remark came the nickname "the Legend," then "Lawrence Of Legendville," and finally "Larry The Legend." Whether you know him as Larry, or by John Duffy's favorite appellation for him, "Mr. Clean," there is no mistaking the man behind the myth. Mike Auldridge is to the dobro what John Williams is to the classical guitar and Bill Keith is to the 5-string banjo: an artist so thoroughly identified with his instrument that the mere mention of his name conjures up a complete picture of masterful technique, trend-setting music, and uncompromising professionalism.

Mike was born in Washington, D.C. in 1938. There were no musicians in his family except for one uncle, Ellsworth Cozzens, who played dobro. Mike heard his uncle at family gatherings; but Mike's eight brothers and sisters were into swing and big band music, so it was only natural that the Benny Goodman and Tommy Dorsey orchestras became Mike's first musical love.

Mike's family moved to Kensington, Maryland, around 1950. It was there that he first heard dobroist Josh Graves, who was performing with Wilma Lee And Stoney Cooper. "I wasn't sure it was the same instrument my uncle played, because Josh played it so differently," Mike recalls. "My uncle played this real old-timey single-note type thing. It was like harmony, like he was singing harmony with Jimmie Rodgers." Josh had "More of a banjo sound," which Mike greatly enjoyed.

Mike started playing the guitar when he was 12 or 13, and as he got interested in hillbilly music, he heard Josh Graves with Earl Scruggs. "When Josh went with Scruggs, that to me was heaven. It seemed like a perfect idea to have a dobro in bluegrass."

Mike had a couple of junior high school friends who played mandolin and banjo. They got a job on a little radio station in Maryland. When the mandolin player quit, they needed another musician within one week, so Mike taught his brother to play guitar. "We only knew about four songs, but we played them about six hours a day during that week and we really had them. Once my brother learned guitar, I had someone to play with and it really helped my music. I've always been serious about it in my own mind."

Mike's interest in dobro was suppressed for several years because he couldn't find a dobro or a teacher. He used to go into music stores and ask for one, but "nobody knew of them in the early '50s." When Mike was 18, he finally found an instrument. The only way he could learn was by slowing down Flatt And Scruggs records. "I didn't really realize how important music was to me until I got into college." he says now. "I studied commercial art at the University of Maryland and minored in music theory. Actually, I didn't realize the importance of music until 1976, when I went full-time with the Seldom Scene."

Mike began as a full-time dobroist with Bill Emerson and Cliff Waldron in 1969. Waldron left in 1970, and Mike stayed with Emerson until 1971. Since then he has performed as a sideman with such artists as Linda Ronstadt, J.D. Crowe, Emmylou

Harris, Dolly Parton, Bill Harrell, and Charlie Waller and the Country Gentlemen. Mike adjusts his musical style for each situation.

"When I play with Bill Harrell," he says, "I play completely different than I would with Emmylou Harris or the Seldom Scene. It's not anything I do consciously, it just happens. I think you have to be able to do that when you do studio work."

Most of Mike's studio playing is spontaneous. He comes in, hears a piece once or twice, and has one or two goes at it. The studio is his favorite place. "I think I'm kind of a bashful person," he admits. "Crowds scare me. I don't know how to entertain people. In the studio I only have to entertain me. There's a great kind of satisfaction to doing something and hearing it right back. You know whether it's right or wrong. If it's right, gosh, it's one of the most wonderful feelings in the world; and if it's wrong, you can fix it."

Like many musicians, Mike doesn't see himself as a "businessman." The financial rewards of his work are just icing on the cake. "When somebody calls me up to do a session," he says, "I am at the point where I ask how much money I am going to make, because that's how I earn a living. But when I am asked to join somebody as a sideman, I usually don't worry about it. I just want to get in and do the music."

Since Mike joined the Seldom Scene in 1971, his bashfulness hasn't seemed to keep either his voice or his playing away from the microphone. Along with banjoist Ben Eldridge, bassist Tom Gray, mandolinist John Duffy, and the band's newest addition, guitarist Phil Rosenthal, Mike has played to countless audiences and done innumerable encores.

Mike was a regular monthly columnist from *Frets'* March '79 debut issue through 1981. During that period he shared his wealth of dobro expertise with *Frets* readers. Following is an extensive, in-depth interview with Mike about his polished technique and his sure-handed approach to recording and performing.

*W*HEN YOU PLAY a lead break, are you thinking in terms of following a vocal line?

Sometimes, if it's a real emotional thing, where I'm not sure what I'm going to do, but just do it. Then I think I play it as I would sing it. If it's something that has a real weird progression, then I would sit down and work it out in a theory sense, sort of a mathematical approach. Like my version of Vic Jordan's "Pickaway." I would play it the same every time.

Can you change the mood on a piece like "Pickaway," or is the performance strictly mechanical?

Parts of it are mechanical. Like the "A" part of the song; I do it exactly the same every time. The "B" part I can play around with a little more, and I'll throw in some vocal-like things. A song like "House Of The Rising Sun" is where I can really put in a vocal-like feeling. Sometimes I can play it in a way that I can't believe myself, and yet sometimes I play it dry. It just depends on my mood, and in that way it's like singing. In order to bring something off emotionally, you have to really have your soul into it.

Can you make adjustments for your mood so you are always up?

No. Sometimes I think, "I'm going to play the hell out of this piece tonight," and it stinks. And sometimes I think I'm so tired that I can hardly stand up, and all of a sudden the piece is singing.

As a traveling musician, is your music often affected by your being tired or not having had a good dinner or something like that?

It's more a spur-of-the-moment kind of thing. One thing that really affects the mood when you're playing on stage is the sound. If I'm playing into a real dry sound system and the tone is barely there, I can hardly play. Whereas if what I'm playing sounds good when I hear it back, right away that charges me.

In that case, would it be worth it to bring along your own sound system, to have some sort of control?

Yes, and that's something that I am just starting to work on. There are so many bad sound systems and problems when you go out traveling. You're depending on a sound company, and a lot of them have never done acoustic music. I decided that it was stupid to be making my living playing music and just walking out somewhere with my instrument when I should be bringing a lot of gear with me to make sure that it's perfect every time. We played a show with Doc Watson up in New York, a couple of weeks ago. Merle [Doc's son and playing partner] broke his arm, and there is a guy named Cliff Miller sitting in for Merle. Cliff also is a soundman down in Nashville. We sat down and talked for an hour or so about what I should do for the dobro, and he was telling me about a little microphone. We played together again a few weeks later in Washington, and Cliff brought me this Teledyne microphone that I stick into the coverplate.

Is it a lavaliere-type microphone?

Right. It has a little battery pack. It's a condenser-type microphone. I'm not sure that this is what I am going to continue using, and I will continue experimenting with other things. But I do like the mobility of it, because I can move around on the stage and still give the fill lines as I am going over [to the vocal mike] to sing. The tone isn't exactly what I want. There's a guy named Bobby Goodman that has a sound company in Washington [D.C.], and he built me an EQ thing that I will be bringing on the road. It has everything in it, and it's going to cost me a bit of money; but once I have it, and know exactly how to work it, then I hope I'll always be able to sound exactly the same whenever I'm playing.

Where do you have that microphone set up on the instrument?

It's sitting in one of those bigger holes on the coverplate. As you are looking down and playing, it's situated somewhere between 11 or 12 o'clock on the plate. It doesn't touch anything. Instead of suspending it, I just have tape wrapped around it to give it a cushion. It's just sort of stuck between the sides of the plate. I might build a little stand for it, to mount it off the coverplate.

It seems to be fairly quiet. I didn't hear any pick or hand noises when you were performing.

There's no noise. The only problem

with it right now is that there is no volume control, so if I want to tune between pieces, you can hear that through the PA system. I'll have a volume control added to it. I have an on-off switch, but it bangs over the sound system when I switch it, so I don't use it.

Do you think of the dobro, in its truest sense, as a fretted or unfretted instrument? In other words, could you play it in the dark?

Well, just for fun sometimes I'll look away. Most of the time I look at what I'm doing. If I'm doing real fast hammer-on things down around the first fret and second fret, I don't have to look because I keep my little finger kind of anchored on the nut so I know where I am. But if I have to do a slide from the 5th fret to the 9th fret, for example, I've got to look. The intonation on the dobro is so critical you have to be right there. You don't have 1/16" to be off. I don't think I could play it in the dark.

But aren't you really hearing the intonation more than looking for the fret line?

I guess basically, it's something that you are hearing. I really don't know. It's funny that you mention it. Well, last night — I don't know what made me think of it — but every once in a while you get in these weird moods and you think of what would happen — like if I were blinded. I would have to go get a job, I think. I don't know if I could pull off playing the dobro blind.

But Tom [Gray] looks at the fingerboard of his bass, and he's not looking at frets.

Yeah, but it's probably a combination. It's both visual and what you're hearing. I really don't know.

But it's just as critical, even more so, on the violin.

That's right, but the violin neck is only five or six inches long, whereas on the dobro, you have long moves all the time. When you end that fast, you've got to be within 1/16th of an inch, or less, of where you're trying to go. And there are differences from dobro to dobro. I've got two identical dobros that were made during the same week in 1935, but they don't "fret" exactly alike, because the necks are just a little different. One is a little warped. When you look down at it, you can't see that; but when I play on the warped one, I have to make adjustments.

What kind of dobro are you playing now?

The instrument I use the most is a 1935 Regal. It was made by Regal in Chicago and sold under the Dobro name. The company was licensed by Dobro to make its resophonic guitars. They were mostly cheaper models, such as those made for Sears. Then they got into making better models. This one has a three-ply mahogany body. [*Ed. Note: Laminated maple is standard today.*]

Have you tried instruments with non-standard stringings?

Right now I'm experimenting with an

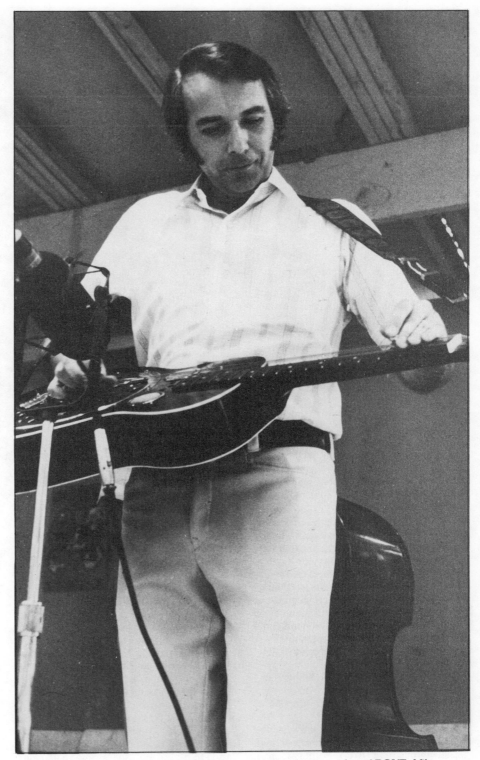

OPPOSITE: *Close-up of Mike Auldridge's dobro resonator, showing pickup.* **ABOVE:** *Mike Auldridge, dobro artist and member of Washington, D.C.'s the Seldom Scene.*

8-string dobro. A few years back, when I got interested in pedal steel guitar, I wondered what a 10-string dobro would sound like. I tried one, but it really didn't work. The problem with a 10-string dobro is that the instrument can't handle the tonal range covered by the strings. So I decided to string it up as an 8-string, and it worked better. I've been fooling around with some tunings on that one. I've got another 8-string on order from Rudy Jones which I should be getting soon.

What are the tunings you've been trying out?

Right now I'm trying a G6 or an A6 — I'm not quite sure which it will be, yet. And on the other one I'll use a G9, which is kind of a strange thing. It's all pretty experimental. I'm getting ready to do another album in the next month or two, and I'll have a few songs that came out of these tunings. They let you do things that you could never dream of doing on a 6-string guitar.

What kind of strings are you using now?

I'm using Guild phosphor-bronze for the wound strings — the medium-gauge set, right from the package. I don't use the first and second strings because they're a little light. I use a .016″ for the first and an .018″ for the second.

Can you describe the optimum sound quality that you like to get from a dobro?

I've always found it hard to talk about sound quality. You know, in 20 years of playing dobro, I've played hundreds of instruments. I don't think I've ever found two of them that sounded alike. The metal-bodied ones are just too metallic-sounding. With the wood-bodied ones, what I look for is something that will record well. Mine records beautifully. It has all the overtones and everything, and it's real balanced. I've played a lot of dobros that have a rich, beautiful bass, but nothing on the high end.

How do you account for that?

I really don't know. I guess it's just the construction. My other guitar was made with the same kind of three-ply mahogany, and I think the mahogany gives a warmer sound.

Do you think it has a lot to do with the spider [bridge support] and the cone [resonator-like disc]?

Yes, it really does. I've tried different resonators in this guitar, and it doesn't sound the same with them.

Why do you keep calling it a "guitar" rather than a dobro?

It *is* a guitar. A steel guitar. What do you call it?

Well, there have been controversies in

the past about the Dobro trade name, and I was wondering whether you were avoiding the issue.

Oh, I didn't do that consciously and I do agree with Ron Lazar [owner of the Original Musical Instrument Company, makers of the Dobro] on that. He's real protective of the Dobro name, and I think he should be.

Do you think of yourself as a guitar player, or as a dobro player?

Neither. No, I think of myself as a steel player.

Does that include pedal steel? What's the difference?

These days the term does include pedal steel, but I always have thought of myself as a steel guitar player, and the steel guitar to me doesn't mean pedal steel or electric steel. It just means that you play with a bar. I even call my pedal steel a "guitar."

Do you favor the Stevens bar over the bullet bar?

No, not really. I do use the bullet bar on pedal steel because of the weight, and because the string span is so wide [ten strings, rather than six] that you have to slide across them, and the rounded end of the bullet bar slides across easily. The main reason I use a Stevens bar on dobro is that I can do quick pull-offs because of its blunted end. On dobro, the bullet bar to me is like playing with hubcaps. It's real awkward.

When you do harmonics, you have to bring your right arm out from under the strap. .Doesn't that slow you down?

Well, the only way to keep from doing that is to keep your arms inside the strap all the time. "Bashful Brother" Oswald [*Grand Ole Opry* dobroist] plays like that; he just hangs the dobro around his neck and keeps his arms inside the strap. To me, when I'm playing a real fast, hard-driving piece, I'm really pushing the thing, and having my arms inside the strap anchors the dobro against my body. If your arms are long enough, you might be able to reach up there and get the harmonic without going outside the strap.

What technique do you use when you finally hit that harmonic?

I use the back of my right-hand palm to hit the string, an octave higher than the barred note. So if the bar is at the 5th fret, the back of my right hand is at the 17th fret, and then I just touch the thumbpick to the string — like a little karate chop. You can get a lot of different harmonics that way.

What do you do to set up an instrument for its optimum sound?

I don't play with it a lot. Once I get the best sound I leave it alone. I do use birch wood for my bridge inserts. I use a bone nut. That's basically it.

How much do you tighten the resonator cone?

The resonator should only be tightened a few turns past the point where the screw contacts the spider. If it's too loose, it has this real "hollow" sound. If it's screwed down too hard, it has sort of a "tight" sound. Once I get it set, I never move it. Twice a year I take everything apart and reshape the resonator, because the string pressure on the spider tends to flatten out the edge of the cone.

Do you change your strings very often?

I generally change them every time I play. I like to change them a few hours before a gig and let them set up a little bit, and then I play on them for a while. Those are optimum conditions. Sometimes I have

to put them on and just go out [onstage]. I've found that if you play on them right away, they'll die right away; but if you let them alone at first, they'll stay bright for an extra day or two.

But you wouldn't keep them on there for a month, would you?

Oh, no. I'm a nut about having a bright, brand-new-string sound. One time when I was doing one of my albums, I changed my strings seven times in one day. It was ridiculous, but they just kept going dead on me. Maybe it's a psychological thing, but I just keep changing them.

Where do you position PA or studio mikes?

I usually use two, especially if I'm in the studio. I put one somewhere around the end of the fretboard, a little bit towards the coverplate. The other one I put at 2 o'clock, as you look at it. At the Birchmere Club [Arlington, VA] I just use one Neumann microphone and put it at the 12 o'clock position. If you want the sound to be brighter, you put the mike back towards the 2 o'clock part of the resonator; but if it's too bright, put the mike back near the end of the fretboard. I keep the mike about five or six inches over the instrument.

Do you use a capo frequently?

I have a custom-made capo for my dobro. There are several types available, but the only other one I've found that I like is the one Liberty Banjo [Bridgeport, CT] has put out. My custom capo just clamps to the strings. This one sounds as if you had a bar sitting on top of the strings. It's got the weight of a bar.

When you're using a capo, do you use it more to get new open notes than to just change the key?

Yes. As much as possible, I avoid using the capo, because you end up doing the same kinds of things you would have done — the same kind of fills, as if it was in G. It really limits what you sound like. Let's face it, you only have so many open-type licks that you can do. You start sounding the same after a while. So I'll use it if we are playing a song that I don't know. It's easier than trying to find tags in some new key.

You did some backup work on the Country Gentlemen's album Sit Down Young Stranger. *For the introduction of "Come And Sit By The River With Me," how did you conceive the off-the-beat, high drone-like line behind the other instruments?*

I really can't answer that. When I do these things, I just do them. I'm not really thinking about them.

Then what stimulates you to do a given line? The lyrics?

Yes, I'll listen to the piece first and then I'll try to do something that complements the lyrics. Often it's a lick that I've never done before and probably will never do again. It just kind of happens right then and there. If it's something I really like, I'll try to go back and learn it. I often wonder what makes me come up with things like that, but I really don't know how to explain it. I do know that a lot of my playing comes from a direct thought process, where I sit down and work something out. It's very mechanical.

Would you play those mechanically worked-out breaks the same way every time?

On the kick-off of a tune, always. If I do something different, it will throw off the timing of whoever's going to sing. And on a break, I'll try to come out of it the same way each time, so that the singer will know where I am. But before that, to keep it interesting for myself, I'll try to improvise a lot.

Is practicing something you still make time for?

I don't look at it as a sacrifice. I get up in the morning, and half an hour after I'm out of bed, I'm playing. That's all I do. I probably play ten hours a day. I hope it doesn't go away some day. I worked for a long time at a day job, wishing I could play music and have the time for it. Now I'm like a guy who was poor all his life, and all of a sudden came into a lot of money. I've got this time, and I just can't learn enough about music. I can't develop my technique enough, you know. I'm always working on it. I love playing music.

— **Roger H. Siminoff**

A SELECTED AULDRIDGE DISCOGRAPHY

Solo Albums: *Blues & Bluegrass*, Takoma (Box 5369, Santa Monica, CA 90405), 1041; *Dobro*, Takoma, 1033; *Mike Auldridge & Jeff Newman*, Flying Fish (1304 W. Schubert, Chicago, IL 60614), 080; *Mike Auldridge & Old Dog*, Flying Fish, 054; *Southern Rain*, Flying Fish, 029. **With The Seldom Scene** (on Rebel, Rt. 12, Asbury, WV 24916): *Act I*, 1511; *Act II*, 1520; *Act III*, 1528; *Baptizing*, 1573; *Live At The Cellar Door*, 1547/48; *New Seldom Scene Album*, 1563; *Old Train*, 1563; *Act IV*, Sugar Hill (Box 4040, Duke Station, Durham, NC 27706), 3709. **With The Country Gentlemen:** *Award-Winning Country Gentlemen*, Rebel, 1506; *Country Gentlemen*, Vanguard (71 W. 23 St., New York, NY 10010), 79331; *Sit Down Young Stranger*, Sugar Hill, 3712; *Sound Off*, Rebel 1501. **With Bryan Bowers:** *View From Home*, Flying Fish, 037. **With Emmylou Harris:** *Elite Hotel*, Warner Brothers, MS-2236; *Luxury Liner*, Warner Brothers, BSK-3115. **With Tony Rice:** *California Autumn*, Rebel 1549. **With Linda Ronstadt:** *Heart Like A Wheel*, Capitol, 11-358; *Mad Love*, Asylum, 5A-510; *Simple Dreams*, Asylum, 6E-104. **With Phil Rosenthal:** *Indian Summer*, Flying Fish, 078. **With Peter Rowan:** *Medicine Trail*, Flying Fish, 205.

Recent Seldom Scene albums include *After Midnight* and *Greatest Show On Earth*, Sugar Hill (Box 4040, Duke Station, Durham, NC 22706), SH 3721 and SH 2201, respectively. This article originally appeared in the May '81 issue.

TOM GRAY

CONDUCTING A POLL to determine the best performer on each different instrument associated with bluegrass music would probably be a confusing job. If you asked who the best banjo player, guitar player, or fiddle player was you'd get at least four or five nominees. However, if you were to apply that question to the category of acoustic bass, you might get a virtually unanimous response: "Tom Gray!"

The foundation of the Seldom Scene's sound since the Washington, D.C. group formed in 1971, Tom Gray's unique walking-bass technique has altered the entire concept of the role of the bass and its relationship to the other components in a bluegrass band. His playing style has, over the years, convinced performers and listeners alike that the bass has the potential to be much more than a supporting instrument thumping out monotonous, simple patterns of notes.

Tom Gray is an intense, quiet, 38-year-old Chicago native who has lived in the Washington area since he was a child. He became hooked on bluegrass as a teenager, and although he first played the guitar and the mandolin, it was the bass which truly captivated him. He became preoccupied early with bass notes and patterns and chord structures, even though he had never played one of the instruments. His chance finally came at age 17.

Gray's musical career started when he was in high school, beginning when he joined the youthful Rocky Ridge Ramblers; it has since run the bluegrass gamut to include stints with Benny and Vallie Cain, Cliff Waldron, Bill Clifton, Buzz Busby, Bill Harrell, the Country Gentlemen, and finally, the Seldom Scene. Today Tom Gray is a seasoned performer who has definite opinions about the role of the acoustic bass.

"I prefer the acoustic bass for bluegrass because it sounds better and more compatible with bluegrass instruments," he says. "An electric bass can easily overwhelm an otherwise acoustic band on stage. Many times I've listened to such combinations and have only been able to hear bass and voice. Electric bass, when played aggressively with much improvisation, tends to transform the music into rock or progressive jazz — and that is good with such groups as the Newgrass Revival or the II Generation, two groups I admire. An electric bass played simply and unaggressively is not so disruptive; but neither is it very interesting to play or to hear. An *acoustic* bass played with much improvisation *is* compatible with the sound and feeling of traditional or contemporary bluegrass. If it is played tastefully, it can enhance the group's overall sound, creating exciting, hard-driving acoustic music. A steel-string acoustic bass played through an amplifier can assume many of the properties of the electric bass."

Tom's own aggressive, tasteful, exciting playing has earned him universal acclaim as the best in his field. That honor has, in fact, been bestowed upon him in writing for the last five consecutive years in the annual *Muleskinner News* poll. Although they couldn't quite be called the Academy Awards of bluegrass music, the *Muleskinner News* selections offer a fairly representative picture of the way bluegrassers feel about their genre's most talented pickers. Tom jokes about his *Muleskinner* awards, but he is truly appreciative of their significance. "I get a certificate with my name spelled wrong and the wrong date on it, which has been crossed off with the right one added," he says, tongue-in-cheek, "but that's okay — I get credit for it anyway. It makes me feel good."

Vocal quartet by the Seldom Scene (L to R): John Duffey, Mike Auldridge, Tom Gray, and Phil Rosenthal.

Tom Gray's predominant influence has been George Shuffler, a member of the Stanley Brothers band in the '50s and one of the originators of the bluegrass walking-bass style. "Most other bass players before him played a simpler rhythm, not that there's anything wrong with that," he says. "What George played was a challenge for me to learn. It sounded great, but it's the kind of thing that only works well with certain groups. A bass player has to feel out the group of musicians he plays with to find the best way to accompany them. With some there's room for improvisation, and he can greatly supplement their sound. In others there's just not enough room for that."

Tom found room to improvise and experiment when he joined the Country Gentlemen. "I was lucky back in 1960 when I joined the Country Gentlemen, because they were an ideal group to improvise in just as freely as I liked," he recalls. "As a matter of fact, I was encouraged to do more all the time. The thing that made it good for the walking-bass style I played was that the lead instrument players were singing in the trios, and that left nobody with a lead instrument to play backup. That left a clear path for me to use the bass as a backup instrument, playing a bit of counter-melody along with the usual rhythm functions."

Tom left the Gentlemen in 1964 to return to his day job as a cartographer with the National Geographic Society, a position he still holds. A wife and child, and bills to pay, influenced that decision, but he looks back on his Country Gentlemen days with Charlie Waller, John Duffey, and Eddie Adcock as an important period in his development as a musician.

From the time he left the Gentlemen until the Seldom Scene formed in 1971, Tom was relatively inactive in bluegrass. He and his wife, Sally, had two more children, and his spare time was devoted to renewing and tending the family Christmas tree farm in West Virginia. During this period, Tom did a brief stint as a member of a jazz band.

"A lot of people have gotten the impression that I came to bluegrass music after playing jazz, but I didn't," explains Tom. "I've been a bluegrass fanatic since I was 13 years old, before which I played classical music on the piano. But back in 1969, when I wasn't playing as much bluegrass, I met some people that played traditional jazz and I asked if I could practice with them."

The group was the Washington-based New Sunshine Jazz Band. Unlike the bluegrass music to which Tom had been accustomed, the band's material required following precise, written arrangements and chord charts. Tom's piano training gave him sufficient background in reading music, but he remembers one time when the written arrangements didn't help.

"We played one night for a party on a barge that was towed up and down the C&O Canal in Washington," he says. "When the barge was halfway out it got dark, and nobody could see their charts anymore. That was the first time I had to improvise jazz, and all of a sudden I realized that it was not that much different from playing bluegrass."

Tom eventually found improvising on the bass in jazz less difficult to do than improvising in bluegrass. "It's easier, in that I don't have to be careful," he says. "I could play many things that would just pop into my head. In bluegrass — especially now with the Seldom Scene having a smooth sound — I try to be careful not to play things that might upset a feeling someone else might be creating in the band. In jazz, you don't have to be as careful of that — at least not in the jazz groups I've played with." Tom also worked with several other professional jazz groups in Washington. He recorded an album with the New Sunshine Jazz Band in 1973, *Old Rags* [Flying Dutchman (dist. by RCA), BDLI-0549].

With the Seldom Scene, Tom has recorded seven albums and is currently completing work on an eighth, due for release in the fall. On the new album will be an original Tom Gray bass instrumental, "Walkin' The Blues," a powerful song that expresses Tom's walking style of playing and his feel for both blues and jazz music. He says about the new song: "I realized that I had been playing 'Grandfather's Clock' as my tour de force for what seemed like the last 15 decades, and I thought it was high time that I started playing something else. So I just started messing around at playing a bunch of jazz tunes and making up a bunch of things."

Regarding bass instrumentals in general, Tom believes that they should be used sparingly. "The bass instrumental, or any bass break in a song, is a novelty, and if it's overdone it's not novel anymore and it loses its effect," he says. "When we do a show, if we play 'Grandfather's Clock' the first time we come out it won't get near the response that it will if we play it later on. The novelty isn't novel until the norm is well established."

Tom uses a 3/4-size German-made Karl Meisel bass. "I bought it five years ago when I realized that the plywood bass I had been playing for years just didn't compare with a good carved-top bass," he recalls. "I listened to Mike Auldridge's first dobro albums, which had several bass players on it — both acoustic and electric — including me and Ed Ferris, and Ed's bass sounded so much better than anybody else's that I decided that it was time for me to get another bass."

He found the replacement for his old bass in a Washington violin shop. The Meisel was a slightly used instrument that met his chief requirements. "When I bought it I considered two things: the sound of it and the price," he says. "I wasn't in any position to pay more than $1,000, but I knew I wanted to get something better than what I had been using."

Like most musicians, he feels that his own instrument produces its best sound when it is set up in a particular way. "Action-wise, I like to have it slightly higher than the standard setting," he explains. "I think the standard setting is for people who play mostly with the bow or for jazz musicians who usually play through amplifiers. I like to have the action a little higher so I can pick harder without it rattling so bad. I like to have the lower strings a little bit higher in action than the upper strings. When I get a bridge, I tell the man at the shop that I want it slightly high on the *G* string side and a little higher still on the *E* string side."

Of the basses on the market, which ones does he prefer? "As basses go, there are several German brands that come from good, reputable companies," he says. "You can't compare basses to guitars, which have say, a Martin that sets the standard for the industry. In basses, the most expensive you can get is a Pollman, but that's not necessarily the best buy. There are several other companies — Meisel, Roth, and Schroeder — that are good, but I really haven't been able to compare them enough to say that one is a whole lot better than another. I found one good carved-top Japanese bass called a Chaki, and if all their carved-top basses are as good as *it* was, I'd kinda like to have one of those! I'm not that interested in the technicalities and the brand name. As long as I have something that I like to play and that sounds good to me, I'm happy. I'm not a craftsman as far as the technical aspects of the physical instrument go; I just play it."

In his efforts to capture the best sound of his bass, Tom has found that nothing beats studio reproduction techniques. "I have never found a way to mike the bass onstage that makes it sound as good as it does in the studio," he admits, "and it usually never sounds as good there as it does when I'm at home playing it by myself. What I generally do onstage is take the microphone — it doesn't have to be an expensive one; I've used Shure and Electro-Voice models — wrap it in foam, and put it between the *G* and *D* strings about halfway from the tailpiece and the bridge. I'll point the microphone toward the arch of the bridge so that it can pick up vibrations from the bridge and from the top of the bass. Having the mike on the bass like that leaves me free to move around the stage. If I want to go and sing, the mike always stays in the same relationship to the bass. If I knew I wasn't going to be singing, I would just aim the microphone toward the f-hole on the *G* string side of the bass." When in the studio, Tom uses a KM-86i Neumann

microphone, which he says is "prohibitively expensive for someone to use onstage."

Miking arrangements vary according to the musician's individual preferences and the type of sound required, says Tom. What works for one player might not work for another. His own objective is a rich tone overall, with extra brightness on solos and breaks.

Tom uses strings from three different manufacturers: Golden Spiral brand for his *G* and *D* strings, Artone for his *A* string, and Dr. Thomastik for his *E* string. He replaces his strings about every ten months on the average, though he says it is not uncommon for him to get a bad string that has to be replaced sooner.

Although Tom is a fervent acoustic bass devotee, he has occasionally used an electric bass in the studio to achieve certain effects. The Seldom Scene's former lead singer, John Starling, preferred an electric bass for several of the group's songs, among them, "Wait A Minute" and "California Earthquake." When taping those numbers, Tom used his Fender Precision bass. "In those slow songs, it was better to have a longer-sustaining note," Tom explains, "and the electric bass sustains much better than the acoustic bass." He doesn't mind plugging in his bass in the studio, but he says, "The appearance of the group onstage is better if I have an upright bass." He also admits that he can play the acoustic bass a lot better than he can its electric counterpart.

In talking about his role with the Seldom Scene, Tom Gray is a satisfied and secure instrumentalist. "I'm quite content with my position there," he says. "You can ask, 'How does it feel to be the bass player?' I feel important. The bass line behind the song is what establishes the feel of that song. It can be light and gentle or it can be strong and hard-driving; the tone can be deep and mellow or it can be percussive and bouncy. A bass player can create any of these moods. The people singing their songs and the lead instruments taking their breaks are always in the front of the stage, it's true. But the bass is an integral part of *all* these things — in just about *every* song and every performance."

— *Robert Kyle*

JOHN DUFFEY

PERHAPS IF JOHN DUFFEY had lived in another era and had been something other than a musician, he would have been an inventor, explorer, entrepreneur, pioneer, gambler, daredevil, or humorist. Because in the quarter-century he has spent in bluegrass, John Duffey has personified a composite of all these identities.

The tenor singer and mandolinist has been the key figure in the formation of two of the most influential and sought-after bands in the business. With the Country Gentlemen from 1957 to 1969, and then with the Seldom Scene from 1971 to the present, Duffey was the catalyst in the creation of a new breed of bluegrass. He became the first to sow the seeds for the hybrid variety of bluegrass known as "progressive," and some critics have gone so far as to dub him the "Father of Modern Bluegrass."

His impact has been felt universally. When Duffey decided that playing straight melody lines was "pretty boring," he introduced jazzy improvisational licks that caught the bluegrass world with its picks down. In doing so, he gave the music a new freshness and energy, and had musicians young and old scrambling to copy his style. When he demonstrated that folk songs penned by urban writers lent themselves nicely to bluegrass adaptations, traditionalists frowned, but an entirely new audience was captured. And in live performances, his comic antics proved that bluegrass artists could be complete entertainers rather than stereotypical musicians who produced music according to a cut-and-dried formula.

Though Duffey has taken a different road than traditional bluegrass artists, he has kept their respect. Bill Monroe, the man who virtually created the genre, has often shared the stage with Duffey during recent years. The two exchange wisecracks and make faces, and invariably Duffey snatches a trademark Blue Grass Boy white hat from one of Monroe's band members, then launches into a Monroe impersonation. "He's gotten to be where he's really fun to fool around with because he's pretty quick himself," says John. "It's no fun to pull somebody's leg when he doesn't know what the hell you're doing, but it's fun to goof off with somebody who will come back at you, and he's doing that. Monroe is really a joy to be around and to do things with onstage."

When Duffey is onstage himself, there is no mistaking him. His 6-foot-2, 220-pound frame houses a high, piercing, tenor voice, which can only be unleashed with safety several feet away from a microphone. His graying hair is perennially cut in a flat-top, and arms the size of oak trees thrust out of one of his characteristic short-sleeve knit shirts. His hefty forearms seem ready to reduce his mandolin to a pile of splinters. Offstage, John looks less like a bluegrass musician than like a high-average man in a local bowling league (which he is) or like a coach/infielder on a men's softball team (which he is).

John Duffey never meant to be a professional musician. Born in Washington, D.C., Duffey grew up in a musical family. Although his father sang with the Metropolitan Opera, John was attracted to the music of Flatt And Scruggs and Bill Monroe, and while in high school he tried to learn to play the banjo. He recalls, "I was about 17, which I understand is pretty late for people in this kind of business; most of them are raised with it from the cradle. But I just couldn't get anything out of that banjo. This fellow who lived around the corner played the guitar, and I said,

'Boy, that really sounds nice.' He showed me nine chords, and it took me about a week to pick them up — to be able to change from one to the other. I used to run home from school and grab the guitar and stay there until my fingers hurt."

John remembers that the bus delivered him and most of the other students to school more than an hour early each day. To kill time, students who had guitars gathered in the cafeteria to play until classes began. This gave John added practice time, but eventually it also inspired him to learn the mandolin. With a room full of guitar players and one bass player, he felt another instrument was sorely needed. He borrowed a mandolin from the bass player's father.

"When I first started to mess with the mandolin I didn't know what in the hell to do with it, so I started playing it like a guitar," he says. "I know it was probably perfectly awful, but it was something different, and I progressed from that." He progressed despite the lack of any instruction book. "I didn't have a thing," he says. "I just had to sit down and figure out that instrument."

The ability to carry a tune was something that came naturally to John, and since he also could accompany himself on guitar and mandolin, he entered and won several school talent shows. After graduation he went to work for a print shop, later getting a job with a surgical supply company. Around this time (1955) he joined his first bluegrass band, Lucky Chatman And The Ozark Mountain Boys, who played 50 miles away in rural Frederick, Maryland.

In the mid-'50s there were just a few bluegrass bands working in the Washington area. One was Buzz Busby And The Bayou Boys. Their banjoist was Bill Emerson, one of Duffey's friends. One night Buzz and some of his musicians were in a car wreck. Emerson, who wasn't in the car at that time, realized that the band would probably lose its weekly job unless he could put together another band in a hurry. He got hold of a bass player, asked John to play mandolin, and called a young Louisiana singer/guitarist named Charlie Waller who was playing in Baltimore with Earl Taylor. While Buzz Busby was recuperating, they formed a new version of the Busby band; but after a couple of weeks they no longer wanted to be Bayou Boys. Their voices and music had jelled so well that they decided to start a new group.

"I thought up a name for us," Duffey reports. "I said, 'We're not going to be Mountain Boys, we'll be something else.' Everybody was 'Mountain Boys' then. I said, 'We'll be *Gentlemen*'." So, In July 1957, the Country Gentlemen were born.

After the first year with the band, John knew music would be his career. He bid farewell to the surgical supply business, and he and the other band members vowed to play whenever and wherever they could. By 1960 their name was relatively well known, and they arrived just as the folk

Three of the original Seldom Scene (L to R): John Duffy, Mike Duffey, and John Starling.

music boom began.

It was also during this period that the Country Gentlemen broke ranks with their colleagues, in terms of their material and their approach to it. The Gentlemen began introducing a more urban, updated style of bluegrass that bordered on popular folk music of the day. Songs in their repertoire like "Copper Kettle" and "Long Black Veil," hits for folksinger Joan Baez, pointed which way the band was heading. Because neither Charlie Waller nor John Duffey put the same country edge on the nasal "high lonesome" sound as their bluegrass predecessors, their voices seemed better suited for the contemporary style.

If a single song could be said to have vividly set the band apart from the rest of bluegrass, the instrumental "The World Is Waiting For The Sunrise," which also featured banjoist Eddie Adcock, would be it. In 1961, after four years of playing mandolin in the accepted Bill Monroe style, John opted for a new technique. "It came from the realization that you cannot play like somebody else and expect to create anything that's your own," says John. He remem-

bers telling himself, "I'll just find the chord pattern and improvise all the way and see what happens." What happened was "Sunrise," and John Duffey the explorer, gambler, and pioneer had blazed a fresh trail in mandolin playing. "I never touched on the melody, just to see what would happen," he says. "As it turned out, I guess I started something."

The altered technique indeed started something novel for bluegrass, and Duffey found himself in the role of trendsetter. "All of a sudden I started to become *some-body*," he recalls. "After a few years, I began noticing that people were copying what I was doing. And in later years — in fact, right up to now — they're still taking a few things from me. But dammit," he laughs, "some of them are playing it *better!*"

After a dozen years with the Country Gentlemen, John Duffey quit them — and music — on his birthday, March 4, 1969. He had logged thousands of miles on the road and spent many nights away from home, and realized he was earning no more than less nomadic nine-to-fivers did at their day jobs in the city. There was also a problem with album royalties, which were often nonexistent; but the primary motivation in John's decision to abdicate his position came out of an attempt by the band to appear on a popular late-night television show.

The show's band director controlled all musical acts that appeared on the program. Before agreeing to audition the Gentlemen, he made it clear that he expected something in return for the national exposure he was in a position to give them. Rather than the band getting paid for the appearance, the deal was for them to slip their fee back into the pocket of the music director. The Gentlemen realized that meant they would be playing for free, and that an illegal kickback of funds was involved, but they decided the exposure was worth it. However, as John recalls, there was more to the reckoning.

"He said, 'Well, that will do for a start.' He wanted *more* money to put us on. But we said, 'No, goddammit!' because in the first place we couldn't afford it. It was payola, a bribe — whatever you want to call it. We'd have to pay him to be on the show." The experience was a rude awakening to the realities of big-time show business, and it left John embittered and resentful. "It became not *what* you knew but *who* you knew," he says. "That was really a blow, to have to pay to be on that thing when I think we really had something to offer."

The Country Gentlemen's hectic performance schedule also contributed to John's departure. He felt the group was spreading itself too thin by wanting to play a much as possible, and he suggested the band become more selective in where it played and how much it was paid. "I thought that even if we had to pump gas to keep eating, we should make a demand instead of saying, 'Columbus, Ohio? 150 bucks? Sure, we'll be right there,'" recalls John of his philosophy then. "I said, 'Let's create some sort of demand for it, and let's make the act scarce!'" John was outvoted, but a few years later he got the chance to put his ideas into practice.

After leaving the Country Gentlemen (Jimmy Gaudreau replaced him), John went into the instrument repair business, operating out of a music store in Arlington, Virginia. It was a successful venture, and repair orders increased beyond the point where John could handle them alone. He looked for an experienced helper to share the workload, but found no one. With the urge to play bluegrass music still in his blood, John accepted an invitation from Country Gentlemen manager Len Holsclaw to attend a local pickin' party. Len wanted John to meet an Army surgeon, John Starling, who had a distinctive style of singing bluegrass even though he had never been with a band. Among others at the get-together were two members of the band Cliff Waldron And The New Shades Of Grass: dobro player Mike Auldridge and

banjo player Ben Eldridge.

More pickin' parties followed, bringing the four musicians together, and out of that came a smooth new vocal trio sound featuring Starling, Duffey, and Auldridge that surprised even the singers themselves. Former Country Gentleman Tom Gray, who worked locally for *National Geographic,* was beckoned out of musical retirement to play bass, and the new group decided to put itself on the road — at least for one night a week — for the fun of it. "It was going to be our weekly card game," according to Mike Auldridge.

In late 1972 the fledgling band landed a weekly job in a Washington bar, but after just six weeks they packed up and left over a difference of opinion with the bartender, who insisted on keeping the bar TV turned up louder than the band. In January 1972 the band secured a regular Tuesday night gig at a small Bethesda, Maryland, club called the Red Fox Inn. Before long it was standing room only with a waiting line outside. Realizing that the combination of musicians was indeed something special, Duffey had them in the studio just two months later cutting their first album. When *Act 1* appeared in mid-'72 on the Rebel label, it established the band as a major bluegrass entity. And as the album's title implied, listeners were experiencing only a small part of what was to come. The band left the intimate Red Fox in 1977 and moved to the more spacious Birchmere Restaurant in Arlington, Virginia, where they performed each Thursday to crowds that still overflow outside.

The Seldom Scene, whose name was supplied in jest by Charlie Waller when he heard that John Duffey was playing with a new group no one had seen yet, provided John with a chance to try his "make it scarce" management tactics. As a result, the group worked only one night per week, recorded just one album per year, and rarely played the same festival — or even the same state —more than once a year. The technique has proved successful. Although festivals keep the band busy from April to October, covering territory from Canada to Georgia, a live appearance by the Seldom Scene is invariably regarded as a unique treat.

The band had to break in a new lead singer in September 1977, when John Starling left for Alabama to pursue private medical practice. His replacement was Phil Rosenthal, already familiar to the group through his compositions "Muddy Water" and "Willie Boy," recorded by the band on its album *Act 3.*

A primary key to the band's popularity is its vocal blending. John Duffey's knack of producing polished harmonies was clearly evident with the Country Gentlemen, and he has carried that over to the Seldom Scene. "My bag is arranging and harmonies," he says. "The guys tell me that's what I'm best at, so that's what I do. I either hear harmonies or I don't. If I don't hear them I

say, 'Well, what can we do with this song, because I don't hear anything in it from my particular corner?'" He says that a new arrangement will often reveal fresh potential in song, and band members will spend time exchanging feedback after working up varied presentations.

"We'll try them a lot of different ways," John explains. "Like things with a high lead or with a regular tenor and high baritone. And then sometimes parts switch off in a song. Let's say Phil's singing the lead; we may wind up in a part of the song where we get into harmonics and I've got the lead, and the parts are going down under. Somebody with a trained music ear would be able to figure that out pretty quick, but people who just listen to music because they like it wouldn't really notice and say, 'Hey, Duffey's got the lead on the chorus.' But it would be the way we arranged it, because after everything we tried, that's the way it sounded best."

John and his fellow band members pay just as much attention to their sound in the studio as they do in rehearsal. Once a satisfactory version of a song is taped, John's practice is to wait a couple of weeks before listening to it again. "What I want to do is go back and have them turn the machine on so I can sit and listen to it as a new piece of

material — as if I'm hearing something for the first time," he says. "If you make yourself a little copy and take it home and listen and listen to it, you're going to pick that thing apart. I don't care how perfect it was; you're going to sit there and find something wrong with it that nobody else is ever going to find. Sometimes you can make an improvement, but most of the time you'll wind up just picking it apart. If you go back and listen to it fresh, though, you'll either say, 'That doesn't have it, we'd better do it again,' or, 'Hey, it's better than I thought it was.'"

Talking about live performances, John says that while audiences deserve to hear a band's old favorites, a group also has an obligation to keep its show fresh and entertaining. Prearranged sets with a well-rehearsed joke here and there virtually kill any chance for spontaneity. "You don't go out with 'Show #1' and 'Show #2' for the 1980 season," he explains. "You go out like we do. You say, 'Anybody know what the first number is? No? Got any ideas?' And we decide on that. We have gone onstage with maybe three numbers in mind, and that's the most ever. We just play it by ear. That also keeps everybody onstage thinking, instead of just standing there waiting for their cue. I think another possible rea-

son for our success is that we're sometimes haphazard, even though we do it right. People know they can go and see us next week and they're not going to be able to set their watch by the songs we do."

John has observed that Seldom Scene audiences — and bluegrass audiences in general — include age groups "from 8 to 80." In recent years he has witnessed a significant increase in younger listeners, most of them new to bluegrass, and he believes that live performances, rather than recordings, are what win young fans. "When young people see bluegrass performed live," he says, "they suddenly discover that these people are for real — that they know what they're doing and that they're doing it right there without any gimmicks. I think this is one of the things that's making younger people say, 'Hey, man, there's something going on here. There are no gadgets, no lights, no laser beams, no freaky costumes!' Seventy-five to 80 percent of the converts have to be introduced visually — to see a band work. That's when they find out. They can't tell by a recording. There may be 25 guys playing on the record, for all they know. But when they see it happen in person, that's the clincher."

John's own playing was first honed on a Gibson F-7 mandolin, which was later stolen. He then purchased a 1936 Gibson F-12, which he modified by carving down the thick top, adding a longer neck, and elevating the fretboard. (The F-12 also was stolen, but eventually both instruments were recovered.) In 1970 while John was out of music and doing instrument repair, he created his own mandolin. Swooping, curved points at each end went boldly beyond all traditional designs, and the unique instrument became a John Duffey trademark when he returned to performing.

Duffey's new mandolin became known as "the Duck" because of a friend's wisecrack. "All of a sudden, all over the world, it was a 'duck.' I didn't name it that!" John proclaims. "I used it on the first four albums the Seldom Scene cut, and on the live album I happened to be using the Gibson [F-12], which is loud. The one I made has a richer tone." In 1976 he decided to replace richness with volume and returned to the F-12. He still has his pet "Duck," but doesn't plan to use it again until he straightens a bow in its neck. There are other Duck-modeled mandolins in bluegrass music, but only one is sanctioned by John. It is a Duffey-built duplicate of the original, made for Japanese mandolinist Akira Otsuka (formerly of the Bluegrass 45, now playing with the Grass Menagerie out of Washington, D.C.). The other "ducks" are in Japan, the product of a manufacturer who neglected to get John's permission to copy the design. John first became aware of the Japanese copies when bass player Tom Gray showed him an ad from an Oriental music magazine. The name "Duffey" and a photo of the mandolin were the only things John could make out. Everything else was in Japanese.

The veteran picker has developed definite ideas about what strings work best for him. "I still, through all the years, have used Gibson steel, except for the second strings. With them I'll take any brand I can get hold of that are gauged .016". I started doing this 15 years ago when I found out that the [second course] A strings are the biggest problem. I started experimenting one day with different gauges of strings, and I figured I'd go a couple of thousandths heavier. I found out they gave a more solid sound and stayed in tune better. Hell, you can't break 'em. I've never broken one yet since I started." He prefers steel over bronze because, he says, the latter tend to be affected more by perspiration and go out of tune quicker.

Duffey's mandolin gets the same microphone placement for both studio work and live performances. "I like to keep the microphone between my hands, up toward about the 18th fret," he says. "It seems to pick up a balanced tone from the instrument there." He says that placing a microphone near one of the mandolin's f-holes will cause an overbalance of treble or bass. "And also," he adds, "I don't stick the instrument right on the microphone. Let the mike be turned up. Hold the mandolin back far enough so the sound of it will actually carry to the microphone."

Although he confesses to being "out of touch with the retail market" regarding who makes the best mandolins these days, he says the reproduction Lloyd Loar F-5L Gibsons are "the nicest things they [Gibson] have produced in a long time." Nevertheless, he believes there is still plenty of room for improvement. "The dummies still won't cock the neck back on it!" he exclaims. "You can't raise the bridge up. It's such a simple thing to do, especially when you're starting from scratch — to cock the neck back so you can have the bridge anywhere from 1" to 1⅛" high and yet still have it real easy to play. Why those guys at Gibson have not done it, I'll never know; it's so

simple. They'll probably read this article and do it."

Duffey's playing preferences include using his mandolins without a finger-rest. "It gets in my way" he says, "and it also covers up half of the soundhole on the treble side." He likes his mandolin's action to measure 1/8" at the 12th fret, explaining, "any higher and it's hard to play." He uses only picks made of real tortoiseshell.

John is reluctant to recommend specific practicing techniques or technical exercises to other players, simply because he feels that his background as a self-taught mandolinist disqualifies him. "I'm not a teacher," he says. "I wasn't taught. I had to learn in the basement and closet, teaching myself totally from scratch. I don't know how to pass anything along or how to tell somebody something, unless they come to me and say, 'Show me that lick.' I can do *that*, but I don't have the ability to teach whatsoever. I've been asked a couple of times to give a lesson and I tried it, but the people never came back. I guess I can't slow myself down and pass things on the way a teacher should."

He does, however, have a few suggestions to pass on to younger groups planning to record for the first time. "When you put that album out, don't go through Flatt And Scruggs' 1948 repertoire," John advises. "The first album we came out with, for example — I don't think you'll find much traditional material on that. I had a decent arrangement, I think, of 'Darlin' Corey,' which I had in the back of my head for years. But it's not a traditional album of old Stanley Brothers or old Flatt And Scruggs songs. Before you cut that first album, put something new into it — more than just one new song. It could make a difference in how you're accepted. They'll say, 'Hey, here's a bunch of guys with new songs, nice arrangements — some thought went into it!'"

In handling bookings and other business for the Seldom Scene, John saw the '70s erase prior years of hard financial times for bluegrass bands. But even now, he says, promoters don't fully realize how much of a

band's salary is eaten up by travel and lodging expenses.

"Let's face it, this is a business," John asserts. "We're not in it to save up to go on tour; I had enough years of that. We're in the business to make a living at it. If the money is there, somehow or other we'll find a way to get there. But I once got a call from a guy in California, for instance, who wanted us to come for one day and said he could afford $3,000. I said, 'Which member do you want?'"

Bands themselves can cause each other unnecessary anguish through what John views as "petty jealousies." Though 10 or 15 years ago there was more of it, he says, it still exists. Offering an example, he recalls that the Seldom Scene was the object of an uncomplimentary remark delivered in public a few summers ago by a well-known bluegrass musician who felt the band played longer than it should have. "That bugs me," John asserts, "because I always feel that if somebody has something to contribute, then there's room for them in the business."

With the Seldom Scene, John has recorded eight albums, and he estimates that he has been on about 25 discs all together. With the Country Gentlemen he wrote several songs, but he now prefers arranging. He did the music for a pair of Seldom Scene numbers, "Don't Bother Me With White Satin" and "Reason For Being," and arranged many others. His original "Christmastime Back Home," written while he was with the Country Gentlemen, is a seasonal favorite that gets airplay year after year.

While it is not uncommon for bluegrass musicians to drift into other types of music, John has been content to make bluegrass his life. "I like it," he says simply. "I don't see anything wrong with trying to put new things into the music and upgrade and update it, which has been one of my ambitions. Something for years that I've always tried to do is bring new things into the music — keep the music moving with the times rather than just lying stagnant."

— *Robert Kyle*

A SELECTED DUFFEY DISCOGRAPHY

With the Country Gentlemen: On Folkways (43 W. 61st St., New York, NY 10023): *Country Songs Old And New,* 2409; *Folk Songs And Bluegrass,* 2410; *On The Road,* 2411; *Going Back To The Blue Ridge Mountains,* 31031. Others: *Bluegrass At Carnegie Hall,* Starday (out of print), 174; *Hootenanny,* Pickwick International, AK 227 (reissued as Hilltop, JS 6156); *Folk Session Inside,* Mercury, SR 60858; *Bringing Mary Home,* Rebel (Box 191, Floyd, VA 24091), 1478; *The Traveler And Other Favorites,* Rebel, 1481; *Play It Like It Is,* Rebel, 1586. **With the Seldom Scene:** On Rebel: *Act 1,* 1511; *Act 2,* 1520; *Act 3,* 1528; *Old Train,* 1536; *Live At The Cellar Door* (double album), 1547 and 1548; *The New Seldom Scene Album,* 1561; *Baptizing,* 1573. On Sugar Hill (Box 4040, Duke Station, Durham, NC 27706): *Act 4,* 3709. **With Mike Auldridge:** *Mike Auldridge / Dobro,* Takoma (Box 5639, Santa Monica, CA 90405), D 1033; *Blues And Blugrass,* Takoma, D 1041. **With Bill Clifton:** *Code Of The Mountains,* Starday, 271; *Soldier Sing Me A Song,* Starday, 213; *Carter Family Memorial Album,* Starday, 146; *Christmastime Back Home* (45 single), Rebel, F 264; *Come By The Hills,* County (Box 191, Floyd, VA 24091), 751; *Mountain Ramblings,* London, HAU 8325. **With Others:** *Your Old Standby,* Rebel, MLT 102; *North Mountain Velvet,* Adelphi (Box 228, Silver Spring, MD 20907), 1028.

CHARLIE WALLER

GUITARIST/SINGER CHARLIE WALLER is the only original member of his band, one that he helped to form more than a quarter of a century ago when the rising tide of the folk boom carried bluegrass to a national audience. He owes some of his durability to his knack for surrounding himself with gifted musicians — such artists, over the years, as banjoists Eddie Adcock and Bill Emerson, mandolinists John Duffey, Ricky Skaggs, and Doyle Lawson, bassist Tom Gray, and dobroist Jerry Douglas, among others. But beyond that, Waller has endured because of his own remarkable musicianship, a blend of taste, technique, and timing that has made him the heart and soul of the Country Gentlemen — a bluegrass institution whose alumni could make up a Bluegrass Hall of Fame.

Since the band started on July 4, 1957, Charlie's distinctive vocal style and his definitive rhythm guitar work have kept audiences coming back for more, and have helped the band's nearly three dozen albums to achieve worldwide success. While the other Gentlemen harmonize on vocals and dazzle audiences with their instrumental mastery, Charlie sings and unobtrusively strums. But Waller doesn't *just* sing; nor does he *just* stand up and strum utilitarian rhythm on his Martin guitar. His unmistakable voice ranks him among the top lead vocalists in the business, and his rhythm guitar playing is among the best in bluegrass. If his instrumental work hasn't stood out prominently over the years, that's because he has experienced the happy misfortune of having his playing overshadowed by the exceptional picking of his band members.

In the early days, before the rise of such lead guitarists as Tony Rice, Norman Blake, Dan Crary, and Doc Watson, Charlie Waller often took instrumental breaks. But when he found himself flanked by flashy virtuosos, Charlie left most of the lead work in their capable hands.

"Occasionally I would do an instrumental, but there weren't many," he recalls. "I didn't work on it, and I'm a little sorry that I didn't learn any more in the early days. Mainly backup and runs is all I've ever really done, other than two or three instrumentals."

Charlie's lead guitar work is featured, however, in the tune "Electricity" — an early Country Gentlemen song revived — on the band's current album *River Bottom*. His rhythm playing can be characterized as hard, loud, and steady, a style shaped in an earlier period of bluegrass when microphones were scarce, honky-tonks were loud, and musicians had to belt out their singing and playing to be heard.

"I came along in a little different era, when the drive was pronounced more in the music," recalls Charlie. "Lester Flatt had the G run, Red Smiley had the D run. They all played in the early days with a little more drive. Jimmy Martin has a lot of drive now. We all used to sing in one mike and there wasn't a guitar mike. You just *needed* to play loud."

If anyone appreciates Charlie Waller's rock-solid rhythm it is bass player Bill Yates. Bill has known Charlie since 1957 and has performed with him as the Gentlemen's bassist since 1969.

"I've picked behind a lot of people in the business," Bill says, "and as far as rhythm and always knowing it's there, he's one of the greatest I've ever played with.

Charlie Waller of the Country Gentlemen, at a show in Massachusetts, 1972.

If you want to learn to pick rhythm, listen to him. His rhythm is easy to play with, and he does such neat little things, like the run on the top string. A lot of people put that in there, but it's not strong. If you can do that and still keep the same rhythm it's really a neat thing. And it's a selling point to the audience. Anything you can do to get the audience's attention is where it's at, and that's what he does. If things sort of get in a rut he'll throw in something a little different on the guitar that will get their attention. I've heard people come up and say, 'How did you do that little ditty on the guitar?'"

That "little ditty" is a Charlie Waller trademark lick. In nearly every Country Gentlemen show he will suddenly race up the neck two or three times with his finger on the low *E* string, as a way of livening up a song and adding something to the rhythm chops. "Just getting a little fancy," is how Charlie describes it.

Charlie's initial interest in music developed when he was eight, growing up in Louisiana. "I wanted a guitar so bad I got me a cigar box and made one," he recalls. "It had copper wire for strings. Needless to say, I couldn't play nothin' on it; I just *thought* I did." He also wanted a harmonica, but had to settle for a plastic pitchpipe

and a plastic flute. World War II was in full swing, and anything made of metal was hard to come by.

At the war's end, Charlie's mother moved to Washington, D.C., to find work. When Charlie turned ten, his mother got him his first real guitar, a $15 Stella. "It took me a long time getting started because I didn't know how to tune it, and I couldn't find anybody to tune it for me," recalls Charlie. "Finally I got the strings right, except the bass string was too low. I think I started learning four or five times over, with it tuned differently each time. But finally I got it, and when my friends would stop by the house I'd pick up the guitar and they'd say, 'Oh, no, we're never gonna get out of here now!' But later it was the opposite; they all wanted me to pick some. My first good guitar was a small Gibson. I got it for $35 off a friend."

Charlie's primary influence always has been Hank Snow, the Opry's country singer from Canada, and there is a marked similarity in the vocal styles of the two performers. Charlie made his professional debut in 1948, singing country tunes by Snow and others, at a bar in Washington, D.C. He was part of a trio of 13-year-olds. "It was not a nice place for young kids to be in, but they paid us," says Charlie, who earned $3 a night plus tips playing twice a week. He says the trio never worked up any harmony; the members simply took turns singing lead.

Through his teens, Charlie continued to perform several nights a week. The music ultimately interfered with his high school studies and he realized that one or the other had to go. The music won out. He left school and got a day job banging out dented fenders in a body shop. But his music got in the way of that, too, as he tried to divide his after-hours time between bands in Washington and Baltimore. "It [the job] didn't last too long because of the pickin'," he says. "I started playing more in bars and actually made more money. I couldn't make much as an apprentice [at the day job]. I did both for a while, but it caused me to have a few hangups on the highway. I wrecked my car two or three times because I was sleepy."

At 20 Charlie was a full-time bluegrass and country performer in the Bayou Boys Band, led by a fellow Louisiana native, mandolinist Buzz Busby. With that group Charlie made his first recordings — on such historic labels as Carol, Jiffy, and Starday. In 1955 the band appeared on the *Louisiana Hayride*, a popular stage show based in Shreveport. While there, Charlie saw other hopeful country artists perform — among them Elvis Presley, Johnny Cash, and George Jones.

After nearly two years in Louisiana, playing mostly in small schools, the Bayou Boys returned to Washington. One night Buzz Busby and another band member were injured in a car wreck. Quick reinforcements were needed if the band was to keep its regular club job. Bill Emerson, then the Bayou Boys' banjo player, recommended a tall young mandolinist whose father was an opera singer.

The mandolinist was John Duffey. Duffey agreed to fill in until Buzz returned, and his powerful high tenor blended beautifully with Charlie Waller's deep, rich lead voice. With Larry Lahey on bass, Waller, Emerson, and Duffey created a group sound that they soon recognized as unique enough to stand on its own. They decided to break off from the Bayou Boys and form their own band. Duffey suggested that they call themselves the Country Gentlemen. The name stuck.

Eventually Eddie Adcock replaced Bill Emerson on banjo. "When we got Eddie on banjo, that's when the sound of the early Gentlemen started taking off, because of his unique style," says Waller. "What we had, I thought, was kind of magic. Nobody knew it then, but now people look back on it and say it was a pretty hot group."

Fans — and critics — rate the current edition of the Gentlemen as a "pretty hot group," too. In addition to Waller and Yates, the band's present roster includes Jimmy Gaudreau on mandolin and Dick Smith on banjo. After more than 25 years of making music, the Country Gentlemen continue to be one of the major international bluegrass bands. Although the personnel changes over the years have left a succession of new faces looking out from various Gentlemen album jackets, the focal point always has been Charlie Waller — his unique vocal style and the musical bedrock of his clean, reliable rhythm playing.

"There's been a lot of changes," says Charlie, "but mainly we just take a song and start doing it. And if I'm singing it, it'll have the Country Gentlemen flavor."

A flavor that nobody has ever been able to beat.

— *Robert Kyle*

A SELECTED WALLER DISCOGRAPHY

With The Country Gentlemen: *Country Gentlemen*, Vanguard, VSD 79331; *Remembrances And Forecasts*, Vanguard, VSD 97349; *River Bottom*, Sugar Hill (Box 4040 Duke Station, Durham, NC 27706), 3712. (On Rebel, c/o Record Depot, Box 3057, Roanoke, VA 24015): *Bringing Mary Home*, 1478; *Calling My Children Home*, 1574; *The Traveler*, 1481; *The Award-Winning Country Gentlemen*, 1506; *Joe's Last Train*, 1559; *Play It Like It Is*, 1586.

PETER WERNICK

PETER WERNICK HAS a unique position among contemporary banjoists; he probably exerts a greater influence over his fellow practitioners through the printed word than he does through his extensive performing and recording. An entire generation of young banjo enthusiasts are learning their first rolls and chord positions from Wernick's classic instruction book *Bluegrass Banjo*, published by Oak Publications (33 West 60th St., New York, NY 10023). Wernick also has authored *Bluegrass Songbook* (Oak Publications), an introduction to traditional bluegrass songs. In addition, Wernick has played key roles in two major bluegrass bands: the seminal Country Cooking, and his current group, Hot Rize. Two of Wernick's tunes, "Pow Wow The Indian Boy" and "Orange Mountain Special," have become bluegrass banjo standards, frequently heard at bluegrass festivals and banjo contests around the country.

Wernick was introduced to the banjo when he was 12, through Earl Scruggs' version of "Shuckin' The Corn." Wernick's exploration of the instrument actually began in the late '50s while he was living in New York. Pete and some friends, who also were intrigued by the folk boom, gathered together regularly to play music.

Wernick began his career by frailing an old banjo that his father had purchased at an auction; but as soon as Pete began to understand the instrument, he started imitating Scruggs — his main inspiration. "I got his records, and it was a total trial-and-error thing for well over a year before I was even able to play in time," Wernick recalls. "From that point on, I tried to find people to play with. I got to meet Jody Stecher and David Grisman and other excellent people."

While attending Columbia University in New York City, Peter ran the school's bluegrass program on radio station WKCR. "It really helped me with *Bluegrass Songbook,*" he says, "because it acquainted me with the whole spectrum of bluegrass."

Pete made his first serious bluegrass performing efforts with the Orange Mountain Boys, which he joined in 1964. Pete, mandolinist Bob Applebaum and the other members of the group spent hours practicing three-part vocal harmonies and writing new material. This was Pete's first chance to get a feel for the dynamics of a bluegrass band. Meanwhile, he was working for a degree at Columbia, and eventually earned a Ph.D. in sociology. (Pete's fans have synthesized his doctorate and his musicianship into the sobriquet "Dr. Banjo.")

Despite his advanced academic pursuits, Pete was tantalized by the prospect of becoming a professional musician. "I suddenly realized in graduate school that all my friends were musicians," he recalls. "David Nichtern [author of 'Midnight At The Oasis'] and I used to do a lot of playing, and Jody [Stecher] and I go back quite a way. A lot of people I knew were people I had met through music, and I only knew a few sociology students as real friends. I started realizing that music was where I really had my heart. It seemed like the academic world was unreal, and the music world was something incredibly exotic."

When Wernick moved to Ithaca, New York, to work at Cornell University in 1970, he was entering a fertile breeding ground for young bluegrass talent. He soon met and jammed with players who would become the core of Country Cooking; guitarists Russ Barenberg and John Miller and banjoist Tony Trischka. The band began as a country and western group, with Peter writing material and Trischka

Pete Wernick as "Waldo Otto" on steel guitar with Red Knuckles and the Trailblazers, 1983.

recorded his first solo album, *Dr. Banjo Steps Out,* and through that project, Wernick assembled the core of the band that was to become Hot Rize.

Musically, Hot Rize has combined the traditional styles of Flatt And Scruggs, Don Reno, and Bill Monroe with the musical incandescence of Tim O'Brien's hot fiddle and mandolin playing, Sawtelle's fluid lead guitar work, and Wernick's phase-shifted banjo sound. It has been an excellent forum for Pete's development of a mainstream bluegrass banjo style for the '80s, continuing the venturesome explorations that began during his days with Country Cooking.

WERE YOU WORRIED about finding musicians to work with in Colorado after you left Country Cooking?

There are talented people everywhere in the country. I feel that what's necessary is a structure that lets those musicians apply their talents. If they just get together and jam all the time, they can blow each other's minds. If you want to be a professional musician, the music has to jell into something beyond a jam session — something that can somehow go out into the marketplace.

How have you been dividing musical duties within Hot Rize to apply those talents to best advantage?

Since May 1978 the band has had me on banjo, Tim O'Brien on lead vocals, mandolin, and fiddle, and on acoustic guitar in the country swing tunes where I'm playing an 8-string steel guitar, Nick Forster on electric bass, electric guitar, and vocals, and Charles Sawtelle on lead guitar and vocals.

Besides using some non-acoustic instruments in your band, you're also known for running your banjo through a phase shifter. How did that come about?

In 1974 I heard a guitar player using one of those in a music store in New York City, and I thought, "I wonder if the banjo could possibly turn out anything like that?" And when I rigged it up, it did. After I discovered the sound of the phase-shifted banjo, the thing that struck me was that it sounded really good and that there were musical sounds I could make which I enjoyed hearing. My motto is "If it sounds good, it must be good." I didn't worry about what people would think or about what traditions might be violated. Then I started playing with the shifter and dreaming about the idea of three people being able to record what came to be known as Niwot music, because it started in Niwot, Colorado. That's phase-shifted banjo music, heavily rhythmic mandolin playing, and electric bass. I didn't put out the album *Dr. Banjo Steps Out* to make a gimmicky statement. I had the chance to do an album and I just wanted to do the very best music I could. But as a person aware of the business considerations of music, gimmicks definitely have a way of

playing pedal steel guitar. But soon, the lure of bluegrass brought the banjos out of the closet and an exciting bluegrass band was born.

Playing with Trischka gave Peter's banjo style an immense boost. "When I met Tony, it made a big difference," he says. "It was the first time I'd met a banjo picker that I really could get off trading ideas with. He's really into working out harmonies, and that made it easy many times because he'd be the one playing the harmony part. We'd sit around and try to think up something that would sound good with twin banjos, and it suddenly occurred to me that we could make a record that would be good enough for people to want to hear. That was the turning point. I called Tony from my office at Cornell, where I was working, and said, 'I just thought of this idea.' Some friends of ours happened to be starting Rounder Records at the time and were beginning to produce albums."

Wernick made two classic records for Rounder with Country Cooking before he left New York in 1976. Another album, *Country Cooking With The Fiction Brothers,* followed; but Wernick was soon pursuing his own musical vision in the mountains of Colorado. For two years, he played banjo in a Colorado bluegrass group known humorously as either the Drifting Ramblers or the Rambling Drifters. It was with this band that Peter met future Hot Rize guitarist Charles Sawtelle. He also helping, as long as they're not just a flash in the pan."

Did you use the phase shifter with Country Cooking?

In Country Cooking's last phase — no pun intended — around 1974 with the Fiction Brothers, I tried to use it onstage with my big, old-time radio ribbon microphone. I did use it at some bluegrass festivals.

How do you set it up today?

I've got an MXR Phase 90 phase shifter and a good banjo mike, a Shure SM-57. The mike goes into the phase shifter via a transformer. It's a very simple connecting box. I step on a switch when I want that effect.

Have you ever tried to put a pickup on a banjo?

Yes, and I do not like the sound. I've never heard a banjo with a pickup in it sound like anything even close to what I think a banjo *should* sound like, except John Hartford's amplified banjo. His instrument has a really unique sound.

You mentioned using an old ribbon-style radio microphone. What kind was it, and where did that idea come from?

It was a real antique, like a 1940 RCA 44BX, and I liked the effect it had. It made the low end of the banjo sound incredibly fat. [Music promoter] Carlton Haney lectured me on those old records by Don Reno and Earl Scruggs, and he said Reno and Scruggs sounded so good because they were playing into announcer's mikes that made the banjo sound bassy. That's a very attractive part of the sound, and it makes a great combination with the phase shifter. I used it for a song on the Fiction Brothers album and for several *Dr. Banjo Steps Out* tracks. It's also on a few cuts from our *Hot Rize* album.

Are you using a vintage banjo along with the vintage microphone?

I got my banjo from Porter Church, a real traditional Scruggs-style player who was playing with Red Allen And The Kentuckians at the same time David Grisman was with the band. They played on my radio program, and the next day I had Porter's banjo. It's an original Gibson RB with an original 5-string neck. The bottom is an RB-1 from somewhere in the late '20s or '30s. Somebody who was fairly authoritative told me that the tone ring isn't original, though. It's certainly not the loudest banjo, but I've gotten used to its sound. I think that it and my touch have sort of grown up together; it doesn't sound the same when someone else plays it.

How do you string your banjo?

I use medium-gauge Liberty strings, which seem to fight back just the right amount. I like the heavier feel of the strings, and I like a higher bridge and a higher action than most players. I like being able to really belt the strings. The first and fifth strings are .011" gauge, and the fourth is a .024", so the set is heavier than most medium packages. I've been using them so long I can't think of the other gauges.

Why the high action and the heavy strings? Do you find that it gives you more power?

I heard J.D. Crowe playing one night, and I thought, "My God, his stuff is so much better than all these little doodle-do licks I'm working on right now." So I went up to him and practically did a full-scale interview to find out what he was doing that turned me on so much. He had a high action on his banjo, and it was pretty clear that he set it up so he could hit the strings real hard. The bridge was the same, but the strings were high off the neck. Later I found that a higher bridge seemed to help, too. The combination worked.

Who was the biggest influence on the development of your style?

Earl Scruggs, definitely. At different times I've been taken with the styles of Don Reno or Bill Keith, or Tony Trischka, who I think is brilliant. But sooner or later — usually sooner — I end up hearing a Scruggs record and it blows me away on a different level. I keep having to realize that what really communicates with me — and, I feel, with the great majority of listeners — is not the particular licks of certain variations of the style, but being able to use a three-finger roll and make a 5-string banjo really ring and sound gorgeous as well as hard-driving; that and having a cleanliness in your touch, a sense of precision and dynamics, and being utterly tasty. Those are the things that make Scruggs such a great model. Beyond Earl, of course, there's the emotional side of the music. Tony Trischka is a model in that sense, because he plays so spontaneously and speaks through his banjo in an uncanned way.

What aspects of Trischka's style most interest you?

For one thing, he has the best chops I've ever seen. Considering what he can do, he seems able to practically make up styles at will — just doing brand new moves on the banjo. I find it very exciting to listen to him and play with him.

Do you like the chromatic, or melodic, style of playing?

I enjoy listening to well-played chromatic style when it's not just rattled off as a series of notes. I love hearing chromatic passages where somebody actually takes the trouble to bend a note in the middle, the way Bill Keith did on his version of "Camptown Races." But as far as playing it myself, in general I find that I have to face it as programming my right hand to do a bunch of stuff that I don't have a natural feel for. I don't like having to think very hard when I'm playing; I'd much rather listen to what the whole band is doing and concentrate on the group sound. That's the ultimate thing, to me.

Do you suggest that beginners try to work within a group as early as possible, to get that same musical perspective?

I tell people that if they can play in time and change chords at the right time, then they're ready to play with somebody else. The only way they're going to go far as musicians is just to play with other people. To me, it means the world to get with good musicians and have that interaction. I think inspiration is the basis of music. If a banjo player can get together with people and have fun playing, then that's great, because he or she will go home and practice more to be better for the next jam session. If you can just find joy in the instrument, you'll go back to it; and if you go back to it, and if you're in the right frame of mind, you'll keep getting better.

— *David McCarty*

For the past three years, there has been an addition to Pete Wernick's Hot Rize. That addition, or alter-image, is none other than Red Knuckles And The Trailblazers, an electrified western swing and honky-tonk group. If you can corner one of the band members — Red Knuckles, Wendell Mercantile, Waldo Otto, Slade — they can tell you all you want to know about them. Other Hot Rize developments since the March '81 publication of this article are two albums on Flying Fish: *Radio Boogie*, 231, and *Hot Rize Presents Red Knuckles And The Trailblazers*, 279.

A SELECTED WERNICK DISCOGRAPHY

Solo Album: *Dr. Banjo Steps Out*, Flying Fish (1304 W. Schubert, Chicago, IL 60614), 046. **With Hot Rize:** *Hot Rize*, Flying Fish, 206. **With Country Cooking:** *Country Cooking*, Rounder (One Camp St., Cambridge, MA 02140), 0006; *Country Cooking*, Rounder, 0033; *Frank Wakefield/Country Cooking*, Rounder, 0007; *Country Cooking/Fiction Brothers*, Flying Fish, 019.

ALAN MUNDE

ALAN MUNDE IS ONE of America's leading banjo players, as renowned an innovator as he is a picker. His credits include records, film tracks, and tours in Japan and Europe with his current group, the Country Gazette. He has, in addition, performed with a host of stellar musicians, such as guitarists Jimmy Martin, Red Allen, and Clarence White; mandolinist/ fiddler Sam Bush, fiddler Vassar Clements, and singer Linda Ronstadt.

Alan has been a *Frets* columnist since the magazine's inception and has published two volumes of banjo music featuring original compositions and arrangements of traditional tunes. Besides those activities, Alan has participated in community arts programs through the Oklahoma Arts and Humanities Council and the Mid-America Arts Alliance.

* * * *

IS IT TRUE THAT you became interested in the banjo by accident?
Yes. I was born in Norman, Oklahoma, Nov. 4, 1946. When I was 15 years old my oldest brother returned from the Navy and brought me back a guitar and an instruction record. The guitar was unplayable, so I went out and bought another one for $40. The instruction record was by Pete Seeger and when I played it, I was disappointed to discover that he played banjo. I thought that he was a guitar player. I eventually began to enjoy the sound of the banjo, and after a year of playing guitar I bought a banjo. I found a guy in Oklahoma City named Gary Price, who taught me the basic roll. After I had been playing for about one year, I joined a little group in Norman, Oklahoma.

What kind of music did you listen to?
We listened to recordings of Bill Monroe, Earl Scruggs, Bill Keith, and the Dillards. I especially like Doug Dillard.

How did you meet fiddler Bryon Berline and banjoist Eddie Shelton?
I met Byron Berline at the University of Oklahoma, where we both went to school, and we began to play together. He and Eddie Shelton played on a local television show. They had tapes of the Kentucky Colonels, Bill Monroe, and the Dillards, and it was a big thrill to hear them. Eddie taught me a lot.

What about Jimmy Martin? Where did you meet him?
I met him through a group of people at a music store in Oklahoma City. The shop had a little recording studio. One of the guys who worked there, Harlo Wilcox, was a guitarist who needed a banjo player for an album he was cutting. He asked me to play a bluegrass song on it. In October 1969 I went to a DJ convention with Wilcox and picked with him at the Old Knoll Hotel. While there, I learned that Jimmy Martin was looking for a new banjo player. When Jimmy came later that day I auditioned for him and he told me to "be back next Thursday because we're going on the road."

How long were you in his band?
For two years, from October 1969 to October 1971.

Did you record with him?
I recorded songs that appear on his albums. I played on *Singing All Day And Dinner On The Ground,* and I played four or five numbers on *I'd Like To Be*

NORMAN, OKLA.
U.S.A.

The Country Gazette in 1978. (L to R): Roland
White, Michael Anderson, Alan Munde, and
Joe Carr.

Sixteen Again. I cut about 13 songs with
him altogether.

*What is the most important thing you
gained from being in his band?*

I developed a professional attitude.
Prior to joining his group, I never really
worked to perfect any aspect of my playing.
Jimmy helped me to learn the basics: producing a good tone, developing a good
sense of timing, and playing clearly.

*Where did you go when you left his
group?*

I joined the Country Gazette. I had
written a letter to Byron Berline, who was in
California. I had heard that he was trying to
form a group. Both he and [bassist] Roger
Bush called me and asked if I wanted to join
the Country Gazette by way of touring
Europe as the Flying Burrito Brothers. I
went on the tour, and when we returned to
the States in January 1972, we formed the
Country Gazette. Our first album was *Trait-
or In Our Midst.*

*There is a certain sense of freshness
about that album. What was your approach?*

We had a producer, Jim Dickson, who
was really good for us. I give him a lot of
credit for the way the first album sounded.
We didn't have any real innovative ap-

proach or attitude. A lot of people wonder
how we come up with all of the different
arrangements. It's relatively simple. For
instance, "Just Keep On Pushing" is a song
that Roger Bush picked off a Gene Clark
record. Originally we did it in the key of *B*. I
put my capo on and played that way and it
sounded ordinary. One day I was sitting at
home just fooling around trying to play it in
B♭ and it worked out fine without a capo. I
asked the group if we could lower the key
and play in *B♭*, and we did. We played one
part of the song in *C*. We used the same
chords from an old fiddle tune called "Wag-
goner." The cut starts out with that and
changes immediately into the song. It even
has "Fisher's Hornpipe" in it.

*Besides yourself, who are the other
members of the group?*

Roland White on mandolin and guitar,
Michael Anderson plays acoustic bass and
does the vocals, and Joe Carr plays guitar,
mandolin, and does vocals, too.

*How would you describe the Country
Gazette's sound?*

I view it as a kaleidoscope of music. If
you're really listening, you can focus on any
one of the instruments and find something
interesting going on.

What kind of banjo are you playing?

I play a Stelling Staghorn. I also own a Stelling Scrimshaw model, but I haven't played it in quite a while because I don't usually take it on the road with me. I used to play a Gibson that had an old pot assembly with a new neck.

Is your banjo set up any special way?

I like the head to be medium tight. Not real loose, and not as tight as it can get. I use a 3/4" bridge [the normal height is 5/8"] made by Snuffy Smith of Springdale, Arkansas. I think that the extra height and the special aged maple give the banjo a clearer, louder tone. As for the tailpiece, I don't have it clamped down. A lot of people tend to have the tailpiece clamped down to the drum. I like it up almost as light as it will go. I let it all the way up and bring it down just a wee bit. That tends to give the banjo a more open sound.

What kind of system do you use to amplify your banjo?

I use a pickup that is not commercially available — I borrowed it from someone. It's a single pole from an electric guitar pickup mounted on the coordinator rods of the banjo, and it's positioned under the middle foot of the bridge — next to the head, but not touching the head. Underneath the middle foot of the bridge there is a little piece of metal, between the middle foot and the head. When you pluck a string, the banjo head vibrates that little piece of metal, which in turn activates the pickup. I also use an L-5 Lab Series Amp. I use the pickup and the amp as a stage monitor. The amp is also miked and goes through the PA. The sound of the amp/ mike is used to reinforce the volume of the banjo more than the tone.

Where do you position the mike on the banjo head?

It faces the lower half of the banjo between the neck and where my hand plays.

How far away from the mike do you stand?

I play about three to four inches away from the microphone during my solos. When playing backup, I play about a foot away from the mike.

What kind of strings have you been using?

I use Stelling light-gauge strings that are [from first to fifth] .010", .011", .012", .020", .010". The heavier first string gives a good solid feel. Also, the middle finger of the picking hand is closer to the bridge and has a tendency to shear strings off. If they're real light, you'll break the first string. With the lighter strings on the inside, I can get a better feel for the pull-offs.

Would you say that the first and fifth strings are sounded the most?

Yes, especially the first string.

When you play, do you deal with the neck as a series of chords or as a series of scales?

I would say it's both. I see a chord position and then I see an accompanying scale. What I do is try to flow from one position to another. For example, if you play a G on the fourth string at the 5th fret, you could play in a position where the scale would lie below the 5th fret, or you could play in a position where the scale would like above the 5th fret.

Why do you use triads or other chords built around the first three strings?

I don't like the tone of the fourth string in the higher register. I do most of my thinking on the first two strings. On "Huckleberry Hornpipe" and "Blackberry Blossom" [*Don't Give Up Your Day Job*] I play mostly on the first two strings and the fifth string. I can get more volume from the first two strings than from the middle strings. It is easier for my right hand to hit those than to move onto the middle strings.

Do you use any particular chord substitutions to fill out some of your backup?

Yes. There's a chord substitution I like to use in which I substitute a minor chord for a dominant seventh chord. In that substitution, the root of the minor chord is the fifth of the dominant seventh chord. It works because the chords are closely related. For instance, you can substitute a *D* minor chord for a *G7* chord because *D* is the fifth tone of the *D* scale, and both of those chords contain two important common tones: *D* and *F*. Sometimes I play an *Am* chord instead of a *D7* chord. The theory behind that substitution is exactly the same. Some players make these chord substitutions without realizing it. You can also get a nice sound by adding a ninth; for example, by adding a *D* note to a *C* chord.

Do you ever practice with a metronome?

No, but I think it would be a great help. Usually when I want to learn something, I slow down a record. I used to slow down Earl Scruggs records so I could hear each note evenly spaced.

How did you develop your "chugging" [playing two or three strings at the same time] style of playing?

I learned how to control the emphasis. Practicing slowly is something that I always felt was a great help to my playing. You get a chance to hear what you've been playing. Some people just stomp the tunes to death and don't know what they're doing. They get sloppy. They're just sliding over what they are playing, instead of trying to bring the notes out. I enjoy playing slowly when practicing. Banjo music goes by so fast that you don't hear all the harmonies that are going on. There might be an interesting note that appears every so often, but you won't get a chance to hear it because of the speed.

Is there something special you do to maintain a sense of freshness in your playing?

I approach each performance as a challenge. I feel that I want to play my best. I may not get up and say, "I'm gonna go and do something that I've never done before," because I feel it wouldn't be as interesting as what I have already worked out. My playing is well thought out in advance. One of the joys of music is discovering new things about familiar pieces. It's a real charge.

— *Jim Tarantino*

Since The October '80 publication of this article, bassist Michael Anderson has been replaced by Bill Smith. The following albums have been released: *Festival Favorites: The Nashville Sessions* (Rounder [One Camp St., Cambridge, MA 02140], RRR0031); and *The Southwest Sessions*, RRR0032; and *America's Bluegrass Band* (Flying Fish, 1304 W. Schubert, Chicago, IL 60614), FF 295.

A SELECTED MUNDE DISCOGRAPHY

Solo Albums: *The Banjo Kid Picks Again*, Ridge Runner (7121 W. Vickery, Unit 118, Fort Worth, TX 76116), RR0022; *Banjo Sandwich*, Ridge Runner RR0001. **With Country Gazette:** *All This And Money Too*, Ridge Runner, RR0017; *Don't Give Up Your Day Job*, United Artists, UALA090-F; *Festival Favorites* (soon to be released from Ridge Runner); *Live*, Antilles (dist. by Island, 444 Madison Ave., New York, NY 10022), 7014; *Out To Lunch*, Flying Fish (1304 W. Schubert, Chicago, IL 60614), FF027; *Traitor In Our Midst*, United Artists, UAS-5596; *What A Way To Make A Living*, Ridge Runner, RRR0008. **With others (on Ridge Runner):** *Acoustic Steel*, RRR0023; *Country Store Live*, RRR00012; *I Wasn't Born To Rock And Roll*, RRR0005; *Jazz Grass*, RRR0009; *One Legged Gypsy*, RRR0025; *Otter Nonsense*, RRR0024; *Poor Richard's Almanac*, RRR0002; *Somewhere Over The Rainbow And Other Fiddle Tunes*, RRR0003; *Stone Mountain Boys Reunion Album*, RRR0015; *Sam And Alan Together Again For The First Time*, RRR0007; *Why Is This Man Smiling?*, RRR0004; *Dad's Favorites*, Rounder, 0100; *I'd Like To Be Sixteen Again*, Decca (dist. by MCA), DL7-5343; *Singing All Day And Dinner On The Ground*, Decca, DL-75226.

J.D. CROWE

THROUGHOUT HIS CELEBRATED 25-year career, J.D. Crowe has been in the vanguard of bluegrass musicians — first as a banjo picker, and later as a group leader. He is regarded as the quintessential Scruggs-style picker, a consummate craftsman with flawless timing and classic tone.

His driving, bluesy style first came to national prominence in the mid-'50s when, as part of Jimmy Martin And The Sunny Mountain Boys, he recorded such classics as "You Don't Know My Mind" and "Hold Whatcha Got" [*Good 'N' Country*]. By the mid-'60s he had formed his own group, the Kentucky Mountain Boys, with Doyle Lawson and Red Allen. In addition to powerhouse instrumentals, their sound featured beautiful trio harmonies with Crowe on baritone.

By the mid-'70s, J.D. had recruited Tony Rice, Ricky Skaggs, and Jerry Douglas to form the New South. Their first recording in 1975, The *New South*, created a sensation. The solidity of J.D.'s playing combined with the free-flying inventiveness of the other musicians, produced a stunningly contemporary sound within a traditional context. Their album catapulted bluegrass into the forefront of progressive American music and drew a whole new generation of young musicians into the acoustic fold.

Recently J.D. has steered the New South toward the commercial country market, concentrating his talents on record producing and arranging. Current band members include Bobby Slone on fiddle, Wendy Miller on mandolin and tenor vocals, Steve Bryant on bass, and Keith Whitley on guitar. Crowe has built the group sound around the smooth vocals of Whitley and has added electric instruments and drums in the studio.

This has meant a lower profile for the banjo within the arrangements overall, a change that is more readily accepted by J.D. than by his traditional fans. His most recent recordings have been vilified in the bluegrass press, with his new stylistic forays regarded more as heresy than as progress.

For J.D., however, the change is a matter of expanding rather than abandoning his bluegrass base. He continues to play a full schedule of festivals, while pursuing broader musical recognition in Nashville — both as a recording artist and as a producer/arranger. It is a posture that is uniquely suited for a man with the myriad talents of J.D. Crowe.

* * * *

YOUR SCRUGGS-STYLE *picking was practically learned at Earl's knee, wasn't it?*

In the early '50s, Flatt And Scruggs moved to Lexington, Kentucky — where I was born in August 1937. They had a radio program every Saturday morning, live in the studio. They'd rehearse for two hours, then do a 15-minute show. That's why they were so good. I went to watch them for quite a while, along with my parents, and got to meet them all. It just really fascinated me.

Besides Scruggs, what other banjo pickers influenced you?

I used to listen to Don Reno because I really liked some of the single-note things he did. In 1955 I got my first bluegrass job with Mac Wiseman, and Reno And Smiley were traveling on the same show, so I got to be around Don. He was great,

ABOVE: *J.D. Crowe and his "rock-solid" banjo at a bluegrass festival in 1979.* RIGHT: *J.D. with his group The New South, compared by some critics to country music "outlaws" like Waylon Jennings and Willie Nelson.*

Smiley were traveling on the same show, so I got to be around Don. He was great, always joking and horsing around. Backstage in the dressing room, between shows, everybody would get together and jam. I learned a lot. Back then there weren't many instruction books. You learned the hard way, by watching and memorizing it. There weren't all that many pickers to learn from — maybe two or three, and you took your choice. For me, it was mainly Scruggs. I loved the way his right hand worked.

After 1956, when you joined Jimmy Martin, it seemed like you really started to develop your own style.

Up until then, I'd been playing straight Scruggs, but I couldn't play that way with Jimmy because it didn't fit his timing. It was the basic Scruggs roll, but with a different feel. Jimmy's timing was more outgoing. He wanted all the backup instruments going real hard all the time to match his singing, so I had to simplify my style. I couldn't use a lot of the rolls I'd been playing. It was straighter playing and hard driving. Jimmy always stressed rhythm and timing, and playing what fit the song.

You also added a lot of bluesy licks, like on You Don't Know My Mind. *Where did those ideas come from?*

I was listening to a lot of rock and roll. Jimmy always said it was a wonder I didn't just play guitar and lay the banjo down, 'cause that's all I listened to. I learned a lot of notes and licks off the electric guitar, and pickup notes off the piano. They didn't play many real hot licks, but what they played fit so well.

The stress on rhythm has remained one of the strongest features of your style. Have you always had a gift for timing, or did you really develop it with Jimmy?

When I listened to music years ago, I could always feel when the performers could feel it. I could determine timing before I could hear the notes or the melody. To me, that's what makes music —the beat, the feel, the touch that you have to it. Not the hot notes. That's why I liked Scruggs over any of the rest of them, because I could hear the timing. There was something about it that was so alive, so powerful. To me, timing is 75% of your playing. I could always play in time, about average, but Jimmy was the first one that really helped me get into all the different aspects of timing and feel.

You also first started singing onstage with Jimmy. Was it difficult learning to sing and play at the same time?

You really don't play that much when you're singing. All you do is fill in between the words that you're holding at the end of the line, before getting back to the first word of the next line. There's a slight pause there, and you can throw in some little run or touch the instrument lightly, because everybody's lightened up and it's not necessary to hit the instrument so hard. I'd watched so many people do this throughout the years — especially Flatt And

Scruggs — that I could just do it automatically. As long as the rhythms of the singing and vocal parts are the same, there should not be any problems.

How do you generally go about developing your solos? Is there a specific strategy that you follow?

I start out with the melody and keep the lead line dominant. Then I work on timing to get it precise. I might hit a few off licks, or hot licks, but I'll always have the melody there, without much variation. My solos are always improvised to a certain degree because it gets really boring to play the same thing over and over again. A little idea runs through my mind and I say, "Hey, this'll fit!" So I go ahead and stick it in there and usually it does fit. Sometimes it doesn't work out too well, but the whole secret to that is getting out of it without anybody knowing it.

How similar are your solos on the same song from show to show?

Let's say we kick off a show with a familiar song like "Old Home Place" [*The New South*]. If I didn't kick off just about the same way every time, a lot of people wouldn't recognize it. So I always get that melody line set in the tune, especially the very first kickoff. Even on an instrumental, I try to stick to the melody, especially when playing the first verse or chorus. After the break on the fiddle or the mandolin, or whatever, when I come back in, I may vary it a little bit.

You're well known for the tremendous amplitude you get out of your banjo. Did you develop that powerful sound in the early days?

In the past, when you played with one or two microphones, you had to be able to be heard acoustically, and that meant picking hard. I used to keep my action so high I could get my little finger under the strings on the last fret. That really developed my grip. Of course, it's set lower now.

It seems like you don't have to sacrifice volume to get good tone.

Well, you have to have a good instrument first of all. Then you have to know how to set it up to get the best performance. You have to learn at what volume level to play to get a good tone; and how hard you can pick it. You also have to know how to set it up from the bridge, and how much tension should be on the tailpiece. People used to come up to me and say, "What kind of strings are you using, heavy gauge?" My banjo always sounded like it was blowing the doors open, but it was just the technique I've acquired through years of experience.

What kind of banjos do you have and how do you set them up?

Right now I'm using a 1933 Gibson Granada Flathead. It has a sweet, deep, mellow sound. I also have two Gibson RB-3 flatheads, 1934 and 1937. They're harder sounding and louder. Each of the three has a different tone. When I reach the tone I want on each instrument, I never touch it again until I change its head. I generally prefer a medium-tension head. I use an 11/16" bridge made by Snuffy Smith of Springdale, Arkansas, because I like the strings a little higher up off the head. That way I don't hit the head and it gives me a better grip. I put just enough tension on the tailpiece to keep the bridge taut. Too much pressure will kill the tone because the bridge can't vibrate. I use a capo made by Tom McKinney of Asheville, North Carolina. I like it because it's real small. I don't believe in having any more metal and weight than you need. It's so compact you hardly even notice it when it's on the neck. For strings, I use GHS strings — a set I helped design [from first to fifth]: .0095," .011," .012", .020," and .0095." My picks are Nationals, the standard-gauge metal fingerpicks, and I use a heavy-gauge plastic thumbpick.

Do you follow a particular practice regimen when you're not onstage?

I usually practice when I have a specific purpose. If, for instance, I'm learning a new tune or a song I've already heard or if I'm writing a new instrumental or trying to work out a specific break for a certain song, I'll practice by myself. Then when we get together as a group, I've got my part already down. But usually I play just to stay loose. Sometimes we'll play one weekend, then we won't play at all until the next weekend. That's too long to go without at least picking up my instrument to get loose. Usually a day or two before the weekend, I'll pick a couple of hours. Another thing I like to do is sit around and enjoy the old Scruggs music, mainly just to see if I can go back and still play it. I think it's best to practice what you hear, not just exercises. They're best when you're just starting out to play. After you've learned the basics, though, you should learn to play a song or try to write a tune. Try and play consistently, not at breakneck speed.

As the leader of the Kentucky Mountain Boys and the New South, you've played with a variety of musicians in a number of different styles. How have you managed to continually adapt and still retain a fresh outlook?

Anytime you have a personnel change, there's going to be a change in your sound. A lot of the older, first-generation pickers will stress playing a tune like someone else did years ago. You can't do that because you need to let a man use his talents to the best of his ability. They can't really put forth their best effort, put their heart in it, if they can't do a little of what they want to do. I always try for the best overall band sound, even if I have to bend a little myself.

You've played with a lot of great pickers like Doyle Lawson, Tony Rice, Ricky Skaggs, and Jimmy Gaudreau. Do you regret that the good musicians keep moving on?

No. Four or five years is about the normal length of stay. Then you get tired and want to try something new. It's great at the time, but I don't want to continue doing what I did in 1970. It's like riding a dead horse. Tony Rice wanted to get into the jazz thing. That's fine. I respect him for it. We did good at the time we were together, but it can't last forever. Doyle left the Gentlemen because he wanted to play his own country music, though he wouldn't be making as much money. Ricky's doing his thing now, and he hated country music when he was in the New South; but Jimmy and Glenn Lawson are doing a lot of the same things in Spectrum that we did together. That's where progress comes from, how new groups evolve. Anybody that's been a part of the New South, I don't feel they can say anything but that we enjoyed it, burnt hell out of lot of songs, and put it down like it should have been done. Everybody had a good time, and we all still have a good relationship.

After 25 years in the forefront of bluegrass, do you feel any ambivalence about moving into country circles, where you're not that well known?

I find that it's a challenge musically. I think any musician would rather be judged on what he's doing at the present rather than what he did in the past. We're looking forward to playing new places and for new audiences. Basically, it's a matter of playing what you like and what you feel, and hopefully the people will like it too.

— *Herschel Freeman*

The current lineup of J.D. Crowe And The New South is: Crowe on banjo, Paul Atkins on guitar, Bobby Slone on fiddle, Wendy Miller on mandolin, and Randy Hayes on bass. The album *Somewhere Between* (Rounder [One Camp St., Cambridge, MA 02140] 0153) was released in the summer of '82.

A SELECTED CROWE DISCOGRAPHY

With Jimmy Martin And The Sunny Mt. Boys (On Decca/MCA): *Good 'N' Country*, 81; *Country Music Time*, 91; *Widow Maker*, 101; *Tennessee* (out of print); *Big 'N' Country Instrumentals*, 115. **With Kentucky Mt. Boys** (On Rebel, Box 191, Floyd, VA 24091): *Bluegrass Holiday*, 1598; *Ramblin' Boy* [renamed *Black Jack*], 1583; *Model Church*, 1585. **With The New South:** *J.D. Crowe And The New South*, Starday (c/o Gusto Records, 220 Boscobel St., Nashville, TN 37213), SLP 1489; *The New South*, Rounder, 0044; *You Can Share My Blanket*, Rounder, 0096; *My Home Ain't In The Hall Of Fame*, Rounder, 0103. **With Others:** *The Bluegrass Album*, Rounder, 0140.

McLAIN FAMILY

KENTUCKY'S McLain Family Band boasts a long list of impressive credentials. They have performed in 61 countries, appeared on numerous television shows, including NBC's *Today Show*, and have recently completed their seventh album, called (appropriately) "7th Album."

Raymond ("Daddy") is the group's guitarist, though he is adept at playing a number of instruments. His family helped mold his musical taste. His mother is a folklorist at the University of Alabama, his father played tenor banjo in high school. His sister, Rosemary McLain Stovall, wrote many of the songs the band sang in their early days. Raymond studied music theory and folklore in college, and for the past several years he has been a professor of music at Berea College, Berea, Kentucky.

Raymond Jr., 26, is the group's banjo player though he, too, plays a variety of other instruments. His musical abilities are only part of his talents; he earned a degree in speech communications when he was only 19. Ruth, 21, plays bass and mandolin. In college she studied art and English. Nancy Ann, 15, bass and mandolin player, and Michael, 12, mandolin and guitar player, are two of the three most recent additions to the group. The third is Raymond Jr.'s new wife, Beverly, 21, who joined the group in December 1979, and plays banjo, guitar, bass, and mandolin.

Like many family bands, the McLains started out with the intention of playing solely for their own enjoyment and for local organizations like the PTA. When the family, originally from Hindman, Kentucky, moved to Berea, however, their musical pastime grew into a new career. Raymond's teaching was picked up by the *New York Times, Playboy,* and CBS, which aired an eight-minute segment of the Appalachian musician teaching his class. Shortly after that, Gian Carlo Menotti invited the band to perform at his Spoleto Festival in Italy. With that exposure, their career skyrocketed.

* * * *

RAYMOND, HOW DO you work out arrangements?
Raymond: There are a whole series of decisions that have to be made with every new piece. It's partly the excitement of it. If it's a song, you decide who should sing it and how to harmonize it. You can't start making decisions with the whole group because that would be too overwhelming. Generally we start with two people. We have a whole list of songs that we'll be working on. We've been saving some material. "Fair And Tender Ladies" [one of the band's most popular songs] we saved for years until we thought we could sing it well enough to sustain the feeling. So if there are just two, we find the key by trial and error somewhere in the range of the voices. Then we use a guitar or mandolin to outline the harmony.

Are you concerned with the color of the key, aside from the range?
Raymond: Yes, to be sure, and we like to keep it as bright as we can. We put it as high in the range as we can without straining. You always want to give the impression that you could sing higher if you wanted to or could sing lower if you wanted to or could play faster or sustain the note longer if you just wanted to; you never expose your limits. Anyhow, we'll find the key, we'll outline the harmony, and

then Raymond [Jr.] generally will start making some instrumental reaction in the lead sense.

Tell me about outlining harmony. You are not talking about writing it out, are you?

Raymond: No, it's all in the mind, because this whole kind of music is the kind of music that's played by ear and held in the head. I have a friend who wrote an essay called *The Oral Tradition: Literature Of The Mind.* The mind is capable of a whole lot more than we give it credit for in the way of memory. The music is in our heads, though we change it and add instruments. Raymond [Jr.] has been our instrumental innovator; Ruth is beginning to blossom. After we choose the range, we begin to sing in harmony. We may have to change the key at this point because it may be too high for the supporting voices. You have to be willing to change. You don't get so in love with your choices that you eliminate future choices.

Tell me about your development of the instrumental aspect of a piece.

Raymond, Jr.: Well, mostly it's dictated by the tune itself and by the chords. However, if we decide to have open-sounding chords like in "Fair And Tender Ladies," there's no third member of that chord. It's just *E* and *A* when we start out.

Raymond: The key of the piece is pentatonic; it's only a five-note scale and there's neither a major nor a minor third in it.

Raymond, Jr.: And because there is no third to make it a major or minor, we don't put any third in the beginning of the accompaniment. We just play *E* and *A* instead of *E, A* and *C, C* or whatever. When we do put a third in, about halfway through, it's minor. The most important thing you can do when you're playing back-up is to be aware of the total picture and think of how you can make it sound the way you want. Also listen to the lead singer and decide how to make the lead sound better without competing.

When you started to do "Fair And Tender Ladies" and worked out some of the harmonies, and were just getting into some of the instrumental parts, how did you create the kickoff, the breaks, and the backup?

Ruth: He goes through a lot of different ideas before he decides on a specific one.

Raymond, Jr.: I will have too many ideas, and Daddy will discard most of them and keep the ones that might have promise.

Ruth: And then develop those ideas.

Raymond: Any piece of ours is a combination of unity and variety. It's a good idea to finally hit on, through experimentation, some motive or idea and then repeat it and advance, rather than to go on to another idea. Some of our earlier arrangements were like a whole catalog of ideas, but that doesn't make a cohesive piece.

If you had a piece like that down pat and finally had performed it ten times and thought it was really together and all of a

sudden Raymond Jr. woke up some night and said, "I can do it another way," would you change?

Raymond: We'd try it.

Would any of you, working as a group on stage, take a different route instrumentally from the way the piece was planned and rehearsed?

Raymond: Oh yeah!

And what happens to the rest of the group?

Raymond: They're amused [*laughs*]! Usually it's not as well thought-out as what we have been doing.

When you change instruments is it for audience appeal or is it for what you think you need for the number?

Raymond: Probably for the audience appeal.

Ruth: You learn to put your banjo down and pick up the fiddle fast.

How do you qualify the music that you are playing now?

Raymond: It's music. Every traditional musician in the past has thought that he was going to play string band music, or old-time music, or some phrase that's been put on later. Even Bill Monroe, I'm sure, didn't set out to play bluegrass music; he set out to play music. If you consider yourself a traditional musician, you're not living up to your heritage if you're not creative also and pushing things on in the way that seems to be right. Labels are for other people to put on.

How about the instruments you play? I notice that an accordion has been added to your regular instruments.

Raymond: That's because I happen to play the accordion. It seemed like it would be a good thing to add. If one is looking for a historical precedent, Bill Monroe's mother played the accordion, but I don't think that's necessary [*laughs*].

How about the banjos that you play or the mandolins? Do you have a particular preference for the banjo you play?

Raymond Jr.: It's a Gibson 1932 RB-6 at the moment. The original neck was converted to a 5-string in 1959.

What kind of strings do you use?

Raymond Jr.: I use Gibson medium-gauge with the plain third. It's my preference because they're heavy enough to give some solidity and I can play with force. I have a hard time playing forcibly on lighter-gauge strings because they can break. Their vibrations are so wide that they are apt to buzz and run into each other.

Have you set your banjo up in a special way?

Raymond Jr.: No, I liked the way it was set up so well that I haven't messed with it at all.

Raymond: You keep the banjo head looser than mine, don't you?

Raymond Jr.: Yeah, I do, but on this particular banjo, it's very tight. I keep the banjo's tailpiece down as close to the head as I can get it without touching. My bridge is higher than most; I have a Shubb compen-

sated bridge and I asked Homer Ledford [an instrument maker in Winchester, Kentucky] to laminate the bottom of it, about 1/8″ of walnut veneer, so it's a little higher than usual, which gives it a better sound. I like my strings about 3/8″ off the neck; I like them pretty high because I don't want them buzzing.

Does the high action bother you for anything up the neck? Other than slides, you don't do a lot of up-the-neck stuff, do you?

Raymond Jr.: Well, I do some but I just have to try to be quicker with my left hand to get the string pressed down.

How about the mandolin?

Ruth: My mandolin is a GRT. I got it from George Gruhn nearly two years ago. I just love it.

Raymond Jr.: One of our mandolins that we play all the time was made by Homer Ledford. It's called the Gem. It's got lots of mother-of-pearl and it's a very nice, crisp-sounding mandolin. I've been using a Stelling lately that I got from Geoff Stelling. It's got f-holes and it has black binding and not much pearl inlay, but I picked it because of the tone.

Do you use Gibson strings on the mandolins, too?

Raymond Jr.: Well, for years we have been using Gibson medium-gauge bronze, but they break so frequently that we're going now to D'Addario.

Ruth: There are still Gibson strings on

two of the mandolins and we have a set of D'Addario strings on the GTR.

Do you use them because that's what the mandolin needs for the sound quality you like?

Raymond Jr.: Also because we know that D'Addario strings don't break as fast.

Where do they usually break?

Raymond Jr.: At the bridge.

Raymond: For years we used metal strings on the bass because that's what came on the bass when we got it. We really prefer the bright sound of the metal strings but they're impossible on your hands! The *G* and *D* strings are Golden Spiral and the *A* and *E* are Thomastik.

Ruth, you're amplifying the bass, right?

Ruth: No. We've got a Barcus-Berry [pickup] in case we need it.

Raymond: This summer we played 21 times with only three mikes. When we plugged the bass in, that gave us, in effect, four mikes.

Do you ever use any non-standard tunings?

Raymond Jr.: Yes. On the fiddle, I sometimes use "Wild-Cat" tuning, *A-E-A-C* going from bottom to top. It's the standard "Black Mountain Rag" tuning. On the banjo, I try not to use non-standard tunings because it takes so long to tune in between numbers while we're up on the stage. For instance, for "Pretty Polly," if I did it in *G*, I would tune the strings to *G-D-G-C-D* (fifth to first) — tuning the second

string up a fret — and play it in *G*. For the "Bells Of St. Mary," I might tune the low string down to *C* and the second string up to *C*. Also, on the mandolin for "Joe Clark's Dream," I tune the eight strings of the mandolin to eight different pitches.

Raymond: That's one reason we absolutely have to have three mandolins. We actually have a few more instruments at home. Raymond has a 1928 Gibson banjo and we have several mandolins.

What do you do to improve or enhance your own style?

Raymond: We try to notice every musical performance or theatrical performance. One thing we work on is how we pronounce words in our singing. We try to pronounce them the same way we would speak them. In some forms of music, you try to round off your vowel sounds, but it seems to me that the whole purpose and aim is communication. You want to make it as direct as possible so you pronounce as directly as you would speak.

Are there any particular parts of the country that you think are the nicest to play in? Certainly you haven't missed a state!

Raymond: It's a matter of understanding the region that you're in so you don't misread the reactions of the audience. Some people are enjoying things a whole lot but not jumping up and down, and other people in some places are jumping up and down with apparent enthusiasm but are not

listening to a thing you're doing! So you try to understand the cultural pattern. We were playing in Burma and the audience just wasn't applauding loudly. Then we discovered there was a religious reason for not clapping their hands together — they were forbidden to kill the microorganisms in the air!

Are there any particular picking styles that you use on the banjo that are different from the normal, three-finger picking rolls?

Raymond Jr.: I hope that most of my picking is different.

Raymond: It was kind of shocking to us when a writer for *Muleskinner News* said that Raymond doesn't have any roll.

Raymond Jr.: What he meant was that I didn't use any particular rolls, but broke them all up and used combinations of rolls.

Raymond: The idea was to get the notes where he wanted them, rather than in mechanical sequence.

Raymond Jr.: Someone once asked me what kind of rolls I used. I explained that first I try to get the tune right, and then I ornament around that with whatever notes I think will make it sound best. I try to stay away from any one particular roll.

What technique to you use when you go into your dixieland-like style of strumming?

Raymond Jr.: The same as if I were using a flatpick and playing dixieland. I go down with my thumbpick and up with my first-finger pick.

Have you ever, in the middle of all that, flipped off a pick?

Raymond Jr.: Oh yes, and it flips out in the audience and it's very entertaining to the person who catches the pick. If your thumbpick came off, which is usually the case, you just got two fingers left and that's a little more clumsy than if you have a thumbpick on one finger! You just carry on the best you can, and if you realize that you can't go down anymore downs, you have to go all ups.

How about your mandolin style, Ruth. Where did you get it?

Ruth: From no one person in particular. I guess my major influence has been Raymond.

Raymond: She gets her own breaks for the most part, but in the beginning Raymond [Jr.] pointed out breaks and that kind of thing.

Raymond Jr.: But now she does all of them herself.

Ruth: We all make suggestions to each other.

Raymond: I don't think anybody has more suggestions made to him than Raymond [Jr.] does about working out breaks and backup.

From whom?

Raymond Jr.: From Daddy [*laughs*], but I appreciate every one of them!

Let me just touch on the miking and acoustic aspects of your music.

Raymond: We love to work without

mikes if at all possible.

When you use mikes for the banjo, where do you like to have the mike?

Raymond Jr.: I like to have the microphone below my right hand on the head, close to the head because it gets such good tone quality.

Are you very careful about where it is all the time?

Raymond Jr.: Well, I think about it.

Raymond: If it's a shared mike with the mandolins, he'd better not dare get too close or they'll turn it down for sure, and the mandolin won't be heard. In that case, he won't even put the banjo up to the mike.

And to judge that, you'll work off the monitor?

Raymond: You can't count on them because they don't give the same signal that the sound system has. I'd rather have no monitor than false information as to what's going out.

How do you know what's going out? What do you use as a key?

Raymond: You can hear it, of course, around the corner, but you realize when you hear it 'round a corner that you're hearing a distorted thing. We'd rather have no monitors than monitors that will distort our impression of what the people are getting.

Ruth: You've got to have a lot of faith in the people who work the sound system.

Raymond: We finally have given up and have bought our own sound system.

Ruth: Not that we're going to take it everywhere we go!

Where do you put the mike on the mandolins?

Raymond Jr.: I like it on the bottom f-hole, but if the top one's closer to the mike, I put it there.

Ruth: I like it on the bottom f-hole, under my right arm. Raymond plays the mandolin on the vocal mike sometimes.

Raymond: He plays the banjo on the vocal mike sometimes, too. Well, it looks good and also it's off the mike better. The instrumental mike is too soft sometimes; you can sense this and it's easy to swing the instrument up.

How about the guitar? Where do you position the mike?

Raymond: On the fretboard above the hole, but not directly in front of the soundhole because it tends to be booming. It comes off a little cleaner and crisper off the strings than it does out of the hole.

On the bass, do you ever put the mike under the bridge to minimize vibrations?

Ruth: Yes. In the bridge or over the head. I put it in foam rubber or a towel —either in the bridge or the tailpiece.

Raymond: The advantage of that over a stand mike is that she can move the bass more freely. You lose a lot of visual effect when you use mikes.

If you had a choice between the mike in the bridge or that Barcus-Berry pickup, which one would you choose?

Ruth: Probably the mike, because I'm more used to it. We're not quite as familiar with how to set the pickup to make it sound like we really want it.

Raymond: Also, when you're tying into something like that, you're at the mercy of the people more. The more you can fix yourselves by the way you move two mikes, up and back from them, the better it is. You want to give the impression of choreography even if you are locked into standing right in front of the mike. You can turn your head or your body to give a visual spotlight to whoever is having the action at that time; and it's also not only a cue to the audience as to whom to look at, but if you're on TV, it helps the camera to know which way to aim.

Where does all this information come from?

Raymond: It's from experience and noticing and thinking about it. There are all kinds of things that we try to consider.

When is it discussed?

Raymond Jr.: It's most effective when we're challanged with some seemingly impossible situation and we don't know what in the world will make it come off. If we've got 3,000 junior high school students in a room with acoustics like an empty swimming pool and no PA system, we think "Well, we'll pay close attention to our choreography, think carefully about where we're looking to spotlight people, and play softly while we're singing."

Raymond: We don't want to distract the audience with extraneous movement.

Raymond Jr.: If there's a number that involves two or three of us, whoever is not performing will make a point of looking interested. If you use that chance to get back to rosin your bow and talk to the other person or wink at the girl in the second row or whatever, than everybody's going to be looking at you rosining your bow or looking for the girl in the second row or whatever else. But if you're standing there busily interested in what's going on, then everyone else will be interested. We figured, almost calculated, that you can have an extremely successful program if about 60 percent or more of all your factors are right. Above 60 percent, all the better; but you can still have a very successful program at 60 percent. You should have great confidence in your material, your instruments in tune, and good lighting.

If all those things you said are true, the instruments are in tune, the sound is good, the lighting is good, the weather is good, you're feeling good, and the audience is the worst in the world, what happens?

Raymond: Well, they won't stay that way. I'm confident that the material would bring them out of it. You just have to have that bridge, that confidence in your songs.

What if the audience is great and the sound is terrible and you're good?

Raymond Jr.: The audience has to be pleased somehow.

Raymond: If they're not embarrassed to be too few in number. There have to be few enough that they can all see or all hear.

Raymond Jr.: If enough of the things are right, you'll be able to please the audience.

How many shows have you done?

Raymond: I have no idea. Not even for one year, I don't have any idea. We worked through July but we worked hard always.

Have you done 60 a year?

Raymond: We do 60 in a month!

So it's conceivable that you did 2,000 or 3,000 show dates in 11 years?

Raymond Jr.: I'd say many more.

You have apparently gotten it down to where you're not just playing; now it's a very calculated science. You have it down to where you're perfecting your music, you're perfecting the show aspect of your music. It's not just something that you stumble into; it's something that you really work out to be just right, isn't it?

Raymond: I'll tell you where we have not done this — in our bookings. We can only do so much and my wife can only do so much so our bookings have amounted historically, to accepting or turning down what we've been offered. We've done very little seeking of our engagements. We hardly ever write anybody or ask if we can play here and that kind of thing. But much to my surprise, I find other people do it much more aggressively than I, now being a festival promoter. I never realized that there's all kinds of pressure that we've never put on people. People invite us and we go. If we gave this much thought to where we were going to play, even the most prestigious national TV things and so on, why I think we'd do better still. I would like to add that I think it's terribly important for the future of this kind of music to expand — broaden the base of the material — because there are only so many songs from the '40s that only go so far and will only bear so many repetitions by so many bands. It's also important to try to become a songwriter, even if you're not a songwriter — not that your song's necessarily going to be the best —but at least it's different and it's fresh. Today, when we play "Bill Hill," Raymond's new fiddle tune, instead of "Orange Blossom Special," I'm sure there are lots of grateful people. Although "Orange Blossom Special" is comfortable and familiar sounding, it has been done so many times. It's important to have new tunes.

I think once in a while an old tune is needed in the middle of a program so people can relate to something.

Raymond Jr.: Also, if you're going to be a national group or if you're going to be a nightclub entertainer, you have to do exactly the opposite. If you're going to play in clubs, you have to play the most familiar numbers, like "Foggy Mountain Breakdown," because that's what people expect. It just depends on where you play.

Raymond: Each time we perform, we adjust the program, depending on where we're playing. That's the best way to please the audience.

— *Marilyn Kochman*

The current lineup of the McLain Family Band is Raymond W. McLain, Ruth McLain Riopel, Michael Riopel, Raymond K. McLain, Nancy Ann McLain, and Michael McLain. Since the April 1980 publication of this article, the following McLain Family albums have been released: *Concerto For Bluegrass Band And Orchestra* and *In Concert At Carnegie Hall* (Country Life Records [CPO 1322, Berea, KY 40404], CLR-11, and CLR-12) respectively.

A SELECTED McLAIN DISCOGRAPHY

(All albums are on the McLain's own label: Country Life Records, CPO 1322, Berea, KY 40404). *McLain Family Band* [out of print]; *Country Ham* [out of print]; *Country Life*, CLR 4; *On The Road*, CLR 6; *Kentucky Wind*, CLR 7; *Family Album*, CLR 8; *7th Album*, CLR 9.

DAN CRARY

ONCE IN A WHILE, AS Professor Dan Crary walks across California State University's Fullerton campus, a student will stop him to say something like, "Gee, I really enjoyed your concert in LA last month!" Crary's serious, professorial expression will dissolve into a wide grin. "Thanks," he will say warmly. "Thanks very much." And then Crary, still smiling, will stride off to his office to prepare for his next class.

Crary has been a professor of speech communication at Cal State Fullerton for nearly six years, but that isn't why he is occasionally stopped in the street everywhere from Southern California to Tokyo. To put it simply, he moonlights as one of the best flatpicking guitarists in the business today. A founding member of the Bluegrass Alliance in 1968, he was one of the first contemporary bluegrass guitarists to go beyond fill-in runs and straight rhythm accompaniment, stepping up front with blazing breaks that helped to make "flatpicking" and "hot licks" synonymous; and he was also a pioneer in adapting fiddle tunes to the guitar. Today, as a solo performer, he is in demand in Japan, Britain, and continental Europe, as well as on the U.S. festival circuit. He has continued to refine his fluid style, expanding his repertoire with music from other genres; and, as befits a doctor of philosophy (he earned his Ph.D. in speech communication in 1974 at the University of Kansas), he has become something of a philosopher of the flatpicked guitar, offering insights on the state of the art from his forum as a *Frets* Workshop columnist. "Flatpicking is one of the most powerful and versatile approaches to the guitar," he wrote in *Frets'* premier issue in March 1979. "Flatpicking is one of the most interesting styles, because it's relatively new and unexplored. We are on the verge of something very exciting as flatpicking becomes what it is going to be." And Crary himself is playing a key role in that evolution.

Dan Crary was born on September 29, 1939, in Kansas City, Kansas. His family was not strongly musical (he recalls that his mother, who was fond of classical music, "dabbed on the piano a little"); but before he was in kindergarten he began to dream of being a performer. "When I was four or five," he says, "I played by myself some because there weren't a lot of kids in the neighborhood, and I'd play games where I was in a music contest — I think I was playing the flute or something. I don't remember where that came from, but I always envied people up there making music on stage."

When he was five his mother took him to see a recital by famed violinist Fritz Kreisler. It left a vivid impression. "I was knocked out by it," he says, "by the audience's reactions and by all the flourishes of Kreisler performing. It was an experience. I was really excited by the dynamics of that."

Soon afterward, at his parents' behest, he began taking piano lessons, but boredom soon set in. He quit after a year and didn't give any further thought to playing an instrument until he was nearly 11. Intrigued by radio broadcasts of country music and bluegrass, he began paying attention to what the different instruments were doing. By 1952 he had taken particular notice of a guitarist/singer named Don Sullivan, one of many Kansas City musicians then playing live on local radio stations. "He had a D-28 or some big Martin guitar," Dan recalls, "and apparently he had to tune it way down in order to get it to fit the keys he could sing in. That gave it a real ringing, jangling sound. I think that's what first caught my ear. I

Dan Crary at a bluegrass festival in Colorado in 1978. One of the first contemporary bluegrass guitarists to go beyond fill-in runs and straight rhythm accompaniment, stepping up front with blazing breaks that helped to make "flatpicking" and "hot licks" synonymous, Dan Crary has also been a pioneer in adapting fiddle tunes to the guitar.

really liked the sound of his instrument, so I bugged my folks to get me a guitar and let me have some lessons. I wanted to do that because it was something that I discovered on my own, unlike piano. Miraculously, they bought me a guitar — which was amazing in those days, because for years thereafter, I was the only guitar player I knew of besides my teacher."

Crary's first guitar was an arch-top, f-hole Gretsch that his parents bought from Ernest Caudill, a Kansas City guitarist who had some teaching studios. Dan immediately began lessons with Caudill. "He was a good, systematic teacher," Dan says. "Unfortunately, I was a bad, unsystematic student. I learned a lot from him in my first year, but after that I wanted to play a different kind of music than he was interested in. I didn't have the smarts to recognize that I could learn music from him and apply it elsewhere, but that's what you don't understand when you're 14 years old. Still, I was really lucky to have someone like that as a teacher, because he taught me to respect the instrument. He taught me to think of it as something of intrinsic worth and beauty — something really important. That came through."

A year or so later Dan made his public debut, playing "The Ballad Of Thunderhead" — from a Burl Ives songbook — in a talent show at Kansas City's Granada Theater. He won a baseball glove. ("In all honesty," Crary says, "everybody won

something.") Having thus broken into show business, he began playing in volunteer shows sponsored by different local organizations — entertaining at hospitals, orphanages, and retirement homes in the winter, then playing at city parks in the summer. "There were acts like little girl tap dancers who had grown out of their costumes years before, yet were still doing it," he says. "All of that silliness. But people enjoyed the shows, and all of us doing the shows learned something from it, so it was really a good thing."

In the meantime he had forsaken his f-hole Gretsch for a "fairly cheap but nice-sounding Kay flat-top." He was content with the Kay until he saw some country guitarists with Gibson J-200s. "I wasn't very discriminating about tone then," Dan recalls, "but I knew those guitars *looked* impressive — and anything that looked impressive had to sound good! About 1954 or 1955 my family got the money scraped together to buy me a J-200, and I still have it. It's a lovely guitar, but it's not a bluegrass guitar."

Crary graduated from high school in 1957 and went to Chicago to attend the Moody Bible Institute, intending to study theology and eventually enter the ministry. In Chicago he found a growing interest in traditional music, with artists like Pete Seeger and the Weavers passing through town. Dan took a few lessons on traditional banjo and attended some hootenannies;

but because the Moody Bible Institute frowned on its students patronizing such establishments as nightclubs, he remained on the fringes of the folk movement there.

"I still wasn't performing," he says, "although I played guitar for some parties and stuff like that. I guess I was getting geared up to perform, because I remember working on arrangements of songs. It wasn't long after I left Chicago, in 1960, that I started looking for places to play and make some money."

After leaving Chicago, Dan became a "school fanatic." He spent the next 14 years working on various degrees. His academic quest led him to some places that, in different ways, proved important in his development as a musician. His first stop was Lawrence, Kansas, southwest of Kansas City. While working on his basic bachelor of arts degree at the University of Kansas, he began playing in a folk trio called the Carltons, getting a limited taste of lead work. "I was playing breaks on some songs," he says. "I did sort of a modified Carter family flatpicking thing, which I thought was terribly impressive; but in a word, it wasn't." In Lawrence, Dan also met his wife, Delores. They were married in 1962.

In 1965 the Crarys headed west for San Francisco, where Dan enrolled in Golden Gate Seminary to pursue a degree in theology. He supported his studies by teaching guitar at a music store near the Bay, Marina Music, and by playing occasional coffeehouse gigs as a solo act. His stay in San Francisco coincided with the full bloom of Flower Power and the birth of the psychedelic San Francisco sound; but Dan took little notice of it all. "Just like Chicago, a whole music thing was happening down the street, but it sort of bypassed me," he says. "I lived five blocks from Haight-Ashbury [the intersection that was the geographical center of the hippie movement], but I had my nose so much into my own problems that I managed not to get into it very much. That seems to be a pattern — I wonder what I'm missing now! But most of the people at Marina Music were playing acoustic music of one kind or another, and that was a little esoteric — not directly related to the San Francisco rock and roll thing that was going down."

Five years later and with his theology degree from Golden Gate Seminary in hand, Dan moved to Louisville, Kentucky, to pursue a doctorate in theology at Southern Seminary. Gifted with a deep, resonant speaking voice, he had begun doing part-time work in radio as early as 1958. ("Usually it was vacation relief and weekends," Crary says, "but through 1974 I jocked every kind of music from classical to country to bluegrass — everything except rock and roll.") At Louisville's WINN, a commercial/country station, he landed a job that helped him underwrite his academic work and also gave him access to a variety of music.

"Hanging around a Louisville music store, I met some people who were interested in bluegrass," Dan recalls. "You know how that happens — one acquaintance leads to another, you go to a pickin' party, and so on. Well, a gig came up — a chance to perform with these people. I was in school and was working full time at the station, and didn't think I could do it. But the more I talked to them about it, the more I found myself thinking, 'I cannot allow this to go by without getting in on it myself.' So we put a band together, a very unlikely band, some of the members of which had scarcely even played the instruments they were supposed to be playing."

That makeshift band was the Bluegrass Alliance. Besides Crary, the group included guitarist/singer Wayne Stewart, banjo player Buddy Spurlock, fiddler Lonnie Peerce, and bass player Ebo Walker. "Lonnie had been playing country and bluegrass for many years," Dan says, "Neither Ebo or I knew that much about playing bluegrass, so the rest of them had to tell us what to do — and convince us that what we thought was wonderful really wasn't so wonderful."

The Alliance got its first steady gig at a Louisville bar near the river, the Red Dog Saloon, playing between two and five nights a week. Stewart, who had become the group's mandolinist, left the Alliance early to form Poor Richard's Almanac with an old friend, mandolinist Sam Bush, and with banjo player Alan Munde. Stewart's replacement was mandolinist/singer Danny Jones. The Alliance worked the Red Dog Saloon for a year and a half, learning the finer points of performance and showmanship on the job. Crary, with his diverse radio background, provided a progressive influence on the band's musical direction, and its material expanded beyond the standard bluegrass repertoire.

In 1969 the Bluegrass Alliance left the Red Dog Saloon for the stage of Carlton Haney's Camp Springs, North Carolina, bluegrass festival. The band found itself sharing the bill with such heavyweight acts as the Osborne Brothers, Ralph Stanley, the Country Gentlemen, Bill Monroe, and Don Reno. There was an undercurrent of tension at the festival over the presence of amplified instruments, a first in some groups (such as the Osborne Brothers), but the all-acoustic Alliance caused a stir for a different reason.

"We raised a few eyebrows, and I think we created some interest," Crary recalls. "Not because we were so wonderful, but because we were doing things that not many other young groups were doing. People were real interested in the fact that I was playing some lead guitar breaks — not because it hadn't been done before and better, which it had, but because this was a time when lead guitar playing in bluegrass had kind of subsided and not much of anybody was doing it. Doc Watson was appearing at some of these festivals, with his son Merle, but he was essentially a solo act. In

the context of a band, it was not the usual thing for the guitar player to stand up and take a break. That helped to make us interesting; plus, we were doing some unconventional material. We looked for songs in rock and roll, pop music, Bob Dylan stuff, and whatever other sources we could think of. Obviously we were not the first to do that; the Country Gentlemen, for example, had been doing it for years. But at the time, even that had subsided a little bit. I really think that anything's appropriate within a certain style as long as it sounds good. We got away with it partly because we mixed in some straight bluegrass stuff and because we were playing acoustic instruments. The real tension then was over electric instruments and drums."

The Alliance worked another festival that season, playing at Callaway, Maryland. The appearances and the band's growing popularity led to a recording contract and their first album. *The Bluegrass Alliance,* on American Heritage, got a warm reception that included top honors in a readers' poll conducted by *Bluegrass Unlimited* magazine. The album's success paved the way for two more American Heritage discs in 1970: the Alliance's second album, *Newgrass*; and Crary's first solo album of instrumentals, *Bluegrass Guitar*. But by the time the records were released, Crary was gone.

Skeptical about the possibilities of making a living in music, and with his wife expecting their first child, Dan decided he would be better off teaching. "I had intended to teach in theology," he explains, "but the job market was bad so I immedi-

ately thought of a field that I had a secondary interest in. I had done a major in speech communication as an undergraduate, and I found myself with a last-minute chance to get into the doctoral program in that field at the University of Kansas. So I made a snap decision. I had all my graduate work in theology, but I had to go back to the master's level at Kansas. It took me four years to get my Ph.D. But I figured I'd been in school 90 percent of my life — why not continue?"

The Crarys' first daughter, Jenny, was born at Lawrence in 1970. Their second daughter, Julie, arrived the following year. At first, academic and family responsibilities limited Dan's performing, but toward the end of his studies at Lawrence he began playing more and traveling to festivals around the country. It was at a 1974 festival in Canada that he met fiddler Byron Berline — a veteran of Bill Monroe's Bluegrass Boys, an ex-Flying Burrito Brother, a member of Country Gazette, and already a successful Hollywood studio musician. By that time, Dan had accepted a teaching

post at Cal State Fullerton. He told Berline he was going to move to Southern California soon, and Berline, who had been favorably impressed by the flatpicked versions of fiddle tunes on *Bluegrass Guitar,* invited Dan to drop by some time for a little picking. It wasn't long before Crary took Berline up on the invitation.

"When I finished my degree at Kansas, I started looking around for jobs," Dan says. "I had completed everything but my dissertation, and when you're in that situation and you get a decent job offer, you don't question what part of the world it's in. You take it. There was an opening at Fullerton and they liked my papers, so I went. In the Midwest, Southern California doesn't get very good press, but it's turned out to be a good place to live. I work with some fine people at the school, and the LA area is a great place for a musician to be."

Casual playing with Berline led to the formation of a new group, Sundance, with banjo player John Hickman, bass player Jack Skinner, and rhythm guitarist Allen Wald. In 1976 the band was signed by MCA for a recording date that produced the album *Byron Berline And Sundance.* The record laid the foundation for a partnership — both business and musical — between Berline, Crary, and Hickman, that is still active. Recently, BCH Productions expanded its activities into producing records for other groups.

Crary also made his first tour abroad in 1976, engaged by Tokyo businessman/musician/promoter Robert Tainaka to perform in Japan. Tainaka and Crary happened to meet at McCabe's, a nightclub-cum-music-store in Santa Monica, California, when Tainaka was on his way to Tokyo with Doc Watson. Crary has been making regular trips to Japan ever since. On his arrival in Tokyo, Dan discovered that his reputation — through *Bluegrass Guitar* — had preceded him. "I found out that there were two coffeehouses and one bluegrass band named after the "Devil's Dream" cut on that album," he says. "Everywhere in Japan I found I had friends I didn't even know about, all because of the record. I had no idea. I would be walking the streets of Tokyo and people would come up and introduce themselves to me. It was a fabulous experience."

Crary began work on his second album late in 1976, recording half of the cuts with Sam Bush and members of Bush's New Grass Revival. The recording was completed in early 1977, with Berline, Hickman, and other members of Sundance assisting on the second half. The completed, all-instrumental *Lady's Fancy,* with three original tunes, was released in mid-1977 on the Rounder label. Sundance's second — and final — album, *Live at McCabe's,* came out on Takoma the same year.

In 1978 Dan made his European debut, playing a summer tour of England and Ireland. He returned in 1979 on a tour highlighted by major festival appearances in

Ireland and Switzerland. His experiences in Ireland gave him a taste for Irish music that has since become a consuming interest. That interest is reflected in one cut, the traditional Irish tune "The Blackbird," on his most recent album, *Sweet Southern Girl,* which was released late last year on Sugar Hill. *Sweet Southern Girl,* with two original tunes, also carries his first solo Dan Crary vocal tracks — and not just a few. Nine of the twelve cuts are vocals, a departure from his previous albums that has put Crary back in the eyebrow-raising business, at least among fans who had thought of him as an instrumentalist and nothing but. When people suggest that he is breaking new ground, he replies quietly that he simply recorded the kind of material he has been doing since his first folk-era coffeehouse gigs.

"It's nothing new," he says. "That's what I've always done, for the most part. I did the album that way because I wanted to do something more in keeping with what I do when people come to see me perform. I'm still interested in bluegrass and I still work with some of the hot bluegrass musicians in Southern California when I have a chance to. But I'm very interested in the guitarist/singer approach — people like Jose Feliciano in this country; and in Europe, Paul Brady, an incredible guitarist/singer from Ireland; and equally incredible, Dick Gaughan, a Scot who is a fabulous guitar player and may be the greatest traditional singer in the world. And again, in this country you think of Doc Watson and Norman Blake. I give a lot of attention to the guitar happening as a separate musical thing with the vocals, providing harmonies and little fill lines — whatever comes to mind — as well as playing breaks between verses. I try to explore some harmony playing, some parallel lines, some colorings and phrasings that are more than just strumming a chord. People are not used to listening to two things at once, and it's hard to sing on tune and simultaneously play something parallel but independent; but I'm always pleased when somebody notices that there were two things going on at once and says something about it. I'm interested in the dynamics that come out of one instrument, one singer. To me, it's a fascinating challenge — and I think it's a natural direction for a guitarist/singer to take."

WITH SO LITTLE *acoustic lead guitar playing going on back in the early '60s when you began developing your style, what or who did you look toward for ideas?*

Well, by that time I had discovered some of the main bluegrass pickers, and I had discovered Flatt And Scruggs. I could not miss some of the lovely guitar work that Earl Scruggs was doing on their gospel stuff and on songs like "Jimmy Brown The News Boy." Their version of that song was one of the first guitar records I heard that just blew my hat in the creek — it just sent me reeling and staggering. Flatt And Scruggs essentially played two guitars on it. Flatt played the rhythm and Scruggs played the lead with fingerpicks. It was incredible, and beautifully recorded, too, for having been done in what must have been the early or mid-'50s.

Were you copying licks off records at that point?

No, I wasn't. In fact, I've almost never done that — which isn't something I brag about, because I think it's actually a good idea. The result of just coming up with all this stuff on my own — and I've taken very few licks off anybody else — was that it took me 15 years to learn what I should have been able to learn in two or three, easy. By the time I seriously got into performing and playing bluegrass in the late '60s, man, I'd been going for years and it was almost like I was just beginning to play.

You indicated that starting to play with the Bluegrass Alliance was a rude awakening for you in a few ways. How did that experience change your approach to bluegrass guitar?

Working with these other musicians made it abundantly clear to me that I didn't know what the hell I was doing! So there was a certain amount of pain in response to their pressure: I had to make some adjustments. For example, I was flatpicking using a very lightweight pick, playing way back by the bridge on my Gibson J-200, and the sound was just all wrong for bluegrass. I didn't think so, of course, but *they* thought so, and gradually I came to see what they were talking about. So I got a different guitar — a Martin D-28 — and started holding the pick differently, going for a different kind of sound.

Besides changing your technique, how did working with the Alliance affect your musical directions?

Various people brought different ideas to the group. I guess I was one of the more progressive influences, ultimately. Lonnie Peerce and Danny Jones both knew a lot of the old songs, and we learned those. One of the main things Lonnie Peerce did for me, for which I will always be grateful, was to make me get interested in fiddle music. I was really ignorant of it, and he got out his fiddle and stuck my nose down it and said, "Here, listen to this." Finally it began to soak in. I'd always been interested in banjo and guitar mainly, mandolin a little, but not much fiddle at all. That was dumb of me, of course. He started playing tunes like "Forky Deer" and "The Dusty Miller," and I suddenly began to realize, "Here's some real heavy-duty music happening!" He

taught me a lot about what kind of music was available for the fiddle, and that there was a whole world of music out there that I was not hearing in standard bluegrass instrumentals. It provided at least one direction for my playing that has been very influential.

Did your initiation into fiddle music awaken your interest in Irish tunes?

Actually, I'm just starting to learn Irish music and trying to figure out how to play it on the guitar. "Blackbird," on *Sweet Southern Girl,* was really a first attempt to do that, and not altogether successful. I think it's a nice cut and everything, but there are some subtleties about approaching Irish traditional tunes that have eluded me thus far. I'm working on it. I have high hopes of eventually doing an album of Irish tunes, and I want to use some honest-to-God live Irish musicians. I want to use pipes, fiddle, bodhran [an Irish drum], and the whole shot.

You switched to a Martin D-28 when the Bluegrass Alliance got started; when did you begin using the Stuart Mossman dreadnoughts you play today?

Well, in 1970 Mossman was starting to make guitars. He came up to me at the Camp Springs, North Carolina, festival that fall, showed me some of his stuff, and I got interested in it and we got friendly. Over the years he started making a first-quality guitar, and I was interested enough to start playing one. I felt that his new guitars sounded closest to what I think is just about the optimum guitar for the music I do, which up to the time had been a mid-'50s D-28. The current Mossman Great Plains model I play exceeds my '56 D-28, which I think very highly of. I would rather travel with a new guitar just because it's easier; the finish is more intact, it will take more of a beating, and if it gets lost you can replace it. But in the case of the guitar I'm playing right now, I have never owned a guitar that is equal to it, and it's less than two years old.

How did you cultivate the smooth, flowing quality of your flatpicking?

Somebody once said, about artists in general, that the essence of artistry is to make something difficult look easy. That's one of my goals, but I don't know whether I do that or not — I guess that's for somebody else to decide. Music is a struggle. It's a struggle against the musician's own inadequacies and against the natural barriers that the instrument throws up. Somebody who's winning the struggle will have an effortless quality about what they're doing, so that's what I try to achieve. Sometimes it works, and sometimes you have nights

when the guitar wins, or when entropy wins.

What advice do you have for aspiring flatpickers who want to become professional musicians?

There are an awful lot of very good guitar players in the world right now; but being good is really only your basic point of departure. A lot of them aren't successful professionally, because while they put in a lot of time and effort getting good on the instrument, they never gave any thought to how to make themselves commercially viable. It's true of flatpickers, in particular. These days a lot of really hot flatpickers are getting dismayed at the realization that the world is not rewarding them for being hot flatpickers. There isn't a market for that. What we're talking about is getting somebody to pay you money for your music. So what are people paying money for? They're paying for the kinds of acts you see in nightclubs, the sorts of things you hear on records, and the sorts of things you hear in concerts. That means either guitarist/singers, or guitarist/singer/songwriters, or guitarists who are part of an ensemble — or the very rare kind of guitarist, like Leo Kottke, who can do solo things with a special, unusual style. You have to use being a good musician as a starting point, then make yourself flexible in terms of working in a band, playing accompaniment, or doing something interesting that no one else has thought of. And I don't know if I'm a great example of how a person should be commercially successful, because I'm still hustling to do better. But I feel I know the music business, and I think it's true that the world is not just waiting for another hot guitar player to come along. You have to figure out how to adapt yourself to what people are buying — and when you've done that, then also find a way of being yourself. That's the best advice I have.

— Jim Hatlo

In the late '70s, Dan Crary, along with fiddler Byron Berline and banjoist John Hickman, formed the ensemble Berline, Crary, & Hickman. The band began almost by accident. The three pickers were invited to play a gig in Japan, and there was only enough money to pay them — not their respective bands. The trio played so well together, they decided to remain a performing entity. To date, they have one LP, *Berline, Crary, Hickman* (Sugar Hill [Box 4040, Duke Station, Durham, NC 27706] SH-3720.

A SELECTED CRARY DISCOGRAPHY

Solo Albums: *Bluegrass Guitar,* American Heritage (1208 Everett St., Caldwell, ID 83605), 275; *Lady's Fancy,* Rounder (One Camp St., Cambridge, MA 02140), 0099; *Sweet Southern Girl,* Sugar Hill (Box 4040, Duke Station, Durham, NC 27706), SH-3707. **With the Bluegrass Alliance:** *The Bluegrass Alliance,* American Heritage, LP-21S; *Newgrass,* American Heritage, 10-305. **With Byron Berline:** *Dad's Favorites,* Rounder, 0100. **With John Hickman:** *Don't Mean Maybe,* Rounder, 0101. **With Sundance:** *Byron Berline and Sundance,* MCA, 2217; *Live At McCabe's,* Takoma (Box 5369, Santa Monica, CA 90405), D-106L.

BYRON BERLINE

WHEN ANY OF several dozen (at least) record producers, film score arrangers, or session contractors want the ultimate in heavy-duty fiddle power, or someone to put together a first-class country string section, the first thing they do is dial a number in Van Nuys, California. The phone belongs to Byron Berline. And if Byron isn't on the road or working with any of the three bands of which he currently is a central member, he'll usually give them exactly what they need.

For more than a decade, Byron has been the fiddle kingpin of the LA studio scene. A complete list of people with whom he's recorded, the film scores he's played on, and the bands he's been in would reach longer than all the hairs of a fiddle bow tied end-to-end, but among his credits are gigs with Bob Dylan, David Bromberg, Henry Mancini, Bill Monroe And The Blue Grass Boys, Olivia Newton-John, the Flying Burrito Brothers, Linda Ronstadt, the Dillards, Jerry Reed, and even the Rolling Stones. And for the last three years, sandwiched between performing and session work, he's found time to contribute a regular fiddle column to *Frets*.

It sounds as though Byron always has a fiddle in his hands, and that's pretty close to the truth. Born in Oklahoma in 1944 and brought up in north Texas just across the state line, he doesn't remember a time when he wasn't fiddling. "My dad was an old-time fiddle player," he says, "and I remember the first time I played. I was standing at my dad's knees, and he put the fiddle around in front of me and put the bow up there and put my hand on it. That's how I started."

The Berlines were a musical family, and Byron's father wasted no time in getting the youngster started. "The first thing he did was to get me a small, half-size fiddle," Byron recalls. "Then he taught me the basic scale. I still think that's very important for people who are just learning to play."

Though his father literally brought him up on fiddling, Byron never studied the instrument formally. "I wanted to [take lessons] when I was going to go to high school — I thought that would be a chance for me to get in the orchestra and learn more about music," he says. "Then they dropped orchestra the year I went. But I did learn to play sousaphone in the marching band. I wanted to play trombone —my brother played great trombone — but the director said, 'You're a big guy; you can hold the sousaphone and walk around with it, and just *look* like you're playing it until you learn how.' So I got stuck with that."

He learned to read music for the sousaphone, but it didn't make a lasting impression. He forgot those skills, and today doesn't read music notation at all. (His wife Bette, a former music major who has an MA in piano, is a handy consultant whenever he needs one.)

Though Byron performed with his father on a number of occasions, he never played fiddle in a band until he enrolled at the University of Oklahoma in 1962. "I went there on a football scholarship —broke my right thumb in my freshman year, couldn't play the fiddle for about six weeks, and that made me start thinking," says Byron. "My dad had always told me, 'Hey, if you're going to play that football, you're going to hurt your fingers.' I'd been a javelin thrower in high school, and the track coach at OU said, 'Come over and throw the javelin for the track team and forget football.' So I said, 'Great. You got a deal.' And that gave me more time for

music. About then the folk music boom was real big, '62 and '63, and they were going to have a big folk music hootenanny show on TV. So I got together with a couple of other guys — one of them was [country singer/guitarist] Bill Caswell — and we did 'Cripple Creek,' as a bluegrass group. It was crude, but it was okay — I didn't even know what bluegrass was then. We just stayed together. That group was called the Cleveland County Ramblers. We played that whole year and part of next year, doing a lot of fraternity parties and all kinds of stuff.

"Then finally, the Dillards came to town — that was in '63. Man, they were so hot! I got to meet them and jam with them. I'll never forget it. It was the day [John F.] Kennedy was killed, and it wasn't even certain that the show would go on. But it did, and that started a lot of things for me."

The Dillards were as impressed with Byron as he was with them, and when it came time to record their next album, they enlisted his services. The young collegian made his recording debut on their *Pickin' And Fiddlin'* LP.

Meanwhile, he met a banjo player named Ed Shelton, and the two formed the nucleus of a band that began working on a weekly TV show sponsored by an Okla-

homa City furniture store. While thus employed, Byron ran into a new undergraduate at OU who also had musical aspirations.

"When I first saw Alan Munde," Byron recalls, "he was playing some of the stuff off that album I made with the Dillards, even though it had only been out a short time. He was only like 18 or 19, starting to play the banjo, and he was so nervous when he was playing in front of somebody that I don't know how he kept his hands on the banjo. But immediately I could tell that he had something going for him, the way he attacked the instrument."

Byron introduced Alan to Ed Shelton, who helped Munde begin developing the chops that are among the most respected in the world today. Byron and Alan started playing together, often jamming for hours at a time, and formed a group they called the Oklahoma Bluegrass Gentlemen. That band rounded out Byron's extra-curricular collegiate musical career. He had another job waiting for him as soon as he got his bachelor's degree (in physical education) in early 1967 with Bill Monroe And The Blue Grass Boys.

Byron had met Monroe in Rhode Island at the 1965 Newport Folk Festival where Byron and his father had been invited to appear by eminent folklorist and musicolo-

gist Ralph Rinzler. Rinzler was introduced to Berline's fiddling when he penned the liner notes to the Dillards' *Pickin' And Fiddlin'* LP. Following what was to become a very familiar pattern, he was impressed.

"*Everybody* was at Newport," says Byron. "Bill Monroe. Bob Dylan. Joan Baez. I'd never been anywhere before, and it was something else." By the time he went home, he had an invitation from Monroe to come play with the Blue Grass Boys as soon as he graduated from college.

After taking off his cap and gown, Byron called Monroe, who confirmed the invitation. Berline met him in Nashville at the Grand Ole Opry, and a few weeks later Monroe made it official. Byron succeeded Richard Greene in the Blue Grass Boys lineup and stayed with the group from March through September — when Uncle Sam called Byron's number.

Byron spent a year and nine months in the army, finding himself stationed at Fort Polk, Louisiana as a musician in Special Services. It turned out the commanding officer loved bluegrass, and one of Byron's assignments involved staging a bluegrass festival. He had no trouble in securing Monroe as the headlining act, which impressed his fellow GI's no end.

The day Byron mustered out of the

Army in 1969, he got a phone call from Doug Dillard, who had left the Dillards to form the Dillard & Clark band with ex-Byrd Gene Clark. The group was cutting its second album, and Doug wanted Byron to come to Los Angeles to play on it. Byron accepted. He little realized what was in store for him.

LA had a lot in those days, but one thing it didn't have was fiddlers. Hollywood latched on to Byron like thirsty men latching on to the lone beer vendor at a midsummer baseball game. The word traveled fast, and in the space of four days Byron not only did the Dillard & Clark tracks but did several other sessions and a film soundtrack as well. He went home dazzled. "I told my wife, 'Look, Bette — we're going to California!' It was the best move I ever made."

John McEuen remembers the kind of impact Berline had when he hit LA. "The Dirt Band was recording its *Uncle Charlie And His Dog Teddy* album [Liberty, 7642]," McEuen says, "and we got Byron to come in and do some overdubs for us because at the time my fiddle playing wasn't quite adequate. Byron was kind of new in town; but that was when I realized how good some natural musicians are. Myself, I'd never put in a couple of years as a bar band player, doing stuff like Top 40 and country. I'd only worked with groups where we did songs we'd learned or songs that had been written by friends. But Byron had done a little bit of everything. When we called him in, he sat down and said something like, 'Now, if I can get this thang in tune, I'll try and lay down something y'all like.' Then, bang! He had it on the first take. 'That all right?' He didn't use charts — it was nothing like the approach that the LA musicians took. We just looked at him, glassy-eyed, and kind of said, 'Er, uh, yeah. Yeah. You, uh, got time for another tune?'"

While session followed session, Dillard & Clark stayed on with part of the band. When Clark departed, Berline stayed on with Dillard. A stint with the Flying Burrito Brothers came next, ultimately reuniting Berline and Munde, and from that liaison emerged the Country Gazette. Byron had been working on a record deal that bore fruit in a pact between the Gazette and United Artists, and in 1972 the new band was on its way. Byron remained with it until 1975.

Through the LA music circles Byron had met former Bluegrass Alliance guitarist Dan Crary, who was a professor of speech communications at a Southern California university. Some jamming parties with mutual friends provided the catalyst for the creation of the band Sundance, with John Hickman on banjo, Allen Wald on vocals and second guitar, and Jack Skinner on bass. An MCA record deal solidified the enterprise, leading to the release of *Byron Berline And Sundance* in 1976. That first incarnation of the band soon expired and the chemistry between Byron, Hickman,

and Crary produced a musical and business alliance that continues to this day. As producers, they've directed several successful LPs by different groups, and, as the trio of Berline, Crary, & Hickman, they had their best year ever in 1981 performing to rave reviews on the national festival circuit and concurrently releasing the critically acclaimed Sugar Hill album *Berline, Crary, & Hickman*.

Of course, Byron isn't one to drop all his musical eggs into a single basket. For three years he's also been hatching interesting ideas with the LA Fiddle Band, which teams him with fiddlers Bruce Johnson and Dennis Fetchitt, aided by Hickman, guitarist Roger Reed, dobro artist Skip Conover, and bassist Dennis Reed. "It started out with us just having fun, jamming at each others' houses," Byron says. "Then we finally worked up some tunes and put a band together. We played McCabe's [music store and night club] here in Santa Monica, the gig was recorded live, and we sold the tape to Sugar Hill [for the 1980 release *Byron Berline And The LA Fiddle Band*]. We're still going."

OPPOSITE: *Part of the original Country Gazette, Byron Berline and Roland White both play fiddle and guitar at a 1974 concert in Wisconsin.* **BELOW:** *Byron Berline and Sundance in 1976: Dan Crary, John Hickman, Byron Berline, Jack Skinner, and Allen Wald. The first three members currently perform as a trio.*

Also going is a recently resurrected and reorganized Sundance, now with Conover on dobro and lap steel, Rick Cunha — a recording artist in his own right — on guitar, Steve Spurgin on drums, Don Whaley on electric bass, and Pete Wasner on piano. "It's the most fun group I think I've ever played in," says Byron.

"We have four lead singers. They're all great musicians. They all write, and they're absolutely wonderful."

The versatility of Sundance allows Byron to shift occasionally from fiddle to mandolin, an instrument he began working on while he was first with Doug Dillard — though much of his inspiration dates back to the days with Bill Monroe. "Learning mandolin helped my fiddling," he says, "especially on things like double stops. I can write things on the mandolin sometimes, just sitting around, that I can take right to the fiddle."

Byron also can play guitar, but he seldom does so. "I don't need to," he says, "because I work with people like Dan Crary."

If you live outside of southern California, you aren't likely to see Byron playing anything but fiddle. To see him with Sundance or the LA Fiddle Band, you have to come to LA. "I can't afford to take Sundance and the Fiddle Band on the road," he says, "because there are too many people in each of them. You've got to be realistic. To take a band on the road, you have to be making a lot of money."

The fiddle, of course, is his bread and butter in studio work. "I probably do two or three sessions a week," he says. "There's always something coming up."

Since he can't really read music, just how does he get by when he's confronted with studio charts?

"It depends on the difficulty of the tune," Byron explains. "I read all the bars in the chord charts, and I know enough music to follow timing and chord changes and that kind of stuff," he says. "If I go into a situation where something is written out and they definitely want those exact notes, I'll have someone play it on piano, and I'll write the [names of the] notes over the music. If there's time. But I let producers know that I really don't read well enough to go in and sit in a string section. I suppose if I was going to

be *strictly* a studio musician, I'd have to learn how to read."

Byron uses his *Frets* column as a regular channel to get advice on a variety of subjects across to aspiring fiddlers, but underlying his instructional columns is a basic belief that you learn best by drawing on the expertise of people who already know things you want to learn.

"Get around as many fiddlers as you can and see what's going on," he advises. "See what people are playing. Learn as many tunes as you can, getting the basics, and don't try to rush it. Try not to go for speed at first. A lot of young fiddlers try to play real fast and just slop over the notes. If you want to be a good fiddler, get the notes down before you try for speed.

You'll be a better player for it."

THEY SAY THAT A truly great fiddler can make good music just by drawing a horse's tail over a wire fence. But any professional worth his salt, particularly a picker as salty as Byron Berline, is going to have some definite opinions about what instruments and equipment work best for him. And those opinions are going to be reflected in the kind of gear he carries on stage or into the studio.

Byron performs with both 4-string and 5-string fiddles. We asked him to give us an inside look at what he plays, and why and how he plays it.

What kind of fiddle is your 4-string?

That's a copy of a Guarnerius; probably a German copy, I would imagine. I don't really know. It's just one that my dad had, and I really liked the sound of it. On the 5-string, the guy who made the [5-string conversion] neck, he figured it was made in Austria — real old, probably over 200 years.

Aren't you afraid that's a lot of tension on the body?

Yeah, it is; the body's real thin, and it has a real deep tone anyway, and it's starting to give way a little bit. But I like it a lot.

On your 5-string fiddle, do you use any variant tunings?

Yeah, for instance I'll tune the high *E* down to *D*, leave the *A* and *D* alone, then

tune the *G* up to *A* and the low *C* up to *D*.

What kind of strings do you use on the 5-string fiddle?

They're Thomastik mediums, with a viola string for the low *C*. I use the same kind of Thomastik strings for 4-string fiddle.

Both your fiddles are set up for amplification with Barcus-Berry transducer bridge pickups; but don't you sometimes play straight into the mike?

When everyone else is playing acoustic, I don't like to go direct into the sound system through the pickup. If you go direct you have to really depend on the man working the system. Playing acoustic, I can work the mike. See, I've got French bridges on the fiddles, real hard ones, not the regular Barcus-Berry bridges.

When do you use the pickups — when you play electric?

Yeah, when I play with the Sundance band.

When you are playing acoustic, where do you like to place your microphone in relation to the instrument?

Oh, I like to come down on top of the fiddle so the sound of the fiddle will come up to the mike. And usually I like it around the bridge area, maybe behind the bridge a little. About in the middle, if I can get it — not too much on the bass side or the treble side.

When you're playing into a mike, are you then listening to the fiddle, or are you listening to yourself in the monitor?

Well, it depends on what's in your ear. If the monitor's right there, you can't help but hear that. And you have to work the mike and the fiddle together — you have to know what's coming out. That's a good question; I never thought about it that much before. But I think you listen to what's coming out and try to adjust to that. Naturally I want to get as good a tone as possible, but a lot of times you can't get it.

You use regular horsehair on your bows; what kind of rosin do you use? Do you apply it heavily?

Hill rosin. I don't put it on heavy. I used to. It depends on the weather; if you use too much, it really crystallizes the hair. There's nothing you can do if you put too much on, except play it off a little.

— *Roger H. Siminoff*

A SELECTED BERLINE DISCOGRAPHY

Solo Albums: *Outrageous,* Flying Fish (1304 W. Schubert, Chicago, IL 60614), FF-227; *Dad's Favorites,* Rounder (One Camp St., Cambridge, MA 02140), 0100. **With Dan Crary and John Hickman:** *Berline/Crary/Hickman,* Sugar Hill (Box 4040, Duke Station, Durham, NC 27706), SH-3720; *Lady's Fancy,* Rounder, 0099; *Sweet Southern Girl,* Sugar Hill, SH-3707; *Don't Mean Maybe,* Rounder, 0101. **With Sundance:** *Byron Berline And Sundance,* MCA, 2217; *Live At McCabe's,* Takoma (Box 6359, Santa Monica, CA 90405), D-106L. **With The LA Fiddle Band:** *Byron Berline And The LA Fiddle Band,* Sugar Hill, SH-3716. **With Doug Dillard:** *Jackrabbit!,* Flying Fish, FF-208; *Gospel Album,* Flying Fish, FF-086. **With the Dillards:** *Pickin' And Fiddlin',* Elektra, EKS 7285; *Copperfields,* Elektra, EKS 74054; *Duelin' Banjos,* 20th Century, T409. **With others:** *Burrito Deluxe,* A&M, 4258; *Lone Star,* Rabbit (Box 25038, Chicago, IL 60625), RS-8001; *Urban Cowboy,* Asylum, DP-90002.

3.
THE
ECLECTICS

DOC WATSON

NEARLY TWENTY YEARS have passed since three young folk singers dubbed the Kingston Trio polished up a collection of traditional American folk tunes and sparked what has become known as the urban folk revival of the '60s. The success of their albums not only spawned hundreds of crew-cut imitators but, more important, caused thousands of fans to seek out the roots of the music they were hearing performed. As a result, the general public was introduced to the brilliance of artists like Pete Seeger, Dock Boggs, Jean Ritchie, Clarence Ashley, and Maybelle Carter, among others. Through records and the resurgence of the hootenanny, many American young people were influenced to buy their first guitars, banjos, dulcimers, or autoharps.

Probably the most influential and commercially enduring instrumentalist to emerge from this folk revival was a blind singer/guitarist from Deep Gap, North Carolina: Arthel "Doc" Watson. Doc was not only a compelling vocalist with a rich baritone and a vast repertoire of Blue Ridge Mountain music, but a true virtuoso of the flatpicked acoustic guitar.

The effect Doc had on guitarists was immediate. Prior to his appearance, the vast majority of budding folk guitarists were content to assume the traditional role of vocal accompaniment and rhythmic backup. When Doc exploded on the scene, flatpicking the lead to fiddle tunes at blazing speed, the fallout was immediate. Gifted young guitarists Clarence White of the Kentucky Colonels and John Herald of the Greenbriar Boys were among the most important of those immediately affected. Doc's genius established once and for all the validity of the flatpicked acoustic guitar as a lead instrument.

Arthel Watson's story begins on March 3, 1923. One of nine children of Annie Watson and General Dixon Watson, he contracted an eye disease as an infant that left him blind before he was two years old. Hymns he heard sitting on his mother's lap in church and the old-time ballads she sang around the house formed some of his first memories of music. His father was also a singer, and something of a banjo picker, and led the family every night in Bible reading and hymn singing.

Doc got his first musical instrument, a harmonica, at an early age and thereafter received a new one each Christmas. Before long he had strung a single steel wire to the woodshed's sliding door and tuned it to his harmonica so he could provide his own bass accompaniment while he played.

When Doc was seven the musical world began to open up for him. His father bought a table model Victrola from an uncle, and included in the purchase were a stack of recordings by such groups as Gid Tanner and the Skillet Lickers, the Carolina Tar Heels, and the Carter Family. The collection soon grew to include recordings by Jimmie Rodgers, Riley Puckett, and Mississippi John Hurt.

Because of his blindness and his family's poverty, Doc did not start school until he was ten. His parents sent him to North Carolina's School for the Blind in Raleigh. When he came home the following summer his father offered to build him a banjo. Doc accepted and took to the new instrument immediately, learning to frail several tunes.

A couple of years later, when he was 12, Doc heard a classmate playing a guitar. Soon he had learned a few chords himself, and after he returned home he made a deal with his father and got his first guitar, a $12 Stella. Not long afterward he

teamed with his brother, Linny, to learn many of the region's old-time mountain tunes and many of the new songs he was hearing on the *Grand Ole Opry* and the clear-channel bootleg Mexican radio stations. Doc's early performances were mostly limited to front-porch playing with relatives and neighbors until the pressure of making payments on his first Martin convinced him to try singing in the streets.

Doc acquired his nickname when he was 18. He and a friend were getting ready to play for a remote radio broadcast at a furniture store, and the announcer decided that "Arthel" was too cumbersome to use on the air. "Call him 'Doc,'" a lady in the crowd suggested. The name stuck (Doc says there is no truth to the story that it derives from the Dr. Watson of Sherlock Holmes lore).

In 1947 Doc met and married Rosa Lee Carlton, daughter of a fine old-time mountain fiddler named Gaither Carlton. Gaither was a walking repository of old tunes indigenous to his isolated mountain home and he passed along many that remain part of Doc's repertoire today.

Despite his blossoming talent, Doc was not earning money from his skills. After his marriage he took to tuning pianos to help feed his family. It wasn't until 1953, when he was 30, that he became a successful working musician. That was the year he met Jack Williams, a piano player from Tennessee, who was fronting a country and western swing band. Williams was impressed by Doc's talent and invited him to play lead guitar in the band. Shortly thereafter Doc traded in his D-28 for a 1953 Les Paul Standard and became an electric guitarist. (Even today Doc carries those '50s tunes with him, and he delights in occasionally astounding audiences with a hot encore rendition of "Blue Suede Shoes" or "Tutti Frutti.")

Because the band did not have a fiddle player, Williams called on Doc to provide the lead part on fiddle tunes for square dancing. Ironically, it was on the electric guitar that Doc developed and honed the style for which he was to become so famous on the acoustic guitar.

The association with Williams lasted nearly eight years. The band toured eastern Tennessee and western North Carolina, playing VFW halls and square dances. During that period Doc continued to pick and sing old-time music with his family. He also played with a neighbor, Clarence "Tom" Ashley, who had been an original member of the Carolina Tar Heels.

In 1960, as the folk boom was just beginning, Ashley was sought out by two young musicologists named Ralph Rinzler and Eugene Earle. Anxious to record Ashley, Rinzler and Earle also happened to get Doc Watson on banjo and guitar. The results of that meeting are still available on a pair of albums, *Old-Time Music At Clarence Ashley's* (Folkways, 2355 and 2359).

Rinzler was excited by the sessions,

especially by Doc's unique talent. He immediately began making plans to get Ashley and Doc to New York to perform their old-time mountain music for the growing folk audience there, but Doc was dubious. He simply could not believe that there was anyone there who wanted to hear it.

Fortunately, Rinzler prevailed. In the spring of 1961 Doc Watson made his urban debut at a Friends of Old-Time Music concert in New York. He was accompanied by Ashley, Clint Howard, and Fred Price. A year later he gave his first solo performance at Gerde's Folk City in New York.

Doc was soon much in demand, traveling the country playing concerts and hootenannies and making some television appearances. He was a smash hit at the 1963 Newport Folk Festival, and in November of that year he played a historic concert with mandolinist Bill Monroe at New York's Town Hall. Bootleg recordings of that concert are still surfacing.

About that time the folk music boom began to bottom out. The Beatles had arrived to breathe fresh air into rock and roll, and most of the newly discovered folk artists were returning to a subsistence level as performers. Doc himself came very close to going back to North Carolina for good, though not for lack of an appreciative public. He was homesick, and his handicap made traveling very difficult.

In 1964 Doc came home from nearly three months on the road to find that his 15-year-old son, Merle, had taken up the guitar. It wasn't too long before Merle was good enough to play rhythm guitar for Doc. At 16, Merle became his father's backup guitarist, road manager, and chauffeur, and the two began spending up to 300 nights a year on the road.

Because of Merle, Doc was able to continue his career, reaching a steadily widening audience even during acoustic music's leanest years.

In 1968 the father-son duo was asked by the State Department to represent the United States in a cultural exchange program with African nations. The Watsons went from snow-covered North Carolina to 100-degree temperatures in Nairobi, Kenya, playing at villages in the bush country of Malawi, Zambia, Botswana, Lesotho, and Swaziland to enthusiastic native audiences.

Doc's music touched a new generation of listeners in 1972 when he participated in the recording of *Will The Circle Be Unbroken* (United Artists, UA 9801), a landmark project organized by the Nitty Gritty Dirt Band. The Dirt Band gathered together and recorded with a living country and bluegrass music Hall of Fame that included Doc, Maybelle Carter, Earl Scruggs, Roy Acuff, and Merle Travis. The result was a three-record album that later went gold. Doc's warm humor, his singing, and his remarkable guitar playing sparkle throughout the album.

Today the burden of travel has eased for Doc and Merle. Their commercial appeal is such that they now fly to their many concerts in a private twin-engine plane. The team was joined in 1974 by bass guitarist T. Michael Coleman, and the three continue to perform as a trio.

Doc's distinctive style starts with a Herco nylon flatpick, which he favors because of its embossed grip surfaces, its durability, and the cleaner sound it makes against the strings. The strings themselves are medium-gauge D'Addarios (Merle uses medium-light Gallaghers, from the same company that produces the Watsons' guitars). Doc likes his guitars set with an action slightly higher than normal, feeling that the extra clearance produces more punch and volume. He uses a capo — he calls it a "cheater" — occasionally, most often at the third fret. At times, Doc also fingerpicks.

Although his right arm appears to move very little while he plays, Doc has characterized his technique as three-quarters arm motion and a quarter wrist motion. He leaves the little finger of his right hand slightly touching the pickguard as a depth gauge. Doc believes that flatpicking technique must be light and delicate to be clean, and suggests practicing scales using even up-and-down picking. On left hand technique, he advises guitarists against copying his use of the thumb on the sixth string for barred chords. He says that Merle has developed a better reach on the neck by using conventional barre chording.

By Doc's own count, there have been 15 Doc Watson albums. Not included in that figure are two he recorded with members of his family in the early '60s, *The Doc Watson Family* and *The Watson Family* (Folkways, 31021 and 2366).

His most recent release, *Look Away* (United Artists, UA-LA887-H) has drawn favorable reviews from magazines as dissimilar as *Playboy* and *Guitar Player*. It features a characteristic variety of material with old-time tunes, flatpicked fiddle tunes, and a fine version of Bob Dylan's "Don't Think Twice, It's All Right."

*C*OULD YOU TELL us a little more about that first banjo your dad built for you?

When I came home that first spring from school my dad said, "Son, I might make you a little banjo this summer," and I said, "I ain't never seen one of them." He said, "Well, I used to pick a little and I know where to get ahold of some of them tension hooks, so I believe I can make you one." So he commenced to working on it. He carved the neck out of maple and made little friction tuning pegs like dulcimers have. When he got the top done he stretched a groundhog hide over it, but that just didn't work right. It was too stiff and didn't give a very good tone. We solved the problem, though, when Granny's 16-year-old cat passed on. That made one of the best banjo heads you ever seen and it stayed on that thing, I

guess, as along as I picked it. Dad got it made and tuned it up and the first piece I ever heard him play was "Rambling Hobo." He showed me a few tunes to get me started. Then one day he picked it up and put it in my hands and said, "Here, son. Take this and learn to play it good. You might need it in this world. It's yours now." He never would pick no more after he got me started.

It seems like your father left you with a fine legacy by giving you that banjo.

Making that banjo and encouraging me into music, knowing that it was a trade I could learn, was a mighty fine thing he did for me. The best thing my dad ever did for me in my life, though, was to put me at one end of a crosscut saw. He put me to work and that made me feel useful. A lot of blind people weren't ever put to work. I remember the morning when he leaned back in his chair, took a big swig of coffee, and said, "Son, do you think you can learn to pull a

crosscut saw?" and I said, "Yeah." I didn't know what I was getting into but I soon found out, I tell you right now.

Could you run down a progression of the guitars you've gone through since you've been playing?

Well, I got the Stella when I was 12. I had heard a friend named Paul Montgomery in school playing guitar and learned a couple of chords. When I came home that summer, my brother had borrowed my cousin's guitar. Daddy heard me messing with it one morning and said, "Son, if you can learn a tune on that by the time I get back from work this evening we'll go find you a guitar of some kind." He didn't know that I already knew a chord or two, and when he came home I could pick the chords to "When The Roses Bloom In Dixieland." That's when we went and got the Stella. I kept that for a while and I worked out the price of my second guitar myself at the end of a crosscut saw. That was a Silvertone

from Sears. I traded around a time or two between that and when Mr. Richard Green, an old man who ran a little music store in Boone, helped me get my first Martin.

Do you remember what model it was?

It was a Martin D-28. That must have been about 1940. It was a new guitar and he let me have a year to pay it off. I played on the street nearly every Saturday, when the weather was warm, at a cab stand in Lenoir, South Carolina. Sometimes I'd make as much as $50, and I paid that guitar off in four or five months. I didn't aim to lose that thing. I kept that guitar right up until the time I joined Jack Williams.

Is that when you bought the Les Paul?

Yeah. I tried to use a pickup on the Martin for awhile but I finally got enough nerve to trade it on the Les Paul.

Did you get into altered chords with the Jack Williams band?

Some. Jack played pretty decent piano, mostly honky-tonk, and I'd improvise with the three- and four-note chords. I didn't worry about learning all the barre chords because we had a rhythm guitar player. The hardest chore I got into with that group was playing the lead fiddle tunes for square dancing. That man would just keep you going for twenty minutes. He'd break your arm off.

What do you think you gained from that experience with Jack Williams?

I still use some of the hot licks that I played on the electric, but they come out sounding a little different to the ear when you play them on the flat-top. I got a lot of technical practice with the flatpick during those years. It helped me build my knowledge of using the flatpick enormously.

Did you always flatpick, right from the start?

I started off playing with a thumb lead, Maybelle Carter style. Then when I began to listen to Jimmie Rodgers, I figured out there was something being done there besides the thumb and finger. So I got me a pick and started working on it. It was Hank Garland who inspired me to learn fiddle tunes on the guitar. I did learn some fingerpicking from a fellow named Olin Miller. I loved Merle Travis. That's who my son is named after.

Was your work with Jack Williams your first real performing job?

Well, of course there were the street things, and people who heard me on the street invited me to come to amateur contests and fiddler's conventions, and I went. I began to win a few, but I found that people didn't want me in their shows no matter how good I was because I was a little trouble to them and I didn't have a flashy stage show. It just wasn't accepted then for you to just sit on the stage and pick, unless you were a super musician, and that I wasn't. I

did win some contests, though, and I remember one time when I entered once in the professional category and won it. That really helped my ego.

Your music shows a wide variety of influences. Were you exposed to different kinds of music early?

We had the records and they were pretty varied. In 1939 we got a battery-set radio and we could pick up anything from Del Rio, Texas, to Minneapolis, Minnesota. I heard a lot of big band music. I remember getting interested in dixieland jazz. I thought that was some kind of fine. And later I began to like the Dorseys and Phil Harris. You name it and I began to like the sound. When you begin to understand music and your ear is being educated to the theory, then you can really learn to love it. You can't really love something until you can understand it.

At what point did you start using the custom-built J.W. Gallagher [Wartrace, Tennessee] guitar you have now?

I don't remember the exact year that happened. After I stopped playing electric and went on the road I borrowed a Martin from a boy named Joe Cox who couldn't play a lick. He gave me that guitar to play as long as I wanted and I used that for quite awhile. Then I played some on a D-28 that Ralph Rinzler had. Merle and I both had Martins for awhile. Then one Easter, J.W.

and his son dropped by our house with three or four of their guitars. The house was full of people who had just come back from Union Grove [the nearby music festival]. I played all of the guitars and just before he left he came over and handed me the guitar that I'd liked the best. He said, "I want to give you this, and there are no strings attached except the ones on the guitar. We'll just let the thing endorse itself if it is any good." I used that guitar for eight years. Three years ago this September he came up to me in Nashville and told me he wanted to do something for me because I had sold more guitars than he could make, just by playing that guitar. I told him he could build me a new guitar with a neck to my specifications, and I sent him my '53 Les Paul to copy. He copied the neck and shape, the fretboard, and the type of frets, and made a guitar to suit himself. That's what I have now.

Is that what he calls the Doc Watson model?

Yes. He heard me playing it and asked if he could produce it and put it in his catalog. Then in January he brought me a twin to it and I've got that at home. I played it on the road for two or three months to break it in so if something happened to one, the other wouldn't have to hit the road straight brand new. When a guitar is green you might be able to hear the good in it, but they're not like they are once you've played them awhile and you break them in. They have to be played to season them properly.

Do you ever play the banjo anymore?

Maybe one out of ten shows I'll pick it up and play something. I let Merle do most of the banjo work these days.

What other instruments do you play besides banjo, harmonica, and guitar?

I tried the fiddle for awhile but I never could get that bowing hand right. I've picked around a bit on the mandolin and I do think I could learn to play that. I never could find a mandolin that had a neck wide enough to suit me and a tone fittin' for beans, though. I did find a beautiful old Gibson A model that I done my damnedest to buy, but the lady that owned it didn't want to sell.

When did you get the notion to try to play fiddle tunes on the guitar?

I guess I actually started trying to do that pretty early. I'd made up my mind that I couldn't play the fiddle, but I wanted to play with the same kind of bounce and rhythm that the fiddle did so I started working them out on the guitar. You can't do the same things that are done on the fiddle but you can do the tunes to where they are pretty. I spent a lot of time practicing. I hadn't heard anyone else do that on a guitar before, and I'll tell you it really surprised Bill Monroe when we played together at the Ash Grove in Los Angeles. Ralph [Rinzler] had got the idea for me and Bill to do some of the old Charlie and Bill Monroe things together as an extra short set on the shows. The first tune we did was "Paddy On The Turnpike,"

and all at once I took a break on the guitar. Bill came over after we got off the stage and said something like, "Mighty fine guitar playing." Then in a few minutes he said, "Do you know 'Tennessee Blues'?" and I said, "Yeah, I think I can pick it." We got back up there the next time and we flat got on it and I played just as fast as he could go with it. When we got off the stage he said, "Man, you got after that tune. I've never heard a guitar played like that before." You can imagine how I felt. I'd been listening to Bill Monroe for maybe 20 years.

What kind of process do you and Merle go through in working out a tune?

Well, I don't ever tell Merle how to play a tune. I might suggest something like, "Try this and see if it will work," but you can't mold a guy if he's a true musician. He's got to pick the way he picks. We'll sit down together and get the melody line straight and he will pick around a bit on it. I'll let him think about it for awhile and in the next day or two he'll sit down again and he will pick it. He does his own arrangements. He'll play a tune one way one night and a different way the next. Same with me. There are one or two songs that have definite arrangements. I play "Sweet Georgia Brown" about the same way every time, maybe adding different phrasing here and there occasionally, but basically it's the same arrangement. The country songs that I'm so used to I'll play a little different each set, depending on how I feel. "Milk Cow Blues" is one we vary quite a bunch.

Do you consciously do things with your voice and harmonica to play against the guitar?

I think the combination comes out according to your feelings. If you are really into a tune, not forcing yourself or nervous, and really into playing for an audience, those sorts of musical things happen as a result of your feelings. It's not a conscious thing. You may practice at something to get it a certain way but find it comes out different when you do it onstage.

Do you use a pickup on your guitar?

Yes. Merle and I both have Barcus-Berrys installed in our guitars. We got into that because of shoddy sound systems at a lot of the festivals. If you turned it loud enough for them to hear your guitar you got feedback. Well, if you put a padded-down signal into their board you can play as loud as you want. It might not sound as sweet and clean all the time, because of their system, but it will be the sound of the guitar.

What kind of amps are you and Merle using?

We've used Fender Twins for years. I don't believe you can hardly whip them for what we do. We rent them wherever we go.

What is your general opinion of the festival circuit these days?

I'd really rather not say what I think about some of those festivals. There's about 70 percent of them that I wouldn't take Rosa Lee or my daughter Nancy to. People go to certain festivals just because

they can raise all the hell they want. The security is bad and there's a lot of drinkin'. There's too many who don't go to listen who spoil it for those that do. It's just downright rudeness. Those festivals are sure a far cry from the quiet, very attentive audiences of the '60s folk festivals. That Newport festival was something. I remember when Clarence, Fred, Clint and I played it in 1963. We'd go out onstage and eight to ten thousand people would go dead quiet and listen to the music. Man, you couldn't believe the ovations for those simple old tunes that Clarence did. You knew the people were there to hear the roots of their music.

Do you hear many new pickers who excite you?

Lord, yes. There are a lot of fine ones coming along. Norman Blake is surely one. That last album I heard by him has some licks on there I don't think I could do. The left-hand parts I believe I could handle, but I don't know about that right hand. I'm going to ask him what kind of operation he had on that wrist to loosen it up like that. Tony Rice and Dan Crary are two more mighty fine pickers. In fact, Tony is recording a couple of cuts with us for this live album. There's also a real fine young fingerpicker named Guy Van Duser. He can pick himself a guitar. There are so many guitar players that play for show and then there are some that play for the love. Man, you can sure tell the difference when you sit down and listen to them. Too many people are just trying to see how many notes they can play on the guitar. Fast and tasteful *can* be combined. Two musicians can play a riff and the choice of notes and the phrasing is what makes it tasteful or not — no matter how fast or slow it is played.

Do you get much of a chance to jam with new musicians these days?

Once in a while I will if I'm rested and their playing interests me. I'm ashamed to say, though, that I don't have the passion for the music that I did at one time. I seldom jam anymore because I play so much on the road that I get it out of my system with audiences.

How much of your musical repertoire is made up of the old time tunes?

I'd say about 30 percent of my music comes from family and relatives and the rest from records, radio, and what-not. One new tune we're doing for this live album is the old Everly Brothers song called "Dream."

Do you have any ambitious concept albums that you are anxious to do? Do you still have a good backlog of old tunes to draw upon?

Well, there are quite a few old ones that I could dig out. We've got one more album under this contract and I haven't even thought of half of that. We just kind of take them one at a time.

— *Jon Sievert*

DOUG DILLARD

CLEANLINESS IS NEXT TO Dillard-ness." The comment comes from John McEuen; the subject is the banjo artistry of Doug Dillard. McEuen — a charter member of the Dirt Band, a popular solo performer, a successful promoter, and a longtime *Frets* columnist — is perhaps the best-known of Dillard's Disciples. Hardly a cult (well, not exactly), quite unofficial, and impossible to number with any accuracy, the Disciples are a still-growing group of banjo players with one thing in common: they all cite as their first and foremost musical influence the remarkable picking of Doug Dillard. In many cases, they point to Dillard as the reason they are playing banjo at all.

The story of McEuen's conversion is a case in point. He was dragged unwillingly by excited friends to a Southern California club one night in 1963 to hear a band that had been in town a few months. The group hailed from Salem, Missouri. They were called the Dillards.

"If I've ever had any mystical experiences in my life, that was one of them," McEuen recalls. "Before the Dillards even came on stage my hands started sweating and my leg starting jumping. When they began playing, I don't think I breathed for another half hour. Doug Dillard was *real* hot! And that's how I got interested in banjo. For the next two years, I was at their shows on an average of at least two or three nights a week."

Banjo author and recording artist Bill Knopf, who eventually collaborated with Dillard on *The Bluegrass Banjo Style of Douglas Flint Dillard* (Almo Publications [dist. by Columbia Pictures Publications], 1980), met the master three years later. Knopf had just come to Los Angeles as a college student.

"I'd been struggling with the banjo a little over a year," Knopf says in his foreword to the Dillard book. "I had never heard the Dillards live, but I knew of them through their first two albums and their TV appearances. A fellow music student at UCLA heard I played banjo and asked me if I wanted to go to Doug's house. My jaw dropped to the floor, because I'd never met a famous picker before, but Doug made me feel right at home. I played a few tunes I had worked up in my own mediocre style, and Doug pointed out a few things I could do to improve. From that day on I spent many hours parked in the front row at Dillard performances, and in front of my phonograph — slowing Dillards records down to 16 rpm and trying to figure out just what Doug was doing."

Dillard, a soft-spoken man with a perpetual ear-to-ear grin, hardly seems cut out to be a musical Svengali. What was it about him and his playing that inspired this kind of awe and dedication among musicians who heard him? "One of Doug Dillard's main influences on me," McEuen says, "was the fact that he could play an instrument with a high level of proficiency and make it look *enjoyable* — making people that weren't into that form of music like it. He physically expressed his music in such a way that people *watched* him play, and enjoyed watching him — as opposed to the kind of player who can be really good, but who just stands there and bores you. It was Doug's attitude that I liked."

And then there was the music itself. "Of all the banjo players I listened to, Doug was my favorite," says Knopf. "His style was different from the other 'big names,' no matter how fast he played — and boy, could he play fast!"

McEuen agrees. "He had a unique tone," says John. "Real bright — partially

because of the arch-top banjo he used and partially because of his attack. He was a real hard player. Consistent and hard. He'd really bear down on the strings.

"And then, in retrospect, the music of the Dillards was as perfect as anyone has done, as far as sheer technical accomplishment. I don't think anyone could play 'Hickory Hollow' the way Doug did — ever. Just like it's kind of hard for anyone to play 'Foggy Mountain Breakdown' or 'Shuckin' The Corn' like Earl Scruggs."

Given all this, you might think that Doug Dillard walked down from the top of one of his native Ozark Mountains one day, a smoking banjo in his hands, and immediately began calling the faithful with divinely inspired hot licks. Actually, he started out like just about everybody else, copying banjo breaks off records — just as McEuen and Knopf were to copy Dillard's own breaks ten years later.

"One of the first tunes I learned to play was 'Earl's Breakdown' by Earl Scruggs," recalls Dillard, now 46. "I learned it off the record. I'd play 78 rpm recordings by Earl Scruggs, Don Reno, and other guys at 33-1/3 rpm to slow them down, to try to figure out exactly how they were playing their licks."

The second of the three sons of Homer and Lorene Dillard, Doug grew up in Salem, Missouri. Homer Dillard was a Tennessee fiddler, and Lorene was a guitarist, so the Dillard boys grew up with music as a daily activity. Homer Earl, Jr., Doug's older brother, took up piano and accordion. Rodney, the youngest son (five years Doug's junior), gravitated to guitar. Doug started out on guitar at the age of five, but his interest in banjo was sparked some years later when Homer, Sr., took him to see a *Grand Ole Opry* show featuring banjo great Uncle Dave Macon.

"I got my first banjo as a Christmas present when I was 15 years old," Doug remembers. "It was a Kay, a real nice one with a resonator on it. A friend of mine in Salem started me out by showing me how to play 'Green Corn,' picking with the thumb and one finger. But I got into three-finger picking about the same time, through trying to learn things off the records."

Doug made his debut in Salem as part of a family band. "We'd play for square dances and pie suppers, mostly," he says. "My dad would play fiddle, and both my mother and Rodney played guitar with us. My older brother, who's an engineer for McDonnell-Douglas now, played keyboards, so he'd sit in on piano and accordion. We'd play all the old-time numbers like 'Sally Goodin' and 'Bill Cheatham.'"

Doug credits his square dance picking with fostering the hard, bright tone that has become his trademark. "I wouldn't know how else to explain it," he says. "When you play square dances, you have to play loud."

His playing expanded beyond the family music circle in 1953 when he joined the Hal Teague band, a group that played for

dances around Salem and did some radio work. In 1956 he and Rodney became part of the Ozark Mountain Boys, featured periodically on the *Ozark Mountain Jamboree* during the next two years, and in 1957 Doug got into television performing on *The Ozark Opry.*

The Ozark Opry was where Doug met a young fiddler and banjo player named John Harford. "I was working a day job as a bookkeeper in St. Louis, then," says Doug, "coming home for the shows. It turned out that John was living in St. Louis, too, so after that we got together and played a lot." That marked the beginning of a long association between Dillard and Harford —better known today as John Hartford. (Hartford added the "t" because he found people invariably spelled his name with it anyway.)

In 1958 Doug and Rodney formalized their musical partnership as the Dillard Brothers by cutting two singles on the K-Ark label. Meanwhile, they began performing with Hartford, bassist Buddy Van, and mandolinist Joe Noel in the group Joe Noel And The Dixie Ramblers. The following year Doug and Rodney cut a gospel EP for K-Ark. Their third recording effort came with Noel in 1960, a single for Marlo Records that featured Doug playing "Banjo In The Hollow."

One night in 1960 a mandolinist from upstate Independence, Missouri came to *The Ozark Opry*, playing with multi-instrumentalist Dale Sledd. The mandolinist's name was Dean Webb, and he and the Dillards struck up a friendship that led to a date in St. Louis the following year to cut some demos. A local disc jockey liked their sound and joined them on bass — and the Dillards were born.

Mitch Jayne, the bassist, had arrived in Salem seven years before to teach school, but he found doing a bluegrass radio show on Salem's KSMO to be a more interesting line of work.

"We'd known him for a long time," Doug recalls. "Rodney and I would go down to his house and play music a lot. But the four of us didn't really play together much as a group before the time we all went out to Los Angeles.

"We had the feeling that it might be a good point to take bluegrass to the West Coast. We didn't know of much bluegrass happening out there then, and Mitch decided he wanted to strike out with us."

Jayne became the advance man, heading out to LA to scout up a manager. That done, he came home, and the newly constituted Dillards played their first and only big show in Missouri before heading west — a successful debut concert at Washington University in St. Louis.

Loading themselves and their gear into Webb's '55 Cadillac, they set out, only to be stranded in Oklahoma City when the car broke down. After doing odd jobs for a few weeks, the boys landed a one-week gig at a local club. It paid $300 — but they turned out to be such a popular draw that they picked up a $100 bonus. That was enough to get them to California.

(The unscheduled Oklahoma City lay-over also brought Doug one of his main instruments, a vintage Gibson Bella Voce tenor banjo that he picked up in a pawnshop there for $295. He had a 5-string neck made for it in Los Angeles.)

It was November 1962 when the Dillards hit town. They checked in at the Ash Grove, one of Southern California's leading folk clubs. A jam session there with the Greenbriar Boys established their credentials in a big way, and before the week was up, they had a contract with Elektra Records.

The Dillards' guess about the LA market being wide open proved to be shrewd. Doug in particular had a clear field, because there were only a few banjo players in town — notably Billy Ray Latham, who later joined Clarence White in the Kentucky Colonels; and Don Parmley, who later formed the Bluegrass Cardinals.

With their personable stage act, the Dillards had no trouble going Hollywood; they soon became regulars on TV's *The Andy Griffith Show*, playing the slow-thinking but hot-picking backwoods Darlin Family. The show brought them national exposure until it finally went off the air in 1965.

In 1963 they cut their first Elektra album, *Backporch Bluegrass*; made their New York debut at Gerde's Folk City in Greenwich Village; appeared as featured guests on a Judy Garland TV special; and worked some instrumental sessions with a rising studio player named Glen Campbell. A second album, *Live — Almost!* came out in 1964 — the year the group also began experimenting with amplified instruments and drums. That was a controversial move, but it cast the die for the Dillards' subsequent development.

The Los Angeles music scene was ripe for experimentation in the mid-'60s. The Byrds found a winning formula in 1965 with their hit recording of Bob Dylan's "Hey, Mr. Tambourine Man," ushering in the folk-rock era. The chemistry that brought about sweeping changes in the music set up a subtle chain reaction that ultimately led to major changes in the Dillards, as well as in other groups.

New faces had an impact. Byron Berline, starting to carve his niche as a studio fiddler, joined the Dillards for the recording of an all-instrumental LP *Pickin' And Fiddlin'*. It was the last Dillards LP on which Doug played as a regular band member.

Old faces had an impact, too, as cross-fertilization between the various LA-based groups continued to encourage musical hybridizing. The Byrds' Gene Clark, who had been a member of the New Christy Minstrels when he first met Doug, began work on a debut solo album in 1966 and called in Doug to help. Within two years, Doug made the transition from sideman to full partner.

It was a two-step process. In 1968 the

Byrds asked Doug to join them for a tour of Europe. Feeling that the time had come to step out on his own, he accepted. Rodney kept the Dillards name, and Herb Pedersen filled the vacant banjo slot in the lineup. Gene Clark, meanwhile, had taken his leave of the Byrds. After Doug returned from Europe, he did some session work and then connected with Clark to form the first several incarnations of Dillard And Clark. The initial 1968 roster included Don Beck on dobro and mandolin, David Jackson on acoustic bass, and Bernie Leadon — who later became a charter member of the Eagles — on guitar. The group's first album was *Fantastic Expedition*, recorded for the A&M label.

After the A&M sessions, Dillard And Clark made their first tour, taking along ex-Byrds drummer Michael Clarke. Several members of that band, along with John Hartford, thereafter joined Doug as he recorded his first solo LP, *The Banjo Album*, for Together Records. (Long since out of print, the album is now a sought-after collector's item.)

Beck and Clarke left Dillard And Clark, but the slack was taken up by the addition of Byron Berline, guitarist Donna Washburn, and drummer Jon Corneal. Though Leadon was the next to go, he made guest appearances on the band's 1969 LP *Through The Morning, Through The Night*.

Close-up of Dillard's unusual picking position.

Clark himself left in 1970 to return to solo performing. "When Gene went his way, Byron and I kept the group going as Dillard And The Expedition," Doug recalls. "We got [ex-Kentucky Colonels] Billy Ray Latham and Roger Bush at that point; Billy Ray played guitar and Roger played bass."

Doug's musical path from 1970 to 1980 was a convoluted one, taking some offbeat digressions and making several switchbacks upon itself. Besides doing film work in 1973 he recorded two new solo albums — with Rodney acting as producer — for the 20th Century label: *Dueling Banjos* and *Douglas Flint Dillard*. Doug grew increasingly active in session work, doing dates with artists as diverse as the Beach Boys, Harry Nilsson, the Monkees, and Glen Campbell. (Interestingly, it was Doug who played banjo on Campbell's Grammy-winning version of "Gentle On My Mind," originally written by John Hartford — who was the resident banjoist on Campbell's TV show.)

Doug launched a short-lived ensemble called Dillard And The Country Coalition, successor to Dillard And The Expedition. The Coalition included John Kurtz on drums, Peggy Bradley on fiddle, Dick Bradley on guitar, and David Jackson on bass. The band never recorded. Doug's next important album date after Dillard And Clark came in 1976 when he, Rodney, and John Hartford (who'd launched his own

Early photo of the original Dillards, Hollywood 1964 (L to R): Dean Webb, Doug Dillard, Rodney Dillard, and comic emcee Mitch Jayne.

solo career in 1972) were reunited for an LP project that became the 1977 Flying Fish release *Dillard/Hartford/Dillard: Glitter-Grass From The Nashwood Hollyville Strings.* The album included a spirited banjo/fiddle duet between Doug and John on "Bear Creek Hop"; but it owed most of what success it achieved to Hartford's reggae-influenced "Two Hits And The Joint Turned Brown," which got enthusiastic airplay on underground FM stations.

A sequel, *Dillard/Hartford/Dillard: Permanent Wave,* was eventually released by Flying Fish in 1980. It was an even stranger assortment of tunes, largely an amalgam of old rock songs and country pop, with such unlikely highlights as Doug's middleweight tenor tackling the lead vocals on revivals of Buddy Holly's "That'll Be The Day" and the Coasters' "Yakety Yak." The musicianship contributed to a sense of self-indulgence, too. One banjo track, on the Hartford song "Same Thing," was so heavily electronically processed that it sounded strangled.

Dillard's explorations may have won him a few new fans, but it lost him — at least temporarily — some old ones. "I quit listening to him for several years, although I still loved him as a person," says John McEuen. "I started looking forward to hearing him again."

The road home began in 1978 with the recording of Doug's first solo gospel LP, *Heaven,* released by Flying Fish in 1979. On it he played banjo and guitar and sang the lead vocals. Among the sidemen were Byron Berline, John Hartford, Herb Pedersen, Dan Crary, Billy Constable, David Jackson, and (doubling as producer again)

Rodney Dillard. Out of that effort was born the Doug Dillard Band: Doug on banjo, Skip Conover on dobro, Ray Park on fiddle and guitar, Billy Constable on lead guitar and mandolin, Bill Bryson on bass, and Byron Berline sharing the bill as the group's featured instrumentalist.

In the summer of '79, that edition of the band made its first and only recording, but it was a memorable one: *Jackrabbit!* Firmly grounding their music in bluegrass and leaving the mid-'70s experimentation behind, Doug and Byron had built the song list with numbers like "Hamilton County Breakdown" and Doug's classic "Hickory Hollow." They appeared at the 1979 Telluride Bluegrass And Country Music Festival in Colorado, and as the band ripped through tunes like "Rolling In My Sweet Baby's Arms" and "Byron's Barn" to repeated ovations, Rodney Dillard supervised the taping of a dynamic live album.

The summer of '79 marked the opening of a successful new chapter in Doug's career as a bandleader, but it also brought him back to his roots. On August 8 his hometown of Salem proclaimed "Dillard Day," honoring its native sons for their achievements in music and the entertainment industry during the preceding 17 years. The tribute to the Dillard family was part of a three-day celebration, and family members and friends came from around the country to attend the festivities. Musical events included reunions of the Dillard family band, with John Hartford sitting in, and a reunion of the original Dillards. The performances were documented on the Flying Fish album *Homecoming And Family Reunion.*

Through all the personnel permutations of the bands Doug has been with, he has remained consistent with his performance instruments: a Gibson Mastertone that he bought new just before the Dillards left Missouri and the vintage Bella Voce that he picked up not long afterward on the journey west. Both are archtop instruments. Recently he's begun including a Fender "Leo Deluxe" model, which he is endorsing for Fender, in his arsenal.

Both of Doug's Gibsons are set up with standard frosted heads that are "as tight as you can get them before they break," he says. How do you find that point — without rupturing the head in the process? "It's hard to do, Doug admits. "You just have to push on the head a little bit as you're tightening it, to get a feel for how tight it's becoming."

The taut head is one element of Dillard's renowned bright tone. Another is the tailpiece adjustment. "I don't like the tailpiece cranked right down on the head," he says, "but I do like it to be only a little ways up. That setting brightens the sound somewhat." He uses standard Grover three-footed maple/ebony bridges. Each of his Gibsons' necks is fitted with a Rick Shubb [Oakland, CA] sliding fifth-string capo, while the Fender banjo has HO-gauge railroad spikes in its fretboard for capoing the fifth string at specific frets. The strings themselves are Vega medium gauge. "If we're playing a lot, I'd change strings every two or three gigs," he says. "If I'm recording, I like new strings to set a little bit before I use them. They have sort of a wiry tone right after you uncoil them and put them on."

Dillard's highly individualistic right-hand picking position is another element in his tone production. The classic right-hand posture for three-finger bluegrass picking is with both the ring finger and the little finger braced firmly on the head. Some players just brace the little finger.

But Doug usually doesn't rest *any* of his fingers on the head. Instead, he hooks his little finger around the treble end of the bridge, anchoring his hand there, and holds his ring finger close to the palm — so that it is floating out of the way above the bridge. He says he developed the unusual position half-consciously when he was trying to play louder at Salem square dances — partly because it seemed to give him more picking leverage and partly because it just seemed comfortable.

Doug's right-hand hardware includes two metal National fingerpicks and a plastic National thumbpick. "I file the edges of the fingerpicks down a little bit," he says. "It makes them lighter. I don't use the real heavy thumbpicks; I like the ones that are thinner. If we're playing a lot, I can wear out a thumbpick in a night. That's probably because of how hard I play. They get rough on the edges, and you can't use them."

Aside from a short fling with a prototype Rickenbacker solidbody banjo in the '60s, Doug has never used a pickup on any of his instruments. For both recording and performing, he prefers to use a microphone. He isn't especially particular about his mike ("Wherever we go we generally just check the different mikes and see which ones have the best sound"), but he *is* particular about where it is placed. "I put the mike right below where the neck comes into the pot," he says, "with the mike pointed at the

resonator holes. Generally I play about six inches away from it. That's where I get the best sound."

To maintain the bright, hard, cutting edge for which his sound is known, does he have to do much practicing? "Not really," he says. "Once you get it, it's kind of like learning how to swim. You don't have to do it over again later. If I do practice at all, I'll just play through some tunes or try out some new licks."

His new licks today are played with the latest edition of the Doug Dillard Band, a quartet lineup featuring Doug on banjo, Billy Constable (the only other holdover from the *Jackrabbit!* crew) on lead guitar, Ginger Boatwright on rhythm guitar, and Kathy Chiavola on bass. It's worth noting that the band is based in Nashville, not Los Angeles. Still keeping an eye on trends, Doug relocated to Music City a couple of years ago, after two decades in Southern California.

His music continues to evolve, but it is doing so within a traditional framework. "Our music is a little bit different than standard bluegrass," he says, "especially the vocals. We don't do completely traditional bluegrass all the time. We get into different kinds of material, and I imagine my banjo playing will be different as we go along. If music has got the basic components of bluegrass, I like that — but I don't see anything wrong with adding other things. I don't see anything wrong with putting in drums or electric guitars or anything else you want to add to it. Music is music, to me."

ON SCREEN

FILM WORK HAS BEEN a significant part of Doug Dillard's studio banjo career. Unlike most studio musicians, however, Doug's cinematic musical activities have several times led to him doing his picking on camera.

Dillard broke into film session work in 1967 on Arthur Penn's highly successful *Bonnie And Clyde*. But wait — wasn't that the movie that made "Foggy Mountain Breakdown" a national hit for Earl Scruggs? Yes, but that was because Flatt And Scruggs' 1948 recording of the tune was selected as the movie's theme. (Ironically, in selecting a fast-paced bluegrass banjo tune for the theme, the producers didn't stop to consider that bluegrass as a musical style — let alone bluegrass with Scruggs-style banjo picking — didn't come along until years *after* the action in the film took place.)

"Foggy Mountain Breakdown" may have been Earl Scruggs, but every other banjo lick in the *Bonnie And Clyde* soundtrack came from Doug Dillard. Since then, Doug has worked on the soundtracks for such films as *Vanishing Point, Junior Bonner, Bound For Glory*, and *Bunny O'Hare*, among others. He also composed and played the theme song for the NBC series *Dean Martin's Country Music*.

He made the transition from session man to onscreen picker in 1979, doing a cameo appearance with Rodney Dillard and Byron Berline as part of Bette Midler's band in *The Rose*. Early the following year Doug took a sabbatical from his own band to go to Malta, where Robert Altman was filming a movie version of *Popeye*. Doug had a speaking part this time, as the character Farmer Clem. ("Basically, I was supposed to be the town banjo player.")

Doug has enjoyed his stints in front of the camera, but he has found that the management of time and materials is a lot different in filming than it is in the economy-minded, clock-conscious world of the recording studio. "Movie work is a lot of fun," he says, "but of course, you always have a lot of waiting around to do on the sets. And I would say that with *Popeye*, about half of the film they shot ended up on the cutting room floor. They could make a *Popeye II* out of the outtakes."

— *Jim Hatlo*

A SELECTED DILLARD DISCOGRAPHY

Solo: *Jackrabbit!*, Flying Fish (1304 W. Schubert, Chicago, IL 60614), FF-208; *Heaven*, Flying Fish, FF-086; *You Don't Need A Reason To Sing*, 20th Century, T-426; *Duelin' Banjos*, 20th Century, T-409. **With the Dillards** (on Elektra): *Backporch Bluegrass*, EKS 7232; *Live — Almost!*, EKS 7265; *Pickin' And Fiddlin'*, EKS 7286. **With Gene Clark:** *The Fantastic Expedition Of Dillard And Clark*, A&M, SP 4158; *Through Morning Through The Night*, A&M, SP 4203. **With Rodney Dillard and John Hartford:** *Glitter-Grass From The Nashwood Hollyville Strings*, Flying Fish, FF-036; *Permanent Wave*, Flying Fish, FF-233.

TONY TRISCHKA

WHETHER HE IS playing experimental banjo from the twilight zone or a driving bluegrass breakdown, Tony Trischka's music comes out of a powerful personal style. It is an eclectic music, with jazz, classical, rock, and traditional elements grafted onto bluegrass roots; and it is often witty, though never frivolous. Since Tony's first recordings with Country Cooking nearly a decade ago, his work has always pointed toward new directions for the banjo. His musical vision has earned him the kind of recognition reserved for musicians like Don Reno, Earl Scruggs, Allen Shelton, and Tony's friend and mentor, Bill Keith — all banjoists whose creativity has not been bound by convention. Tony's music is fresh and exciting because he is constantly exploring the limits of his instrument — searching back to draw upon the styles of Scruggs and Reno, and the traditions of classical and ragtime styles; and exploring ahead into still-uncharted technical and stylistic territory.

Tony was raised in Syracuse, New York, where his first musical studies were on piano and flute. Those early lessons gave him a good footing in music theory and in reading music notation, a background that was to prove useful in later years. With the advent of the '60s folk boom, he focused his attention on a new instrument, the banjo. He had grown up with the music of Pete Seeger, Woody Guthrie, and the Weavers, but it was Dave Guard's banjo playing with the Kingston Trio that really fired his imagination. An unused guitar was sitting in his father's closet and Tony set out through Pete Seeger's banjo book [*How to Play The Five-String Banjo,* self-published, 1962] with the guitar strings tuned to banjo pitch. After a while he got the genuine item, a long-neck Christy banjo.

Technical refinements were rudimentary in 1962. "Back in those days it was a thing to scrape the head to get a crisper sound," Tony recalls. "You could either use solvent, or do what I did — I took a jackknife and hacked at it. It didn't pop on me, but the head was hacked to pieces."

Several people influenced Tony directly in those early years. Tony got his first lessons — and worked his first paying gigs — with Jon Gaines, a black musician who played guitar and clawhammer banjo. Gaines guided Tony through the day's folk and political scene, and the two performed together regularly. But as Tony began studying banjo with Hal Glatzer, his heart was stolen by bluegrass music.

"In one lesson I knew how to play Scruggs style, or pretty close to it," he says. "I was enraptured by the sound, and that was it from then on." From the start, Glatzer pointed him on the progressive direction of Don Reno and Bill Keith, teaching Tony tunes like "Follow The Leader," "Banjo Signal," "Devil's Dream," and "Sailor's Hornpipe."

Tony's first bluegrass band was the Southern Planters — sponsored by a local embalming school. It included Joel Diamond and Harry Gilmore, who later played on the first Country Cooking album. "Gilmore was a very strong influence on all of us in Syracuse," says Tony, "an incredibly intuitive musician. He taught us a lot about rhythm and timing — taught me to get away from hot licks, go back to Ralph Stanley and Bill Emerson."

Tony became a blugrass fanatic as the band evolved into the Down City Ramblers. He was listening closely to Lester Flatt and Earl Scruggs, Bill Monroe, Don Reno, the Kentucky Colonels, and other influential artists. In 1964 he began

sending tapes to Bill Keith, seeking criticism and advice. "I was totally influenced by that man," Tony says. "Now people are sending tapes to me and it feels funny, flattering."

The Down City Ramblers continued in various incarnations (even today they are likely to turn out for an annual gig), but by 1970, Tony was playing pedal steel guitar with Country Granola, a Syracuse country-rock band. He then met banjoist Peter Wernick, however, and the meeting was a turning point for Tony's recording and performing career. The two musicians hit it off, and Tony began playing banjo and pedal steel with Country Cooking, which then included Wernick, Nondi Leonard, Russ Barenberg, and John Miller. The group's first Rounder album came quickly, born in the excitement of working out new music right in the makeshift recording studio. A second album followed a year later. Many of the musicians on those albums (Wernick, Barenberg, Miller, Ken Kosek, and Andy Statman) were to play important parts in Tony's musical life through the ensuing years.

Tony had one original tune on the first Country Cooking album, "Hollywood Rhumba," written at Wernick's urging. Tony explains, "The tune wasn't that good, but it got the ball rolling. I wrote 'Bluegrass Light' and 'Kentucky Bullfight' right after that. So I owe Peter a large debt of gratitude for getting me back into writing."

Recording dates have come pretty regularly for Tony since then, counting solo albums, feature roles with Country Cooking and Breakfast Special, and frequent session work as a sideman. Through it all, Tony has made a distinctive rhythmic feel his musical trademark. "Even in the '60s I was doing various syncopated things," he says. "I'm not sure where they come from, but this was something in my musical mind. Scruggs does a lot of syncopation, and Keith too; but I think I take it out a little farther."

Another characteristic stylistic element is what Tony calls *pinching*, "playing two strings at the same time, which Scruggs would do a little. But I got into three-note pinches, which give me more power. You can hit a chord and slide it down, then hit another chord and slide it, instead of always having a roll going."

He has also been perfecting and teaching a single-string approach reminiscent of Don Reno. "There's more sense of power using the thumb and index finger alternating," he says. "It's not as flowing as the melodic style, but it gives me a punchier sound for a bluegrass band."

Tony advises his students to master the rudiments of bluegrass banjo before pressing on. "Even though I have a distinctive sound, I'm reworking techniques that were invented by Scruggs, Keith, and Reno," he says. "Of course, there's a lot of intuitive musical input, but I'm also learning licks now that I should have learned years ago.

It's been a constant thing of going back and learning the basics — back in one direction, then off into future land."

The banjo he uses in these musical safaris is a hybrid Gibson Mastertone that was assembled by Eldon Stutzman of Rochester, New York. Although Tony has played several other instruments onstage, he has used this particular instrument for recording since 1973. The rim and resonator date from the Thirties, with some new hardware. The neck is a recent Gibson RB-3. "It's sort of a composite," Tony says, "but it's my favorite banjo; I come home to that."

Tony looks at the banjo as a tool, something to play music on, not as an item to be worshipped by collectors or rationalized in enginering terminology. He uses medium-gauge strings (whatever brand happens to be handy) and National picks. "Everything's gauged now," he says, "but I never thought in those terms. I just pick it."

A list of his current listening indicates where Tony's ideas are coming from. "I've followed jazz for the last ten years or so," he explains, "and I've had a classical influence from my earliest days. Right now I'm listening to Robben Ford, a great electric jazz-blues guitarist who was with the LA Express; and Larry Carlton, another studio guitarist from Los Angeles. [Guitarist] John McLaughlin's new record has a lot of nice information on it, too. Interestingly enough, [young fiddler/guitarist] Mark O'Connor is also listening to Larry Carlton. All these supposed bluegrass musicians are stepping out and listening to things that are different from what one would expect."

Another source of inspiration and technical challenges for Tony is classical music, such as Bach's Inventions and Paganini's "Perpetual Motion" ("which makes a great fiddle tune in C"). Several months ago, a friend sent Tony a copy of *Cadenza*, a magazine published in the early 1900s for classical banjo, mandolin, and guitar enthusiasts. Slowly he's been working through difficult pieces like "Turkish Towel Rag."

Tony has a lot to say about theory and technique. "Theoretical knowledge is important if you want to stretch out on the banjo," he asserts. "That's something I want to work on, something I think everyone serious about music should try to do. Music is a very logical thing and there's been so much theoretical work done. Bill Keith is the king of that. Yet, most banjo players can't read music. I think that's a great shortcoming — in myself as well. I read very slowly. But I'm trying to get better at it."

Tony Trischka's albums, *Bluegrass Light, Heartlands,* and *Banjoland,* convey the strongest expressions of his broad musical vision. His bluegrass influence is usually evident, but he often combines rock elements, jazz, classical music, poetry, and bluegrass with a fine, adventurous touch. "The first album had a lot of new ideas,

unrefined," he explains. "Then *Heartlands* was even more that way; it was throwing in the kitchen sink — very experimental, and I enjoy it for that freshness. But *Banjoland* is a little more mature, if I can use that word. I pared it down and took out the blatantly experimental things."

Tony's own compositions are always challenging to other musicians and to himself. He works them out carefully with very little improvisation. "The tunes themselves may be kind of weird, but I play them consistently, true to the melody," he says. "If I'm playing a Scruggs tune, I can go crazy on it. But my tunes are more complex chordally and sometimes more complex rhythmically. I'm not yet as comfortable playing on those changes as on a three-chord bluegrass tune. I had all these wild ideas in the early '70s, and since then I've been whittling them down to play what fits rather than what's crazy for craziness' sake. That really doesn't work. I was with Hazel Dickens and Delia Bell some months ago at the Brooklyn Academy of Music. We played 'Will The Circle Be Unbroken,' and I took this break that was so straight it surprised me. I thought, 'did I play that?' Totally sticking to the melody, with no fancy syncopation, it was very satisfying. It's good to be able to play that way, almost as a discipline."

Still, even while refining his music, Trischka will always take plenty of chances. "To my mind, bluegrass music was predicated on taking chances," he says. "Look at what Bill Monroe did to the music in 1939, then what he did by adding Scruggs in 1945. That was pretty revolutionary in those days. Then time went on and it got caught in that state with little sense of newness. There's very little bluegrass that excites me now. I need to hear something really compelling, something that moves me. I get bored listening to a band play the same music they've been doing for years without any progression. I like progression in music."

His earliest banjo influences were progressive, players with their own styles and music. It follows that the modern players Tony admires are the ones who are opening new territory.

"Alan Munde knocks me out, playing some incredible breaks on jazz tunes," Tony says. "Or Pat Cloud, stepping so far out on a limb you can almost hear it cracking behind him. Butch Robins plays perfectly straight with Bill Monroe, then on his own records he really takes it out. He's a good composer too. Lamar Grier still amazes me. Last summer at the Berkshire Bluegrass Festival he was with Peter Rowan. I got this old excitement I used to have back when I saw Lamar with Monroe in 1966 and 1967. He has this punch and drive that won't be denied. Bela Fleck is an amazing banjo player. He can play the most intricate avant-garde banjo anyone's doing today or play the straightest Scruggs-style as he does with Tasty Licks. Peter

Tony Trischka with his new group, Skyline (L to R): Larry Cohen, Tony, Dede Wyland, Danny Weiss, and Barry Mitterhoff.

Wernick is another great player. He'll come up with a very original sound, and yet it will be an easy right-hand roll. He's really doing something new, but in a comfortable, banjoistic way. I admire him for that."

Lately Tony's life has been filled with travel, and he spent almost four months abroad in the last year or so. With help from Bill Keith, Tony went to France with Russ Barenberg for a 1978 summer festival and workshop in Courville. Last January, Tony returned to France for six weeks, along with Danny Weiss (a guitarist friend from his Country Granola days) and fiddler David Jaffe, joining some musicians from Keith's French band — Christian Seguret on mandolin and Lionel Wendling on bass. Their 14-concert tour culminated in the recording of their album, *Illinois*. Their warm reception made it possible for Tony, Danny, and Ken Kosek to return for an extended stay this summer. In between these European jaunts, Tony was recruited for a trip to Japan with Peter Rowan, Richard Greene, Andy Statman, and Roger Mason, playing in five cities and recording two albums for Japanese release. He also joined Stacy Phillips in the spring for two weeks in Australia. All this wandering has broadened the audience for Tony's music, has brought him some new cultural inputs, and has given him more options as a performer.

Tony's future seems to beckon in two directions at once: toward a steadier band format and toward more solo work. The groups Breakfast Special and Heartlands were both attempts at finding a common sound among a community of brilliant players. The problems they had could be attributed in part to an overabundance of talent. As Tony explains about Heartlands, "It was a great band, and we are all great friends [Russ Barenberg, John Miller, Matt Glaser, and Tony]. But it just couldn't work because there were too many diverse musical directions. Matt had to be playing more jazz, I had to be playing more bluegrass. We all had to compromise too much to stay in the band, which is a shame."

The result is that Tony has been working with groups organized only for particular jobs or tours, and he has found there are some advantages to that. "You can have a freshness to the sound," he says. "There's an excitement in playing with people for the first time. But at some point I think I have to settle down and get into a steady band, basically a bluegrass band, and start promoting my music. That's easy to do on record. But when you get up onstage and you're the front person and it's your music, that's putting yourself on the line. I guess I'm not quite ready to do that yet."

As the ensemble possibilities continue

to ripen, it has been natural for Tony to explore solo banjo. He has given some solo concerts on the West Coast, and he plans to do more. "It's an exciting prospect," he says. "I've been writing banjo tunes that just stand on their own. They don't need a whole band to play them."

Along with solo work and deeper probes into classical and ragtime styles, Tony has become interested in orchestral playing. "Several months ago I did a gig as soloist with the South Orange [New Jersey] Symphony Orchestra," he says. "We played one of my tunes, 'Song For Aurora,' from the *Banjoland* album. It was arranged by the conductor, who happens to be one of my banjo students. We played the hoedown movement from Aaron Copland's 'Rodeo.' I improvised around that. Then we did the Boston Pops 'Fiddle Medley,' which has nine or ten good tunes in it. It's hard to get used to an orchestra. I'm accustomed to a mandolin backbeat and very steady, solid rhythm. This was a 70-piece orchestra, and the rhythm was spread out all over the place. Still, it was a great experience.

"And that's one more thing for the future."

— *Alan Senauke*

A SELECTED TRISCHKA DISCOGRAPHY

Solo Albums: *Banjoland,* Rounder, 0087; *Bluegrass Light,* Rounder, 0048; *Heartlands,* Rounder, 0062; **With Country Cooking:** *Barrel Of Fun,* Rounder, 0033; *Country Cooking,* Rounder, 0006; j2Frank Wakefield, Rounder, 0007. **With Others:** *Back Road Mandolin,* Rounder, 0067; *Catfish For Supper,* Rounder, 3026 *Cowboy Calypso,* Rounder, 0111; *Dance Like A Wave Of The Sea,* Front Hall (Box 843 Ithaca, NY 14850), 017; *Dr. Banjo Steps Out,* Flying Fish (1304 W. Schubert St., Chicago, IL 60614), 046; *Duets,* Rounder, 0075; *The Robber Bridegroom,* CBS (51 W. 52nd St., New York, NY 10019), P14589; *Things Are Coming My Way,* Flying Fish, 204.

TONY
RICE

ONLY A FEW YEARS AGO a small circle of musicians in the San Francisco Bay area, led by mandolinist David Grisman and violinist Richard Greene, took the first steps toward what was to become known as "Dawg" music, a genre that looked to bluegrass for its roots, and to the small-combo jazz of the late 1940s for its future. Dawg music (taking its title from Grisman's nickname) made a tremendous impression on the acoustic music world, in no small part because of Anthony "Tony" Rice, perhaps the most innovative contemporary exponent of the flatpicked steel-string acoustic guitar. Rice's three-year tenure with the seminal David Grisman Quintet, which Rice left last fall, forged what amounted to a new conception of the guitar's role in both solo and ensemble contexts.

By the mid-'70s, Tony Rice had established himself as a major bluegrass artist as guitarist with J.D. Crowe And The New South, and his style was already attracting attention. Rice's rhythm playing took as much from the late Clarence White as from the classic bluegrass rhythm work of Lester Flatt; and Rice's lead work already pointed to a style beyond bluegrass. Not only did he play the extended guitar solos first attempted in a string-band context by White, with some harmonic twists of his own; Rice had developed a guitar sound that altered the balance of small acoustic combos.

Volume, or amplitude, has always been one of the critical restraints on the role of the acoustic guitar. Few guitarists could overcome the difficulties of balancing projection and tone, particularly in soloing. As a result, while many of the "newgrass" bands of the '70s offered guitarists a prominent role, generally with the help of amplification, it was more often than not at the expense of the group sound. But Rice, playing first with the New South and then, brilliantly, with the David Grisman Quintet, proved that an acoustic guitar could serve as the rhythmic focus of a drumless acoustic combo, and as one of the dominant lead voices, without sacrificing the quality and nuance of the individual player's sound.

Rice's uniquely powerful playing made possible another innovation for the string band format, related to a discovery made by jazz musicians in the '60s. At that time the straight-ahead rhythmic foundation of mainstream jazz was replaced by a "circle of sound" concept, pioneered by drummer Elvin Jones of the great John Coltrane Quartet. In Jones' system, the beat of a tune became a framework within which different time signatures were played against each other, substituting a circle of rhythmic tensions for the driving momentum that had served previous stylists. In effect, Rice performed the same function for the Grisman band. The Quintet had already freed its bass player from the conventional two-step bluegrass role, substituting walking bass lines that opened far more possibilities for harmonic and rhythmic exploration. Rice exploited those possibilities, transforming the linear thrust of bluegrass into a whole new set of grooves, thus creating a current of sound that in turn opened new opportunities for expression and gave a broadened dynamic range to the other soloists in the Quintet.

If Rice had absorbed a critical development of modern jazz, his lead guitar work was adding something new to the jazz tradition. The Quintet's original music, though making use of harmonic and rhythmic conventions from the jazz tradition, was firmly rooted in bluegrass time and tonality. The same could be said of individual soloists in the band—particularly Grisman and Rice. Certain techniques that Rice used extensively in his solos with the Quintet, and which he continues to use, come directly out of bluegrass: his fondness for beginning solos in the lower register, his extensive use of hammering-on and slurs, and a tonality that makes as much use of the "butter notes" of white country music as it does of the dissonance of black urban styles.

In a certain sense, both Rice and the Quintet were traditionalists, for all their innovation. Their insistence on the integrity of the acoustic group sound, in an age of amplification, opened the door to a kind of chamber jazz that relied on its complexity for interest, rather than on its rhythmic pulse. Something similar was attempted by jazz cornetist Bix Beiderbecke in the early 1930s, but Beiderbecke's highly idiosyncratic music is now rarely performed (a few tunes can be heard on Ry Cooder's *Jazz* [Warner Bros., K-3197].) Thus the Quintet's members and a few other musicians, like Richard Greene and mandolinist/fiddler Sam Bush (one of Rice's old friends and pickin' partners) are the lone practitioners of perhaps the only jazz style based on a white musical tradition.

Rice's background is strongly colored by his friendship with Clarence White. Rice, born in Danville, Virginia, was nine when he met White in Los Angeles. From carrying Clarence's guitar cases, Rice went on to consciously expanding White's flatpicking legacy, which had the acoustic guitar a literally established lead instrument in bluegrass. White's chief guitar, a 1934 Martin D-28, belongs to Rice now. (Tony also owns a custom dreadnought made by the Santa Cruz Guitar Works [Santa Cruz, California], his primary instrument for performance.)

At the age of 14 Rice moved from Los Angeles, where he had played with his brothers Larry and Ronnie in a group called Haphazards. Sam Bush recruited Rice for the Bluegrass Alliance in Reidsville, North Carolina, in 1970. A year later Rice, then 20, joined the New South. His first appearance with that group took place at a festival where he was also the featured guitarist with the Bluegrass Alliance. Rice's years with the New South were marked by a superb group LP and two solo LPs, but he was dissatisfied with the band's amplified sound. In October 1974 he moved to California and joined Grisman in the original David Grisman Quintet, with mandolinist Todd Phillips, violinist Darol Anger, and bassist Joe Carroll (who was soon replaced by Bill Amatneek, then by Phillips, with Mike Marshall taking over on second mandolin).

Rice's work with the Quintet was documented on *The David Grisman Quintet* and *Hot Dawg,* and he also contributed to Anger's 1979 album *Fiddlistics*. His own *Acoustics,* released on Kaleidoscope early this year, is his latest solo effort, and another solo album, *Mar West,* is due on Rounder soon. He has recorded a duo LP with mandolinist/fiddler Ricky Skaggs (another New South veteran) and several tracks with country vocalist Emmylou Harris, all awaiting release. The only recent Tony Rice music that has gone unrecorded has been that played with Ook'n'm, a band comprised of Rice, Anger, Marshall, and Phillips. In their West Coast performances last fall, the group offered off-the-wall techniques and music that at times approached free jazz.

Rice now devotes himself primarily to recording, his first love. He lives in Corte Madera, California, in a house filled with recordings of saxophonists John Coltrane and Eric Dolphy, keyboardist McCoy Tyner, and numerous bluegrass and jazz artists.

WHAT EVENTS LED to the formation of the David Grisman Quintet?

I'd heard the Great American Music Band [*Ed. Note: Originally a pickup group with Grisman, formed by Richard Greene; never recorded*], and then David and I played together on Bill Keith's *Something Bluegrass* album — it was pretty straightforward bluegrass, with the exception of Jim Rooney's singing. Grisman wasn't headed in the direction of Dawg music at the time, and neither was I. He wasn't out scouting musicians to play that kind of music. Richard Greene put together a lot of the Great American Music Band himself. That's a key to the whole sound of that band, which a lot of people didn't realize. David didn't have a concept for the Quintet, he didn't wake up and say, "Two mandolins!" It just came together. I was in California on my way to the Orient, and I stopped ahead of time to spend a week with Grisman. Right after the night I got there, David arranged a jam with myself, Todd Phillips and Darol Anger, and Joe Carroll, the bassist. After five or ten minutes there was an element that wasn't in a band before, and we all just stuck it out for a while.

Did you all have bluegrass backgrounds?

Except for Darol, who was classically taught, though I don't think he ever got really formal. And Joe Carroll didn't know a thing in the world about bluegrass — he didn't know who Flatt and Scruggs were, or Bill Monroe, or anybody. He was into jazz.

So that changed the bass concept?

Yeah, exactly. For one thing it changed the *group* sound —intricate walking bass lines. The bass was one of the dominant factors. Of course, Grisman was impressive. Music of this genre is difficult to separate from its performers, when you think about it.

In bluegrass, the bass and guitar work as a unit, don't they?

It depends. A lot of people are skeptical about that, me included. A bass and guitar should be able to work completely independently. If they've got it together, they'll collaborate in some legitimate form. In too many bands, the guitar player will say, "It's the bass player's line," and the bass player will say, "It's the guitar player's rhythmic pattern," and it usually ends up to be a bunch of crap. If they both just play in time — they've got all the basic essentials of music right there.

You weren't a traditional bluegrass player, in that your rhythm guitar work differed from the usual "boom-chick" style.

Anything you played would fill in a hole, an emptiness that would normally be there. By not playing a steady beat, or what people have heard for years, a guitar could be made to sound a lot fuller than a lot of people think it can be made to sound, particularly in bluegrass. I don't just mean the tone, though that *is* one of the essentials. I played rhythm similar to Clarence White, and he *really* played differently. A bluegrass rhythm is "boom-chick" and there's another that's "boom-chicka," and there's yet another thing that Clarence did and I do, which is an

Tony Rice with David Grisman.

extra note in there, an extra upsweep with your pick, which certainly adds a fuller sound.

What is your goal as a rhythm player?

I like beating the sound into the band. That's what it's all about. If you put on an old Flatt and Scruggs record from the Fifties, you'll hear what bluegrass rhythm is all about, on a diehard level. The guy's doing it right: tone, time, and articulation. If you've got those elements in there and you mess up, it'll be all right. It's always good to mess up with dignity.

You've commented that you didn't like the amplified sound of the New South.

I *never* liked it. In fact, I was disgusted with it. I never really saw any purpose in it. At some point somebody started convincing people that with an electronic transducer you could pick up the instrument's tone directly off the soundboard, and supposedly you'd get what the human ear hears, but it *can't* work that way. A mike is essentially gonna capture what the human ear would, a sound pressure level, but a transducer makes an electronic sound. A lot of people record with a mike, and then use a transducer to get an added EQ, to make it brighter. But they could just play it right in the first place. A lot of guys need a transducer for specific applications. If they want a lot of volume, they should probably go with a transducer. If they're using a mike, they're going to have to roll off so much of the high-end and low-end frequencies, it's not even going to sound like a guitar anymore.

You tend to play from the wrist more than from the elbow.

Yeah, though I don't put a lot of energy into any particular point. If I'm playing right and feeling good, it's usually balanced from my elbow to the pick. Richard Greene once made a good statement: "If it doesn't feel comfortable, you're doing it wrong."

What sound do you look for in a guitar?

What I want is a pounding sound on each note; not a crispy crackle, or a booming bass — just a richness, a tone that contains higher frequencies and lower frequencies, for a balanced tone.

You like to play loud, don't you?

Some people say I'm the loudest acoustic guitar player they've ever heard. I don't know why that's so, unless it came from

doing it a long time. When I'm doing a phrase I've done for five years, I can beat the hell out of it. If it's something I haven't done, I don't have the confidence to really bang it out.

Do you use particular scales when you solo?

A lot of times I play whatever my fingers will allow me to play. If my hands feel good, I can stretch out. If not, I quote myself a lot. In bluegrass, a lydian scale goes real good against a diatonic scale. That goes back to Blind Lemon Jefferson, Eddie Lang, Lonnie Johnson — those cats all used that, stuff like raised fourths, major thirds against minor thirds. I still stick with that; every tune I write has some of that lydian scale in it. I also like to use raised fifths now and then, in conjunction with a flatted seventh. A lot of people reject playing a minor scale over a major chord, but I like to do that sometimes. There's some of that on "Key Signator," Darol's tune on *Fiddlistics*. In a minor key I use flat thirds, sixths, or sevenths; you could use a raised fourth and make it sound bluesy — that would sound good in a major or minor key.

Do you pay a lot of attention to rhythm playing in jazz?

People ask me if I sit down with jazz records and try to learn stuff. I don't think I've caught myself doing that. Anything you listen to enough, it'll rub off on you.

What jazz guitarists have influenced you?

I've listened to George Benson for years. I've got to credit that guy with having the most amazing set of hands of any guitarist. I listened to Django Reinhardt enough to know he was pretty amazing. Some duets I heard a few years ago, of [jazz guitarists] Lonnie Johnson and Eddie Lang, put them on my all-time lists. My favorites are from different genres — Johnson, Lang, Benson, White, Earl Klugh, and Philip Catherine are some of them.

Let's back up for a moment and talk about why you left the Grisman Quintet.

It never really came down to my leaving. David had the opportunity to play with [jazz violinist] Stephane Grappelli, and I refused the gig. Grappelli's music is his, David's is David's. Tunes like "Dawg's Rag," — to me that's Dawg music. If it didn't have that quality, it wasn't Dawg

music, and I wasn't interested in playing it.

So you're trying to develop Dawg music?

That's hard to say. I'm sort of trying to correct what I didn't like about it. I didn't really favor the two-mandolin sound; one good mandolin player can cover the ground. I also thought that with Grisman I was adding more on rhythm than on lead, beating sound into the unit. If I'm soloing half the amount I was doing it with Grisman, every time I'm soloing I have more to say. Some tunes just don't need guitar solos. Norman Blake came over a while back, and we were picking, and I said, "I just did a new album, but there ain't a lot of guitar on it. I get tired of hearing guitar solos blasting out all the time." He said, "You know, I just did a new album like that, and I'm tickled to hear that you feel the same way."

Who would be in your ideal group?

I'd like to be part of a unit with the same group I've used for my last two albums: Richard Greene on violin, Sam Bush on mandolin, and Todd Phillips on bass, but at this time it's not feasible. Right now, for the near future, I don't see myself leading a band. I want to be an integrated part of a unit. I favor the format of mandolin, fiddle, guitar, and bass; the one I've been working in for the past two or three years. It's been proven that a lot more can be done with it than people had imagined. I'm open to anything that could expand that, and I'm open to different instrumentation too. I'd like to do some playing with an English horn or oboe, soft woodwinds — just one of everything. I like the concept of *one*. Then you can hear what a guy stands for.

— **Mark Hunter**

Since the April '80 publication of this article, Rice has cut a number of albums on Rounder (One Camp St., Cambridge, MA 02140): *Still Inside*, RRR 0150; *Backwaters*, RRR 0167; *The Bluegrass Album, Vols. I, II,* and *III*: RRR 0140, 1064, and 0180, respectively. *Church Street Blues*, on Sugar Hill (Box 4040, Duke Sta., Durham, NC 27706), SH 3732, also was released. Recent gigs have included performances with bluegrassers J.D. Crowe, Doyle Lawson, Bobby Hicks, and Todd Phillips; and with the eclectic David Grisman Quintet.

A SELECTED RICE DISCOGRAPHY

Solo Albums: *Acoustics*, Kaleidoscope (Box O, El Cerrito, CA 94530), F-10; *California Autumn*, Rebel (Box 191, Floyd, VA 24091), 1549; *Mar West* (Rounder, One Camp St., Cambridge, MA 02140), 0125; *Tony Rice*, Rounder, 0085; *Tony Rice Guitar*, Rebel, 1582. **With The David Grisman Quintet:** *David Grisman's Rounder Album*, Rounder, 0069; *Hot Dawg*, Horizon (1730 Kings Rd., Waycross, GA 31501), SP-731; *The David Grisman Quintet*, Kaleidoscope, F-5. **With Others:** *Catfish For Supper*, Rounder, 3026; *Duets*, Rounder, 0075; *Fiddlistics*, Kaleidoscope, F-8; *Manzanita*, Rounder, 0092; *Ramblin'*, Rounder, 0110; *The New South*, Rounder, 0044; *Something Bluegrass*, Rounder, RB-1.

FRANK WAKEFIELD

F RANK WAKEFIELD HAS "split the mandolin atom," according to mandolinist David Grisman. Anyone who knows bluegrass mandolin music knows about the fallout Wakefield has produced.

From his early appearances and recordings with the bluegrass group Red Allen And The Kentuckians in the '50s and '60s, Wakefield has proven to be a virtuoso of striking talent and originality. "New Camptown Races," his $B\flat$ tour-de-force instrumental (documented on his recent album *End Of The Rainbow*), moved mandolinists only an inch away from G major, but light years away from tradition. Wakefield also has become known for his classical-style solo pieces for mandolin, for his striking autoharp work, and for his innovative special mandolin tunings.

Frank's shows are notorious for his outrageous wit and stage antics, his "backing talkwards," puns, verbal frenzy, tricks and stunts with the band, and rousing exchanges with his audience.

Frank Wakefield was born June 26, 1934 in Emory Gap, Tennessee — a place, he says, "that wasn't big enough to whip a cat in." He was the tenth in a musical family of 12 children. He took up mandolin because few other musicians in his area played it, and it wasn't "so worn out." He had played guitar, tried the harmonica, and even played the steel guitar before trading his $1.50 guitar for his brother-in-law's $2 round-back "tater-bug" mandolin. In 1951 mandolinist Red Allen saw him playing it on a porch in Dayton, Ohio and soon the two of them — with Allen's Kentuckians — were performing and recording early bluegrass classics. The group also featured many of Frank's original songs, mandolin leads, and singing. Their 1964 album, *Bluegrass* (produced by then 17-year-old David Grisman), is a showcase of Frank's early work.

In the '60s Frank played with the Greenbriar Boys in and around New York City. Their 1967 Vanguard release *Better Late Than Never!* features Frank's playing and singing as well as three original songs. One of them, "Up To My Neck In Muddy Waters," was popularized by vocalist Linda Ronstadt.

The breakup of the Greenbriar Boys resulted in one of the most important phases of Frank's career. He moved to Saratoga Springs, New York in the early '70s, and there created a unique style characterized by his playing both lead and rhythm on one mandolin. The mandolin alone sounded "too lonely," Frank recalls. He used the technique primarily in his "classical" solo pieces. During these years he also developed his highly original autoharp style. His 1972 Rounder album *Frank Wakefield* contains 16 songs that reflect this period of his stylistic development. Most of the tunes were his own compositions, written for mandolin, banjo, and autoharp, with a stylistic scope that encompassed religious, country, bluegrass, calypso, and classical pieces, some of which he played in special tunings.

In the mid-'70s guitarist David Nelson, of the country/rock group New Riders Of The Purple Sage, brought Frank to Marin County, California where Frank and the Good Old Boys recorded *Pistol Packin' Mama*. Frank has been in California ever since.

WHEN DID YOU develop your fondness for unusual key signatures and
minor keys, such as the key of B♭ in "New
Camptown Races" and the key of Dm in
"End Of The Rainbow?"

I first wrote "New Camptown Races" in
1953 because all the tunes that were being
played then were played in major keys. I
thought that many tunes sounded the
same, so I thought I better do something
that doesn't sound like everybody else. I
started writing songs in minor keys. I don't
think I ever made any recordings without
including some minor-key songs. It's a challenge to play in minor keys. I once wrote a
tune in F♯ minor — a key that has no open
notes [on the mandolin] at all.

*When did you start writing your "clas-
sical" pieces?*

I think it was right after I wrote "New
Camptown Races." I was playing it on a
bluegrass show — before country people
even considered listening to classical
music. I just got brave and did a solo. It got
such a good reception that I started writing
a lot of things like that. I found out it would
go by itself, and that people would listen to
it if you played it for them. I'm still writing
classical-style pieces, probably more now
than ever. I want to get a record out someday with all the outrageous stuff I do.

*Most of your classical-style songs are
solo mandolin pieces and don't have the
same requirements as those of accompanied songs. How did you start writing
those solos?*

It was when I started doing shows by
myself around Saratoga Springs in New
York State. I invented a way of doing two
parts, of carrying the rhythm and the lead
at the same time. I thought, "If I have to play
solo, I have to *do* something. I have to figure
out some stuff to make this sound really
different."

*You're an excellent guitarist and banjo
player, and you also play a number of other
instruments. When did you learn to play
them?*

The guitar was the first instrument I
could play. I also played some harmonica
when I was a kid. I took the banjo up years
ago, but didn't pursue it until I recorded
"Hallelujah On The Fives" [*Frank Wake-*

field]. I started playing autoharp because I
needed more variety in my shows. I wanted
to make them sound different from anybody else's. I use five picks on my fingers,
play the autoharp on a table, and fingerpick
it like a banjo, playing behind the bar and
the buttons. I don't use the cross-hand
technique, as many other players do,
because it's too haphazard.

*When you play the autoharp on a table,
it has a completely different sound. It
almost sounds like an organ. Was that the
effect you were aiming for?*

Not really. I just wanted to be able to
play it better than anybody else. I don't
know if I've gotten that far, but I play pretty
good.

*What are some of the unusual tunings
you use on your instruments?*

On the autoharp, I "tune" the chord
bars to get more majors instead of so many
sevenths. On the mandolin, when I play
"The Greek" [*Blues Stay Away From Me*],
I raise the lowest pair of strings from *G* to *A*
and lower the highest pair of strings from *E*
to *D*, so the tuning is [from low to high]:
A-D-A-D. When I play "Little Snake And
The Dreadful Girl" during performances, I
do not tune the lowest set of strings in
unison. They are tuned to *F♯* and *A*, and
the remaining three sets of strings are
tuned [from low to high] *D-A-D*.

Have you ever thought about teaching?

I'm teaching mandolin now for the first
time in 20 years. I got real good when I
started teaching 20 years ago, and my
teaching is helping me a lot now, too. It's
got me doing things over and over again —
real simple. When you're showing somebody how to do something, you suddenly
find all kinds of ways to do it. It helps a lot. It
makes you understand those notes much
more clearly. It makes you want to perfect
your technique.

When did you meet David Grisman?

We met at a bluegrass festival in 1961 in
Maryland, and after that he used to hitch-
hike from New York to my place in Maryland for lessons. Then he started to get
bookings for me, such as in Carnegie Hall.

*It seems that most mandolinists are
into the F-5 style instrument. What kind of
mandolin are you playing now?*

A 1923 Lloyd Loar [Gibson F-5] that I
got in 1960.

*What gauge of picks do you prefer to
use, and is there any special way you like to
hold them?*

I usually use medium-gauge picks. I
used to use heavy because I could play
harder. Now I've learned that by lowering
the mandolin bridge and by using a softer
pick, you can play just as loud as you can if
you play real high with a stiff pick. I also like
to play with the rounded end of the pick,
because when I play with the pointy end,
the sound is too tinny. I used to use picks
that were as round as quarters, but if I lost
one, it was too hard to learn to use the
other kind of pick. If I had enough round
picks and could keep them I'd still use
them.

*Have you found any particular kind of
strings to be more suited to your style of
playing?*

I'm now using specially made strings. I
used to use Gibson, but stopped because
they wouldn't match. You'd get a couple of
D strings and they wouldn't note together;
they wouldn't be in unison.

*Are you satisfied with commercially
available instrument bridges, or do you
also use specially made bridges?*

I make my own bridges. They're made
from epoxy glue and fiberglass, and they
produce a pronounced treble sound.

How do you see your musical future?

I see myself concentrating more and
more on music I created — for example, my
arrangements of classical pieces. I want to
show people what I have done. I think that
performing original music suits me more
than anything else.

— Randall Colaizzi

This article originally appeared in the April
'81 issue of *Frets Magazine*. The current
lineup of Wakefield's band is David Nelson
on guitar and vocals, Tom Stern on banjo,
and Wakefield on mandolin.

A SELECTED WAKEFIELD DISCOGRAPHY

Solo Albums: *Blues Stay Away From Me,* Takoma (3105 Pico Blvd., Santa Monica, CA 90405), TAK 7082; *End Of The Rainbow,* Bay (1516
Oak St., Suite 320, Alameda, CA 94501), 214; *Frank Wakefield,* Rounder 007. **With Others:** *Better Late Than Never,* Vanguard, 79233;
Bluegrass, Flying Fish (1304 W. Schubert, Chicago, IL 60614), FF 049; *Bluegrass,* Folkways (43 W. 61st St., New York, NY 10023), FA 2408;
Pistol Packin' Mama, Round (dist. by United Artists), *The Early Days Of Bluegrass,* Rounder, 1014; *Early Dawg,* Sugar Hill (Box 4040, Duke
Station, Durham, NC 27706), 3713.

David Grisman with Frank Wakefield at the Greenmountain Festival in Vermont, July 4, 1976.

RICKY SKAGGS

"**S**OMEDAY," RICKY SKAGGS laughs, "someone is going to come up to me and say, 'Gee, I saw you 20 years ago with Ralph Stanley!' I'll be 25, and I'll feel like the oldest man in the world."

Skaggs, 26, already has more years of active performing behind him than some artists half-again his age. He cut his teeth on the mandolin when he was five, made his television debut when he was seven, and has been going strong ever since. Today he is a key figure in Emmylou Harris' Hot Band, a frequent guest with Buck White And The Down Home Folks, and a solo recording artist in his own right. His latest venture on vinyl is the new release *Skaggs & Rice*, which features Ricky and guitarist Tony Rice playing and singing old-time country music in an affectionate tribute to their parents and to their musical roots.

Skaggs' musical roots go back to July 18, 1954, when he was born in Lawrence County, Kentucky. Hobert Skaggs, Ricky's father, was a welder who enjoyed playing the guitar; Ricky's mother was a singer. Ricky began singing with his parents at three. Two years later, Ricky's father returned from a welding job in Lima, Ohio, with a mandolin. "He got snowed in there," Ricky recalls, "and bought the mandolin and brought it back to me. He showed me three chords, your basic *G, C,* and *D,* and then went back to Ohio and got snowed in again. When he came back I was singing and changing chords at the same time, and it freaked him out! So he got interested in music again in a hurry, and went out and bought himself a real good guitar — the guitar I'm playing now, in fact: a '59 Martin D-28."

With Hobert Skaggs on guitar and Ricky on mandolin, the Skaggs family formed its own band. "Me and my mom would do a lot of duets," Ricky recalls, "and my dad would sing baritone or bass, so we would have lead and tenor and bass, and it would sound real haunting and neat. We used to work a lot of churches, and we played in high schools and at pie suppers and theaters and stuff. Sometimes we'd be guests for the Stanley Brothers or whoever came through town. I got a chance to play with Ralph and Carter Stanley a couple of times while Carter was still living, back in '61 or '62, and they were just incredible."

Idolizing the Stanley Brothers as a youngster, Ricky had no inkling that before he left high school he would actually be performing with Ralph Stanley. Meanwhile, Ricky was finding his niche as an instrumentalist.

"I was mostly playing rhythm when I first started out," Skaggs says. "I wasn't much of a soloist. Then about a year after I started playing and learning chords, my dad would want me to take little solos, so I would play real simple breaks. My fingers weren't trained to go to those positions, but even though I technically didn't know how to do it, I was hearing it in my head."

By the time Ricky was seven the family had moved to Tennessee. An audition landed him an appearance on the Flatt And Scruggs television show, his first taste of widespread public exposure. As the gap between what he could hear and what he could play narrowed, he took up guitar as a second instrument. When he was 13 he discovered the fiddle, inspired by one of his father's cousins, Eulas Paul Wright, who mixed hoedowns with Joe Venuti and Stuff Smith swing tunes.

Ricky became proficient enough on the fiddle to begin working square dances with his father. One night the Skaggs father/son duo was invited to perform in a show at a high school in Ezel, Kentucky (the family had since moved back to

Ricky Skaggs at the Corinth Bluegrass Festival in 1977. Ricky's versatility has earned him a reputation as a sideman par-excellence, but his plans for the future go far beyond supporting roles.

Kentucky, where I was going to high school. Daddy told us to take our instruments, just in case somebody might want us to play. Well, Ralph was late for the show, and the owner of the club knew who we were, so he asked if Keith and I would get up and sing because the people were getting restless and wanted some music. So we got up and entertained the crowd, and they were liking it — and in walks Ralph Stanley, my hero. We were singing 'Little Glass Of Wine' or something like that. He set his banjo case down on the barstool, and I glanced over at him out of the corner of my eye. He wasn't really smiling; he was looking off somewhere like he was reminiscing, in a way. It turned out that he was. Afterward he said, 'Boys, the first time I saw y'all it just brought back so many memories of me and Carter.' That really blew me away."

Stanley and his band did their show, then asked Skaggs and Whitley to come back for an encore. Later he invited them to see him at the same club in a month, when he was due back for a return engagement. After the second meeting, Stanley asked the young musicians to pay him a visit at his home in McClure, Virginia. The boys made the drive and spent a long time playing and singing with their host on Stanley's porch. Stanley then offered them another invitation — to appear with him at an upcoming bluegrass festival in Reidsville, North Carolina. Ricky cites that festival as a turning point in his career.

"I was 15 at the time," he recalls. "It was a big year for me. We got called back for three encores in our first time at Reidsville, and everybody just took to us and kind of put us under their wing. After that, Ralph asked us to start working with him full-time in the summer."

Skaggs stayed with the Stanley band for the better part of the next two years. "It was a good training ground," he says, "and I learned a lot of things about feel and music — I learned what *not* to play. I was playing mostly mandolin, and then I would trade on twin fiddles with Curly Ray Cline. Those were really great days."

In 1972, discouraged because times were hard for bluegrass bands and because his expenses were running beyond his income, Skaggs quit and moved to Washington, D.C. There he married and got a job as a boiler operator for a Virginia power company. He lasted on the job six months — which he recalls as the worst six months of his life. He was rescued when Bill Emerson of the Country Gentlemen asked him to play fiddle on a new album that the group was recording. It was a departure from Country Gentlemen tradition, because the group had never used a fiddle before; but it was a successful experiment, and it earned Skaggs a regular spot in the band's lineup. He stayed with the Gentlemen for two years, then left to do his first solo album: *That's It,* for the Rebel label, featuring his parents on a number of the cuts.

Kentucky). "When I went in," Ricky recalls, "this boy was up on the stage singing with three or four other people. I liked his singing a lot. After a while it was time for my dad and I to go on, and this same guy came back and listened while we did a couple of duets. We saw each other downstairs later and introduced ourselves. It was Keith Whitley. We got to talking about the music we liked and discovered we had a lot in common."

Whitley came to visit the Skaggs family the following weekend, and soon Ricky and Keith were working as a trio with Keith's banjo-playing brother, Dwight. In 1970 the group began doing radio shows on station WLKS in West Liberty, Kentucky. The programs — a half-hour Saturday bluegrass show and a half-hour Sunday gospel show — were taped in the Whitleys' garage.

"One night Keith and I went with my dad to see Ralph Stanley," Ricky says. "He was going to be playing in Fort Gay, West Virginia, across the river from Louisville,

He had almost finished the album when he got a call from J.D. Crowe, asking him to temporarily fill a vacancy in the New South that had been created by the departure of Larry Rice (Tony Rice's brother). Ricky was more interested in putting a band of his own together, but agreed to come down to Lexington, Kentucky, Crowe's base of operations, for a weekend. He then went home, finished his recording work, returned to Lexington, and decided to stay. He remained with Crowe for nearly a year. The stint gave Ricky his first opportunity to work regularly with Tony Rice and later with lightning-fingered dobro artist Jerry Douglas, who joined the group in June 1974.

After the New South made a successful tour of Japan, Rice left to play with David Grisman. Still eager to have his own group, Skaggs recruited Douglas and, with guitarist Wes Golding and banjoist Terry Baucom, formed Boone Creek. Organized in October 1976, the group stayed together for two years, with a succession of bass players that included Vince Gill and Steven Bryant. The band recorded one album for Rounder (*Boone Creek*) and another for Sugar Hill (*One-Way Track*).

The members of Boone Creek went their separate ways in early 1978, after completing their second album. Skaggs' own way led to Emmylou Harris' Hot Band. Ricky had met Emmylou while he was working with Country Gentlemen. He was introduced to her and to Linda Ronstadt during a picking party at the home of John Starling, then lead singer with the Seldom Scene. Emmylou invited him to perform on her first album, *Pieces Of The Sky*, and in 1978, as Boone Creek was finishing *One-Way Track*, she asked him to join her for a concert tour through Europe.

Ricky's second solo album, *Sweet Temptation*, was recorded the following fall and released in 1979. Guests included Rice, Harris, Douglas, mandolinist/pianist Buck White, steel guitarist Buddy Emmons, and electric guitarist Albert Lee, among other artists. That recording effort was followed by *Skaggs And Rice*. Ricky is currently finishing a third solo album, as yet untitled, that will feature appearances by Ralph Stanley, Dolly Parton, Linda Ronstadt, Buck White And The Down Home Folks,

and members of the Hot Band.

Skaggs uses several guitars, a couple of mandolins, and a 5-string fiddle that was custom-built for him by Arthur Conner, a Floyd County, Virginia, violin maker. "I hardly ever use a 4-string fiddle anymore," Ricky says. "It throws me off. I keep thinking of all the low parts I can play in a song, and when I don't have that [low string], it kind of freaks me out. I use it a lot with Buck and the girls — we play a lot of western swing and jazz and stuff like that. The girls [Cheryl White and Sharon Hicks] sing a lot of slower country stuff, and that gives me a chance to play a lot of low and pretty things. Working with them has kept my fiddle chops up. I don't actually get to play enough fiddle with Emmy, because I'm playing guitar, singing, and playing mandolin so much."

Ricky strings his fiddle with a 5-string set made by Thomastik. He favors relatively heavy pernambuco wood bows with bleached horsehair, using fairly tight bow tension and dressing the bow hair with either Hidersine or Hill & Sons rosin (both are English brands).

Skaggs' principal performance mandolin is a Gibson A-O model, dating roughly from the early 1920s. He says he prefers the mellower sound of the round-hole model for amplified work. The instrument is on indefinite loan from Jim Smith of the Pinnacle Boys. Ricky's other mandolin is a 1924 Gibson F-5, signed by Lloyd Loar, which Skaggs has owned since 1975. He uses GHS nickel-wrap mona-steel guitar strings on his Loar mandolin, snapping out the ball ends and using the remaining loops to attach the strings. His gauge preferences, high to low strings, are .012", .016", .028", and .038". He prefers the nickel wrap because it is "slicker and smoother."

Ricky's main guitars are all Martins: a 1942 000-21 that has been in his family since 1942, his father's 1959 D-28, and a 1961 D-21 (named "Red") that he bought in Nashville. Ricky had the D-21's tone bars and braces scalloped at the Nashville Pickin' Parlour by luthier Danny Farrington. Skaggs strings his guitars with bronze GHS strings, favoring medium-gauge sets but occasionally using light-gauge and heavy-gauge strings for particular effects.

He uses different picks for different

purposes, alternating between heavy genuine tortoiseshell picks, Fender heavy picks, and Fender medium picks. He usually prefers a Fender medium for his A-model mandolin and heavy tortoiseshell for his F-5.

Skaggs occasionally plays banjo, too. He owns a Stelling Staghorn model and plays in a frailing style. His *That's It* album and Emmylou Harris' recent *Roses In The Snow* album are the only discs that document his banjo work. "I started playing banjo when I was 14 or 15," he says. "A real old-time musician named Sanford Kelly, in West Liberty, Kentucky, taught me to play clawhammer style. I actually just wanted to learn to play clawhammer. I *can* play Scruggs style, but I feel that I'm a lot better clawhammer player than I am a three-finger picker." He uses a plastic thumbpick and either National or Dunlop metal fingerpicks.

Ricky's versatility has earned him a reputation as a sideman par-excellence, but his plans for the future go far beyond supporting roles. Skaggs still has ideas for a band of his own.

"I'd like something for myself," he says matter-of-factly. "It's time to get my own career started."

— **Jim Hatlo**

Since the August '80 publication of this article, Ricky Skaggs has soared into the limelight and has become a major country star. He has had several hit singles that made it to #1 on the Country charts, and he's earned a handful of prestigious awards. In 1982 he was voted Top New Male Vocalist by the Academy of Country Music, Best Band of the Year by *Music City News*, and Best Male Vocalist by the Country Music Association. These honors were repeated in 1983 when he won the *Music City News'* Best Bluegrass Act Of The Year award, Star of Tomorrow award, and the Academy of Country Music's Band of the Year Award. In the spring of 1982 Skaggs was inducted into the Grand Ole Opry — the 61st artist and the youngest.

His current band include Bruce Bouton on steel guitar; Ray Flacke on lead guitar; George Grantham on drums; Jessie Chambers on electric bass; Mickey Merritt on piano; Lou Reid on fiddle, guitar, mandolin, and dobro; and Bobby Hicks on fiddle.

A SELECTED SKAGGS DISCOGRAPHY SOLO ALBUMS:

Solo Albums: *That's It*, Rebel (Box 91, Floyd, VA 24091), 1549; *Sweet Temptation*, Sugar Hill (Box 4040, Duke Station, Durham, NC 22706), SH-3706. **With Boone Creek:** *Boone Creek*, Rounder, 0081; *One Way Track*, Sugar Hill, SH-3701. **With Emmylou Harris:** *Pieces Of The Sky*, Reprise, 2284; *Blue Kentucky Girl*, Warner Brothers, 3318; *Roses In The Snow*, Warner Brothers, BSK 3422. **With J.D. Crowe:** *The New South*, Rounder, 044. **With Jerry Douglas:** *Fluxology*, Rounder, 0093. **With Tony Rice:** *Skaggs & Rice*, Sugar Hill, SH-3711.

MARK O'CONNOR

O VER THE PAST 25 YEARS, younger and more technically gifted musicians have emerged from the explosion of string instrument players. But the arrival of a true prodigy is still a signal event in the world of music. A 14-year-old kid who can rip through an Al Di Meola guitar break or an Earl Scruggs banjo solo at top speed is one thing; but a 14-year-old kid who can step into a long-standing musical tradition and add significant *new* dimensions to it is quite another. Mark O'Connor is quite another musician.

Consider the following statistics: By the time he was 14, O'Connor had already won two National Junior Fiddle Championships, a Grand Masters Fiddle Championship, and the National Guitar Flatpicking Championships — and had produced two albums under his own name. O'Connor, 23, has repeated all of those wins at least once and is the current Grand Masters Fiddle Champion. Last year he revealed a new dimension to his talent by capturing first place in Buck White's World Mandolin Championship at Kerrville, Texas. To date O'Connor has recorded eight albums under his leadership, performed on many others, and played in two of the world's leading-edge instrumental bands —"dawg" music's pioneering David Grisman Quintet and the electric rock/country/jazz fusion Dregs.

Judging Mark O'Connor's talent by mere statistics, however, is shortsighted. The proof is in the listening and in the wonder and awe in which he is held by his peers. Nashville fiddler Buddy Spicher has called him the greatest fiddle player in the world. David Grisman says that Mark is perhaps the most imaginative, adventurous, and versatile musician Grisman has ever worked with. Roy Acuff introduced him from the stage of the Grand Old Opry when O'Connor was 12 and informed the audience that Mark had made him reconsider the concept of reincarnation. Violinist Darol Anger, who worked with him for a year and a half in Grisman's band, is more specific.

"I find it very difficult to talk about Mark, because he has really put himself in a category that very few people have reached in the history of music," explains Anger. "He seems to have been blessed from birth with the ability to express a sense of truth about what moves people musically. It's not anything he did to get there. He just seems to be tapped into something that the rest of us get to experience only on occasion. He also has unbelievable physical attributes that allow him to express any idea he has in his head immediately. There's no blockage, no matter how physically impossible it may seem to express an idea. His coordination is one-in-a-billion; he can memorize anything instantly and has monstrous hands. Mark has helped us all in looking at what we do in pursuit of technique for technique's sake. It makes us wonder what it means when somebody comes along who can do things that we could work at for years and still never achieve. He's a very leveling influence."

There is little in Mark's background to account for his prodigious talent. He was born on August 4, 1961, in Seattle, Washington to essentially non-musical parents (although his mother, Marty, listened to a lot of classical music). His parents' first sense of his musical gift came when he was three, and demonstrated the ability to recognize specific composers and albums and put them on the turntable. His first instrumental lessons began at age six as soon as he was able to wrap his already

Mike Marshall, Stephan Grappelli, Rob Wasserman, David Grisman, and Mark O'Conner.

long fingers around a classical guitar neck. Though he studied for nearly three years and demonstrated promise, the rigidity of written music offered little appeal to him and he came close to quitting. Recognizing that, his teacher recommended that he switch to flamenco guitar where he could study by ear from Normando Breniz, a Peruvian player living temporarily in the Seattle area. No longer bound by written music, his talent began to grow at the same time his musical interests were widening. He entered, and won, his first contest at the age of ten — a formal classical/flamenco competition sponsored by the University of Washington.

Despite his obvious talent, by the age of 11 Mark had lost interest in formal guitar study. In an attempt to revive his flagging enthusiasm, his parents bought him the violin he had been wanting for three years, and the doors were unlocked. Within a half hour after picking it up he could play the melody to Doug Kershaw's "Louisiana Man" on one string. Three weeks later he was playing fiddle at a square dance, though he only knew three tunes. His first fiddle lessons were from a 14-year-old girl named Barbara Lamb who was experienced in contest fiddling. She also introduced him to bluegrass through records that, in turn, inspired him to acquire a banjo, a dobro, and a steel-string guitar.

Seven months after acquiring the violin, he made his first trip to the National Old-Time Fiddle Championships in Weiser, Idaho, and finished second in the Junior-Junior (12 and under) Division. There Mark experienced his first Texas-style fiddle jam, led by the acknowledged King Of Texas fiddle himself, 65-year-old Benny Thomasson.

Texas-style fiddling is characterized by a slower, more swinging feel and more complex improvised variations than, say, bluegrass style. Its roots can be traced to Bob Wills' bands in the 1930s, where Eldon Shamblin's guitar laid down a running pro-

gression of jazz chords with moving bass lines and a heavy sock rhythm, giving the fiddle breakdowns a totally different feel. Mark taped that jam session and took it home with him, and Thomasson became his most important musical influence.

Over the course of the next year, Mark kept running into Thomasson at various fiddle contests. Each time, Benny would take him aside and work with him. In June 1974 Mark returned to Weiser and won both the Junior-Junior and Junior (18 and under) Divisions. The wins started an amazing streak that was ended only by a change in the contest rules. He won the Junior Division for the next three years and, because he was so clearly dominant, he was allowed to compete in the Open Division at age 16. Finishing second that year, he followed up with three consecutive victories — and again the rules were changed. A winner has to sit out for one year after winning three straight championships. He was eligible to compete again this year.

At the end of a summer of touring on the 1974 festival circuit, Mark and his mother made their first trip to Nashville. There they looked up dobro player Tut Taylor, whom they had met at a Seattle bluegrass festival. Taylor plugged Mark into a jam session at Nashville's Old-Time Pickin' Parlor. When it was over, Dr. Perry Harris, the founder of the Grand Masters Fiddling Championship, invited Mark to compete the following year. Two nights later, Harris introduced Mark to Roy Acuff in Acuff's dressing room at the Grand Ole Opry. Astounded by O'Connor's talent, Acuff gave Mark a spot in his Opry set that same night.

While in Nashville Mark also recorded his first album, a collection of fiddle tunes now named *Mark O'Connor, 4-time National Junior Fiddle Champion* [Rounder (One Camp St., Cambridge, MA 02140), 0046]. Norman Blake and Charlie Collins backed him up on mandolin and guitar,

respectively. Closing out a busy summer, Mark entered the National Guitar Flatpicking Championships at Winfield, Kansas, and finished second. He returned the following year and won it — at age 14. The rules were changed so that a one-time winner would have to wait five years to try for a second victory.

Mark, accompanied by his mother, continued to tour the festival and contest circuit for the next few summers, though he went through a period when his wins began to drop off. Old-time fiddle contests have somewhat rigidly defined parameters aimed at preserving the purity of a unique style, and Mark's outside musical influences — mainly jazz — began to creep into his playing. It took a period of rededication and listening to himself on old tapes to get back on the track. In the meantime he continued to record a new album every year and started playing short engagements with artists like Jim & Jesse, Buck White, J.D. Crowe, and Dan Crary. By the time he was ready to begin his senior year in high school, he either held or had held every major fiddle championship in the U.S. and had five albums to his credit as a soloist. Because his grades had slipped badly, he decided to take the year off from touring and concentrate on graduating.

Following graduation in 1979, he again hit the festival circuit, with vague plans to land in Nashville and find occasional session work to supplement his touring. In late August David Grisman called Mark, seeking a guitar player to tour with his band and violin great Stephane Grappelli. Mark accepted, but first had to fulfill a two-week commitment to tour Japan (as a fiddler) with Dan Crary. He returned just three days before the Grappelli gig and learned the chord changes to nearly two dozen jazz standards. The tour went so well that Grisman asked him to become a regular member of the band. He played guitar and some fiddle with the quintet for a year and a half.

In February 1981 Mark broke his arm above the elbow in a skiing accident, and the Grisman band became a quartet. While recuperating, O'Connor got a call from Steve Morse, the leader of the eclectic electric Dregs, who was looking for a fiddle player. Ten weeks after breaking his arm, Mark played his first gig with the Dregs. During his tenure with them, he was selected to appear as part of a PBS series called *Young Artists In America*, which paired an established star with a prodigy of the star's choice. Mark was selected by Merle Haggard, and the show culminated in a concert for Ronald Reagan and the presidential entourage at Reagan's California ranch.

In 1983, Mark left the Dregs to pursue a more independent career. Since then he has made brief tours with John McEuen, Peter Rowan, and Chris Hillman. He also did a brief tour of France and Ireland with Doc And Merle Watson and performed on their just-released Flying Fish LP *Doc And Merle Watson's Guitar Album*. Other artists he has recorded with this year include John Hartford, Dan Crary, and Bela Fleck. Rounder will soon release Mark's eighth album, *False Dawn* — a true solo effort on which he plays all the instruments, and for which he wrote all the music. Last August Mark was about to end a brief swing through the Middle East that included stops in Syria and Egypt and culminated in a command performance for King Hussein of Jordan. He spoke with *Frets* just before his departure.

WHAT INSTRUMENT DO *you feel capable of making your most advanced musical statement on?*

Probably the violin. Mainly because I feel that I can do some things on it that I haven't heard before. Whenever I pick up a plectrum instrument, I always feel that no matter what I play I must be quoting somebody, just because there are so many players. That's particularly true of the guitar. I don't think there have been that many violin players who have tried to play a fusion of styles like country, rock, and jazz, like I'm doing now.

Does that make the violin your favorite instrument?

Actually, my two favorite instruments are ones that I can't really play — piano and drums. I really love 'em. The instrument I most like to sit around the house and play is an acoustic guitar. I write all my tunes on the guitar because I can play a bass line, melody, and chords. It's the closest thing I can get to a piano.

What instrument do you feel is the most difficult to master?

I think the answer to that is different for different people. Any instrument is hard if you hope to play it very well, though some are more difficult to play physically. I can't imagine anyone playing a [jazz saxophonist] Charlie Parker solo on an acoustic bass, for instance. There is an old saying that the violin is the hardest to play, but I think that idea came from its role in an orchestra where it is usually given the lead — the hardest part. But is a violin really any harder to play than a cello?

Do you interpret a tune differently depending on what instrument you are playing?

Yes, because each instrument suggests a different approach to me. I've seen people play a tune on the fiddle and then pick up a mandolin and play the same notes. I don't do that, but I do think I physically play the guitar and mandolin like a fiddle player because that's the way I hear things. I finger the top three strings [G-B-E] of the guitar in a fiddle position because the space is about the same width as a violin neck. The mandolin has the same scale as a violin, of course, but you can't get as much freedom with the left hand because of the double strings and frets.

How did you maintain your identity when everyone was calling you a genius, and you were still just a kid?

There was a lot of pressure, because everybody makes such a big thing out of it because of your size. Fortunately, I grew tall real fast. I was almost six-foot by the time I was 13. My mom helped me keep it in perspective. She wasn't the pushy type. She'd get me to the contests and festivals, but she didn't go up and hype me to people. When I was 11 or 12, I didn't have any idea what life was about. It wasn't like a learning thing I was doing. It was just something that happened. When I went on the *Grand Ol' Opry* I didn't know it was a big deal for Roy Acuff to give me a spot on his part of the show and then introduce me as some kind of genius. I barely knew who he was. I was more interested in meeting [fiddler] Howdy Forrester and in getting back to Seattle to hang out with my skateboarding friends.

Do you think anyone resents your talent and presence?

I sure hope not. The fiddling world is different than the bluegrass world. There's not the petty jealousy between amateur and professional. Every fiddle player I know — if they're any good —makes money playing. They either play at dances or in a country/western band or something. When I didn't enter Weiser last year, people were complaining. They want a chance at you.

What instruments are currently your most-played ones?

I have an 1850s Maggini copy violin that I find is very stable for traveling. For guitars, I'm using Ovations and a Takamine dreadnought with a cutaway. All of them have pickups. I'm going to be endorsing Ovation and they're building me a beautiful 12-string Adamas with a thin body and stereo piezo pickups so each double string can be split between two amplifiers. My mandolin was built by Luke Thompson [Zachary, LA] and I won it at Buck White's contest. I've had John Monteleone [Bay Shore, NY] put an arched fretboard on it.

How do you amplify your violin?

I have a Barcus-Berry bridge pickup mounted on the bass side of the instrument. To avoid feedback, I stuff each f-hole with foam and put some foam under the tailpiece. That pretty much takes care of all the parts that vibrate.

Have you ever considered using a solidbody electric violin?

I've thought about it but I've never heard one that sounded or played as good as my acoustic with a pickup. I also like to be able to hear it acoustically for tuning. If you have a solidbody, you have to totally rely on the amp sound to hear the pitch, which can fool you. It's really tough to tune to electric sounds on a violin because it creates harmonics and distortion. Actually, someone is building one for me and he wants to put things like active EQ inside.

How are you able to get so much volume out of an acoustic violin?

I have a very strong right arm — and you have to play loud to drown out the guitar player in contests. Texas-style guitarists are the loudest. I remember playing with [fiddler] Richard Greene, and he would grab my fiddle from me and wonder how I was projecting. It just comes from that powerful snake-like motion. I'll get my shoulders arched up and just play as loud as I want.

What gives you the most problems in music?

The emotional factor still gets to me. When you're playing with a band 150 nights a year like I was with the Dregs, there's a tendency to say, "What the heck. I don't feel very good tonight so I'll just play lousy. I don't care. The audience won't know the difference." The band knows and *you* know, though. The other side of that is that when you're playing the same tunes and the same parts over and over, if you mess up one little part it can really bum you out even though you're the only one who knows it. Physically and technically it's no problem. Keeping it together in my head, from an emotional standpoint, is the hardest thing.

As a veteran musician at 22, would you say you've arrived?

So far I've had a lot of mini-triumphs in my life, like contest wins and band opportunities that are little things but also big things. Everything seems like a big step at the time, and when it happens you say, "This is it. I've arrived!" But the next day you realize it's just a false dawn. You know that one day you're going to go over it and that will be a real dawn. I'm not exactly sure what that means, but I think one part of it has to do with being financially stable. That means, in my mind, the real dawn will come when I can travel anywhere in the world and just go play music on the street wherever, and with whomever, I want.

— *Jon Sievert*

A SELECTED O'CONNOR DISCOGRAPHY

Solo Albums (on Rounder, One Camp St., Cambridge, MA 02140): *Four-Time National Jr. Fiddle Champion*, 0046; *Pickin' In The Wind*, 0068; *Texas Jam Session*, OMAC 1; *In Concert*, OMAC 2; *Markology*, 0090; *On The Rampage*, 0018; *Soppin' The Gravy*, 0137; *False Dawn*, 0165. **With Others — David Grisman Quintet:** *Quintet '80*, Warner Bros., BSK 3469. **Fred Carpenter,** *Cuttin' Loose*, Grass Mountain [dist. by Richey Records, Box 12937, Fort Worth, TX 76114], 1004. **Doc And Merle Watson:** *Guitar Album*, Flying Fish (1304 W. Schubert, Chicago, IL 60614), FF 301.

BELA FLECK

BELA FLECK, IN SOME WAYS, is a typical 5-string banjo player. He uses two fingerpicks and a thumbpick and plays mainly in the three-finger-roll style a la Earl Scruggs, whose recordings he has closely studied. Bela plays most tunes in *G* tuning. Like thousands of other banjoists, he originally was inspired to play by such classic tunes as "Dueling Banjos" and "The Ballad Of Jed Clampett," popularized in the '60s. He's been part of five or six bluegrass bands. He's 24 years old.

There are other ways in which Bela (rhymes with "*Lay*-la") is *not* such a typical banjo player. He was named after the twentieth-century Hungarian composer Bela Bartok. When Fleck was a teenager he practiced banjo seven hours a day. He attended the New York High School of Music and Art — which accepts only musically and artistically gifted students. He has written 200 banjo tunes. And in the 1982 *Frets* Readers Poll he was voted Best Country and Bluegrass Banjo Player, and Best Dixieland and Jazz Banjo Player.

The key to Bela's appeal is his amazing mastery of every known technique for the 5-string banjo played with fingerpicks. Not only has he assimilated every chapter of the bluegrass banjo "book" to date, but he has written a number of new chapters and is working on several other "books" at the same time.

In the last year Bela played note-for-note harmony arrangements of Earl Scruggs' classic tunes along with Earl; he played note-for-note Irish melodies along with DeDanann's fiddler Frankie Gavin; he was invited to participate in an onstage jazz jam at the prestigious Telluride Jazz Festival in Colorado. He released his second solo album, *Natural Bridge*, an eclectic work of original compositions and arrangements, featuring such leading acoustic musicians as Mark O'Connor, Ricky Skaggs, Jerry Douglas, David Grisman, Mike Marshall, and Darol Anger.

Born and raised in the heart of New York City, Bela played enough guitar to pass his audition for the New York High School of Music and Art. Many of his classmates were classically trained. Because of the school's requirement that students become proficient on orchestral instruments, Bela studied the French horn and joined the chorus. But in his free time, he relentlessly practiced the banjo, and he studied privately with three of the best banjoists in New York — Tony Trischka, Erik Darling, and Mark Horowitz. When he graduated from high school in 1976, he was ready to opt out of the expected college path and go fulltime with the Boston-based bluegrass band Tasty Licks.

Bela first came to national attention on records and through appearances with Tasty Licks. But his graduation in 1979 to Spectrum, a super-band that included Jimmy Gaudreau and Glenn Lawson, along with the 1980 release of his first solo album, *Crossing The Tracks,* gave him the increased exposure that led to his being heralded as *the* up-and-coming banjo player of the 1980s.

In November 1981 he left Spectrum to join superpickers Sam Bush, John Cowan, and Pat Flynn in the re-formed New Grass Revival, the most musically innovative and dynamic band ever to challenge the borders of bluegrass music.

As busy as Bela is with the band, he still finds time for other musical pursuits. He is recording another album for the Rounder label, so far untitled, which will consist entirely of duets with such players as Tony Rice, Mike Marshall, and David Grisman, in a variety of musical styles. He also is recording a Dan Crary instrumen-

tal album, along with Sam Bush and others. Bela tries to play as much jazz as possible, and when time allows, he plays with an informal, strictly bluegrass all-star band called the Dreadful Snakes, which soon will release an album of its own on Rounder. erson who wears his banjo crown casually and humbly. His young age is undoubtedly part of the reason for the groundswell of interest in him. It is impressive for anyone to have achieved such success; but it is astonishing for someone to have done it within ten years of having started to play the instrument. In that sense, Bela is more than a masterful creative artist. When it comes to fast learning, he is something of a phenomenon.

TONY TRISCHKA HAD a big influence on you. You once said you learned everything that he recorded. Was that just by listening, or did he actually show you things?

I would start out by trying to figure things out by myself. I would come up with a way to play it that usually was the hardest way you could ever imagine. Then I would take it to him and he'd usually crack up. He thought it was pretty funny how I had figured out how to do it, and then he'd show me that all I had to do was pull off to an open

string instead of stretching my hands six frets over in the other direction. A lot of what Tony does sounds harder than it is, though a lot of what he does is incredibly hard. Trying to figure out what Tony is doing without seeing him play is pretty difficult. When you have seen him play a little bit, you get some idea of what he is doing. I think that at one time I could play everything he'd done on those albums that he did with Country Cooking, as well as on the first two or three of his own albums.

Did you get much out of going to the New York High School of Music and Art?

I learned a lot of basic theory and got to know a lot of very good musicians at a pretty early age.

What kind of practicing were you doing during high school?

I put in a half hour in the morning before I went to school, and then as soon as I got home I'd play until I fell asleep. That would be from about 3:30 to about 11 p.m., subtracting a half hour for dinner. Every possible minute I was locked in the room, trying to figure it out.

Was there anything in particular that you were practicing?

I spent a lot of time working out scales. I had devised some kind of strange system of playing melodic scales from the 1st fret to the 22nd fret, melodic style, but I found very little use for them. I also wrote melodic

exercises; that is, I thought I was writing great music at the time, but now when I listen back to them they sound a lot more like exercises.

When you were in Boston with Tasty Licks, weren't you part of another band that played in the streets a lot?

Yes. The summer before I joined Tasty Licks, and the summer after it disbanded, I was in an eclectic group. Gene Schwartz was a pretty good fiddler who could play classical and jazz, and some bluegrass, too. Mark Schatz was playing bass, and we had this lady who sang Broadway-type songs. We would do some bluegrass tunes, jazz, Irish-type material. We did play in the streets a lot. Playing in the streets is one good way to find out whether you can hold a crowd. Whatever you play has to be able to appeal to somebody who might not really know what you're doing.

Didn't you go back on the streets again before getting involved with Spectrum?

When Tasty Licks decided to split up, Mark Schatz and I went looking for work and we did some street performing in Boston to make a living, hoping that the Spectrum gig would come through. When it did, we moved down South. It was really exciting to play with these guys who had worked with J.D. Crowe. I always felt that I had to follow J.D.; I don't know if that was really true, but Jimmy Gaudreau and Glenn Lawson had worked with J.D., and I was the next guy they worked with.

How did you tackle that one?

I spent all month when J.D. was playing at the Holiday Inn in Lexington, Kentucky, sitting in front of him and watching his hands — listening like a madman. I tried to figure out what he was doing — how he got the sound he was getting. A good friend of mine, Steve Cooley [banjoist with the Dillards], and I used to sit at the tables and watch J.D. Crowe play. Then we'd go home and try to figure out what he was doing. We'd bend our picks funny ways, try different gauges of strings, high bridges, low bridges, thin bridges. I was too scared of him to really pick his brain in person. He made me nervous, but eventually we became friends.

Does your approach to timing change when you play different kinds of music?

When I play jazz, I notice that people tend to phrase well behind the beat, and in bluegrass there's a tendency to play on the faster side — or on the front side of the beat. If you sit with a metronome and play — think of that metronome beat as the point. If, when you're playing with the metronome, it beats a tiny bit before you play, then you're not quite with it. I think that all the greatest bluegrass bands play together on the front of the beat.

How did you go about becoming a member of the New Grass Revival?

The hardest part was plugging in [playing amplified]. The first night I used a Barcus-Berry transducer. It was the only thing I could get in time for the show. I had just returned from Japan five days earlier and had done intensive rehearsals those five days before we went and played our first show. I didn't have time to experiment with anything. I thought, "Boy, that sounded horrible." The Barcus-Berry was really disappointing. So I spent the next six months experimenting. I got a friend of mine named Chuck Adair [Willicutt Guitar Shoppe, Lexington, Kentucky] to help me design a pickup that I am still using. It is an electric guitar pickup mounted under my bridge, and it picks up the sound through a sliver of metal I've got taped to the head, exactly under the bridge. The sound goes from the bridge through the head into the metal, and then from the metal, magnetically, to the pickup. The pickup doesn't touch the metal. That's been the best sound I have been able to get so far.

How does the banjo work as a rock instrument?

As a rock and roll instrument, the banjo is limited in sustain. You have to approach it as a piano player approaches his instrument — you can't depend on sustain when you are a piano player. I play some electric guitar licks and imagine the sustain — even though it's not there.

Do you ever think of adding an effects device like a delay unit, which would enable you to put sustain on a particular note?

That would be nice. Everything I've tried so far didn't sound right to me. I have tried some effects, and right now I'm not using any at all; but I am not opposed to them. If I find some I like, I will use them. I figure if you plug in, you might as well go all the way.

Is there an attitudinal difference between walking out onstage as part of a bluegrass band and as a member of a "new-grass" band?

I feel free to express myself a little more in this band because they are not expecting me to come out and be a bluegrass banjo player. It seems like they are ready for whatever wild curveball I throw. I just think there is stuff you express when you play bluegrass and there are other things you express when you play other kinds of music. I like to do them all.

Could you elaborate on what you mean by "expressing yourself?" I used to have difficulty with the idea of "expressing yourself." When people say the guy's really saying a lot with his saxophone, I used to say he's just playing the sax.

I remember a similar thing when I talked to Tony Trischka, trying to get him to tell me how to improvise. He'd say, "I kind of play off my feelings." I'd say, "Oh. How do you improvise?" It didn't really tell me much at that time, and now I find myself in a similar position. Someone asks me how I do it, and I say I don't know, I just kind of play.

Do you think, for instance, of the lyrical content of the song and try to get yourself in that mood, and then just play whatever a person in that mood would play?

I think I do that unconsciously. In New Grass, after playing the song for a year, when it comes time to hit the tunes, I don't have to think too hard about what I am trying to express; but how I am feeling that day might affect how I improvise on the tune.

Most banjo players would be interested to know what happens when you show up at a jam session of jazz musicians and start playing the banjo.

I always try to be real low key about it when I show up. I won't come and sit in if I don't know somebody who might tell those guys it's okay. I think it is really important that you come into a jam session and be prepared to lay back.

Even when you lay back, I imagine that the standard thing that happens at a jazz jam session is similar to what might happen at a bluegrass session. While players trade breaks, a horn player might just stay in there and hold his horn and watch other soloists. Would the banjo player do that? Do you?

It depends on how many guys are playing. If there are two guitar players, I will tend to play less backup, than if there is just one. If there is one guy playing backup, when he

OPPOSITE: *Pat Flynn, Bela Fleck, John Cowen, and Sam Bush of the New Grass Revival.* RIGHT: *Tex Logan, Benny Martin, Bela Fleck, Bill Monroe, and Pete Rowan at the Station Inn in Nashville, 1983.*

plays a solo then there isn't anybody comping. I think if you can learn to play jazz, you should be prepared to comp. You should be ready to comp in several different ways. One is in a very sparse way — adding an accent now and then. The other is to be the only guy comping, and playing a good deal more. It's all just like bluegrass in that you have to find your place in every setting. If you're playing with three guys, you'll play a lot more than if you're playing with eight.

What unique characteristics does the banjo contribute to jazz, and what are the problems of playing the banjo as a jazz instrument?

The first problem is going to be amplification. A banjo is not going to be as loud over a microphone as a saxophone will be. So you are going to have to plug in. When you plug in, you had better make sure it sounds good. You don't want to get too shrill, but on the other hand, maybe that harshness — that punchiness — is also valuable, in that it is different. It's a different sound than those other instruments have. I think jazz always has been an idiom where people could come in with new ideas — that's sort of the whole point. When guitarists started playing guitars in jazz — which really wasn't that long ago — a lot of people were skeptical, and others were more open-minded.

What kinds of attitudes do you run into about the banjo's role in jazz?

Some guys will say that jazz is only the stuff that Charlie Parker played in the '50s, or whatever, and the banjo wasn't part of that, and we'd rather you didn't jam with us. Some are going to say well, jazz is whatever we play on this song, and if you want to play, feel free. I think you have to respect their views about that kind of thing. Just like if I were a piccolo player and heard a bunch of guys playing Flatt And Scruggs music and wanted to sit in, and they said it might not really fit, I would respect that and not do it. But if they said, "Go ahead and try something," I would try it.

Do you ever feel as though playing a lot of bluegrass banjo and jazz banjo get in each other's way?

I think as I go along I find it easier and easier to reconcile playing both at different times. The more jazz I play, the less I feel that I have to throw the kitchen sink into my breaks when I am playing bluegrass. The more bluegrass I play, the more free I feel to express myself in jazz. It's starting to work out pretty good.

I have seen fear totally dismantle a number of players —including myself.

Well, take my word for it, it has done it to me a number of times.

With your busy schedule of recording and performing, do you get much chance to practice?

It really varies. Sometimes, after playing ten days in a row, I really don't want to play. That usually passes after a day or two and before I know it I'm playing again. On the average, when I'm home, I get up, have a cup of coffee, and play for three or four hours. Nowadays I'll try and write something rather than just practice, unless I'm working on a new technique or something. I'm the kind of guy who leaves his banjo case open and stops every once in a while throughout the day, hits a few licks, and then puts it down.

When you tackle a new problem, how do you approach it?

I always sit down with the metronome on and just work with it slow — build it up. Usually what I end up doing is working at it for a half hour or so. I would probably progress more quickly if I had the kind of patience to sit down and turn on the metronome and work on one idea until I had it right. I kind of get bored. I just go on and try something else after I have done it for a while.

Do you practice certain kinds of music differently?

If I am working on a bluegrass piece, I might work on doing pull-offs for a while, not in any particular tune. I'll just play a few songs and do a bunch of pull-offs.

You mean playing a break in the song using as many pull-offs as you can?

No, not using as many as I can, but putting special emphasis on doing them right when I come up to them. But if I'm playing a jazz tune, I might attack the way I approach the tune. For instance, I'll ask myself what the hardest parts to improvise are. It might be a chord passage or getting to a certain chord passage. I'll figure out what notes are in those chords and what positions I could work out that would be melodic.

When I practice, I have left-hand things I work on and right-hand things. Usually if I'm into something technical that I need to work on, it makes my hand hurt after a point. Then I just switch hands.

I don't think you should ever let your hands hurt when you play. I used to think that you should play as hard as you could,

and that would make your hands hurt. Lately I have come around to thinking that if you are doing something that makes your hands hurt, then maybe you shouldn't be doing it. There is always a little bit of pain involved in playing, you know — like breaking calluses once in a while, building new muscles, or the pain that comes from not having played in a while. I guess there is a level of discomfort that must be tolerated, but every player must decide for himself what that level is.

The hurt is evidence that you are going up against your physical limit, and that itself is what stretches the limit. It's called "the wall" in running. If you keep at it, it backs off slowly and after a while it isn't there anymore.

I'm worried about things like tendinitis. I think playing with a lot of tension is unhealthy. I think there is a level of intensity you can maintain without getting too tense. Nowadays when I am working up a new technique — a lot of times I'll find that my hands are starting to feel tense or tired or hurt, and then I decide whether to stop or rethink my approach. Ideally, most playing can be effortless.

You are in a unique position in the bluegrass world. In the liner notes to Natural Bridge, *David Grisman wrote: "Bela Fleck will be the first banjoist/composer since Earl Scruggs to gain mainstream exposure and acceptance." I wonder — apart from considerations of whether you feel you really are that good — how do you think a person in your position could exert that much influence?*

The first thing I thought when I read that was, "How in the world am I going to live up to something like this." I finally decided that I wasn't going to try and if that it happened organically, fine. I think I just have to follow the path where the music leads me and play as many different kinds of things as I can. If that's a by-product of all that — great. Basically, I try not to take it all too seriously. As Alan Munde once said, "It's only a banjo." I mean, how seriously can you take it? It's like being the best kazoo player in the world."

But you take it seriously enough to sometimes play for eight hours a day.

I take the musical side of it as seriously as I can — and I try to keep the side effects from affecting me too much.

— *Peter Wernick*

A SELECTED FLECK DISCOGRAPHY

Solo (On Rounder, One Camp St., Cambridge, MA 02140): *Natural Bridge*, 0146; *Crossing The Tracks*, 0121. **With Tasty Licks:** *Tasty Licks*, 0106; *Anchored To The Shore*, 0121. **With Spectrum:** *Opening Roll*, 0136; *Too Hot For Words*, 0161; *Live In Japan*, 0184. **With Jerry Douglas:** *Tennessee Fluxedo*, 0112. **With Bill Keith and Tony Trischka:** *Fiddle Tunes for Banjo*, 0124.

4.
THE
INNOVATORS

BILL KEITH

DURING THE FIFTIES, when the banjo playing of Earl Scruggs infected enough musicians to cause a virtual epidemic, there were a few experimenters who ventured off to conquer stylistic plateaus above and beyond the foundation Earl had formed. One such enterprising young man was William Bradford Keith.

Bill grew up in Brockton, Massachusetts, a town just south of Boston. The Boston/Cambridge area was a wellspring for many folk musicians who developed their styles and fame in that era. Bill played tenor banjo with some local Dixieland bands, but he soon became captivated by the fingerpicking styles of Earl Scruggs and the multistyle playing of Pete Seeger.

While at Amherst College in Amherst, Massachusetts, Bill bought a 5-string banjo for $15 and a copy of Pete Seeger's book *How To Play The 5-String Banjo* (self-published, 1962); he then set out to learn finger styles rather than plectrum styles. After developing some proficiency, Bill found that the eight-note units of the basic Scruggs style could be altered to accommodate whole strings of notes played in a sequence. From that developed a quest to fit other music forms to the 5-string banjo.

Bill met guitarist Jim Rooney at Amherst. Rooney was a year ahead of Bill and was also running the college radio station. The two musicians hit it off, and they began playing in many campus concerts and at many local coffee spots.

Keith and Rooney met a promoter named Manny Greenhill (today Doc Watson's promoter) and with him organized the Connecticut Valley Folklore Society to promote folk music in New England. Many college performances followed, with folk groups from area universities invited to take part. One Saturday show featured Bill Keith and Jim Rooney, banjoist/guitarist Winnie Winston, guitarist/singer Buffy Sainte-Marie, and a few college groups. When it was Bill's turn to come to the microphone, he announced a tune called "Noah's Breakdown." It was a historic moment. Though the tune may be rudimentary by Keith's present standards (he refuses to play it today), it was nonetheless a glistening example of a picking form that people came to call *chromatic* banjo playing.

When Bill finished school, he moved to Washington, D.C. to live with legendary banjo maker Tom Morgan and learn the art of banjo making. Washington was (and still is) another music hot spot. It was through Tom that Keith and Rooney met guitarist Red Allen and mandolinist Frank Wakefield, and their group, the Kentuckians. Bill was invited to become the band's banjoist.

One thing led to another. Earl Scruggs was playing in Baltimore, and Manny Greenhill (who was then booking some of the Flatt And Scruggs shows) introduced Bill to Earl. Earl thereupon invited Bill to come to Nashville to write out the tablature for the banjo instruction book that Earl was preparing (*Earl Scruggs And The 5-String Banjo*, Peer International, 1968). During Bill's stay with Earl, the two went to the Grand Ole Opry a few times, while the Opry was still at Nashville's old Ryman Auditorium. During one of the visits, Bill managed to find a banjo and sat in a dressing room playing "Devil's Dream." That caught the attention of another musician who happened to have an ear for fiddle tunes: mandolin legend Bill Monroe. Before the night was over, Keith had a job as the banjo player in Monroe's band, the Blue Grass Boys. However, Monroe used to introduce him as *Brad* Keith

— because, as Monroe put it "there's only one Bill in my band."

The constant traveling, and conflicts with Keith's responsibility to attend Air Force Reserve weekend drills, kept him from continuing with Monroe on a regular basis. Keith stayed with the Blue Grass Boys for about a year.

Early in 1962 Bill and Jim Rooney cut an album entitled *Livin' On The Mountain* (Prestige, 14002). Although sales distribution of that album was minimal, people who *did* purchase it soon came to respect the then-unknown banjo player who set fire to two cuts: "Salty Dog Blues" and "Devil's Dream."

Since then, Bill has stepped out in a thousand directions. Formerly the banjoist in the Woodstock Mountain Review, he still performs regularly with Jim Rooney, and he devotes a great deal of time to giving specialized banjo workshops around the U.S. He travels regularly to France, where he is highly respected by fans and musicians, and of course, Bill is one of *Frets'* charter columnists.

*W*HAT GOES INTO *developing a chromatic banjo style?*

Well, I would say that the basic difference between that and the regular Scruggs style is that the hands are working together with a much higher degree of cooperation. With the regular Scruggs style, you can play a certain right-hand pattern or roll and you can do a lot of different things with your hand. The way Scruggs plays "Home Sweet Home," the same right-hand pattern is used for the up-the-neck break as is used down the neck. Even in the regular "Foggy Mountain Breakdown" lick at the 2nd and 3rd frets, the same thing happens up the neck for the high break. There must be examples in the chromatic or melodic styles where the same right-hand pattern is used too, but I would say, basically, that there is a lot more planning necessary, and that you cannot even think of it in terms of right-hand patterns. There's a lot of working things out in advance, too. I don't feel that the style lends itself to improvisation as well as, or in the same way as, the Scruggs style. That could be contested, but it would be just a question of how many elements you had to learn before you were ready to go improvise. When you play chromatically, you're pretty much playing note for note, whereas in the regular Scruggs style it's more apt to be lick for lick. One of the big differences in the way the left hand is used is that you're using different kinds of chord positions than are used in the regular Scruggs style. And of course you use open strings, so very often you're fretting on the second string and the first string is open, or you're fretting on the third string and the second string is open. They are sort of partial positions up the neck, done in such a

way that they don't really look like the chord that's actually being played. For example, if you take the whole *G* scale and then cancel out the notes that are in the *G* chord, which is the open tuning of the banjo, what you're left with are the "odd numbered" notes of the *G* scale — which make an *Am7* chord. So, you can actually fret an *Am7* chord up the neck and use the open strings, which are the *G* chord, and you've got the *G* scale out of it.

Must you learn those chords and the whole neck before you can start playing chromatic banjo styles?

No. It's as simple as saying, "Here are your first and second strings, a *D* and a *B*." Now, some kinds of scales contain those notes, and there will be a note in between that *D* and that *B*, and it will be either a *C* or a *C* — the only two that are possible. So that's only one note you have to fret, and you can fret it on the third string most conveniently at the 5th or 6th fret. And there you have three notes in a row on three different strings, so you can play them going up or down or alternating, or whatever. That's how it starts. It's like learning normally or playing the Scruggs style. You don't have to learn everything inside out before you get to play. You learn a couple of licks, and then you play them, and then you slowly work them into your style, and then you learn a few more and work them in, too.

Can you give me some guidelines about backing up another musician or singer?

I was very impressed by a remark made by Glen Hardin, who played piano with Emmylou Harris. I was at a concert she did in Paris, and I went backstage while the warm-up act was on. Emmylou's group was getting ready and doing what some or a lot of musicians do before they go out onstage — psyching up for the show. Then Glen Hardin said, "Okay, boys, let's go out there and make our star shine." What he meant was, you go out and you play in such a way that the attention is on the star, and that the star is in a good light. You don't try to steal the show, you don't try to rob the limelight, you don't try to upstage the person out front.

How about playing in different keys? You don't usually use a capo to switch keys, do you?

It depends on what the keys are. I feel that certain keys are really convenient, some are practical, others are possible, and some others are completely impractical and impossible. Basically, it revolves around the open tuning of the strings. If you're tuning to a standard *G* tuning, then the key of *G* is eminently possible and feasible. And looking at the circle of fifths, the keys on each side of that are feasible until you get too far away, and that's the point. In other words, *C* would be convenient and so would *D*, and the next step away would be *F*, and in the other direction it would be *A*. So, *F* is feasible. And look at the circle of fifths, the keys on each side of that string. If

you keep shifting around the circle, you'll find that there are no open strings that are convenient in that key, so everything you do has to be fretted. And there you are locked into single-string, or the [Don] Reno style, because there are no available open strings to be the sort of in-between notes. It really does revolve around open strings and the notes that are in the scale that you're trying to play; and since the banjo is tuned to the *G* chord, the *G* scale is quite convenient. And looking at the circle of fifths, the scales immediately to the right and immediately to the left are only different by one note. My concentration these days is on that type of thing: taking the *G* scale for example, and just changing one note in it and making the next adjacent scale.

You don't think it is improper to use a capo?

No, I don't. In fact, look at it this way. Let's suppose you can only play in *G*, *C*, and *D*. Then by reverse logic, or by logic, there must be three different positions on the neck where you can play *G*, *C*, or *D*. And if you can play in five tonalities without the capo then you can play any one of those tonalities five different ways with a capo. Do you see what I'm saying? Your capo can be a really productive thing. It's not a cheater, it's just a way of doing something a little differently. I don't think you should feel guilty — I certainly don't — if you have a capo on your instrument. Some people feel proud that they don't need one. Well, let them. I feel happy that it is there and that it gives me a variety of ways to play in the same key.

If there is another instrument like a mandolin or a fiddle playing a lead, my tendency is to want to play rhythmic stuff to back that up. Whereas if there is a singer I might go into countermelodies, or let's say, leading lines — lines that lead into a chord change. I don't know why I make that differentiation, and it may be different between a picked instrument or a bowed instrument. Obviously a mandolin, I feel, is very different to back up when you're playing banjo, because first of all you have to make more room for the mandolin. So my tendency is to either stop playing or to play soft, rhythmic stuff. Whereas, with a fiddle, the sound of the instrument is different. The long notes that are sustained don't get confused with banjo notes as much as the plucked notes on the mandolin. Pete Seeger has a remark in one of his instruction books: "One of the things to know is when *not* to play." That's something that I don't even feel I do as much as I should — taking advantage of a real change in texture just by stopping. Taking a breather. The resting instrument is all the more welcome when it comes back in; it can change a monotony into a variety. Just not playing is maybe the first thing to consider, but the next thing is to stay off whatever the lead person is going to do. Either stay off of his octave or the range of his instrument or voice, and also off of the melody, because that's probably what he'll be doing. That leaves you with a choice of either rhythmic "drumming" on your instrument, or well-chosen lines that lead into and out of chords.

Do you have any feelings about miking a banjo?

First of all, I'd say that it has been my experience, as far as microphones go, that dynamic microphones are much more satisfactory than condenser microphones when it comes to getting a good banjo sound. I recommend any of the dynamic microphones in the $100 range — more so than a $200 or $300 condenser microphone or ribbon mikes or expensive microphones.

Is there a line separating the regular Scruggs-style bluegrass player from the chromatic bluegrass player? Does one have to more musically educated than the other?

I don't like to draw lines. If I said there was a line there, then people could point their fingers at me for drawing it. I think people generally will admit that there is a difference between newgrass and traditional bluegrass and I think the difference is in the material that is dealt with. These days, there is a higher percentage of material that has more complicated harmonies in it. Also, newgrass, jazzgrass, and what I call fusion music are taking bluegrass instrumental styles and playing other kind of music, including jazz and old standards — like Fred Geiger's stuff, or whatever. There's more of a variety of chords. In fact, you get into this kind of variety when you include more notes in the chord that you're playing. And the old-time bluegrass could be done with three-note chords of majors and minors, and the dominant — which is a four-note chord. Well, in modern styling, four-note chords seem to be the minimum, which include sixths and sevenths and the sevenths of all chord types: major, minor, and dominant. And even five-note chords like the ninth and the *9add6* [13th] chords — those are coming more into use, and so it's only logical that there are more things there to learn or to get a handle on.

— *Roger H. Siminoff*

A SELECTED KEITH DISCOGRAPHY

Solo Album: *Something Bluegrass,* Rounder, RB-1. **With Others:** *70 Songs Special,* Rebel (Rt. 12, Asbury, WV 24916), R-1473, R-1474; *Banjo Paris Session,* Musigrass-Diffusion (25 rue Carnot, Cournesville sur Eure-28, France), PV-1002; *Banjoland,* Rounder, 0087; *Bluegrass Time,* MCA, 116; *Bill Clifton And Company,* County (Box 191, Floyd, VA 24091), 765; *Christian Seguret-Old-Fashioned Love,* Cezame (dist. by Rounder), 0069; *Jazzgrass,* Ridgerunner (dist. by Richy, Box 76116), RRR-0009; *Livin' On The Mountain,* Prestige/Folklore (dist. by Fantasy), 14002; *Marcel Dadi And Friends Country Show,* MMO (43 W. 61st St., New York, NY 10023), 4; *Mud Acres-Music Among Friends,* Rounder, 3001; *Muleskinner,* Ridgerunner, RRR-0016; *Newport Folk Festival Evening Concert, Vol. 1,* Vanguard, VSP-79184; *Philadelphia Folk Festival, Vol. 2, Sept. 1962,* Prestige International, 13072; *Pierre Bensusan,* Rounder, 3023; *Red Allen, Frank Wakefield, And The Kentuckians,* Folkways (43 W. 61st St., New York, NY 10023), FA-2408; *Woodstock Mountains,* Rounder, 3018.

SAM
BUSH

WHEN HE WAS 11 YEARS OLD, Sam Bush bought his first mandolin. It wasn't long afterward that he took a shine to the fiddle, and he has been drawing the admiration of fellow musicians ever since. By the time he graduated from high school in 1970, Sam had won three Junior National Fiddle Championships and had produced a landmark album, *Poor Richard's Almanac*, with banjoist Alan Munde and guitarist Wayne Stewart. Today, at 30, his mandolin and fiddle are at the cutting edge of the newgrass movement, and Sam is one of the most wanted studio musicians in his profession.

"I think the guy is the world's greatest all-purpose mandolinist," says David Grisman. "He's got everything: incredibly powerful rhythm, great solos, and he can play in any style. Everything he plays is just *there* — not just headed somewhere, but fully realized."

Born in Bowling Green, Kentucky, on April 13, 1952, Sam began training in a hurry once he became serious about music. For years he immersed himself in the recordings of fiddler Tommy Jackson and tried to copy the mandolin licks of Red Rector and Hank Garland. He found other models as he went along. "A lot of things I learned that were first exposed on records like *Poor Richard's Almanac* were definitely influenced by Byron Berline, and by Texas Shorty [Jim Chancellor], the unsung hero of Texas fiddle," he says. But despite his early fondness for Texas swing, Sam got hooked on bluegrass in 1965 when he went to Virginia to attend Carlton Haney's Roanoke Bluegrass Festival.

Sam's visibility rose markedly in bluegrass circles in 1970 when he joined the Bluegrass Alliance, one of the more progressive young bands struggling to make a living in a soft market. Rock and roll ruled the consciousness of American youth, and when the Alliance broke up, Sam rallied the survivors and pushed further in that direction with the formation of the New Grass Revival. (The first lineup included Curtis Burch on guitar and dobro, Courtney Johnson on banjo, and Ebo Walker on bass.)

The Revival's hard-rocking rhythms and long improvisational jams almost immediately thrust them into a musical no-man's land. Vilified by much of the traditional bluegrass community for straying so far from the fold and ignored by rock and rollers, the band was forced to establish its own circuit. By staying on the road 42 weeks a year — while seeking a breakthrough hit — the band has created its own fervent audience. And, despite its virtual ban from the bluegrass festival circuit, the Revival has managed to leave its mark — particularly in the area of improvisation and rhythmic variations — on a number of contemporary bluegrass bands.

In 1979 headlining rock singer/pianist Leon Russell invited the Revival to become his backup band. For two years they toured with him, opening each Russell show with an extended set of their own. Toward the end of the stint with Russell, Courtney Johnson and Curtis Burch departed to form their own group —leaving Sam and bassist/singer John Cowan to finish the tour. By that time, the band's sound had hardened considerably and their volume had reached hard rock levels. In addition to mandolin and fiddle, Sam was playing acoustic and electric guitar, electric mandolin, and electric slide mandolin.

At the end of 1981 Sam and John re-formed the Revival, bringing in the brilliant

Sam Bush playing with Leon Russell at the Great American Music Hall in 1981.

njo and Pat Flynn on guitar.

Throughout his New Grass Revival career, Sam has managed to keep a relatively high profile among acoustic music fans. He has made frequent appearances as a session player with such musicians as Doc Watson, Tony Rice, John Hartford, Vassar Clements, Norman Blake, Mark O'Connor, Tut Taylor, John Prine, and Butch Robins. Thanks to his campaigns on the road and his operations in the studio arena, Sam has had a powerful impact on other musicians.

"I would say Sam influenced me much more than any other mandolin player," says Mike Marshall, a Florida state mandolin and fiddle champion before he went west to make a name for himself with the David Grisman Quintet. "He always played so loud and clear and smooth — one note would blend into the next, like a fiddle player. He is just outrageous!"

LOOKING BACK ON the last two years, what do you think you got out of your rock and roll touring with Leon Russell?

All in all, it was a very good thing for us to go through. One thing it taught me was the importance of how you present yourself onstage. I learned to not be afraid to look at the audience. That may sound like a very elementary concept, but it's very hard to make eye contact sometimes. I also learned that they are there to watch, so you'd better give them something to look at. There's a possibility that it went on a little too long, but it was hard to leave. It's easy to get caught up in the kind of working and travel conditions you have with a star like Leon. It was also a lot of fun because he is such a great musician who really kicks it.

What kind of decisions were behind forming the New Revival?

In May of 1981 we were trying to decide as a band if we wanted to leave Leon. When we talked about it, we discovered that we all no longer had the same goals. Courtney and Curtis left to form a new band [Barren County Revival]. When they first quit, John and I were just devastated. We didn't know what we were going to do. It's like a very painful divorce. I really love those guys. We decided the only thing to do was to form a new Revival. We had met Pat Flynn at the Telluride Festival and knew he was a great guitar player; Bela Fleck was an old friend. But they both had a few commitments to honor first. We stayed with Leon until it could all come together.

How do you think the sound of the band has been affected by the change?

Well, we don't rock out quite as hard as we used to. And I don't think we play nearly as loud as we did with Leon. Even with the mandolin we were playing at 110 decibels onstage. One of the objectives of the new band is to quiet down and to get more finesse in the dynamics. Part of that change has come from deciding to drop some of our rock tunes because we had been doing them for seven or eight years. "Fly Through The Country" [*Too Late To Turn Back Now*] is one of those tunes we used to play every night, and we just kind of had enough. Some people might begrudge your not doing a song they want to hear, but they should realize that once you have a band together for ten years, the only way to stay interested is to change the tunes. And when new guys come in that's the perfect opportunity to change.

Are you writing any new tunes?

I don't make specific efforts to write and I guess I've always been kind of lazy in that regard. The bottom line for me is that when I try to write a tune and use all of the correct compositional things that I learned in high school, it just never comes out as well as

when I wake up and naturally hear a tune in my head. Then I can just go to my instrument and it comes out. That's not necessarily the most productive way to look at it, but I just want every tune that I write to count. Now I'm in a position where I don't have to write, because the other guys are so good at it. I feel I'm more of a player than a writer, though I think I have some talent as an arranger.

The mandolin is your primary instrument, but you're also proficient on a number of others. Which of those are you using with the new band?

I've found that I like to play the mandolin more than I'd been playing it. After working in a louder atmosphere with Leon, I'm rediscovering what it sounds like to play quietly — even though we're still plugged in. Most of the time I play mandolin, and I play fiddle about as much as I ever did onstage. I'm also playing slide mandolin on one tune that Bela wrote. Basically with the new group, Pat plays the electric guitar in places where I used to. I like the way he plays electric, for low volume things, a lot better. I like to play electric guitar loud, and that doesn't really fit in with what we're trying to do now.

What kind of acoustic instruments are you using with the Revival?

I have a Stuart Mossman Tennessee flat-top that I use for acoustic guitar parts. My primary mandolin is a 1930s Gibson F-5 that I acquired in 1973 from Tut Taylor. It used to belong to Norman Blake, who decided that he didn't like the finish, so he scraped it off. I think John Hartford has a tape of the finish being scraped off my mandolin. Norman had Randy Wood of Savannah, Georgia rework the top and tone bars and Randy engraved the block inlay. Norman then sold it to Tut, who put a varnish finish on it and sold it to me.

Are you still interested in pursuing electric mandolin?

Yes, but I haven't been able to work it into the new band yet. I plan to get it in there, especially since Washburn has come out with a 4-string Sam Bush model. I'm not going to just work it up to show off my mandolin, though. We wanted to start with the basics for a while, until we got used to each other and got really solid. That's already started to happen.

Are there any particular amplification devices that you prefer to use?

I still use Barcus-Berry Hot Dot transducers on my mandolin and guitar, and I've started using a Barcus-Berry bridge pickup for my fiddle. The sound is good, but I sure don't care much for the jack assembly. I sweat a lot, and sometimes I'll actually short it out. I'd like to see them build a jack assembly for a violin that will take a regular guitar cord and not just a standard minicord. For some reason, the cords just don't last very long for me.

Which kinds of microphones and amplifiers have you found most suitable for your sound?

I usually carry around an old AKG D-190E mike for the mandolin, and we use Shure SM-58 mikes for vocals. I still use a Polytone Mini-Brute Two amp, which has developed a rip in the speaker — but I like the way it sounds. I didn't realize how bad it was until Bela pointed out it was sounding weird. It didn't transfer to the P.A. because we have a direct line coming out of the amp, so you don't get the speaker sound. I like the Polytones because they're so easy to carry around and they have a real flat tone. The Fender amp I did use had more of a metallic high end because, like most amps, it was made for guitars. When I was with Leon, I used the Polytone cranked up to 9½. I kept expecting it to blow, but it never did.

How do you characterize your style? How do you hear yourself as a mandolin player?

One thing that I hope would characterize my style would be my timing; that no matter what I play, you'll hear the right-hand time. I think being a fiddler has made me more aware of things I could do all over the fretboard, as opposed to just the standard mandolin licks. Maybe one thing I've done is to bring the fiddle influences back into mandolin playing. At one time fiddle tunes were just about the only things played on the mandolin, until Bill Monroe came along. Of course, Jethro Burns was always playing the far-out stuff, but in a different kind of showcase. But there seemed to be a period there where hardly anybody was playing fiddle tunes.

What about the way that right hand works? Do you use a stiff wrist or a loose-wrist picking action?

I'd say I use a combination of both. When I see a videotape of the band, I'm amazed at how stiff I look, sometimes. I hope it doesn't sound like that. On rhythm, I seem to play with more of a free hand. There are certain [jazz guitarist] John McLaughlin-style phrases that I've adapted to the mandolin, and when I do those fast runs it seems that's when I look the stiffest. It's something I've developed out of not being able to do other things. John Hartford once said that a style is based on limitations, and I think that's right.

Are there any other particular techniques that you use?

Another thing I do that affects my style is to brace my hand on the top. The very first week that the New Grass Revival was

together I had a car door slammed on my right hand. Up until then I had always played without bracing my hand; but I guess I must have chipped something, because whenever I tried to hold my pick the same way, it really hurt. I developed a style of resting my hand on the top. I don't think I'd want to teach young players my right-hand technique, because I don't know if it's a good idea. It's just something I ended up doing because I had to.

What kind of similarities do you see between your mandolin and fiddle styles?

Since I started playing the mandolin first, I'd say that approach affects any instrument I play. When I was first learning to play the fiddle and I wanted to learn a tune I would always learn it on the mandolin first, because I could see where the notes were. I could understand the tune better, and that's still true today. I think even when I play guitar, I think like a mandolin player. I find myself approaching the guitar vertically rather than horizontally. Instead of playing across the fretboard, I tend to go up and down. It definitely has a different sound when you play it that way.

Have you ever taken any kind of instrumental lessons?

When I was a senior in high school, I took violin lessons from a lady named Betty Pease. Even though I'd already won those junior fiddle championships I started off as a beginner — learning all the standard exercises. She helped me understand why you would use certain fingerings and things like that. I studied for about ten months because I had planned to go to college and study strings and arranging. But I got married instead and moved to Louisville to play in the Bluegrass Alliance. I've never been sorry.

Did your lessons add up to a strong technical education?

Somewhat. I understand basic theory, but I'm not all that educated. I can't really read music today, even though I could in high school. That's simply because I haven't applied that knowledge to any kind of music I've been playing since I left high school. I can read a Nashville-style number chart, but that's about it. Hopefully, anybody I get to work with can accept that. I'm not one of those guys who says that reading won't help you, because I know it will. I know if I could read right now, I could learn things a lot faster.

Do you still have any musical heroes?

Sure, lots of them. David Grisman and Mark O'Connor are two of the first names to come to mind. Jethro Burns was and always will be my main inspiration to go further on my instrument. I met him in 1973 when we were playing in a town near Chicago. My wife Kathy had met him earlier and told him about me. He said, "Sam Bush? Who the hell *is* he! I've been playing all my life, and now people have been coming up to me and asking them to teach them how to play like Sam Bush!" So I called him, and he was nice enough to say, "C'mon up, I'll show you some stuff." And, boy, did he. After that we played a few jobs together. Sometimes I'm fortunate enough to run into him when he's in Nashville for *Hee Haw* or something. One day I walked into the set at Opryland and there were Jethro, Chet Atkins, [pianist] Floyd Cramer, [fiddler/mandolinist] Johnny Gimble, and [saxophonist] Boots Randolph. I have heroes on other instruments, too. My guitar heroes go from Norman Blake, Tony Rice, and Pat Flynn to Eric Clapton and John McLaughlin. I love to play electric guitar on the side.

What kind of musical image are you hoping to project?

When you see a band with a mandolin and banjo — I don't care if you do play like us — you would tend to think country music marketing. That would be okay with me if we made a country music chart. The group Alabama plays rock and roll, but they're a number-one country group. The difference between them and us is that we're still trying to present the mandolin, banjo, and acoustic guitar. What we're really up against in the marketplace is that we don't carry a drummer or really play drum music. We still play string-band style music. We just have to find that balance to enter the mass market. I don't think we'll have to compromise *that* much to do it. Grisman's telling me that we just need to get the right percussion on record — Grisman, of all people. He believes in getting the best players around him, and that's one thing he taught me. They make you sound better. Maybe within a year we might have a major record label deal. We've almost got somebody committed to put some money behind us. I'm waiting.

— Jon Sievert

A SELECTED BUSH DISCOGRAPHY

With The New Grass Revival: *New Grass Revival,* Starday, SLP 482498. (On Flying Rish, 1304 W. Schubert, Chicago, IL 60614): *When The Storm Is Over,* FF-032; *Fly Through The Country,* FF-016; *Too Late To Turn Back Now,* FF-050; *The Festival Tapes,* FF-068; *Barren County,* FF-083; *Commonwealth,* FF-254. **With Leon Russell:** *The Live Album,* Paradise (dist. by Warner), PAK 3532. **With Tony Rice:** *Manzanita,* Rounder (One Camp St., Cambridge, MA 02140), RR-0092; *Mar West,* Rounder, 0125. **With Alan Munde:** *Poor Richard's Almanac,* American Heritage (1208 Everett, Caldwell, ID 83605), 401-255; *Sam And Alan Together Again For The First Time,* Ridge Runner (7121 W. Vickery, No. 118, Fort Worth, TX 76116), RRR0007. **With Mark O'Connor:** *Markology,* Rounder, 0090; *On The Rampage,* Rounder, 0118. **With Bela Fleck:** *Crossing The Tracks,* Rounder, 0121.

DAVID GRISMAN

WITH SO MUCH UNIMAGINATIVE, derivative music pouring out of the radio 24 hours a day, it is refreshing when a truly original musician comes onto the scene.

To call the music of mandolinist David Grisman "original," and leave it at that, would be a colossal understatement. The development of a new musical movement within an existing idiom is a rare enough occurrence; creating an entirely *new* form of music, which is what Grisman has done, is a monumental achievement.

None of the hyphenated hybrid categories (jazz-rock, folk-rock, etc.) collectively known as fusion or crossover can pigeonhole what Grisman has been cultivating in recent years. The antecedents are numerous and well in evidence, but still don't describe or define the music — unless you want to call it bluegrass-jazz-Gypsy-rock-Middle-Eastern-Hebraic-folk-classical-Grisman. And even then, the most important element, Grisman himself, would be the hardest to pinpoint.

What people have been calling it thus far is "Dawg" music, after Grisman's nickname. And while it remains to be seen whether the mandolinist's musical excursions will initiate a full-blown movement, *The David Grisman Quintet* album, released in April of 1977, has definitely opened a few ears. *Billboard,* listing it as a recommended LP in both the jazz and pop categories, described it as "fire-breathing acoustic string music that fuses the emotional freedom of rock to the tight precision of bluegrass to create something new and unique in contemporary instrumental groups." *Billboard*'s concluding remark was "Best cuts: all of them." As of this writing, album sales have passed the 60,000 mark. That places *The David Grisman Quintet* second in all-time sales for an independently released acoustic LP. Only Leo Kottke's *6- & 12-String Guitar Instrumentals,* issued eight years ago, has done better.

If one LP for a small label by an all-acoustic, all-instrumental band that has never toured much outside the San Francisco Bay Area can cause such a stir, there's no telling what the release of Grisman's follow-up album will do. *Hot Dawg,* on A&M Horizon, features Grisman backed by such jazz notables as 70-year-old violinist Stephane Grappelli and former Bill Evans bassist Eddie Gomez, along with guitarist Tony Rice and the other members of the David Grisman Quintet.

Because so much recent attention has been focused on Grisman the Quintet leader and innovative composer, his accomplishments as a superb instrumentalist have been almost overlooked. But performing was the trade Grisman learned first, and for years he was what he describes as "the hot mandolin player in the second generation New York City bluegrass scene."

By age 18, only two years after discovering the mandolin, he was producing the album *Red Allen, Frank Wakefield, And The Kentuckians* (Folkways, FA 2408), and playing on his first LP as part of the Even Dozen Jug Band [*Jug Band Songs Of The Southern Mountains*] with a cast of "future all-stars" that included Stefan Grossman, Maria Muldaur, Steve Katz, and John Sebastian. A year later, his group, the New York Ramblers, won the award for best bluegrass band at the prestigious Union Grove fiddle contest in North Carolina.

To date, David Grisman has appeared on more than 45 albums with such stars as Linda Ronstadt, Bonnie Raitt, James Taylor, Judy Collins, Martin Mull, Tom Paxton, the Pointer Sisters, and the Grateful Dead. He has been a key member in several short-lived but innovative bands, including Earth Opera (with Peter Rowan),

David Grisman working on a new score in the office of his home in Mill Valley, California.

Muleskinner (with Bill Keith, Richard Greene, and the late Clarence White), and Old And In The Way (with Vassar Clements and Jerry Garcia).

Grisman has been acclaimed by critics as well as by such musical peers as Stephane Grappelli, Doc Watson, and Bill Keith, who wrote in the liner notes to his *Something Newgrass* album, "I've had the pleasure of playing music in several different contexts with David during a friendship spanning almost fifteen years, and his unequivocally eclectic style never ceases to amaze me."

Born March 23, 1945, in Hackensack, New Jersey, David was exposed to music at an early age. "My father was 47 when I was born, but earlier he had been a professional trombone player," he says. "My mother was an art teacher, but she also played the piano. Piano was my first instrument, beginning when I was seven. My father died when I was ten, and I sort of slacked off — he'd kept me practicing. I didn't have the discipline to go home and practice my lessons."

At ten, David and his mother moved to Passaic, New Jersey and by the age of 16 he was caught up in the folk music boom of the early 1960s.

"I got interested with two friends in school, Fred Weisz and Jack Scott," he recalls. "We quickly progressed from emulating the Kingston Trio to being into the New Lost City Ramblers in about six weeks or so. Jack had an FM radio, so he was in touch with the *Oscar Brand Show,* which had Roger Sprung playing banjo. One day Jack came back from New York with a record called *Mountain Music Bluegrass Style.* He put on a cut called 'White House Blues' by Earl Taylor, and it just totally flipped me out. It was so fast! We played it over and over."

Around this time, David met noted folk music enthusiast Ralph Rinzler, who played mandolin with the Greenbriar Boys. "Fred, Jack, and I wanted to start a folk music club

at school," Grisman recounts, "so we asked our English teacher, Elsie Rinzler, if she would be the advisor. She said, 'Oh, I have this cousin named Ralph who plays folk music.' Ralph came to class one day with his mandolin, guitar, and banjo, and gave a demonstration. He was the first guy I saw play a mandolin who affected me."

Grisman was soon hanging around Rinzler at every available opportunity. "We just started bothering him," he laughs. "He was a ticket agent for BOAC Airlines at the time, so he'd get home around midnight, and we'd go over there [*laughs*]. He'd play for us or play tapes of Bill Monroe. Some of it was too strong for me at first, but I started developing taste real fast. At first Bill's voice was too high for me. His records had fiddles on them, and I rebelled against that, because my initial flash was the mandolin and banjo — I liked those kinds of sounds. But on August 8, 1961, Ralph took me to see Bill Monroe perform, and it all changed; I loved his voice. But I had to see it come out of a real human being."

Following along wherever Rinzler went proved to be the best education the three aspiring bluegrassers could ask for. As Grisman puts it, "Ralph was always trying to turn us on to the real stuff — which is what he's always been into and still is. He'll get around to discovering me in a few years; in about thirty years Ralph will show up on my doorstep with his Nagra tape recorder [*laughs*]. We worshipped him. We'd sit at rehearsals of the Greenbriar Boys with our mouths open. I remember when Ralph brought Clarence Ashley and Doc Watson back from North Carolina; he discovered them and later managed Doc and Bill Monroe for awhile."

By this time David had been noodling around on his first mandolin, a Kay he got for $16 in New York City. "It was a really crummy mandolin," he admits. "I didn't know a thing about it. I worked out 'Woody's Rag' from a Weavers record where Pete Seeger

played it. But it was so alien to me, I figured it all out on one string [*laughs*]. Ralph came over and showed me that I had to go on to the next string. I never took formal lessons from him — I probably should have — but I just hung out and he showed me a lot of stuff."

Soon Grisman was making his own hitchhiking journeys to ferret out that "high lonesome sound."

"In 1963, during Easter vacation from school," he recalls, "I made a pilgrimage to Washington, D.C., to meet Frank Wakefield. I'll never forget it. It was this *tiny* little bar, and he and Red Allen were sitting at the table in front of the stage, drinking beer. I just walked right up to Frank and introduced myself and told him I played mandolin. He just took me home with him! Frank was a huge influence on me."

The boys' folk music club soon progressed into a bluegrass band, the Garret Mountain Boys. Eventually they recruited Steve Mandel, who later played guitar to Eric Weissberg's banjo on "Dueling Banjos" in the movie *Deliverance.* The group then merged with a rival bluegrass band, the Downstate Rebels, to become the New York Ramblers. In 1964 — with Grisman on mandolin, Winnie Winston on banjo, Gene Lowinger on fiddle, Eric Thompson on guitar, and Fred Weisz on bass — the Ramblers went to North Carolina and won the Union Grove competition.

"We won first prize of the whole contest, World Championship Bluegrass Band," David states proudly. "It's like the Olympics of bluegrass. We mainly wanted to play there, but the way to play was to enter the contest. We played several tunes, one of which was 'Rawhide.' Unfortunately, they didn't have a mandolin category in those days."

During this period Grisman was studying English at NYU. Living in an apartment on Thompson Street in Greenwich Village, he became a part of the folk music scene that was developing in the early Sixties.

"I don't know what I was doing at school," he admits, "because I was a bluegrass mandolin player first; that was my existence. We used to play at Gerde's Folk City every Monday night, Hootenanny Night. We had a good following. We started hanging out in Washington Square. Bob Dylan and those guys were there, too — I used to see Dylan walking down the street. But I didn't appreciate that singer-songwriter sort of music, because those guys were just singing songs and not tuning their guitars. I'd rather listen to Roscoe Holcomb. I was into the real thing, *real* folk music — like Clarence Ashley. I could walk down the street to Ralph Rinzler's house and hear the greatest Doc Watson stuff that ever was. I'd spend entire afternoons listening to Ralph's collection of tapes."

Despite his purist sentiments, it was with some of these young New York folkies that Grisman cut his first record, *The Even Dozen Jug Band.* He recounts, "Stefan Grossman was friends with Peter Siegal, and we were all sort of friends, but we were into different areas of music. I was really into bluegrass mandolin and Stefan was into blues guitar, but we were both hanging out in Washington Square, along with everybody else. So Stefan put together a jug band for this album, with himself, Steve Katz, John Sebastian, Maria D'Amato [Muldaur], me, Fred Weisz, Peter Siegal, Joshua Rifkin on piano, Danny Lauffer on jug, and a guy named Bob Gurland who could imitate a trumpet with his mouth."

Even though Grisman was playing bluegrass almost exclusively, he was already beginning to incorporate some of his own ideas. "I was just back in New York," he notes, "and I heard a tape of an unreleased album by the New York Ramblers. There are tunes on there like 'Fanny Hill,' which I still play, and I noticed there's a little part in there where I played a solo with only bass accompaniment — it just went into this other zone. I think I always had a certain streak of wanting to do something with that kind of music. But first I had to get a grasp of something to hang on to, so I really studied Monroe and Wakefield. I got into sounding more like Bill Monroe than anybody *should* sound."

Besides providing David with the basis of his early mandolin style, Monroe and Wakefield also instilled in him the value of writing his own songs. "That's something I consciously tried to do," he explains, "because I noticed that Bill and Frank wrote. My first composition was 'Cedar Hill,' which we still play. I patterned it after a song of Frank's called 'Leave Well Enough Alone' [a version of "Cedar Hill" played by a group called Country Cooking appears on Rounder 0006]. I wrote 'Opus 38' [*The David Grisman Rounder Album*] around 1964."

A virtual trademark of Grisman's recent work, his penchant for minor keys, dates back to before he began playing the mandolin. "In synagogue, I remember certain melodies," he says. "I've always been attracted to minor melodies and Hebraic music. I've always liked sad music, and there are a lot of sad melodies in the Jewish faith. Some people have said that the minor sound sort of defines my style, but I've written a lot of tunes in major keys, too — like 'Janice' and 'Dawg's Bull' [on *Hot Dawg*] — and some of my most recent pieces are more away from tonality."

Grisman continued to move upwards in his succession of mandolins, eventually acquiring a Gibson F-5. "Ralph Rinzler had reworked his F-5," he recalls, "so I tried to do it to my A-Junior. I regraduated and refinished it, and one night there was a loud snap, and the top caved in [*laughs*]. So I put a huge lug nut inside it to prop the top up, and it acted like a tone bar — it was actually louder. Then I made the big move and got together $150 and bought an F-4 that had belonged to Mike Seeger. I had that during the latter part of the Garret Mountain Boys and the New York Ramblers. I eventually sold it and bought a 1951 F-5 for $325. But it was real garbage; it had a mahogany neck and didn't even have black and white binding! I had it reworked and doctored up and sold it for $475. In 1965 I bought a 1920s Lloyd Loar

Grisman playing a Cmaj7 chord high on the fretboard of his Moneteleone Grand Artist mandolin.

Gibson F-5 from Harry West for $550."

In 1967 David made his first deliberate move away from bluegrass and with Peter Rowan formed a rock outfit called Earth Opera. "Pete had left Bill Monroe," he recounts, "and I wanted to form a bluegrass band with him and maybe Bill Keith and Richard Greene. But in 1967 there was no place for bluegrass. There wasn't anything like *Frets* or *Pickin'* magazine — and I could have used that stuff back in 1962 [*laughs*]. Players like me are cropping up now, but we were happening back then. We were sort of the lost generation in that whole evolution. There was Ralph Rinzler's generation and people like Bob Yellin, John Herald, Mike Seeger, and Roger Sprung before us, but my generation of bluegrass pickers never continued what we started. Anyway, Pete Rowan was on sort of a reactionary trip after leaving Bill Monroe's band, and Bill Keith and Richard Greene were in the Kweskin Jug Band, so Peter and I got together and started doing some songs he'd written as an acoustic duo. Then we decided to put together sort of a rock band. Looking back on it now, I think we should have stuck with the acoustic duo. We got a contract with Elektra Records, and they set us up with Simon And Garfunkel's manager, who suggested that we be an acoustic duo. But we decided we wanted to have a band."

It was with Earth Opera that Grisman finally found a use for the mandocello he'd bought in 1964. [*Ed. Note: A mandola is tuned a fifth below a mandolin; a mandocello is tuned an octave below a mandola.*] "I figured if I was playing a different kind of music, like Earth Opera, it would be fitting to have a different instrument. I was attracted to mandocello because no one else played one. I got my Gibson K-4 model for $300 then, which was sort of a fluke. I electrified it with a Johnny Smith pickup mounted in the fretboard — I had some frets taken out. I used

fuzztone with it and everything."

Grisman, Rowan, and a few others thought of themselves as the "bluegrass dropouts." Grisman, however, stayed in touch with the bluegrass world, even though he was living in California and getting more deeply involved in his own music.

In 1972 David and some of the other "dropouts" formed a sort of rock-bluegrass outfit, Muleskinner, which produced one LP by the same name. The band consisted of Grisman on mandolin, Rowan on rhythm guitar and vocals, Richard Greene on violin, and Bill Keith on banjo, along with the guitarist some have called the greatest flatpicker of all time, the late Clarence White.

"Clarence was the greatest, as far as I'm concerned," declares David. "I spent a week in 1964 playing with him in the Kentucky Colonels. They were in New York, playing at the Gaslight, and Roland White's wife was having a baby, so I subbed on mandolin. That was the best bluegrass band I ever played in — it was Clarence, Roger Bush [bass], and Billy Ray Latham [banjo]. One of my big regrets of my musical life is that they asked me to go to Chicago with them the following week and I didn't go.

"The thing I loved about Clarence's playing," Grisman continues, "was the way he would mess with time; he'd play a whole bar ahead or behind. He also played real light and delicately. When he died, I thought that was just gone forever, but Tony Rice has that spirit and that awareness of time. He's the only other cat who does. I mean, people can learn the notes or licks, but that's not really what Tony has done. He's got the same *feel*, that attitude. I always dreamed of doing some of my own songs with Clarence, but it just seemed too remote. I got to do one, 'Opus 57,' on *Muleskinner*. See, I could never get guys to *learn* stuff like that."

Although the members of Muleskinner now represent the cream of the progressive

"What I've done is to put the mandolin at the center of attention . . . It seems to me that the instrument has the potential to be heard by a lot more people in all kinds of music, and I want to stimulate people to play it if I can."

bluegrass at its beginning and the album has become a collector's item, Grisman admits, "I never really liked the record that much. There was so much music that could have come out of Clarence in two hours, but we were doing these songs. An interesting thing, by the way, which isn't mentioned on the original album jacket, is that Roland White played mandola on the intro to 'Opus 57.'"

The next group Grisman and Rowan played in, Old And In The Way, also featured bassist John Kahn, Vassar Clements on fiddle, and Grateful Dead guitarist Jerry Garcia playing 5-string banjo. "I had met Jerry," David reminisces, "at a Bill Monroe show in West Grove, Pennsylvania, in 1964. I made my first trip to California a year later and stayed at a house in Palo Alto where Eric Thompson was living, along with [bassist] Phil Lesh, Garcia, and all the guys in the Grateful Dead — at that time called the Warlocks.

"In 1973," he continues, "we were all living at Stinson Beach. One day we were sitting in Garcia's living room and he said, 'Let's pick some bluegrass.' We started playing in clubs like Paul's Saloon, and for Jerry it was his musical outlet — but Pete Rowan and I could use the hundred bucks, you know [*laughs*]. Jerry was, of course, a big name, a big entity, so I wanted him to call the shots — because, let's face it, I'd already played in hot bluegrass bands in 1966. And Old And In The Way wasn't a tight band, because those guys were out of shape and Jerry doesn't like to rehearse. We got Richard Greene to play fiddle on a few gigs, but he was in another band, so we called Vassar Clements, who I'd never met; he was like a legend to me. After a while I decided to devote more time to my own music. A live album was released after the band dissolved."

Grisman's next group began even more casually than Old And In The Way and never even recorded. But the Great American Music Band (originally the Great American String Band) finally gave David a platform for his original compositions as well as some jazz playing.

"A gig came up at the Great American Music Hall [in San Francisco]," he recalls, "which was supposed to be Richard Greene and Vassar Clements, each with his own band. Richard asked me to play with him, so we got Eric Thompson on guitar, Sandy Rothman on banjo, and Bing Nathan on bass. Some promoter got a local group called Skunk Cabbage to back Vassar, and on the afternoon of the opening night both bands played a radio show. After Skunk Cabbage heard us play they said, 'We can't play with Vassar; he belongs with you guys.' They were honorable enough to do that. So they opened the show for us, and we had Richard *and* Vassar and called it the Great American Fiddle Band. The second night Jerry Garcia played banjo, and Sandy Rothman switched to guitar. Bing Nathan couldn't make the second night, so Taj Mahal played upright bass. Another musical friend of mine, [guitarist] David Nichtern, who wrote 'Midnight At The Oasis,' had been interested in my stuff — to the point where he'd make cassettes of the songs and learn them. So he showed up the second night and knew all the tunes — played right out of the audience."

The group eventually settled with Grisman, Greene, guitarist John Carlini, bassist Joe Carroll, and singer/guitarist Ellen Kearney.

While David was playing with the Great American Music Band he was also teaching mandolin at the Family Light Music School in Sausalito, California. Coincidentally, the day after the school fired him over a disagreement, he received a phone call from none other than Bob Dylan, asking for mandolin lessons.

"He had a blonde F-4," explains Grisman, "and he wanted to learn all about it. He took the 3-day crash course. I showed him some basic fingering exercises and some chords; we listened to Charlie Monroe records. One day he hung out for 13 hours. The third day, he came back and had written a song on the mandolin, which is probably what he wanted to learn."

The following week, the Great American Music Band was playing at the famous Palomino Club in Los Angeles, opening for Bill Monroe. "Dylan was real interested in Bill Monroe," says David, "so I told him about the gig. So here we are playing our new music at a gig opening for Bill Monroe. After our set — Bill had come in after we'd started — I was out in the parking lot and Richard Greene came out and said, 'I just saw Bill Monroe, and he ignored me. I stood next to him for ten minutes and he didn't acknowledge my existence.' See, not only had Richard played in Bill's band, but Bill had always praised him — he's still complimentary towards him — but this night he was giving him the cold shoulder. I said, 'Well, he ain't gonna do that to me.' We were tight; he used to call me up onstage; I named my son Monroe Grisman; he'd once even said he wanted to manage Pete Rowan and me. He was into me when I was playing successor to the throne. So I went inside, and I'm standing in the doorway to the dressing room, wondering if I should go say hello or what, and all of a sudden who shows up but Bob Dylan with Robbie Robertson. He says, 'I really dug the set. Hey, I want to meet the man!' So here I am about to be possibly snubbed by Bill Monroe, and I have to introduce Bob Dylan to him. Suddenly Bill turns towards me, sticks out his hand, and smiles. He was real impressed when I introduced Dylan to him; they sang 'I Saw The Light' together backstage."

While still teaching at Family Light, Grisman met future Quintet member Todd Phillips. "He was my ace student," the leader boasts, "and we got into playing with two mandolins." The rhythm-and-lead-mandolin sound became an essential element when the David Grisman Quintet was finally formed in late 1975.

Phillips, who played bass on *The David Grisman Rounder Album*, became second mandolin in the group, with Darol Anger on violin, Bill Amatneek on bass, and Clarence White's apparent successor, Tony Rice, on guitar. "I met Tony cutting Bill Keith's *Something Newgrass* album in Washington, D.C.," remembers Grisman. "We picked a few tunes, and Tony asked me what I was up to, so I played him a tape of the Great American Music Band. I put on 'Dawgology' and after about ten seconds of it, he said, 'That's the greatest music I've ever heard.'"

Tony recalls that day: "We were compatible right there on the spot; I liked his playing and he liked mine. When I heard a tape of his Dawg music, with Richard Greene and John Carlini, that idea really appealed to me — playing without vocals and without a banjo. I figured I could play this stuff after a little training. As it turns out, I didn't get any training; I had to do it myself [laughs]. We kept in touch, and finally I left J.D. Crowe And The New South to see if David and I could get something going. I moved out to California about four months after I'd first heard his music."

With the formation of the David Grisman Quintet, Grisman got to really flex his jazz chops. "The very first jazz record I got turned on to," he states, "was a very obscure record called *Bass Ball* on Philips by a bassist named Francois Rabbath — just bass and drums. Then I got *A Love Supreme* by John Coltrane and *Eric Dolphy At The Five Spot* in around '67, and started becoming a jazz freak. Of course, I already had a couple of Django Reinhardt-Stephane Grappelli records. I began to see that jazz was a category of music where it was *all* good; it was a style of music where you *had* to be good to play it. I admire all those guys; Jim Hall, Bill Evans, Charlie Parker, Duke Ellington, McCoy Tyner, Wes Montgomery, Oliver Nelson, Oscar Peterson, Dizzy Gillespie, Charles Mingus, Keith Jarrett, Sonny Rollins . . . ."

But in spite of Grisman's love of jazz, he views his own music as a form of classical music. "The style I'm trying to play in," he explains, "has a lot of elements that aren't jazz. I think I like the idea of classical music; that is, composing something that's fixed, and playing it every time. It's working on the idea of the execution; the music is already written out, so it's just the interpretation. Of course, there's a lot of improvisation, too. That's one criticism I've encountered: one jazz critic accused us of working out our solos. That's not my total approach, writing out solos, but any musician develops the same kinds of ideas no matter how many times he plays the same song. I had the opportunity on the last album to hear Stephane Grappelli play maybe five takes of the same song — and nobody's schizophrenic enough to play a totally different solo every time. I think there's a tendency among jazz buffs or critics to expect that to be good it always has to be different and spontaneous. But, you know, spontaneity is just part of existence; there are other things, such as thoughtfulness. Classical musicians devote their whole lives to areas such as expression and articulation. That's valid too."

The main thing that differentiates Grisman's Dawg music from the bluegrass he used to play is probably the chord voicings. Mike Marshall, a 21-year-old mandolinist from Florida who recently moved to California and is now playing second mandolin in the David Grisman Quintet, observes, "When I first started trying to learn the stuff on the Quintet album, I had to have David relay some of it over the phone, because it's quite different from just bluegrass, which I'd been playing for about six years. The chords are completely different. In bluegrass you have three or four certain chord forms of majors and minors and that's about it. They're called 'chop' chords, and they're real punchy. In Dawg music, you play more like a barre chord, and you use more colorations, like 6ths and minors. And David has it worked out so that with two mandolins one plays low register and one plays high. He uses three-finger chords a lot, so that between the two you form a six-note chord."

Grisman explains further, "When you start using different chords and progressions, minor sevenths to dominant V7 chords, you have to eliminate something, since you only have four [paired] strings. I've found that on the mandolin, the color notes seem to be more important than playing the roots, because you're usually playing with other instruments that can supply those notes."

Although he keeps on hand a number of method books from which he practices such things as scales and arpeggios, Grisman improvises mostly in terms of melody. "It's hard for me to just take something out of a book and throw it into my playing," he says. "I like to learn the different scales and try to adapt them to something in my style, rather than just play something right out of the book."

David's main instrument today is a 1927 Gibson F-5 he bought from Matt Umanov in New York City. Also included in his collection are the K-4 mandocello, a 3-point F-4 (pictured on the front cover of *The David Grisman Rounder Album*), a Gibson solidbody electric 4-string mandolin, and a Japanese Blue Bell.

Trying to pinpoint the advantages of the F-5, Grisman reflects, "F-5s are loud, and they have a certain tone quality that's kind of penetrating. In a bluegrass situation, it's the mandolin that'll really cut through a loud banjo and fiddle; another model will get swallowed up. I think the most important thing in a mandolin is balance. Some mandolins are bright, others are bassy; some have good high strings, some have good low strings. But to find a mandolin that sounds the same on all the strings is pretty hard."

The David Grisman Quintet as it appeared in 1980: Rob Wasserman, Mike Marshall, Grisman, Darol Anger, and Mark O'Connor.

Grisman has made a few modifications on his Gibson: "I removed the pickguard and the tailpiece cover and end-pin. I took all the weight off of it, which wasn't much. I had another fretboard built for it, then I put on a third fingerboard which was given to me by Mike Apollon, [vaudeville mandolinist] Dave Apollon's son. It's an old Twenties F-5 fingerboard that was a spare of his father's. I've also had the neck slimmed down."

David strings his mandolins with custom-gauge D'Addario phosphor bronze sets. High to low (*E, A, D, G*) they are: .011", .015", .026", and .041". His picks are tortoiseshell, "but not so stiff that you can't bend them. They're about the size of a guitar pick, like a Fender — with one point and two rounded edges — but I like to use the rounded edge."

Among his favorite mandolin players, David lists "Hugo D'Alton, s an English classical player; Buck White; and of course, Bill Monroe, Frank Wakefield, and Jesse McReynolds. Right now Ricky Skaggs, Sam Bush, and Jethro Burns are really playing some contemporary mandolin. Jethro pioneered the whole idea of jazz on the mandolin. He's an inspiration to any mandolin player worth his salt. Another fine mandolinist is Tiny Moore from Sacramento [formerly with Bob Wills And His Texas Playboys], who plays electric 5-string. I produced an album with him and Jethro for Kaleidoscope in January. I think on a technical level Sam Bush has the most going for him of just about anybody. One of my ex-students I'm really proud of is Andy Statman, who came to me when he

was fourteen or fifteen — I was seventeen. He's one of the most progressive players around. Also, Mike Marshall is hot stuff."

David had an opportunity to use several mandolin players and other fine instrumentalists on a recent film project, the soundtrack for the movie *The King Of The Gypsies*. He got the assignment after producer Federico DeLaurentis happened to hear the David Grisman Quintet album at a Tower Records store in Hollywood. On several pieces in the score, Grisman augmented a 56-piece orchestra by adding mandolins, mandolas, and mandocellos to the various string sections. Musicians present on the soundtrack include: guitarists Tony Rice, John Carlini, and Diz Disley; violinists Stephane Grappelli and Richard Greene: bassist Ray Brown; and mandolinists Andy Statman and Mike Marshall. Guitarists Tony Rizzi and Tommy Tedesco also contribute mandolin parts.

This is the fourth movie David has scored, the previous three being *Big Bad Mama, Capone,* and *Eat My Dust*. "One of my fantasies," the mandolinist muses, "is to put out an album called 'Good Music From Bad Movies.'" The soundtrack for *The King Of The Gypsies*, the most challenging film product Grisman has yet worked on, is, in his words, "my conception of Gypsy music. I played it for a real Gypsy lady, though, and she got goosebumps."

— Dan Forte

MANDOLINIST/composer/arranger David Grisman probably has had more impact on modern concepts of acoustic string bands than anyone since Bill Monroe, the legendary "Father of Bluegrass." No name has been more closely identified with today's resurgent interest in acoustic string instruments than that of Grisman, and no one else has made such strides in opening up the commercial jazz and pop charts to the new acoustic idiom.

Grisman was, of course, inspired by Monroe. They use the same instrument as their primary means of musical expression. It was Monroe who created a rhythmic role for the mandolin within a band, playing closed-position chop chords on the back beat to create the effect of a snare drum. Grisman, too, exploits the instrument's rhythmic capabilities as an important element in his music; but it was Grisman who pioneered the concept of two mandolins playing orchestrated rhythm and lead parts. And while Monroe sees bluegrass as an outgrowth of country music traditions, Grisman sees his own music as a new classical form.

Grisman's role as spokesman for and champion of the mandolin goes well beyond that of a player/composer, however. He is also a writer, a publisher, and a record producer. *Frets* readers are familiar with his mandolin column, which has been highly popular since its debut in the magazine's second issue. Back in 1976, as a means of answering all the mail he received from mandolin players, he founded *Mandolin World News* in his basement with Todd Phillips and Darol Anger, members of his Quintet. Though Grisman no longer serves as editor, the magazine is still published quarterly. It allows him to pursue his goal of bringing such unrecognized mandolin greats as Dave Apollon, Jethro Burns, Tiny Moore, and Hugo D'Alton to the attention of mandolin players and the general public.

Two years ago David introduced Tiny and Jethro to one another, provided them with a rhythm section comprised of bassist Ray Brown, guitarist Eldon Shamblin, and drummer Shelly Manne, and produced a smoldering album of jazz standards and original tunes (*Back To Back*, Kaleidoscope [Box O, El Cerrito, CA 94530], F-9). More recently, he assembled and produced at his own expense an album featuring the music of Dave Apollon. Apollon recorded sparingly in the '30s and '40s and is essentially unknown today, but Grisman considers him to have been the first true jazz mandolin virtuoso. Grisman also researched and wrote the extensive liner notes, and donated his entire financial interest in the project (*Mandolin Virtuoso*, Yazoo 1066) to Apollon's widow.

David's music continues to evolve. The film for which he was then writing music, *King Of The Gypsies*, was released in December 1979 and quickly faded from the theaters — but not before David's score was given some highly favorable reviews. Record producer David Rubinson, who produced the *Apocalypse Now* soundtrack, went so far as to call it "one of the three best film scores in the history of the medium." Unfortunately, though a record had been prepared, a *King Of The Gypsies* soundtrack album was never released.

Nevertheless, through the film Grisman fulfilled a personal fantasy by hiring seminal swing jazz violinist Stephane Grappelli to perform on the soundtrack. That collaboration began a warm musical and personal relationship that led to Grappelli making a cross-country tour with the David Grisman Quintet last year, and netted the band its first appearance on *The Johnny Carson Show*.

Y*OU'VE ALREADY MADE a significant contribution to the mandolin in acoustic string music; that's widely acknowledged. But how do you see yourself?*

Mainly what I've done is to put the mandolin at the center of attention. Traditionally, the mandolin has been thought of in an accompaniment role. I've made it the central focus in my music by having two of them. Sometimes I'll put the violin, guitar, or cello out front, but basically the emphasis is on the mandolin. If you do that with *any* instrument, and the tunes and the playing are good, people are going to like it.

In carrying your mandolin music to a live audience, how do you reconcile the

matter of putting acoustic instruments through an electronic amplification system? How do you deal with the problems that creates?

That's something we keep working on. When we first started, we played small rooms without microphones, but of course you can't reach many people that way. When we're rehearsing and working out music in my living room, we sit around in a small circle where everybody can see and hear each other. There aren't any microphones. We're just concentrating on what we're doing, and the rhythm really jells. I've carried a sound man for the past several years. That's the only way you can have a chance of sounding good. My first sound man was Bill Wolf, a really gifted engineer and musician, who recorded most of my records. It makes a difference.

What microphones are you currently using in performance?

I have Neumann KM-84s for the mandolins and violins. We use an AKG 451-EB for the bass and another one for the guitar. Rob also has an amp for the bass. We have our own monitoring system, made by Galaxy Audio of Wichita, Kansas. Two Hot Spot speakers mount in a small cabinet that fits on a microphone stand and sits about a foot away from each guy. The units have their own variable loudness control and they don't interfere with the house system. That's about all we carry with us. Sometimes we have a problem interfacing our equipment with what is available at the gig. We do use a FRAP pickup for the cello, in conjunction with an AKG 452 microphone for definition in the monitors. We also use a parametric equalizer, in line with the guitar channel, for the house sound system. It gives us a fuller, cleaner sound, without feedback.

Have you been resisting an urge to put pickups on everything, and avoid a lot of miking hassles, or is it the other way around?

I must say I really feel that pickups which attach to the instrument produce a characteristically colored sound. To me, it's inferior to a natural sound. An instrument is not made to be heard while you're resting your ear on top of it. If you rest your ear on an instrument and play it, it will sound just like what a pickup sounds like. You're hearing the sound in the wood, rather than the sound in the air. I'm speaking totally out of instinct, but this is what I perceive. I feel that when I'm playing my mandolin, the sound has to go through the air to live. The sound that's only in the wood is stillborn. I just enjoy the sound of acoustic instruments the way they are. I'm not saying there isn't beauty in electric music. Listen to B.B. King, George Benson, or Tiny Moore. I have a good old Gibson solidbody electric reserved for when I want to do that. It just gets too loud for me, for the most part.

How do you view the state of the mandolin-building art today?

I think the custom builders have been doing extremely well, but I haven't seen much out of the factories that I'm impressed with. I did see a nice low-priced Japanese model called a Kentucky. Some of the best builders I've come across are Steve Gilchrist [Warramboll, Victoria, Australia], Mike Kemnitzer [Boulder, Colorado], John Paganoni [Manassas, Virginia], Tom Ellis [Austin, Texas], and John Monteleone [Bay Shore, New York]. An old friend of mine, Tom Morgan [Dayton, Tennessee], issued the first complete set of accurate Gibson F-5 plans. He was the first builder to really share his knowledge. All of these guys make excellent F-5 copies ranging from $1,000 to $2,000. [Portland, Oregon, luthier] Robert Steinegger has built only one mandolin, but it's an exact copy of Orville Gibson's first F-5 model —except Robert made it sound and play much better than the original.

Have there been any big advances in design?

Monteleone was the first guy to make a somewhat substantial departure from the basic F-5 design. His Grand Artist model has a scroll, but unlike Gibson's scroll, it's entirely hollow. He's changed the angle of the upper point so there's more room to get around and he's designed a pickguard that doesn't obscure the f-holes as much and that attaches without any hardware. These are small details, and a lot of it has to do with the new look he's given the instrument. They're very clear and sweet-sounding mandolins.

As a practical matter, do you ever really use any mandolin besides your trademark 1925 Gibson F-5?

I must confess that I almost always use that mandolin. It just seems to suit me. Balance is very important to me, and that instrument is the best-balanced mandolin I've ever heard. Every string sounds the same — bright and clear, with good separation. I also believe that an instrument has to be played a lot to truly sing out. That fern-inlay F-5 sounds much better now than it did when I got it 12 years ago, from all the pounding I've done on it. It always sounded bright, which is a very good characteristic in a mandolin. Often they're too bassy, and microphones tend to accentuate the bass characteristics of a mandolin. Mine just seems to cut better than any other I've ever played, and that's the real test for me. You can sit around and play it and listen to it, but when you get up on the stage, that's when it will either do the job or it won't. And most just can't do it. They just disappear. All this talk is relative, though, because instruments become very personal. They become sort of an extension of yourself. Jethro uses an off-the-shelf Washburn with a tiny, thin pick, and he sounds great.

Didn't you recently reacquire a 1924 Lloyd Loar Gibson F-5 that you had previously owned?

Yes, it was the first old Loar I ever owned. I bought it for a certain amount in

1964 and sold it for about three times that in 1970. I repurchased it in 1979 for three times the price I originally paid. I've got mixed feelings about what's happening to the value of old mandolins. I understand the law of supply and demand, but it's unfortunate that a lot of good instruments are going into collectors' vaults. They should be played. Actually, many of the old instruments are not what they're cracked up to be. A lot of people more or less get stiffed because they'll pay $6,000 for them no matter what they sound like. I have seen and heard a bad-sounding Loar. A player would be better advised to spend a third or less than that and get an instrument from a custom builder. They're the guys who are building the collectors' items of the future. Generally, the Loars are beautiful mandolins, but I think the late '20s F-5s have a brighter quality. Steve Gilchrist described them perfectly as being like F-4s with more volume and a little more crispness.

Do you have any basic technical advice for mandolinists?

I think the main thing is to find something that is comfortable for you. Basically I use a loose-wristed right-hand style. I don't like to tell people how to play, because everyone is an individual, but I think you have to develop both hands and use all the fingers on the left hand right from the start. Play a lot. If you have the advantage of going to a good teacher, take it. I was too much of a renegade to seek out a teacher, and it turns out there might have been some around. There were definitely classical teachers around in New Jersey when I was getting started. I could have studied with Dave Apollon. He was alive for ten years after I began playing. And actually, his wife says he would have welcomed me with open arms. So I blew it. And I started late. Ideally, one should start at age seven.

How has your music changed in relation to changes in your group's personnel?

That's always been an important factor in my music. This is the most versatile band I've worked with. Three of them play several instruments very well, and they play many different kinds of music. Various members of the band, in the past, have objected to certain kinds of music that I wanted to play — like traditional jazz, or gypsy music. These guys are more open-minded and eager to play different styles. And rather than trying to play everything one way, this band tries to play different things different ways. Just having the flexibility to utilize different orchestrations is great for me, because I think variety is very important. I'm interested in orchestration, whether it's something simple like mandolin, guitar, and bass playing sparsely, or several violins doing intricate, interweaving parts.

Would you say that, besides bringing lesser-known artists their due, you're committed to making the mandolin a more popular instrument?

It seems to me that the instrument has the potential to be heard by a lot more people in all kinds of music, and I want to stimulate people to play it if I can. It's the players who will advance the instrument, and there's room for everybody. There are many hundreds of good piano, guitar, and saxophone players, but only a relatively small handful of good mandolinists.

So you don't view personnel changes negatively?

I like the experience of working with a lot of different musicians, and obviously I have to prepare for that because these guys are too talented to stay with me forever. I've never demanded or expected that kind of allegiance. I taught three of my tunes to Buck White's band with Jerry Douglas and Ricky Skaggs and *they* were in my band. There are a lot of musicians that I'd like to work with. I really value my relationship with Stephane Grappelli because he is a

wonderful, inspiring human being. I think we have more things to do with him because he is genuinely interested in this kind of music. He likes the kind of rhythm we have.

Maybe you'll become the Miles Davis for acoustic string musicians — with your band being the place for all the hot young talent to develop.

I hope so. I hope I can be that good. My music is based on a group concept — I can't go out and play it by myself. And what's happening with it is dependent on the guys I'm working with. Everybody who's played with me since I started this thing has helped advance the music, and that includes Richard Greene, David Nichtern, Taj Mahal, John Carlini, Ellen Kearney, Joe Carroll, Tony Rice, Todd Phillips, and Bill Amatneek. Everyone.

— *Jon Sievert*

Since the Mar. '79 and Feb. '81 publications of these two articles, a number of changes have taken place in the Grisman ensemble. First and foremost, the Grisman Quintet became the Grisman Quartet in the winter of '81, when Mark O'Connor broke his arm and was forced to leave the group. A number of albums were released; *Live* (Warner, BSK 3550), featuring Grisman and Stephane Grappelli; *Mondo Mando* (Warner, BSK 3618); *Here Today* Rounder [One Camp St., Cambridge, MA 02140], RRR 0169, without the quartet, and *Dawg Jazz, Dawg Grass* (Warner, 3804-1). The Quartet continues to perform everything from bluegrass to jazz to "Dawg." Quartet members are also cutting albums of their own. In 1983 bassist Rob Wasserman recorded *Solo* (Rounder, RRR 0179); and Darol Anger and Mike Marshall recorded *Duo* (Rounder, 0168).

A SELECTED GRISMAN DISCOGRAPHY

Solo Albums: *Hot Dawg,* A&M Horizon; *The David Grisman Rounder Album,* Rounder, (One Camp St., Cambridge, MA 02140),0069.
Group Albums: *Quintet '80,* Warner Bros., BSK 3469; *The David Grisman Quintet,* Kaleidoscope, (Box O, El Cerrito, CA 94530), F-5; *Muleskinner,* Ridge Runner (7121 W. Vickery, Fort Worth, TX 76116), RRR0016; *Old And In The Way,* Round Records, RX 103; **With Earth Opera:** *Earth Opera,* Elektra, 74016; *Great American Eagle Tragedy,* Elektra, 74038. **With Jerry Garcia:** *Jerry Garcia And Merl Saunders, Live At The Keystone,* Fantasy, 79002; *Garcia,* Round Records, RX 102. **With Maria Muldaur:** *Maria Muldaur,* Reprise, MS-2194. **With James Taylor:** *Gorilla,* Warner Bros., BS-2866; *In The Pocket,* Warner Bros., BS-2912; **With Tony Rice:** *Acoustics,* Kaleidoscope, F-10, *Tony Rice,* Rounder, 0085; *Manzanita,* Rounder, 0092. **With Hazel Dickens and Alice Foster:** *Who's That Knocking?,* Verve/Folkways, FV-9005; *Won't You Come And Sing For Me?,* Folkways (43 W. 61st St., New York, NY 10023), FTS-31034. **With Others:** *The Rowan Brothers,* Columbia, KC-31297; *Andy Pratt,* Columbia, KC-31722; *Crabby Appelton,* Elektra, 74106; Judy Collins, *Whales And Nightingales,* Elektra, 75010; Tom Paxton, *Morning Again,* Elektra, 74019; Bill Keith, *Something Newgrass,* Rounder, RB-1.

5.
5-STRING BANJO

EARL SCRUGGS

On Technique, Style, And History.

Earl Scruggs is the father of bluegrass banjo. His name has become synonymous with a unique way of playing: "Scruggs Banjo." His perfection and popularization of this 3-finger style has had a tremendous impact on the history of acoustic string music. In the following question and answer forum, Scruggs offers his own insights on banjo history, style, and technique.

How did the "Ballad Of Jed Clampett" come about, originally?
Paul Henning, who created *The Beverly Hillbillies,* wrote the song and wrote the music and lyrics for it. Lester and I were working a coffeehouse in Hollywood back in the late '50s — about a year or so before the show was to go on the air. Paul never told me this, but I was told that he came to about three of our sets during the 17 days we were out there. He said if the show was picked up by a network then he would try to get us to do the background theme music. Louise, my wife, was doing our booking and managing at the time, and when they approached her, the term "Beverly Hillbillies" didn't hit her well at all. Mr. Henning said, "Well, it's not what it sounds like." He then sent the show's music director, Perry Bodkin, to our home with a pilot film so we could see that it would be about hillbillies, but common-sense hillbillies. That's how close we came to losing it. But we had worked so hard to get away from what you might call the "hillbilly" image thing — trying to be sure that we were called country music performers, rather than just a bunch of hicks from Tennessee or something like that. So we did a three-hour session and recorded that tune in two or three different tempos, and did a bunch of "shave-and-a-haircuts" [ending tags], and the Kellogg's Corn Flakes ending to fill in. The first sponsor was Winston, until the FCC or whoever came in and said that it was too much a family show to be sponsored by cigarettes. As to Lester's voice, I don't think a lot of people know it, but Lester never did sing the lyrics on the soundtrack. It was Jerry Scoggins. I think Mr. Henning sensed that there might be a change in the vocal lines because of sponsor problems, and he wanted to have a voice right there [in Hollywood] in case a change came up. When we recorded the "Ballad Of Jed Clampett" on our Columbia record, Lester did do the vocal part there.

What were your performances like in the old days? How were they different from today's?
There's quite a difference. In the old days, we'd go out and play three or four tunes, and then a comedian would come onstage for about 15 minutes. Then we'd go back out and do sacred numbers and another tune or two. During intermission, we would also sell things like songbooks and pies for the sponsor of the show. Another thing that was important as a difference was that we would all work into one mike. Today, of course, we're working into several and have special microphones for instruments and others for voices.

When you and the late Lester Flatt wrote songs like "Cabin In Caroline," did one of you always write the music while the other wrote the words?
Basically, it was a combination. We'd compare notes and we'd help each other. A lot of times he'd have an idea or I would have an idea and we would go to work on it. We might have an idea for the words but no tune, or the other way around. I was always better at the tunes and Lester was better at the words. I've always concen-

trated on the sound and the melody, so I would really get serious with the tune and be concerned with the way it was presented and the backup and the whole thing. Likewise, Lester concentrated a lot on the words. Of course, it is pretty hard to pinpoint the exact credit for this or that, and we can't ask Lester how he would remember it. In the same sense, I did most of keeping the band organized and working on the music part of the show, and he concentrated on the types of tunes we would do.

I've had a great deal of trouble finding some of your records, and I've been told that many are out of print and no longer available. Do you know of any stores or record dealers who might specialize in Scruggs recordings?
Frankly, I don't know of any regular record shops or record dealers that have them. I don't want this to seem like an advertisement, but several years ago, when Columbia was trying to close out some of our records, I bought all I could from them so that I could be sure they wouldn't get dumped or sold out in some large department store in a cheap way. I'm more than glad to sell them if I know they are going to someone who wants Lester's and my music. You can write to Flatt & Scruggs Records, Box 66, Madison, TN 37115, for a complete list. I'm selling most of the records for $5.95, with some priced at $6.95 and some priced at $7.95. Among the albums I've got are *Flatt & Scruggs At Carnegie Hall* (CS 8845), *Foggy Mountain Banjo* (LE 10043), *Flatt & Scruggs Greatest Hits* (CS 9379), *Nashville Airplane* (CS 9741), and *Hard Travelin'/The Ballad Of Jed Clampett* (CS 8751). I've also got albums I recorded with my boys in the Earl Scruggs Revue.

Everybody talks about Bill Monroe's "high lonesome sound." Can you tell me how you would define that sound, and what it means to you musically?
Bill, to me, has always had a lot of blues in his voice. And I think in some of his interviews, he refers to the many black people he was raised around — but I'm not sure about that. I remember in his early songs, he had a lot of blues notes that he hit, and a lot of people didn't notice that. When Randy [Scruggs — Earl's son, and a well-known guitar picker] was very young and started to listen to some of our music [with Monroe], he started to talk about the blues notes that Bill hit. I don't know how much came from Bill's background. A lot of people who came up through the depression days would sing bluesy things, and I'm not sure that the depression was really an asset to a lot of singers and pickers, you know. So, I have always seen Bill's "lonesome" sound in a blues way and not in a lonesome way. It's sort of like a blues way of singing bluegrass music.

The other day I was sorting through some of my father's old 78 rpm records and I came across an old Columbia disc featuring Flatt And Scruggs' "Randy Lynn Rag." Your banjo sounded "thunkier" than on your current recordings. Was this because of the less sophisticated recording equipment or because of gut strings or a calfskin head?

Well, I think it might be a combination of things. First of all, I have never recorded with gut strings. I've heard of some old-time players who use gut strings, but I've always used steel strings on my banjo. As for the head, I used skin heads until the plastic ones came along. The skin heads had a good tone, but you couldn't rely on them on account of the weather. On humid days, the banjo would just sound "dead." I would think that the major difference has to do with the recording quality. The microphones we used were just great at the time. They [the studio] would use the same microphone for all kinds of recording. Today, when you go into a studio, there are a dozen types of microphones for you to choose from. Rather than having a sound engineer who only adjusts the volume and tone, you have an engineer sitting in front of rows and rows of controls to do just about everything to your sound. And you can go back after you record and do a lot more fine-tuning until you get the sound the way you like it. Then there is another very important part that I don't want to leave out. The way they make the records — the actual "pressing" of the record — is a lot different today than it was thirty years ago. I'm not just speaking about the change from mono to stereo, but the actual science of making better sound come out of a record has done a lot for the work of all musicians.

I recently heard a Flatt And Scruggs recording of "Foggy Mountain Breakdown" that sounded different from the Bonnie And Clyde *version. Are there several different versions? I could swear that the chord changes went from a* G *major to an* E *major instead of* G *major to* E *minor.*

The original version of the tune was cut on the Mercury label in 1949. Then we recorded it again for the *Bonnie And Clyde* album in 1968, on Columbia. The Earl Scruggs Revue recorded it, too, but that sounded quite different from the versions I think you're talking about. When the producer asked me to do the score for *Bonnie And Clyde*, he listened to the Mercury recording and liked it because it had more of an old-time sound than the way we were doing it at the time, so he chose to use it for the movie. He liked the old tone, which was more in keeping with the time of the story. As to your second question, I never played an *E* major — but you have keen ears, because Lester [Flatt] went to an *E* major many times in the cut. Actually, we recorded it with the intention to go to the *E* minor; I never did question him as to why he played it the other way. It sounded good so we both just carried on.

Are you the composer of "Pike County Breakdown"?

No, I'm not. Bill Monroe is the author of that piece. I've been asked that by a lot of people, I guess mostly because it has become such a popular banjo piece. But it was actually a mandolin tune written by Bill. In trying to remember back, I really can't recall just how much he and I played it together when I was in the Blue Grass Boys. We must have played it together some, because I did get to learn it and I know I learned it from him. But I don't really know if we ever performed it much in the shows back then. When I recorded it, I gave him the credit as the author. Anyway, it did start out as a mandolin tune. I really don't know why Bill didn't use it that much, but I have always enjoyed playing it as a banjo tune, just because it is kind of different from tunes that were written for the banjo to begin with.

Many banjo pickers talk about a "basic Scruggs pattern." What is that, really?

Through the years, I've had some trouble explaining what I am doing with my right hand when I pick the banjo, because for me it is something I do naturally and don't think about. When I wrote my banjo instruction book [*Earl Scruggs And The 5-String Banjo*, 1960, Peer-Southern Publications, 1740 Broadway, New York, NY 10019], I finally did have to sit down and figure it out. Basically, my style is several patterns that I call *rolls*. Each one of these patterns has eight notes in it. There is one called the forward roll that goes thumb, index, middle, thumb, index, middle, thumb, index (*t, i, m, t, i, m, t, i*). Then there is the backwards rolls (*t, m, i, t, m, i, t, i*). I do one that is an alternating thumb roll (*t, i, t, m, t, i, t, m*) and another that goes up and down the scale (*t, i, m, t, m, i, t, m*). Of course, there's a lot more in my style, but I think this is the part people talk

about when they talk about basic "Scruggs patterns." I don't do a lot of those long, chromatic-type runs.

For several years now I've been trying to play "Foggy Mountain Special" and have been unable to develop the same kind of slurs and tonal characteristics that you have. I play it beginning at the 12th fret (which I believe you do) and work across to the fourth string at the 12th fret. Here's my tab for it. Would you mind telling me what I am doing wrong?

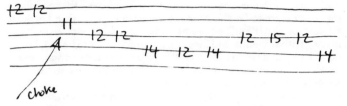

I don't want to say that what you are doing is *wrong* because there are many ways to play the same tune. It's just that some ways may come easier for some people. I've been playing "Foggy Mountain Special" my way for so long that it's the only way I know how. Actually, you are not the first one who has shown me how it can be played your way. But doing it like that you can't get the chokes to come out the same, and I think you just might find my way to be a bit easier. Here is some tablature from my writings so that it can be clearer for you to follow:

You can see that I play most of the lick on the second and third strings. That allows me to get the choke in, and for me, it's real comfortable to play. Even though I have played it for so long now, I believe that I play it slightly different every time, but I think the music example here is about as accurate as I can sit down and write out. I think it's amusing that "Foggy Mountain Special" started out as a practice [run] for me. It was a boogie tune that I used to play over and over.

You recently explained how you do the break up the neck for "Foggy Mountain Special." I have listened to how you do it, and I think you left out a note in the tablature. I can hear a second B string played at the 8th fret [the first G in the break], but the tablature only shows one. Am I wrong?

Well, yes and no. When I play the tune, I often play it many different ways. The way you've heard it on my recordings is just *one* way that I play it. Actually, if you listen carefully, I play it the very first time through with just one *G* note there — when I'm fretting at the second string, 8th fret. But the second time, I add that extra *G*, so I do it both ways. Following is the tablature that shows it both ways. Both are "right," and there are many more ways that are right as well. You know, this is an important point: There is no *one* right way to play a piece. For me, music is like a way of talking, and I can't imagine someone saying the same sentence exactly the same way twice. If you follow what I'm saying, you have to express your feelings when you are playing the banjo, or any other instrument, and there is nothing wrong with playing the same tune slightly different each time, so long as you carry the melody and don't alter it so much that the members of your band don't know what you are doing. I don't purposely try to play a tune different each time I play it, but I don't try to play it exactly the same, either. I might be more particular about how I play the very first break so that my audience can recognize the tune.

Do you ever note [fret] with the fingernails of your left hand?

Yes, I do a combination of that and noting with just the fleshy part of my fingertips. A lot of times when I'm sliding into a high note or when I'm going for a blues type of note, I do use the fingernails of my index and middle fingers. To do that you turn your fingers slightly and just tilt your knuckle over a little, until you get on the end of your finger and your fingernail hits the string. I was doing it for a number of years unaware of what I was doing until somebody got to noticing it and asked me about it. It's a natural thing that comes to me, and I seem to be able to make a clearer slide note and make it sustain longer. It's still not something that I do consciously. If I'm playing with someone and they *ask* me to do it, just to hear it, I can't do it. I just do it when I *feel* that the slide needs more brightness. I don't really think about it. It's not something you can do a lot, because your fingernail just won't last long that way. The fingernails on my index and middle fingers have always stayed worn down ever since I've been duty picking. The right side of each fingernail is worn from so much rubbing against the strings.

I want to be sure that my right-hand position is solid. At about what angle should the right hand be to the strings? In your book, you wrote that the index and middle fingerpicks should be flat against the strings when picking; but if I do that, my arm is way above the armrest.

This is a question that I get asked a lot, and I think it is because the right-hand technique really does take a lot of learning and training. Over the years, I have seen banjo pickers hold their hands all different ways, and I have learned that no way is what you call "right." The way that works for *you* and your hand is "right." I hold the palm of my hand so that it is almost even [parallel] to the banjo head, and I keep the long parts of my fingers — the first bone part nearest the palm of your hand —almost straight with the palm. Then, after the knuckles, I bend my fingers back —more than most players do, I think. Because of that sharp angle, and the way I pick at the strings, I have to bend my picks back until the part that contacts the string is flat with it. Below are some drawings to illustrate this for you because I don't know how else to describe it so that you can fully understand it. Some players don't bend their fingers as much and also don't bend their picks as much, but they get almost the same angle of the pick to the string. Most of my picking motion —in the parts of my fingers that do the most movement — happens after the big knuckle, and it is just the last two parts of the fingers that do most of the picking and moving. When I am chopping at chords up near the neck, I tend to move more of my whole right hand, but that's because I'm pulling at a few strings at a time.

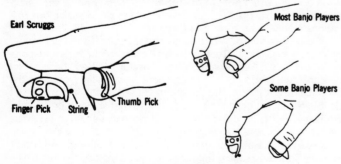

Earl Scruggs / Most Banjo Players / Some Banjo Players / Finger Pick / String / Thumb Pick

Do you use your left thumb for fretting strings?

Yes, I do. I've had several people ask me that, and I think the reason they don't notice it [the sound of the fretted fifth string] is that I don't play it in what you call the chromatic style. Some banjo players fret the fifth string to get notes as part of a special chromatic run up and down the neck. I have used my thumb on the fifth string for years, but it's been for my style and just to add that note to a special run or tag I might be doing. So I don't think you hear it the same way as if you were doing the chromatic styles.

When you are playing two-finger [right hand] backup up the neck, what kind of technique are you using for the "double thumbing"?

I've done that several ways. When I first started it, I was using my [right hand] index and middle finger in what some people have told me

is a classical guitar technique. For me, I couldn't get enough power or speed that way and I started to try it with the thumb and index and the thumb and middle. For a long time I was doing it both ways, doing the one that felt most comfortable at the time. But it's a little more stable using just my thumb and middle finger. I can also get a little more power that way, so I have finally come around to doing that kind of picking with my thumb and middle finger.

You have said that you used a Barcus-Berry pickup in your Gibson banjo. Can you please tell me which one you use?

It's the type that is the little piece [transducer] about 3/4" long — maybe it's 5/8" or so. You put some goo stuff on it and stick it to the head, or whatever — like, you might want to stick it inside a guitar. I'm not quite sure of the number or model name, but it's a small rectangular one. [*Ed. Note: Earl is using the No. 1356 pickup from Barcus-Berry, 15461 Springdale Street, Huntington Beach, CA 92649.*]

I've been playing banjo for over a year and a half now, but still have problems changing chords quickly and accurately. Could you please outline the correct left-hand approach?

Thanks for your question on this one. I think this is one of the most common problems that banjo players have. To be perfectly honest, if I am working out a new tune, I have to practice making the chord changes quickly, too, and it's not until I practice the tune over and over that I have it down right. I think everyone hates to hear the word "practice," but there's just no substitute for it. Moving the fingers of your left hand around to the right spot each time doesn't come natural. It is something you have to learn. You have to practice just how far to move your arm, how to position your left hand [fingers], exactly where to stop, and so on. After a while you won't even think about going from a C chord to — let's say — an F chord. But first you must take the time to sit and go back and forth from one chord to another. Watch your left-hand fingers. Picture in your mind what your fingers are doing. Which ones are you using? Where are they going to end up? Think about the ones that you aren't putting down [on the fretboard] and just how you are holding them up [off the fretboard]. Here's a simple practice exercise that I worked out for you to try: First, play a pattern like 3-1-5-2-1-5-2-1 [*Ed. Note: the right hand fingering for this pattern is T-M-T-I-M-T-I-M.*] with a C chord, and then at the end of the first pattern switch to an F chord. This will force you to keep your left index finger on the 1st fret of the B string while you have to switch your other fingers around to make the F. Then after the second pattern in F, switch back to the C and keep going back and forth. It will seem hard at first, but then you should get it smooth. The second exercise is to play the full G up between the 3rd and 5th frets. Play a pattern in the G and then play the next pattern in the full D chord that is made between the 2nd and 4th frets. Repeat this over and over again. This will force you to leave your pinky on the first string and your ring finger on the fourth string while you have to switch around your index and middle fingers, at the same time sliding your hand down and up one fret each time you make the change. This will seem hard at first, too, but I think working on these practice patterns will help get your fingers working for you.

Is it hard to build up strength to do bends with all your fingers, or do you do all your bends with the left index and middle fingers?

By "bends" I guess you mean "chokes." [*Ed. Note: A "choke" occurs when a string is stopped and forced to one side on the fretboard to raise its pitch.*] No, I use whatever finger is necessary and whatever finger I *can* use at the time. I think that most banjo players have little trouble with their index and middle fingers of their left hand because those fingers are naturally strong. The ring finger is a bit harder to use and the pinky is probably the hardest to use. I can't recall how long it took me to use my little finger to choke the string, but I think I got forced into doing it when I was working out the break for "Sally Goodin." In the beginning of that tune, I'm up the neck at the 8th and 9th frets with my [left] index and middle finger, and have to fret and choke the B string at the 11th fret. The only way to do it is to use my little finger. After some time, you can get the chokes down as easy with the little finger as with any other finger, but you will have to build up your finger muscles with practice.

Some banjo players use the little finger of the right hand for support at the bridge, while others use both the little finger and the ring finger. Which do you prefer? Do you think that two fingers damp the head more than one finger?

I use both the ring finger and the little finger — it comes easy for me that way. Now, there's some people that can't do it [that way]. I even got a letter once from a doctor who told me about the muscles and the position of the fingers and all, because he heard that some people said you couldn't do it physically. Of course, that's not true. In my opinion, it can give you more stability; there is just more support with two fingers than with one. But, if it hinders you, don't try it. As to the question about damping the sound, I've never played any other way. I guess I'd have to say that it might have a tendency to do just a bit of that. I touch the bridge with my pinky finger and use that finger as a way to locate my hand — especially when I go to playing away from the bridge and then move back to the bridge. I also do my muting or tone control for the real high notes with my pinky. On certain notes, if the sound is too bright or ringy, I use my pinky hard against the bridge to cut it [the brightness] back some. The muting comes natural to me, but I am conscious of the sound. I'm always listening to the sound. If I sense that it sounds too bright or too ringy, I'll just naturally move my pinky to mute it down some.

My left-hand fingers get sore after playing for an hour or two. Is there any way I can toughen them up?

The very first thing I have found with that is to try to put a regular practice schedule into effect with about the same amount of time each day. If you choose 30 minutes a day, then be sure to play 30 minutes every day. The continuous practice will build up your hands and fingers. It will also build up the calluses on your fingertips. I've had a lot of young banjo players complain to me about holding their left arm out and having it get tired. Some find that it's easier to hold the banjo neck up higher, but when you come right down to it, it's just practice that you need to build yourself up. Here's something, too, that you should consider: The banjo is heavy, a lot heavier than a guitar. If you always practice sitting down, without the strap across your shoulder, you are not going to get used to the weight of the banjo; and if you have to go out and play standing up for a couple of good hours, you are going to feel very uncomfortable.

I'm in the habit of doing only push-offs [making a note by pushing or pulling the string to one side with a left-hand finger, then snapping the finger free] even when a pull-off is called for. Do you think I should learn both ways?

Yes, you should. I don't believe that you will be able to get as good a sound from a push-off as you can from a pull-off. Another important thing is that there are some tunes where you want the finger doing the pull-off to be able to come back on to another note, or to come back on to do a hammer-on. I don't think you can build as much power if you do a push-off and then try to bring your finger back towards your hand to do the next note. You should also think of the position your finger is in after it does the pull-off. Is it ready to come back to do the next note or to make the next chord? If you find that you are left with your finger up in the air, and you have trouble getting it back down, then I think you should take time and practice learning how to do pull-offs.

What is the best way to learn how to develop speed?

As with anything you do on the banjo, it takes a lot of practice —

you have to decide that you really want to play the banjo, and then spend a lot of time practicing. People have always asked me about *speed*. For my style of playing and for what I like to do, speed alone is not important to me. What is important is how I carry the rhythm when I am backing up; and then how I handle my pick-up notes when I come into a break, and how I go out of a break. I think that good, clean timing — coming into a break right on the beat and with clean clear notes — is more important than just playing fast. Oh, I'll play fast sometimes when I am just sitting home or jamming with some friends. It's sort of an exercise and a way to limber up my fingers. But I never thought of my kind of banjo playing as being a fast style. People have commented on how fast I could play, but I think they were referring to how busy my fingers were, and not that I was playing so fast. I think people learning to play the banjo should concentrate on the music they can get out of the banjo and not just how fast they can play. To me, it has always seemed strange that no one ever asks me how to play *slow*. If you think about it, it is harder to play a piece like "All The Good Times Are Past And Gone" or "Worried Man Blues" and to keep the rhythm and keep the good timing, than it is to just play fast. To answer your question, I think you should concentrate on hitting sharp, clear notes, and if you practice enough, the speed will come.

I recently compared a tape of my playing to your playing on one of your records. Although I think my playing is similar, I am missing the emphasis that you put in. Is there any special way that I can develop the emphasis on certain notes to make my playing sound less mechanical?

Without hearing your picking, I can't give you an answer on that one. The "bounce" or emphasis that you ask about is just a way that I make a difference between the melody notes and the rhythm notes, and that's whether I am playing an instrumental number or playing the break for a song. You see, the instrumental has a melody too. Although I think I can generalize and say that the emphasis is usually on the thumb [of the right hand], it is not always the case. The lead — or what you are calling the "emphasis" — will switch from one finger to another according to whether the note that is being played is part of the melody or part of the rhythm. You have to take the time to study the piece you're trying to play and find out where the melody is — which notes are the melody notes that need to be played harder. And that brings me to another point. It's very hard for me to say whether I am playing the melody notes harder or whether I am changing the tempo of them slightly to make them stand out more — sort of like grouping my rhythm notes closer to each melody note. One of the problems I have always had was to be able to clearly explain exactly what I am doing. I do not play any special way that I *think* about, it's just something that I do; and when I stop and slow it down to analyze it, I sometimes have problems doing the same thing slowly that I do when I play at normal speed and don't concentrate on it. When I think down over the years, I believe that I have kept the melody in my mind when I have played a break, and the rhythm notes just came along. Of course, when I have played backup, I would think of rhythm ideas while the singer would be handling the melody. I hope that this helps to clear up the question, and I really wish I could explain it better.

Instructional Tips
ALAN MUNDE
Syncopation Accents

Alan Munde is one of America's premier banjo players and a member of the acclaimed bluegrass group Country Gazette. Here are some details on his musical career —which includes major recording and film track production plus concert tours throughout the world.

A CONSTANT STREAM OF SIXTEENTH-NOTES forms the basis of bluegrass-style banjo playing. I've found it necessary to develop a technique that accents certain notes in the roll for syncopation or "bounce."

Doing this requires a measure of control over the thumb, index finger, and middle finger of the right (picking) hand. Here's a simple roll to practice that will help you develop the control you need:

Practice playing the exercise with the accents as shown. Putting the accents in those places means using a lot of concentration to send that bit of extra energy to each finger at the right moment. If you are doing the exercise correctly you should achieve a definite syncopated feel.

Now try moving the accents to other places. For instance, try this roll:

Notice how the feeling changes. Experiment with other patterns in your repertoire to discover how many different ways each can sound with slight shifts in the accents.

Here's an excerpt from "Blackberry Blossom" with accents marked as I might play them:

"Blackberry Blossom"

**Traditional
Arranged by Alan Munde**

Forward-Reverse Rolls

THE FIRST ROLL I EVER LEARNED is commonly called the "forward-reverse" roll (see Ex. 1). This roll can be divided (as its name suggests) into two sections, with the open fifth string dividing them. I have found this roll to be useful for moving rapidly from one chord position to another, as in Ex. 2, or for moving from a fingered position to the open position, as in Ex. 3.

Ex. 1

Ex. 2

Ex. 3

Forward-reverse rolls also make up some standard licks, and one such instance is shown in Ex. 4.

Ex. 4

The name of the roll pattern refers to the general nature of the right-hand picking sequence, and not necessarily to the strings picked. For variety, the thumb and fingers can change the strings they strike. (That is true for most roll patterns.) That idea is illustrated in Ex. 5 and Ex. 6.

Ex. 5

In general, I have found the forward-reverse roll to be most effective for playing a lead line that has some harmonic movement rather than for playing a more static backup situation.

Ex. 6

Left-Hand Blocking

GETTING YOUR FRETTING fingers to the right place at the right time requires practice.

A friend of mine who had studied piano told me about a method for practicing arpeggio passages — a technique called "blocking." Instead of playing a passage as a series of notes in arpeggio, the student plays all the notes "blocked" into their chordal forms. This is a good way to become familiar with the hand positions in a passage without worrying about the exact order of the notes.

Since bluegrass banjo is primarily composed of a series of rapid arpeggios, "blocking" is an excellent left-hand exercise that helps you to focus your attention on your fretting hand without worrying about your picking hand. It also gives you a chance to hear some interesting (often dissonant) harmonies that fly by your ears too fast to recognize when you're playing at full speed.

Below is the banjo solo that I played on "Gone, Gone, Gone," from Country Gazette's *All This And Money Too*, Ridge Runner Records (7121 W. Vickery, No.118, Fort Worth, TX 76126), RRR-00017. The solo appears in the music as I recorded it. I have added chord ("block") diagrams to help familiarize you with the left-hand positions. Try this as a "blocking" exercise first — it should help you to know the fretting positions before you try the picking.

In measure 11, I use my left-hand thumb to fret the fifth string. Some people prefer not to use the thumb for fretting, so I have included an alternate fingering that does not use the thumb.

"Gone, Gone, Gone" Solo   **Arranged by Alan Munde**

Pull-Off Exercises

PULLING-OFF IS A TECHNIQUE that I am very partial to. A pull-off is created when your *fretting* hand plucks a string, sounding either a fretted note or the open-string note.

Many beginning players misinterpret the pull-off, thinking of it as lifting their finger from the string. You must *pluck* the string with your fretting finger to get a strong, clean pull-off; a lifting motion produces a very weak sound.

To properly execute a pull-off, you need to catch and pull the string with the fleshy part of your fingertip. After your finger plucks the string, you must be careful not to hit any adjacent strings with the pulling finger. That can deaden the adjacent strings, or cause unwanted notes to sound.

The direction that the finger usually travels during a pull-off is down — groundward. Virtually all of the pull-offs I do are in that direction. However, I should mention that some players do their pull-offs by pushing up — skyward. I call that approach "pushing-off." The effect is the same with either approach. You might want to try both methods to see which is most comfortable for you.

The beauty of the pull-off is that it provides another way to articulate notes and to play grace notes (notes with a very short time value). They add variety to your style, and relieve your right hand of some of the often frantic task of plucking the strings.

Below are a few exercises that incorporate pull-offs. Notice that the right hand does not wait for the pull-off to sound before continuing — the pull-off happens at about the same time as the next note that is plucked by the picking hand.

Eighth-Note Pulloffs

PULL-OFFS ARE OFTEN USED in 5-string banjo playing to embellish a normal eighth-note right-hand pattern to create *grace notes* (notes with very short time values). Sometimes pull-offs can be used to replace one or more of the notes in standard eighth-note patterns, thus giving the pull-off note a full eighth-note value.

The technique for an eighth-note pull-off is similar to that of a grace note pull-off, except that the eighth-note pull-off is not done as quickly, and the right hand waits for the pull-off to sound before plucking the next note.

Part of my initial intent in writing "The Earl Of Broadfield" (below) was to create a piece of music that illustrated the technique of eight-note pull-offs. I recorded the tune on my LP *The Banjo Kid Picks Again* (Ridge Runner Records [7121 W. Vickery No. 118, Fort Worth, TX 76116] RRR-0023). One especially attractive aspect of the tune is the cadence that is set up by the pull-offs, especially in the B section.

Remember that the eighth-note pull-offs are as important as the other right-hand eighth-notes, so those pull-offs must be done vigorously, to keep the notes ringing.

Here are two measures that can be substituted for measures three and four of the B section. The term for such substitutions is *ossia*.

"The Earl Of Broadfield"

By Alan Munde

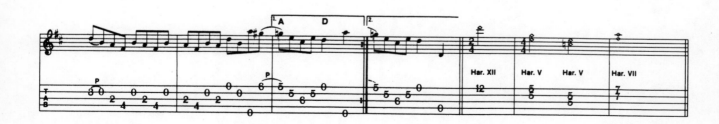

Reno-Style Playing

ALONG WITH EARL SCRUGGS, Don Reno is considered to be one of the major 5-string banjo innovators, right from the early period of bluegrass banjo music. It would require a book to cover this entire technique, but the one aspect of Reno's playing that is most often cited as his unique contribution to 5-string banjo is his single-string approach, or the "Reno style."

That style sounds as though it developed from a desire to lay melody lines more in a sequential guitar style than within the standard bluegrass banjo rolls. To achieve an effect similar to guitar flatpicking, Reno devised the right-hand technique of alternating his thumb and index finger, with the thumb corresponding to the flatpicker's down-stroke and the index finger corresponding to the up-stroke.

Reno-style playing requires good left-hand dexterity because of the fast single-note lines, which are usually more demanding than the position-based left-hand approach of traditional, roll-style playing. Also, in Reno-style playing notes are played and immediately released as the left hand moves to the next note. The result often is a fast, punchy, staccato sound.

Below are some exercises in the Reno single-string melodic style. Start out by getting familiar with both the right-and left-hand fingerings, and then slowly work up to performance speed. As you increase the tempo, be sure to maintain tonal clarity and proper timing.

Modular Endings

THERE ARE ANY NUMBER of popular ways to end a banjo piece. Below, I have outlined a few of the most commonly used endings for instrumentals (see Exs. 1 through 5). After playing through them you may notice that for the most part, the four-measure phrases are divided into two two-measure "licks." The licks are often interchangeable. For instance, the first two measures in Ex. 1 may be played with either of the two-measure licks in Ex. 4; "modular" music, if you will.

Ex. 1 probably qualifies as the classic bluegrass banjo ending. If you listen to Earl Scruggs on the *Foggy Mountain Banjo* album (Columbia, LE10043), you will hear this ending on "Cripple Creek," "Sally Goodin," "Cumberland Gap," and "Sally Ann."

The first two measures of Ex. 2 are similar to Ex. 1, but with enough difference to provide an option. I usually use this ending. The closing two measures come from the playing of J.D. Crowe, the famed banjoist of New South, formerly with Jimmy Martin. Many

players use this ending on "Train Forty-Five." It can be heard on Crowe's recording — with Jimmy Martin — of "John Henry," from the *Sunny Side Of The Mountain* (MCA,4643).

Ex. 3 has a little extra element in it. Again, there is a familiar sound, but each two-measure lick has its beginning in the previous measure. Bill Emerson plays this ending with Jimmy Martin on "Little Maggie, She's So Sweet," from *Big And Country Instrumentals* (MCA, DL 74891).

Ex. 4 is very much in the Bill Keith style, and is used on many fiddle-type tunes.

Ex. 5 gives you an idea as to how you can transpose an ending lick to the key of *C*.

Of course, these endings represent only a few of the possible ways to end your blazing instrumental. There are as many endings as there are players, but these will be useful in getting you started —or rather, stopped.

Vocal Endings

THERE ARE ALSO SOME FAIRLY standard endings for vocal numbers.

The main difference between the two types of endings is that the typical vocal ending is two measures long as compared to the usual four-measure instrumental ending. The two-measure ending for a vocal number is played more as part of an ensemble effort than as a featured solo instrumental finish.

Ex. 1 and Ex. 2 are probably the most frequently used ending phrases in the key of G. Most of the medium-to-fast tempo Flatt And Scruggs songs played in the G position use those endings or some variation of them.

Ex. 3 is a variation that I heard Bill Keith play.

Ex. 4 is the ending that I used on "Look Down That Lonesome Road" from the *Country Gazette Live* LP, Antilles (444 Madison Ave., New York, NY 10022), AN7014. The final G chord can be strummed by dragging the index finger upward across the strings (first to fifth) followed closely by the middle finger. That technique overlaps the two strums, giving an extended, full sound to the final chord.

Examples five and six are Scruggs-type endings that are used mostly for medium-to-slow tempo songs. I used the ending shown in Ex. 5 to end "Sunny Side Of The Mountain" from Country Gazette's *Out To Lunch*, Flying Fish (1304 W. Schubert, Chicago, IL 60614),FF 027.

Ex. 7 is an ending that Earl Scruggs has used both on vocal and on instrumental numbers. Earl's recordings of "Dear Old Dixie" and "Shuckin' The Corn" both employ this ending.

Ex. 8 is in the key of C, and the final note is the third note of the scale *(E)*, which gives the ending a slightly unusual sound.

Ex. 9 is a chordal ending in the key of D that is reminiscent of Allen Shelton's playing. Be sure to tune your fifth string up to A for this one.

Banjo Tunes
"Cripple Creek"

CRIPPLE CREEK" MAY NOT BE the first tune that beginners learn, but it is surely one of the first two or three, because it contains many of the basic elements of Scruggs-style picking, as in Ex. 1. Similarly, the tune also can be arranged to spotlight some of the basic elements required in melodic-style playing (see Ex.2 and Ex.3). We will concentrate on just the first section, because it can provide the best example of a melodic interpretation.

The basic ideas in the first example are the slide from *E* to *G*, which is followed by a pinch, and the open first and second strings. Then there is a *C*-chord arpeggio (beginning on the fifth string), and the section concludes with a slide (or hammer-on) on the third string and a quick *D* chord.

Compare that version with the melodic-style approach in Ex.2. In the first measure, the slide from *E* to *G* is replaced by the two pick-up notes *E* and *F"*. Then, instead of just playing the *G* note twice, the *A* note is added as an embellishment. In the same place in Ex.3, one of the *G* notes is replaced by an *F"*, for another variation.

In Ex.2, the *C*-chord arpeggio is somewhat broader, encompassing the first four strings. In Ex.3, that arpeggio includes a little extra harmonic interest, with the addition of the *A* note (creating a *C6* sound).

For a recording of these different approaches, check out *Festival Favorites, Vol II* (Ridge Runner Records [7121 W. Vickery No. 118, Fort Worth, TX 76116], RRR-0027).

"Forked Deer"

KNOWING WHEN TO USE A CAPO and when to change your tuning is a valuable piece of knowledge for any banjoist. Each technique has its advantage in certain arrangements. "Forked Deer" provides us with a good example of when *to* use a capo.

Harmonically speaking, the dominant chord (*A7*) plays a strong role. It only appears in the fourth and eighth measures of the first section, but almost the entire *second* section is played in the dominant chord. In fact, many players actually change to the key of *A*, and instead of coming back to the tonic *D* in the fourth measure,

they play an *E7* to firmly establish the key change.

The point of all this is simple. Since the *A* chord is used so much, placing a capo on the second fret to achieve an open *A* chord enables you to play the tune much more easily. I've found the first section playable with or without a capo, but the second section is definitely stronger if played in the capoed position.

If you'd like to check out my own recording of this arrangement, it can be found on Country Gazette's album *Out To Lunch* (Flying Fish [1304 W. Schubert, Chicago, IL 60614],FF027). Good luck!

"Old Joe Clark"

LOOKING BACK, I CLEARLY REMEMBER sitting in my parents' garage, struggling with my banjo in hopes of coaxing some semblance of good music out of it. One tune that I devoted many garage sessions to was "Old Joe Clark." The version I was trying to work out was Eric Weissberg's — the one he played with Marshall Brickman on *New Dimensions In Bluegrass And Banjo* (Elektra, 7238).

The element of Weissberg's arrangement that caused me the greatest grief was the phrasing. Each phrase in the first section started before I expected it to (at the end of the measure preceding the first full measure of the phrase). That approach was much different from the other recorded versions of the tune I had listened to (Bill Monroe's and Sonny Osborne's).

After trying many different combinations and spending many frustrating moments, I finally hit upon the right combinations. When at last I got it right, I felt that a barrier had been removed and that I had made some progress in my playing. This month, I'm offering an arrangement of "Old Joe Clark" that includes the passage I struggled for so long to master.

I would like to call your attention to a couple of other points of interest in this arrangement. When we think of the eight-note roll patterns that make up much of the bluegrass banjo style, we tend to conceive of each roll beginning and ending in one measure. That is the way the style is usually taught — one roll begins and ends within a measure, and is followed by another roll that begins and ends within a measure, and so on.

But in part B, there is a roll that begins in the last half of the second measure and continues into the first half of the next measure. Unlike a normal roll, that one is divided by a bar line. The point I'm making is that although bluegrass banjo is primarily modular, you should think in terms of designing an arrangement to *flow* from the beginning to the end, rather than putting together randomly selected modular patterns that conform to a preconceived style.

In measure five of the B section there is a phrase (lick) that I picked up from Doug Dillard's playing. I added it here as a variation of the first measure of the same section.

"Orange Blossom Special"

THERE ARE A NUMBER OF "MUST" instrumentals that a bluegrass band needs to play in order to get through an evening at the local pizza parlor. "Dueling Banjos," "Foggy Mountain Breakdown," and "Orange Blossom Special" are a few of them. The first two can be covered by almost any banjo picker, but what does the group do with "Orange Blossom Special" if they don't have a fiddler? I will be the first to admit that this tune sounds best when played on a fiddle, and not quite right on other instruments. But why not give it a try? It might not be exactly right, but it can be interesting.

"Orange Blossom Special" is divided into three sections, the first of which is in the key of E (D fingering with a capo at the 2nd fret on the banjo). Although the first section (see music below) is played without any chord changes, it can still be the most interest-

ing part. The band holds a steady, rapid tempo while the soloist plays freely over the harmony (without the usual restrictions of chord changes). This type of approach is usually referred to as "modal" playing, and it was popularized by such jazz greats as Miles Davis and John Coltrane in the early '60s. Chubby Wise, one of the composers of "Orange Blossom Special," wrote the tune with this modal idea about 40 years ago.

The music below shows a few ideas that I used on my recording of the tune (*Festival Favorites, Vol. I*, Ridge Runner [121 W. Vickery No. 118, Fort Worth, TX 76116], RRR-0026). There is an infinite number of ideas possible in playing the first section, and I suggest that you search out other recordings of this number — both on the fiddle and the banjo — to help you develop some of your own interpretations.

"Scotland"

AMONG THE MANY PLEASURES I've enjoyed in my ten years as a professional musician is the ever-present opportunity to make music with some very talented people.

Recently I had the good fortune to record with Bobby Hicks, the fiddler on many of the classic Bill Monroe instrumentals. As one who grew up being thrilled by that music, I was equally thrilled to be part of Bobby's recreation of a few of those tunes for his album *Texas Crapshooter.*

One tune from the session that particularly interested me was "Scotland." The original Bill Monroe recording had no banjo solo for me to model mine after. What I devised to play — though simple — has a few techniques that may be of interest to banjoists.

The first statement has a *G-F♯-G* figure used as a kind of pedal point. When this statement is repeated, I use a simple pull-off technique — from a fingered note to the open position. The pull-off is among my favorite devices; in addition to the fluidity it gives you, it

creates the illusion that more is happening than really is.

The second half of the solo is played in a lower position. It was my banjoist's attempt to imitate the fiddle, using two strings to play a unison *G* with two other strings playing a unison *G* an octave higher; *G* on the fourth string with *G* on the open third string, and *G* on the first string with *G* on the open fifth string. Not much, but I tried. Gee.

The closing two measures make up a restatement of the opening, except the major-seventh *F♯* is changed to the flatted-seventh *F* natural. I used my right hand as follows: middle finger on the second string, first finger on the third string, and thumb on the fourth string. This will prove a bit awkward at first because some hand movement is required, but it's the only comfortable way I've found to play passages on the second string and still manage to continue the roll on the third and fourth strings.

"Scotland" Break

Arranged by Alan Munde

"Big Mon"

HERE IS MY BREAK FROM "Big Mon" from Bobby Hicks' *Texas Crapshooter* LP (County Records, [Box 191, Floyd, VA 24091],772).

Bobby Hicks was the fiddle player on Bill Monroe's original recording of "Big Mon." Since there was only a short banjo solo on Monroe's recording, I patterned my playing after the fiddle part. That is especially evident in the first section, which is actually the second part of the original tune. The break requires several position jumps,

so the left-hand fingering must be planned carefully.

The second section is longer, and is more in line with the banjo idiom. Notice that in the first and fifth measures, the index finger of the picking hand plucks the second string and then moves back to its normal first-string work. The last four measures also require a little extra attention because of the unusual note placement.

But the real killer in playing this piece is the tempo. It's one of the true barnburners in bluegrass music.

"Big Mon" Break

As Played By Alan Munde

ARRANGEMENT © 1981 ALAN MUNDE

"Flop-Eared Mule"

THE RENO STYLE OF BANJO playing can be applied to the old dance tune "Flop-Eared Mule," as in Ex. 1. I am also including a melodic-style arrangement for comparison (see Ex. 2).

As you play through these arrangements, remember that besides learning the tune, what we are trying to do is to develop some of the many picking styles you need to know as a banjo player. As you get more into developing arrangements for performance, you will find that it can take all the techniques you know just to perform a single piece.

Although the first arrangement of "Flop-Eared Mule" is in the Reno Style, it is not an exact transcription of his recording. Reno's version can be heard on Reno And Smiley's LP *Country Singing And Instrumentals* (King Records [1900 Elm Hill Pike, Nashville, TN 37210], 776).

If you'd like to listen to banjo players who can really mix the many picking styles, check out any of the recordings by John Hickman, Bela Fleck, and Larry McNeely.

ARRANGEMENT © 1981 ALAN MUNDE

6.
MANDOLIN

Instructional Tips
DAVID GRISMAN
Roots of Bluegrass Mandolin

David Grisman's "Dawg" music has been called "bluegrass-jazz-Gypsy-rock-Middle Eastern-Hebraic-folk-classical-Grisman" Whatever style he's playing, Grisman's technical virtuosity and brilliant imagination make him one of the most original musicians of his generation. In the Instructional Tips and Tunes that follow, however, David has focused his wisdom and experience in some lessons that pertain especially to bluegrass music.

COUNTRY MANDOLIN playing was first heard on commercial "old time" records made during the late '20s and early '30s in the rural South. The great popularity of mandolin societies and orchestras a few years earlier helped to popularize the instrument and make it a catalog item that could be easily obtained by people in the South. At any rate, the earliest stylistic developments were highly influenced by ragtime and blues. Good examples of this earliest style may be heard on records by the Dallas String Band, Gid Tanner and his Skillet Lickers, the Golden Melody Boys, and Yank Rachel, who played in a bluesy fashion on many recordings by Sleepy John Estes. However, these early prototypes are less relevant to bluegrass mandolin than the style that developed along with the smooth duet singing of the mid- and late '30s.

During this period, many performers featured the mandolin along with close-harmony vocal duets. This new repertoire included many sacred songs, sentimental love songs, and strictly traditional material. For the first time in country music, the mandolin was given some definite roles: to introduce or "kick off" the song, to play melodically as an instrumental break between verses, to fill up the background melodically and rhythmically, and to function as an instrumental extension of the singing. For the most part, all of these functions were accomplished with the use of the *tremolo*, or the rapid reiteration of alternating downstrokes and upstrokes. Some of the performers who characterized this new style were Karl Davis and Harty Taylor, the Callahan Brothers, the Morris Brothers, and most notably the Blue Sky Boys (Bill and Earl Bolick) and the Monroe Brothers (Bill and Charlie).

Try playing Bill Monroe's kickoff to the well-known traditional folk song, "Weeping Willow Tree" (also known as "Bury Me Beneath The Willow"), which was recorded in 1937 and can be heard on the Monroe Brothers LP *Feast Here Tonight*, Bluebird (dist. by RCA), AXM2-5510. It's nearly all tremolo in the key of *F* (see Ex. 1).

Another kickoff that was played in a similar manner, by Bill Bolick of the Blue Sky Boys, is shown in Ex. 2. The tune is "Mary Of The Wild Moor," a simple but very beautiful melody; and again, nearly all tremolo. You can hear it on the RCA Camden LP, *The Blue Sky Boys* (CAL-797), which is out of print.

The Father of Bluegrass

RECORDINGS SPANNING A PERIOD over 40 years document the many facets of Bill Monroe's playing as the creator and chief innovator of the bluegrass mandolin style. As Bill will tell you himself, much of his style is "taken from the fiddle." This is evidenced by his vast repertoire of such traditional Anglo-American fiddle tunes as "Sally Goodin," "Grey Eagle," and "Katy Hill," as well as by many fiddle-type Monroe originals like "Monroe's Hornpipe," "Wheel Hoss," and "Roanoke." Interestingly enough, despite the fiddle influence, most of his "trademark" instrumental compositions are completely mandolinistic. Tunes like "Rawhide," "Blue Grass Breakdown," "Kentucky Mandolin," and "Moonlight Waltz" fall into this category.

Bill has also experimented occasionally with variations of the standard mandolin tuning, producing compositions like "Get Up John," written in an open D tuning (DA-AA-DD-F A), and "Blue Grass Ramble," which utilizes an A tuning (GG-DD-AA-EC).

Another important aspect of Bill's mandolin style is the influence of *blues*. This is evident in much of his solo and harmony singing as well as in his mandolin playing on many songs. Bill has also composed a number of blues mandolin instrumentals: "Blue Grass Special," "Blue Grass Stomp," and "Blue Grass Part One," to name a few. (My own version of "Blue Grass Part One," called "Bluegrass Blues," appears on *Red Allen And The Kentuckians* [County (Box 191, Floyd, VA 24091), 710], recorded in the Monroe style in 1966.) I have chosen as an example of Bill's bluesy mandolin playing the kick-off and break (introduction and solo) to the song "I Was Left On The Street," recorded in 1962 and available on the LP *Blue Grass Special* (MCA, 97). The song is in the key of G, one of Bill's favorites for blues, and contains some of his characteristically tricky syncopations.

One of the important things to consider about Bill's blues playing in general, and specifically about this song, is that he uses all downstrokes (   ), except in tremolo or other fast picking movements like the triplet figures in bar four of the kick-off and in bar seven of the solo. This adds a solidity and power to his playing that could not be achieved by using the customary alternating downstrokes and upstrokes. Picking that way may be a little difficult to get used to at first, but try to play with as much strength and force as you can (without overpowering the instrument). Notice also that Bill employs various slides (**s**) throughout the solo. The finger simply slides up to the next note (in this case, one fret) as quickly as possible. Listen to the recording to hear the typically complex nuances and subtleties in phrasing.

Of course, Bill's style has undergone many changes during his long career as a musician. To discover some of the many other directions in which he has taken the mandolin over the years, try to listen to as many of his recordings as possible; and, by all means, hear him play in person whenever you have the opportunity. Chances are, you'll hear something you've never heard before.

"I Was Left On The Street"
Introduction and solo
As played by Bill Monroe

Transcription by David Grisman

Bluegrass Basics

PLAYING IN A BLUEGRASS BAND is one of the most well-rounded musical experiences a mandolin player can have. Blue grass music provided me with an education as a mandolinist, giving me a context for playing rhythm, lead, and backup, as well as a format for developing improvisational skills. A recent tour and recording project with my new bluegrass band, Here Today, gave me the opportunity to reflect upon and put to use those skills that I learned years ago while listening to Bill Monroe, Jesse McReynolds, and many other bluegrass mandolin masters. With those high, lonesome sounds still ringing in my ears, I'd like to share some of my recent observations with you.

Rhythm. As I noticed the first time I saw Bill Monroe play, the mandolin is the snare drum of bluegrass music. It provides punch and drive, and is a major contributing factor to the rhythmic "groove," or "feel." The traditional rhythmic role of the bluegrass mandolinist is to play "clipped" chords, and "chops" on the up-beat (oom-*pah*, oom-*pah*; or oom-*pah-pah* in 3/4 time). The mandolinist interacts with the bass player, who plays the down-beat (*oom*-pah, *oom*-pah), and the two instruments provide the basic rhythmic outline of the tune.

The bluegrass rhythm chop utilizes only a few basic chord positions (see Ex. 1), and requires a quick release on the left hand,

Ex. 1

which dampens the strings and gives the chords a much more percussive effect. The chords are for *B*, a common bluegrass key.

Since most mandolin players also sing in the bluegrass band, you will have to learn how to keep the chop going while you are singing. Interestingly, the best way to develop your playing while singing is to really nail down your vocal parts. The singing comes *first* in bluegrass, and once you learn your vocal part — enunciating all the words clearly, hitting all your notes on pitch, and blending with the other vocalists — you'll find the chopping rhythm on the mandolin will fit in easily. If, however, you're uncertain of the words or the melody, this will detract from your mandolin part.

Listening to the mandolin greats and playing along with records is an excellent way to practice. Old Flatt And Scruggs records are great for playing with, because they have incredible rhythm and "groove," and very little mandolin playing — almost like a bluegrass band minus one.

Backup. One of the nice features of bluegrass music is that it allows a mandolin player to be truly supportive. You are part of a multi-layered musical backdrop for solo and harmony singing, as well as for banjo, fiddle, and guitar solos. In most of these situations the old reliable rhythm chop supplies the perfect background. However, you don't want to do it *all* the time. In addition to keeping good bluegrass time (via the chop), utilize various other rhythmic accents inherent in the tune being played, or in the parts being played by the other musicians. For example, you can rhythmically double the kickoff to a fiddle solo, or sweep a ringing chord across the down-beat of the first bar of a real smoker.

At some point in the tune, a nice effect may be obtained by tremoloing some double-stop harmonies behind the singing. Here are a few standard positions that work quite well (see Ex. 2), also in the key of *B*. Make sure that either the banjo or the fiddle (or both) take over your rhythmic commitment to the upbeat at precisely the moment you start your tremolo. Since this is the background you're going to have to keep it simple to be an *effective* supporter, rather than a detractor.

Finally, there are many backup "fills" or "licks" that sound good when played between verses, or right before choruses. Here are a few basic bluegrass licks (see Ex. 3), also in *B*. The first two are Bill

Ex. 2

Monroe-type licks, and the third one is in the style of Jesse McReynolds. Again, keep it simple — good bluegrass playing involves teamwork, playing a part that makes everyone sound good. Background licks are used to enhance the singing, not obscure it.

Ex. 3

Play the Melody

OFTEN IN OUR QUEST AS mandolinists for newer musical plateaus, higher levels of technical facility, hotter licks, and so forth, we tend to lose sight of the basic original premise of our instrument: *melody!*

Although most musical styles such as swing, jazz, pop, folk, and bluegrass are improvisational in character, the basis for most of the improvising lies firmly within the structures of the various traditional melodies associated with those particular idioms or genres. Many of these tunes are quite *simple* to play, even for a beginner. But in fact, the rendering of a melodic statement or theme, no matter how simple, can easily demand a considerable level of sophistication and taste, phrasing, dynamics, nuance, and subtlety from even the most developed mandolinist.

As a practice technique, try to learn a new *simple* melody each day (or hour, or week, or month, depending on your routine). This will immediately put you in touch with the essentials of fingering and picking, while simultaneously expanding your repertoire. As an example of a simple tune you could learn, I've included a melody which I composed for the recent film *King Of The Gypsies*. This short, somber theme was originally conceived as a funeral lament, but the director of the film had such an affinity for the morose that he decided to use it in a number of sequences.

As you learn any new piece of music, be aware of the numerous possibilities in articulating the melody. First, try playing all the notes with firm downstrokes, letting the longer notes ring for the duration of their time values. As a variation, try tremoloing the entire theme; and finally, experiment with tremoloing the longer notes and picking the shorter ones (in measures 1, 3, and 5, tremolo the top note and let the other [s] ring). Give your left hand a workout and try playing the entire piece an octave higher. If this seems too easy, transpose the tune to any key that seems hard enough, such as *B* minor, using all closed positions (no open strings).

After exhausting all possibilities or your interest in this tune, try your hand at learning a new one of your choice. If you want something happier, try "Happy Birthday" (handy at gigs); or, more seriously, "Blue Moon Of Kentucky," "Solitude," "Georgia On My Mind," "'Round Midnight," or whatever turns you on.

Gypsy Theme
by David Grisman

Position Shifts

HOLDING HIS MANDOLIN CASE, the young man queried, "Ah just want t'know one thing — how do you know where to put your fangers?" This is a very good question; and as in cat-skinning, there are usually several different answers. With one, two, or sometimes even three locations on the mandolin fretboard for any given note, and any one of four fingers of the left hand to use, there can be as many as 12 different ways for fingering any given fretted note.

The reach of the left hand is assumed to extend (with a hearty stretch of the pinky) approximately eight frets at a time. Thus, any notes which fall between the open fourth string 🎵 and the 8th fret of the first string 🎵 may be reached in the first, or open, position. To reach all the notes above this fret, or in order to phrase properly, a *displacement*, or shift, of the left hand is necessary. Thus, if the left hand is placed so that the first finger falls on *C* 🎵 we have the *second* position; if the first finger falls on *D* 🎵 we have third position; if it falls on *E* 🎵 we have the fourth position, and so on.

In playing any piece of music, written or improvised, there are usually several approaches to fingering, even when the range of the piece is safely lodged within the confines of the first position. Given the fact that these different fingering options exist, it behooves us to seek out the most convenient (easiest to play) ones. This will become more apparent, and more necessary, when we try to play tunes or passages of greater difficulty, like bebop heads (melodies) or Paganini caprices! In classical music (particularly music for violin), fingerings are often indicated; but it's good practice to get in the habit of figuring out your own.

First, try playing the major scales below (*F*, *G*, and *A*) in the closed second, third, and fourth positions (see Ex. 1).

To illustrate position shifts, I've selected a passage from the introduction to my composition "Opus 57 In *G* Minor" (as recorded on the album *The David Grisman Quintet* [Kaleidoscope, F-5]. The passage involves several shifts of fingering positions. Of course, there are alternate approaches, and you may wish to search for one that works better for you; but this is what I play. (The right hand alternates downstrokes and upstrokes. See Ex. 2.)

Ex. 1 **Major scales**

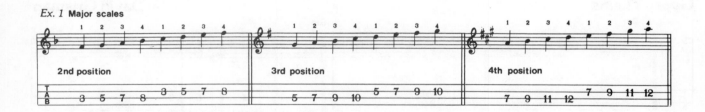

Introduction to "Opus 57 In *G* Minor" By David Grisman

Double Stops

MANDOLIN PICKERS OFTEN ARE credited with producing "colorful" musical effects. Taking this as a compliment, let's examine one of the best ways to sound colorful — the use of *double stops*. A double stop is the simultaneous sounding of *two* notes (on two pairs of strings). There are many musical reasons for using double stops: When tremoloed, they produce lush-sounding, chord-implying backgrounds or lead lines; when picked singly, they add substance to lines, both harmonically and melodically. Practicing double stop positions will strengthen your sense of harmony and chords, your knowledge of the fretboard, and, yes, the fingertips of your left hand!

Octaves

Perhaps the simplest (at least harmonically) double stop that can be formed is the *octave* (the same notes, sounded an octave apart), which involves essentially one left-hand position utilizing the first and fourth fingers. Try playing the G major scale in octaves (see Ex. 1). Octaves are great for embellishing melodic lines, and can be heard in the improvisation of such guitar masters as Django Reinhardt and Wes Montgomery, as well as mandolinists Jethro Burns and Sam Bush. Play the two bars of octave melody in Ex. 2. Can you recognize the tune? Now try playing your favorite melody in octaves. Isn't this fun?

Intervals

All other double stops contain two different notes. The musical distance between the notes is called an *interval*; every interval implies a chord. For example, the major scale may be harmonized and played with double stops. In Ex. 3, the major scale is harmonized with closer intervals (major and minor thirds), and then with wider intervals. Chord progressions, particularly the transition from one chord to another, may be highlighted by the use of double stops, as the music in Ex. 4 illustrates. Double stops may also be used to convey motion within a single chord, as in Ex. 5. That is more interesting than merely repeating the same chord position. This is the kind of backup I use in my own tune "Opus 57" from the *David Grisman Quintet* album (Kaleidoscope, KLD 5).

Try incorporating double stops into your own style and see how many uses you can find for them. You may find that two notes are better than one!

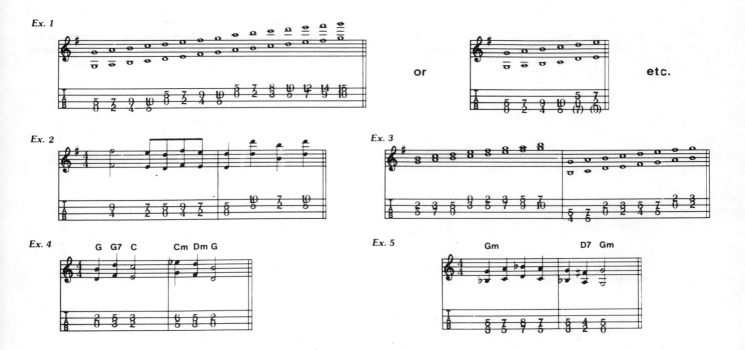

John Duffey Kickoffs

FOLLOWING THE INITIAL IMPACT of Bill Monroe's mandolin style on the world of country music, there was a proliferation of mandolin players and kindred styles (Pee Wee Lambert, Bobby Osborne, and Red Rector, to mention a few), which truly established the idiom of bluegrass mandolin. The process has, of course, continued with the advent of more "progressive" stylists — Sam Bush, Doyle Lawson, Jimmy Gaudreau, and Mike Marshall, and there's a whole new crop coming up! One tends to wonder how it all happened. Just exactly where and when did bluegrass turn "newgrass"?

Musical events are hard to pinpoint, but on July 4, 1957, a new band genre was accidentally formed when guitarist Charlie Waller joined forces with mandolinist John Duffey to found the now-legendary original Country Gentlemen. During the early '60s, their unique approach to bluegrass music (with 5-string banjoist Eddie Adcock and bassist Tom Gray) turned all our ears around!

The Gentlemen were the first bluegrass unit to expand the traditional repertoire and effectively create an entire musical style around it. Of course, there were others who made great departures in specific areas of style: Mac Wiseman (repertoire), the Osborne Brothers (vocal harmony), and Jim and Jesse McReynolds (mandolin style); but the Country Gentlemen sound was a homogenous new sound in bluegrass.

John Duffy was perhaps the spearhead of the new sound, as can be heard in his amazing singing, in his vocal arrangements, and in his inventive mandolin playing — which retains all of the drive, tone, and fluidity of the founding father (Monroe) while exploring many new areas, both rhythmic and harmonic. Duffey's style is centered around an extremely smooth tremolo that has great attack and clarity. His solos are always perfectly integrated into the song at hand, and are unusually melodic and interesting. The tunes are often more sophisticated than average, chord-wise, and Duffey's mandolin playing reflects that sophistication and even adds to it. Naturally, John is still laying down the authentic "Duffey" style in his dramatic work with the oft-heard Seldom Scene. Most of us "contemporary" mandolin pickers owe John a great vote of thanks for helping to bridge the old and the new, way back when we were just getting started.

The following two transcriptions are from my all-time favorite John Duffey "kickoffs," or introductions. Ex. 1 is from the beautiful stately ballad, "Katy Dear," from the LP *Bluegrass Country*, Pickwick Records (7500 Excelsior Blvd., Minneapolis, MN 55426), JS-6156. Ex. 2 is from the up-tempo classic "Two Little Boys" on *Bluegrass At Carnegie Hall*, Starday Records (220 Boscobel, Nashville, TN 37213), SLP 6156.

"Katy Dear" will give your tremolo a workout (nearly all the way through, except for a bit of crosspicking in the first measure), while "Two Little Boys" combines fast downstrokes (a la Bill Monroe) with tremoloed double-stops (measures two and three), all played in the fourth position around the *B* chord.

John is an expert at setting tunes in motion with his mandolin, and these kickoffs will tell you why. They are melodic and inventive, and they convey the total personality of the tune at hand.

Mandolin Tunes
"Auld Lang Syne"
(A Bobby Osborne Improvisation)

WITHOUT A DOUBT, one of the most dynamic influences on bluegrass music has been "old-time" fiddle playing. For years, Bobby Osborne has been transferring fiddle-derived techniques to the mandolin, and consequently had laid the groundwork for the techniques of a whole new generation of players.

As you develop your own skills in the same style, you may occasionally run into licks that are hard to play smoothly — because your right hand wants to pick in the opposite direction from where you want it to go. This difficulty can occur when moving from one string to a higher string with an up-down movement:

Ex. 1

Conversely, it also occurs when moving to a lower string with a down-up movement:

Ex. 2

Practice these examples slowly, making sure that the down-up down-up picking pattern is never altered. Try to play with as much definition as possible, making sure each note rings out clearly.

As an example of Bobby's playing I've included his marvelous improvisation on the traditional tune "Auld Lang Syne" from *The Early Recordings Of Sonny Osborne, 1952-53, Vol. 2* (Vetco Records, out of print). The solo is virtually an Osborne dictionary of improvisation for the key of *G*. Have fun!

"Auld Lang Syne"

Traditional
Arranged By Bobby Osborne

"I'll Never Let You Worry My Mind Anymore" (A Red Rector Solo)

UNSUNG HEROES SEEM TO ABOUND amongst us mandolin pickers, and few players ever really manage to garner the universal admiration and respect of both amateurs and professionals. The exception to the rule is "little" Red Rector from Knoxville, Tennessee, who is truly a mandolinist's mandolinist.

Since the early '40s, Red has been playing inventive, articulate, and exciting mandolin solos on bluegrass-type recordings with such artists as Charlie Monroe, Don Reno and Red Smiley, Carl Story, and Hylo Brown. Red's style has always been characterized by clarity, precision, and taste. Unfortunately, much of his great playing on recordings was uncredited at the time of release, so many of us didn't know who was playing that "hot" mandolin all those years. Lately, Red has been "Rectorfying" that oversight with the release of several albums both under his own name and in partnership with such notables as Norman Blake and Bill Clifton. One trademark of Red's sound is his use of a round-hole Gibson mandolin (model A-4), which gives him a mellower, less harsh tone, but one no less distinctive than the traditional "F-5" mandolin sound.

I've transcribed one of Red's amazing solos on "I'll Never Let You Worry My Mind Anymore," from his recent LP *Red Rector And Friends*, Revonah Records (Box 217, Ferndale, NY 12734), RS-931. The solo is not an easy one, starting in the third position (first finger on the 4th fret), and swooping down to the lowest compasses of the fretboard at the finish. Some of the highlights of the solo are the licks reminiscent of Jethro Burns in the opening five measures (the first measure makes an excellent pinky-training exercise when played repeatedly); some tricky syncopations (unusual rhythmic accents) in measures seven and eight; the progressive usage of "blue" notes (flatted thirds and sevenths) throughout the second eight bars; and a great little bluegrass end tag, complete with a neat little Red Rector triplet, in the next-to-last bar! As Bob Artis explains in the liner notes, "'I'll Never Let You Worry My Mind Anymore' is another one of Red's long-time favorites, with a mandolin break that explains why he is one of Jethro Burns' favorite pickers."

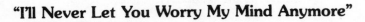

"I'll Never Let You Worry My Mind Anymore"

Traditional
Transcribed by David Grisman

"Cedar Hill"
(The Melody)

HERE IS THE MUSIC TO "Cedar Hill," my earliest mandolin composition, which I only recently recorded for my new Warner Brothers LP *Mondo Mando* (BSK 3610). The piece was originally written in 1964, during the embryonic stages of my bluegrass mandolin-playing career. In fact, the chord progression of the first part (first eight measures) is based on a song called "Well Enough Alone," which was written by one of my early mandolin heroes, Frank Wakefield.

Through the years, slight changes in the chords and the melody have occurred — an accent here, an embellishment there. In 1974 I utilized the tune as the main theme for my first film score, *Big Bad Mama,* a take-off on *Bonnie And Clyde.* The arrangement on *Mondo Mando* is a mandolin duet, played by myself and Mike Marshall. I played the melody shown below, and Mike played the harmony part, which I'll include in a future column. Pay close attention to the fingering, which makes frequent use of the fourth finger (pinky) at the 7th fret on the *A* and *D* strings, still keeping the left hand in the first position. Happy mandolin playing!

"Cedar Hill"

By David Grisman

"Cedar Hill"
(The Harmony)

HARMONIZING A MELODY is a wonderful musical technique that can be utilized quite effectively in adding color to an arrangement, creating various moods that can range from exuberance to mystery. Here is the harmony part to my tune "Cedar Hill."

In this arrangement the harmony line adheres rather strictly to the *diatonic* harmony of the major scale, and is usually played a third (major or minor) above the melody notes. Most of the harmony notes are a major third above the melody in this arrangement, adding a bright, happy sound that is right in character with the tune.

Other tunes with different chord progressions naturally will imply alternate harmonies that are based on various scale types. (For example, a minor-key tune will use primarily "darker-sounding" harmonies, such as minor thirds.) Always keep the particular chord you're working with in mind, because it usually will dictate a "logical" harmony.

As an exercise, you might want to try harmonizing a major scale, or harmonizing another tune you're already familiar with. Just write out the scale or the tune, and try adding the note a third above each melody note. Get together with a mandolin-playing friend and work out some harmonized duets. You'll be surprised at how much this technique can do for your understanding of any tune and its harmonic structure. Have fun with "Cedar Hill."

"Cedar Hill" harmony

By David Grisman

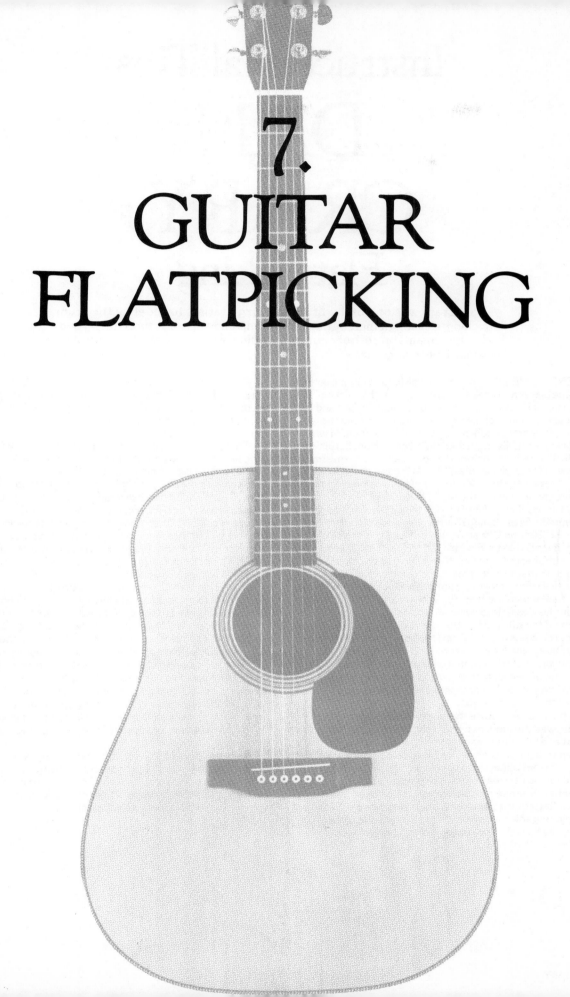

7.
GUITAR
FLATPICKING

Instructional Tips
DAN CRARY
Flatpicking

Dan Crary was one of the first modern guitarists to redefine the art of flatpicking, elevating it thereby from an accompaniment to a virtuoso technique. Today, he remains one of our country's leading players and a veteran of many influential bluegrass groups.

LET'S SPEND SOME TIME trying to define flatpicking and setting forth some biases and goals of this enterprise. "Flatpicking" is a term that, so far as I know, has been around since the '50s and has undergone quite a change of meaning. I first encountered the term during the late '50s among folk music enthusiasts, most of whom played fingerstyle and distinguished themselves from flatpickers with just a little condescension. In those days the term simply indicated how a person picked the guitar. In the '60s things began to change, and there were two developments which seem to me to have changed the meaning of the term "flatpicking."

One change was that guitar players in bluegrass music began to tire of the limited role of playing rhythm only and started trying to play lead. In the '50s and '60s an occasional lead break was played by rhythm guitarists (Lester Flatt played one on "Foggy Mountain Special," as did Charlie Waller on "Aunt Dinah's Quilting Party," and Don Reno sometimes laid his banjo aside to play some nice flatpicking solos). On a more regular basis George Shuffler was playing guitar solos with the Stanley Brothers and Clarence White was flatpicking his classic lead guitar stuff in California. But his early activity seemed to fade and by 1967 it was difficult to find a lead guitar player in bluegass music. When I tried my hand at playing lead guitar in the Bluegrass Alliance from 1968-1970, one of the main audience reactions was surprise that anyone would do such a thing. But by 1970 a lot of lead guitar playing was happening in bluegrass, and the term "flatpicker" had come to refer to bluegrass players who ventured to play some solos.

Another major development that contributed to the redefinition of flatpicking was the emergence of Doc Watson. Although he appeared at a lot of bluegrass festivals, Watson's music was something apart from any convenient musical categories. Rather than developing from within the ranks of folk, bluegrass, or country, Doc created music that was none of these and all of them at the same time. His influence on guitar players has been immense, especially on flatpickers. At a time when very few people were playing flatpicking solos anywhere, Doc Watson was doing it up there on stage by himself! The speed, power, and tastiness of what

he played was a blast of reality which alternately humbled, intimidated, and inspired those of us in the '60s who thought we played pretty hot guitar. Such a style of playing demanded a label, and for want of a better term we called Doc Watson's playing "flatpicking" too.

That little shot of history does no justice to the flatpickers of forty and fifty years ago who played beautiful music in the country bands, and similarly ignores some of the local and regional players who kept the style alive without any national recognition. But the term "flatpicking" as we use it now arose out of what happened to bluegrass guitar and the emergence of Doc.

We're still left with the task of saying what flatpicking is today, so I guess I should try a tentative definition. Flatpicking is an approach to guitar that utilizes a plectrum in playing a steel string acoustic guitar. Typically the music played is bluegrass, folk, country, gospel, and fiddle tunes. Vague definition? I agree, but I think it's realistic given the new and developmental state of the art, and the fuzzy distinctions that are drawn among the current categories of music. Maybe we don't want too specific a definition because there's no point in defining anybody out of the flatpicking category.

Here are some of my biases. For one, I think the guitar is the noblest musical instrument ever fashioned by the hands of man. Like any instrument it has its limitations and difficulties. But for every limitation it has a thousand versatilities. For all its apparent simplicity it offers complexities and subtleties worthy of a lifetime of study. And in spite of its unassuming appearance it is capable of great music in an ensemble or by itself. In the last twenty-five years the guitar has touched more people with music than any other instrument ever did.

Another bias of mine is that flatpicking is one of the most versatile and powerful approaches to the guitar. A third bias I confess to is that flatpicking is one of the most interesting styles because it's relatively new and unexplored. We are on the verge of something very exciting as flatpicking becomes what it is going to be.

Crosspicking

CROSSPICKING IS ONE OF THE most useful and beautiful techniques available to flatpickers. I'd like to get you started in crosspicking; or if you're already started, I'd like to add some new ideas to what you're already doing. But let's get some misconceptions about crosspicking out of the way first.

Misconception number 1: *Crosspicking is a banjo roll transferred to the guitar.* That is rarely the case; guitar crosspicking is quite different from banjo rolls. Misconception number 2: *Once you learn one pattern, that's it.* Crosspicking can be conceptualized as patterns, but it's more like an *approach,* which begins as a series of several patterns. The patterns serve as a sort of springboard for playing music that is beyond the pattern. Misconception number 3: *Crosspicking is random and unstructured.* Most of the crosspicking that I do is rather planned out, and I think that's true of most of the notable players who employ the technique. Improvisation does happen in crosspicking, but most improvisation is based on a structure of some sort. Crosspicking is more structured than, "just get your pick moving and see what happens." Finally, Misconception number 4: *Crosspicking is difficult.* I think the greatest difficulty is in *thinking* it, not in playing it. It *will* seem awkward at first, but it *will* become easier.

A word or two now about what crosspicking is. It is a syncopated sequence of sixteenth-notes (in 2/4 time) that is played in a roll-like pattern on three different strings. The primary activity is the right hand picking on three different strings while the left hand holds a chord, moves from chord to chord, or modifies a chord.

The simplest form of crosspicking can be explained in terms of a simple, familiar tune like Glenn Miller's "In The Mood." The main theme is shown in Ex. 1. Play through it a couple of times and put extra emphasis on the down-strokes. (Make sure that your picking direction follows the tablature.) If you can play that, you can

crosspick. Just by looking at the music you can see some of the characteristics of the technique that make it interesting. Notice that the music is in 4/4 time (four beats per measure), but that you're playing on *three* adjacent strings. So crosspicking is a style that fits series of notes in threes into a measure of four beats. I suggest playing the down-strokes louder so that you can pick up on the built-in syncopation that happens in crosspicking.

Now let's modify Ex. 1 slightly and make it into part of the "B" section of "Beaumont Rag," which is one of the standard flatpicking tunes (see Ex. 2). Notice that it is very similar to "In The Mood." The only differences are that in "Beaumont Rag," the third string is fretted differently, and the chords change after two measures of G instead of four measures. With respect to what the pick is doing, the two examples are identical.

What we've done so far is illustrate a pattern. Without indicating any particular notes, the picking pattern is shown in Ex. 3. You can modify the pattern in the second measure to make the roll last a bit longer, as in Ex. 4. I use "X's" in the tablature to indicate that any notes that sound good together as a chord can be crosspicked by using exactly the same right-hand movements.

Finally, some pointers about how to apply this pattern. First, play around with it; play it on different strings with different chords. Second, *vary* it by changing the notes on any of the three strings. For example, play the pattern with the top-string notes alternating as in "Beaumont Rag" (Ex. 2). Or, try changing the notes on the *bottom* string, leaving the top strings unchanged.

Where does crosspicking fit? It fits almost anywhere that a melody line holds or pauses for a couple of measures. It's a fair substitute for a spot in a fiddle tune where the fiddler plays a low shuffle. It's a pace-changer in a break that has become monotonous because of too much single-string melodic playing.

More On Crosspicking

ADHERING TO THE TRADITION of *Jaws, Star Wars,* and other similar epics, I provide the sequel to *Crosspicking;* namely, *Crosspicking II.* Let's review the basics before moving into the new material.

To progress, you should be fairly comfortable with the "In The Mood" pattern (see Ex. 1 and Ex. 2). Once you've got the basics, you'll be ready for this new material, which falls into two categories: expanding on the basic pattern, and playing new patterns. Recall that the "X's" in the tablature indicate that the same picking pattern can be used with any three notes that sound good together as a chord.

Now let's consider some variations of the basic pattern. One idea for varying the pattern is to change the notes on the top string. Almost any variation on the top string is a possibility, as long as it doesn't create an overly harsh discord. Several variations are shown in Exs. 3 through 6. Ex. 3 is a familiar passage from "Beaumont Rag," while Exs. 4 through 6 are random ideas that employ different string combinations. For reference, a chord is indicated with each example.

In Ex. 7, I've introduced a second variation — the inclusion of a harmony note. That is, instead of playing only one note on the top string, add a second note to it. That's one of the prettiest crosspicking moves you'll ever hear, and it becomes even sweeter when combined with the first variation (the alternating high note), as in Ex. 8.

The possibilities for those variations are endless. Any set of three or four strings that sound good as a chord can be crosspicked with those patterns.

There's still more. A third variation is to crosspick on three *non-adjacent* strings, as in Ex. 9. It takes a bit of practice to smoothly jump over a string, but it's harder in the mind than it is on the hand. When that starts to work, combine it with the second variation, as in Ex. 10. Or, if you want to go all out, combine all three variations — alternating the high note, harmonizing the high note, and using non-adjacent bass notes, as in Exs. 11 and 12.

The last variation I can think of for crosspicking a particular pattern involves alternating notes on the *low* string, creating a moving bass line. An illustration is shown in Ex. 13.

With the four variations, a basic crosspicking pattern can take on new dimensions of flexibility. But before getting too involved in variations, remember the basics: Keep your picking direction straight (down on the beat, and up between the beats). And don't play so fast that the syncopation inherent to the pattern is lost. The optimum tempo for crosspicking is somewhere between "road runner" and "funeral procession."

Finally, let's take a look at a few bars of other patterns that are less flexible than the basic pattern, but have a sound all their own. It's a good idea to mix patterns, going back and forth among them for variety. Not that I'm only giving you one form of each new pattern; they can be varied by employing the same variations suggested above. Pattern II is shown in Ex. 4.

Pattern III is shown with two different chords (see Ex. 15). The first measure (with the *G* chord) features a picking pattern that is very similar to a standard banjo roll.

Pattern IV is a flatpicked version of a standard fingerpicking pattern (see Ex. 16). Although it's easier to fingerpick the pattern, it's not as hard to flatpick as it might seem, and it's excellent practice for moving from string to string. Exotic, perhaps, but it's an enjoyable challenge and useful on occasion.

That's just about everything I know on the subject of crosspicking. The trick now is to turn the ideas into music. To do that requires some discipline, some adaptation of the patterns into tunes, and some patience on the part of the people you live with!

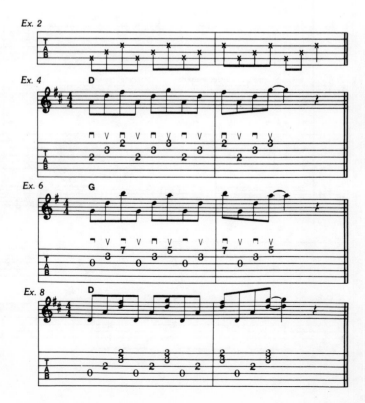

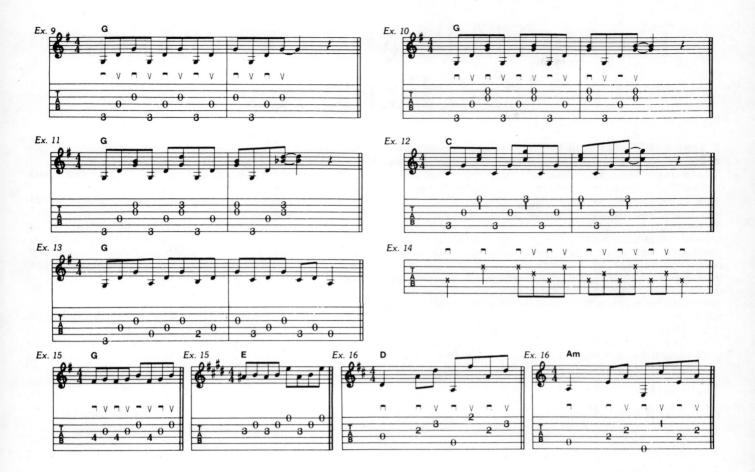

Playing Fiddle Music On Guitar "Dill Pickle Rag"

HERE IS THE TABLATURE to "Dill Pickle Rag," and with it a few ideas on how you can to approach fiddle music on the guitar. I'll continue to develop these ideas, but here are some basic steps.

First, learn the tune itself, preferably as played by a competent fiddle player. Get it in your head. Then get it on the guitar in rough form, but as close to the original as possible. Then, after you've given the tune a chance to educate your playing, begin the adaptive process of arranging the thing into good guitar music. When the exact fiddle version just doesn't work note-for-note, make your adaptations as close to the original as possible. For example, when the fiddle version "shuffles" the guitar may have to brush a chord or do some crosspicking. The goal should be to produce an arrangement that does justice to the original and also sounds right for the guitar.

I hope that as you learn this version you might listen to a record of a fiddler, get the sense of the time from that source, and not be tied totally to playing my interpretation of the thing. I should mention that this version is close to the way I recorded it, but it's not identical. Here are some guides to following this tablature:

1. Picking direction is indicated by ⊓ for a down-stroke, and by V for an up-stroke.

2. Other symbols: *S* — Rather than picking the note, slide up to it from the previous note. *H* — Hammer-on. *P* — Pull-off.

3. Ideas on left-hand fingering: In part A, measures 1, 2, 9, and 10 — bar the first and second string at the 3rd fret. Also in Part A, measures 13 and 14 — hold the fifth string note through both measures. In part II, play measures 2, 6, 10, and 14 holding this position:

'Dill Pickle Rag'

Traditional
Arranged by Dan Crary

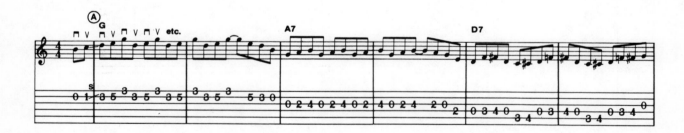

Playing Banjo Music On Guitar
"Foggy Mountain Special"

BANJO MUSIC? "WHAT THE FLYING flatpick is banjo music doing in a flatpicking column?" you might ask. It happens that bluegrass banjo music is one of the greatest untapped sources of guitar repertoire. Let's take on Earl Scruggs' banjo tune, "Foggy Mountain Special," in a flatpicking arrangement for guitar that is very close to the way Earl recorded the piece on the banjo.

"Foggy Mountain Special" is a bluesy little trip that some banjo players dislike, because it's out of the ordinary in that it doesn't allow banjo players to fall into a roll-type picking pattern. But what makes the tune difficult on the banjo makes it fit the flatpick very nicely. However, one slightly unusual thing about my guitar arran-

gement is that the capo is placed at the 3rd fret — the key is *G* — so it's like playing lead out of the open *E* position. It's not that hard to do, but it is something that flatpickers seldom try. Note that the chord positions are given, along with the actual pitches of the chords (in parentheses) with the capo at the 3rd fret.

What follows are the first two parts of the tune. The short sections in the arrangement are composed of a mixture of ideas: some note-for-note recitations from the banjo version, and some ideas of my own. In the third part, which we'll look at next month, I borrow a couple of licks from Lester Flatt's guitar break. I'm sure you'll enjoy this little adventure from the realm of the banjo.

Guitar Tunes
"Salt Creek"

THE ARRANGEMENT OF "Salt Creek" below is a follow-up to the article on crosspicking, since the second section of the tune is usually crosspicked. Here are a couple of notes on the second section: First, be sure to follow the picking directions as indicated above the tablature. Second, note that the quarter rest ( ) gets one whole beat, and that the eighth rest ( ) gets one half beat.

Notice that observing the eighth rest and using the correct picking directions are interrelated. For example, in the second section, following the picking directions will come close to guaranteeing that you will give the eighth rest its proper time value. That's because the notes that come just before and after the rest are both up-strokes, and the extra time it takes to play two consecutive up-strokes is just about the time value of the eighth rest.

It's nice to know that in all this chaos, there is orderliness, at least in music.

"Salt Creek"

Traditional
Arranged by Dan Crary

"Ragtime Annie"

CROSSPICKING IS A TOPIC that comes up in some of my guitar workshops very often, and "Ragtime Annie" is a tune for which the technique was ready-made.

When this tune is played on the fiddle, the bow is likely to be doing something like a "shuffle." On the guitar, the nearest approximation to that effect is crosspicking. This technique gives the tune a sort of "inside" sound that's very solid and satisfying.

This version is similar to that which appeared on Byron Berline's record *Dad's Favorites* (Rounder, 0100). Because it works so well on banjo and fiddle, this tune is a standard at jam sessions, and any basic repertoire should include it.

ARRANGEMENT © 1982 DAN CRARY

"Pike County Breakdown"

THIS TUNE FROM THE GLORY days of bluegrass is a stand-ard in the banjo repertoire. Like so many of Bill Monroe's tunes, it's one you'd better know if you're going to play bluegrass. It's almost certain to be a favorite of somebody in your band, of someone at a picking party, or of that real mean-looking fellow over there at the second table who just requested it.

This arrangement is in two parts. The first is a fairly simple, basic version that sticks close to the straight tune. The second part wanders around a bit, and contains two ascending and descending octave runs. You can play both sections, since the tune usually is played twice through by each player. Note that there's only one 16-bar part, not two or three eight-bar parts as in the typical fiddle tune.

At several places you'll find the first and second strings fretted close together at the third fret. When this happens, I'd suggest fretting the first string with the fourth finger and the second string with the third finger, as indicated in the music. Also note that I play the song with the capo on the 2nd fret, putting the tune into the key of A.

Be prepared to play this tune fast. Flatt And Scruggs powered through it like the last train out of Sodom, and subsequent genera-tions of banjo players have done likewise. But as I've said before, start off at a reasonable speed. Once you can play it perfectly, go ahead and gradually speed it up.

I would also encourage you to use these versions presented in the column as a basis for building your own arrangements. Tunes like these have a loose enough melodic line so that there's room to substitute a run or a lick that you want to contribute.

In any case, you should be able to sleep a little better at night knowing that when that mean-looking guy starts pounding the table with his beer glass, yelling "Pike County Breakdown," you'll be able to pull it off.

"Blackberry Blossom"

SOMEHOW, "BLACKBERRY BLOSSOM" has become one of the most popular tunes in the flatpicking repertoire — actually, the grandaddy of 'em all. I'm not sure exactly why, but *everybody* plays this tune. Maybe it's because of the easy flow of the melody in the A section or the powerful modulation to *E* minor, but the tune does have a very special appeal to it.

The version offered below includes some variations. Note that the B section lends itself to departures from the melody, so any old *E* minor runs, riffs, or amazing moves will work nicely. The A section lends itself to parallel harmony parts, so if you and your band (or casual fellow pickers) want to experiment with some harmony parts, this is a good tune to try out.

It may be a "bandwagon" argument, but you probably should play this standard flatpicker's delight, if for no other reason than that everybody's doing it.

"Blackberry Blossom"

Traditional
Arranged By Dan Crary

"Huckleberry Hornpipe"

"**H**UCKLEBERRY HORNPIPE" IS the masterpiece of my buddy, Byron Berline. This tightly conceived, highly melodic tune has enough ideas to keep a guitar player busy for several weeks. The arrangement below represents an attempt to parallel the fiddle melody and is very close to my recording on *Lady's Fancy* (Rounder, 0099). For a different approach to the same tune, check out Clarence White's break on Country Gazette's LP, *Don't Give Up Your Day Job* (United Artists, UA-LA090-F). White's version is lovely, although a bit looser in following the original melody.

My arrangement is intended for advanced players or interme-diates who would like to stretch out a little. The jump up to the 5th and 8th frets in part C is a little nuts and takes some getting used to, but it's the only way I could play the tune precisely.

I'll make a brief pitch here for learning a very melodic tune like this one *as played by the fiddle*. Some tunes don't have a clearly identifiable melody through all parts, but depend on bow licks and other devices. On those, any old bit of improvising is appropriate. But flatpickers can benefit from the discipline of learning a melodic tune accurately. "Play it like it was wrote" is still good advice, especially when it was "wrote" with as much subtlety and musical sense as "Huckleberry Hornpipe."

Huckleberry Hornpipe

by Byron Berline
Arranged by Dan Crary

"Soldier's Joy"

"SOLDIER'S JOY" HAS EVERYTHING it takes to be high on my personal hit parade of tunes: a beautiful name, a very pretty melody, and it's in the key of *D*. There's something else that is often overlooked — it can be played at a slow tempo. I know that somebody out there is saying, "Why would you want to play anything *slow*, for gosh sakes?" To make music, my friend. Yes, it's true that some tunes just don't make it unless they *are* played fast, but some (like "Soldier's Joy") take on a whole new perspective and a new beauty at a slower-than-usual pace. I once heard a German drinking song sung to this tune at a very plodding, stately sort of tempo, and it worked very nicely. Experiment with the tempo on "Soldier's Joy." You might even want to work up an arrangement that starts slowly and ends at a fast pace, drawing some new feelings out of this old, familiar tune.

There are two levels of difficulty built into the music. The first eight measures of each section are relatively easy, while the last eight measures of each section are more difficult. You can make up an easier version by playing the first eight measures of each section, and then, instead of playing the more difficult second eight measures, repeat the first eight measures of either section to conclude your simplified version.

Note that the series of notes in measures 9, 10, 13, and 14 are sixteenth-notes, which means that they all happen in the space of one beat. It's difficult to count notes that fast, so the best advice is: Play them as fast as you can, and when you've got them going about as fast as humanly possible, they should just about fall into one beat. The combination of one hammer-on followed by two pull-offs should be worked into a single sort of rolling motion.

"Soldier's Joy"

Traditional
Arranged by Dan Crary

"Flop-Eared Mule"

UNDER THE CATEGORY OF "music doesn't have to be complex to be good," consider this s arrangement of "Flop-Eared Mule." Its simplicity resides in straightforward melody lines, several quarter notes, and a moderate tempo. Its beauty comes from a very nice modulation from *D* to *G*, and the effective use of thirds in the tonic chords. If you and your band have thought of working out some tunes with harmony parts for two or three instruments, "Flop-Eared Mule" is a good place to begin.

Notice that instead of writing a repeat section into Part II, I wrote the second eight bars a bit differently than the first eight. If you prefer, you can repeat either one of the two eight-bar segments in Part II instead of playing it as written. For those of you who are relatively new to flatpicking, I think you'll find this tune satisfying but relatively easy.

"Flop-Eared Mule"

Traditional
Arranged By Dan Crary

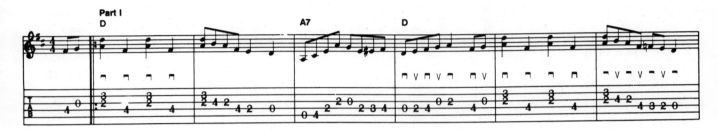

8.
FIDDLE

Instructional Tips
BYRON BERLINE
Bowing Tips

ONE OF THE MOST IMPORTANT ingredients of good fiddle playing is bowing technique. Notice that I *didn't* say "correct" bowing technique! I will surely get an argument from the people who contend that there is definitely one correct way to bow; but results are most important to me. A certain method might be right for you, but not necessarily good for me. Not everyone swings a golf club or holds a bowling ball the same way, so why should all fiddlers have the same bowing style?

Learning to control the bow is the single most important aspect of fiddling, and is probably the most difficult to learn. Naturally, there are suggestions and helpful hints for those who are seeking help; that's why I'm discussing some concepts of bowing.

I have participated in many fiddle workshops, and one of the most frequently asked questions is "How do you use the bow on this tune?" That is really one of the most difficult questions to answer. It is much easier to demonstrate than it is to explain such things as when to use an up-bow or a down-bow, when to employ a rocking motion, and so on. For people who don't read music, bowing directions sometimes need to be discussed or demonstrated. For those who do read music, violin notation usually includes symbols that indicate bowing suggestions (for a down-bow for an up-bow among others).

What is the correct way to hold the bow? It is usually held in the proximity of the frog. People who take violin lessons are usually told exactly how to hold the bow. Those who haven't had any formal training usually hold the bow in any way that seems comfortable for them. I have seen some very interesting approaches to holding the bow — all the way from the "correct" grip (with the thumb between the hair and the stick, next to the curve of the frog) to a very unconventional grip (holding the bow halfway up the stick). I have heard some good fiddlers who use the latter technique.

I hold the bow with my thumb under the frog, a position I learned from my dad. Many Texas-style and bluegrass fiddlers also use this method. I have tried other positions, but nothing works better than my original way. This method seems to free my wrist better than any other grip.

I have been told that my grip is unusual. Vassar Clements, my good friend and a very good fiddler, also has an unusual way of holding the bow. He seems to grasp the bow with his entire hand. At times, he seems to use very little wrist motion — but needless to say, he gets the job done.

If you are interested in pursuing old-time or Texas-style fiddling, the following suggestions may be helpful. Begin the tune with a down-bow. Try to use a clockwise wrist motion whenever possible, and try to end the phrase with a down-bow. I have found that the flow of the music is often interrupted if these suggestions aren't followed. Naturally the tempo and the type of tune will vary the bowing action, but as a general rule these are helpful hints.

Since we are talking about bowing, let's discuss the bow itself. I have talked about how important it is to have good control of the bow. It is also essential to have a decent bow in order to develop good control. I am sure that many of you beginners aren't aware of the importance of having a good bow. You probably wonder how in the world anyone can pay the enormous amounts that are asked for some bows, and sometimes I wonder myself! But the important aspects of a bow are the weight, the grip, and the length.

Whatever kind of bow you have, expensive or not, take care of it. Make sure it is properly rehaired, as necessary, and protect the hair by not applying too much rosin. Too much rosin will crystallize the hair and result in premature breakage. Don't tighten the bow too much, and don't forget to loosen it when you put it away. A tight bow has a tendency to bounce on the strings as you play. Of course, if this is what you desire, OK.

The hairs do wear out. When they break, you should cut them with scissors at the top and frog. Sometimes that isn't possible, especially if you're onstage performing; but you can carefully break the ends, or you can even bite them off.

I might add that when my bow hairs break, they always break exactly in the middle. If you look at my bow after several hairs have broken, there is an open space in the middle, with the remaining strands on each side. Most people break hairs on one side or the other. Don't ask me why mine is different: maybe I play exactly in the middle of the hair. I don't know.

I hope I've sawed out some helpful tips for you on bows and bowing techniques. Happy fiddling!

My usual bowing grip. Two fingers actually hold the bow, with the third finger giving support from the other side.

My bowing grip for a fast shuffle or for a bouncing motion. All my fingers are on top of the bow, with the little finger adding strength and balance to the grip.

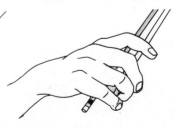

Vassar Clements' bowing grip. His entire hand seems to grip the bow.

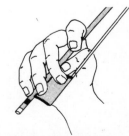

The bowing grip employed by most classical players.

Slide Technique

SLIDING OR SLURRING FROM one note to another is a subject I have often been asked to comment on. Beginning fiddlers frequently ask me which finger they should use to slide from *D* to *C*, or from *G* to *A*. They also wonder how many fingers are involved in executing the slide. There are no easy answers to those questions, because the techniques depend upon the musical context — the style of the tune, the tempo, and so on.

A slide may be executed entirely with one finger, or it may begin with one finger and end with an adjacent finger, depending on the notes that follow the slide. For example, if you are playing a *D* note on the *A* string with your third finger, you can just slide the third finger back through the *C* (a very short distance), and then play the *C* with your second finger. Of course, you will want to perform this as smoothly and flowingly as possible.

A good example of a long slide that is executed with only one finger is found at the beginning of "Brown Skinned Gal" (see music

below). The first note is a *B*, played on the *A* string with the first finger. The slide up to *D* is done with just the first finger. (The *D* note would normally be played with the third finger.) The reason for doing this slide in "Brown Skinned Gal" is that you need to reach the third position with the first finger almost immediately in order to begin the first part of the tune.

The secret of this slide is the speed with which you move your first finger from the *B* to the *D*. If you slide the first finger too slowly, you will hear every note in between; but if you slide quickly and smoothly, the slide is much less obvious.

The technical word for the slide in "Brown Skinned Gal" is *portamento* — a slide that starts on one note and slides straight through to another note without actually playing any of the in-between notes. There are many other types of slides, some of which involve double stops.

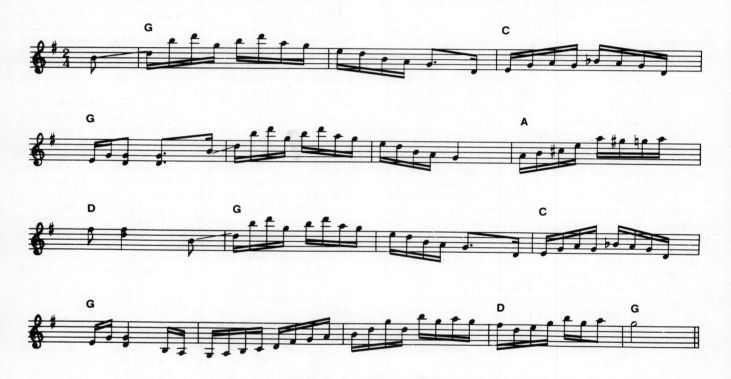

ARRANGEMENT © 1981 BYRON BERLINE

Double Stops

DOUBLE STOP: the execution of two or more simultaneous tones on the violin or similar instruments (intervals, chords, passages in two or more parts). The curved position of the strings, conditioned by the curved shape of the bridge, frequently compels the player to resort to an arpeggio-like rendering, particularly in the case of chords of three or four tones on the piano.

That is what the *Harvard Dictionary of Music* says about the double stop. When I was a kid, I thought a double stop occurred when you were playing a passage that made you stop twice before you could proceed with the tune. Actually, any time you play two or more notes together you're playing a double stop. There's nothing prettier than double-note playing in a waltz or a slow tune. Of course, double stops are used in many types of playing: fiddle tunes, bluegrass music, Cajun music, and so on.

As the dictionary said, the curvature of the bridge determines how the player approaches the double stop. Many bluegrass fiddlers prefer to have their bridges flattened somewhat in order to play double stops (and triple stops) more easily.

One of the simpler double stops is called the "drone," which is often an imitation of a bagpipe sound. For instance, if you stop the A string at the D note and draw the bow on the A string and the D string, you're creating an octave drone. This can be done if there is an open string to drone (see Ex. 1).

You can also get a drone sound by holding a note (usually a low note) as it sounds against changing harmonies in the other parts. This is called a "pedal point" (see Ex. 2).

You have probably heard a lot of drones in Cajun music. A good example is the common introduction that is used to kick off many Cajun tunes. Many record producers ask for Cajun-style fiddling even if the song is not a Cajun tune. It may go something like Ex. 3.

Utilizing fifths on the fiddle is sometimes very effective. Since the fiddle is tuned in fifths, a straight bar across the strings will produce the desired sound. The width of the string separation and the size of the player's fingers determine how easy it is to play fifths. However, most bluegrass double stops are in thirds. A good example of both intervals used in the same tune is Bill Monroe's "Footprints In The Snow" (see Ex. 4).

There are many variations when it comes to playing double stops. "Sally Goodin'"is a good example of drones and thirds played in the same tune. I play the first two parts as shown in Ex. 5.

Anyone who plays the fiddle undoubtedly has played or will play "Orange Blossom Special." Double stops and triple stops really come into play in this tune. I mentioned triple stops earlier. You really have to apply pressure with the bow to execute a triple stop. The late Scotty Stoneman showed me how to get a dissonant train whistle for "Orange Blossom Special." It's almost like playing a C chord on the guitar (see Ex. 6).

Other triple stop effects can be accomplished by rocking the bow from the low strings to the high strings, as in Ex. 7.

If you really want to get wild and crazy, loosen the bow all the way and play all the strings at the same time. Johnny Gimble did this on the tune "What A Friend We Have In Jesus," from his LP, *Fiddlin' Around* (Capitol, ST 11301).

I certainly hope this gives you a better insight on double stops and triple stops. Guess I'll come to a "stop" now.

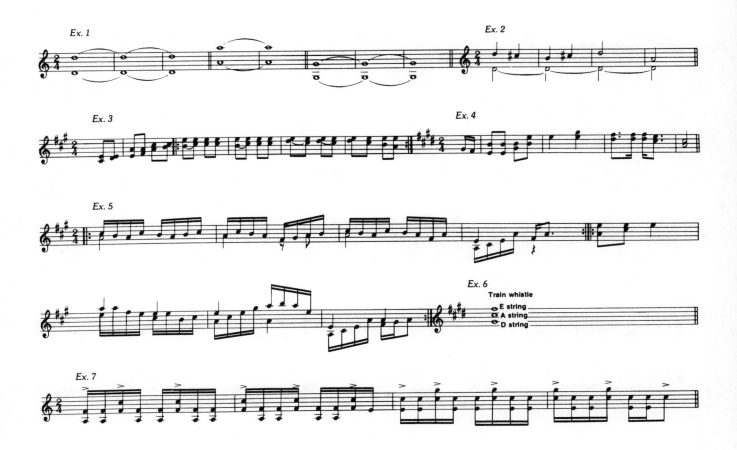

Finishing Touches

EVENTUALLY, EVERYTHING HAS to come to an end, even your favorite fiddle melody. So let's look at some endings that might work for your tunes. The ending, or "tag," for "Ragtime Annie" is illustrated in Ex. 1.

There are thousands of ways to end a tune, a few too many to list here; but I'll mention some that you may be familiar with — and several that may amuse you. For the sake of simplicity, all the tags will be in the key of A. Probably the most widely used basic fiddle-tune tag is shown in Ex. 2.

An ending I've used several times, especially in the key of A, is shown in Ex. 3. The slides on the E and A strings up to the harmonic notes are the same as those in the first few bars of "Limerock." This ending isn't as difficult as it might look, so don't be afraid to try it.

Another type of fancy ending is shown in Ex. 4. The trills (turns) really add interest to the music. Many of the Texas fiddlers use this ending quite often.

A tag that begins with the basic ending and finishes with a rhythm pattern (played with your bow) is shown in Ex.5. Many bluegrass tunes end with this pattern. Notice the variety of chords

that can be played with the bouncing bow.

Ex. 6 is one of the more progressive endings. The descending notes really make it a nice melodic tag. I have heard banjo and guitar players use this ending very effectively. Try it and see how it works for you.

It's sometimes a good idea to end a fiddle tune with a line that bears some similarity to the melody. For example, the tag I use on "Sally Goodin'" repeats some of the theme (see Ex. 7). This is a good example of style continuation.

Another fancy ending — similar to Ex. 3 — is shown in Ex. 8. The difference is that there are no harmonics — just more notes, instead. After all, if you have a good tag, many people will forget all the mistakes you made in the middle. (Nope, just joking!)

And last but not least, there's your basic "shave-and-a-haircut" tag (see Ex. 9). Notice the F instead of the F .

Those are just a few basic ways to end your tunes. Adopt anything you like and find comfortable, and don't be afraid to use your own imagination and improvisatory talents. I hope you all have a "happy ending!"

Beginners' Tunes

FIDDLE IN HAND, YOU'RE ready to learn to play just like that guy with Bill Monroe, or that fiddler with Merle Haggard, or that young fellow who won the National Old-Time Fiddlers contest last year. Well, good luck! On the other hand, if you're a rank beginner and aren't afraid to say so, you may need some guidance.

There are several different sizes of fiddles available. Your age and size are the primary considerations in determining the size of fiddle you need. I was five years old when I started playing, and I used a half-size fiddle. Now that I'm almost grown I use a full-size instrument, and that is what I suggest for all you full-size people. If you already have your fiddle and bow and the necessary accessories (rosin, strings, and maybe a six-pack), you are ready to begin.

It is very difficult to simply pick up the fiddle and just start playing. It's generally accepted that the fiddle (or violin, whichever term you prefer) is one of the most difficult musical instruments to play. So don't get discouraged at first. If you are lucky enough (as I was) to have a friend or a family member who already plays, you are ahead of the game from the start.

The first things you should try to learn are the scales. Basic scales are a *must*! You have to know where your fingers stop the strings to produce the notes of the basic scales. Beginners often want to play a tune without first going over the scales, and they usually find it somewhat difficult to do. As in any field of endeavor, habits are formed in learning fiddle playing. Bad habits are hard to break, so try to catch them early and get started in the right direction.

After you have progressed to the point where the fiddle feels comfortable to you, and you can get a fairly good tone on some basic scales, you are ready to learn a tune. The easier the tune, the better — don't go in over your head, and don't try to do too much at once. Learn a part of the tune and stay with it until you have it, *then* go on to the next part.

The tune I usually suggest for beginners is "Boil The Cabbage Down" (see Ex. 1) in the key of *A*. I begin by teaching a beginner the shuffle rhythms with the bow, and then the rest is easy. The fingering positions are relatively easy, so the tune doesn't take long to learn.

The first tune my dad taught me was the old-time "Mississippi Sawyer" (see Ex. 2). It's a little more difficult than "Boil The Cabbage Down," and it's in the key of *D*. "Mississippi Sawyer" has three sections, while "Boil The Cabbage" has two sections. Both tunes are good for beginners.

There are many different ways to learn and develop your musical abilities. Tape recorders, television, concerts, and record albums of bluegrass, old-time fiddling, and other styles can greatly enhance your listening skills and your knowledge of music. Those are some of the reasons why the younger players of today are progressing at such a fantastic rate. Not so long ago there was very little material on record for fiddle players to hear. LPs by Tommy Jackson and Howdy Forrester were about all you could find, and tape recorders didn't exist! But so much is available now, thank goodness, that fiddlers can hear their favorite tunes or their favorite artists any time.

Fiddle Tunes
"Devil's Dream"

MASON WILLIAMS is a composer, artist, and man of many talents who gave me the inspiration to present this material to you. Some of you already know about Mason's concerts for orchestra and bluegrass band. I have had the privilege of participating in these concerts for several years, and let me tell you, there is nothing like it.

Mason's concept for these symphony concerts is to incorporate the bluegrass musicians into the orchestra itself, rather than present them as a separate band. I thought you might enjoy discovering the mood that Mason creates with "Devil's Dream" as the chordal structure unwinds. Here are some excerpts from the program notes:

"Devil's Dream" is an Irish tune and was included in the great collection of Irish fiddle tunes edited by Captain Francis O'Neill in 1903. It is also known as "Deil (Devil) Among The Tailors" in Ireland. At one time, in certain rural communities, dancing was considered immoral, and because fiddle music incited dancers into particular frenzied gyrations, the fiddle was considered a kind of Pied Piper leading listeners down the road to sin. In fact, some believed there was a special place at the very lower end of Hell reserved for fiddlers and those who danced to their tunes; this lively spot was called Fiddlers Green. Perhaps the picture of evildoers forced by a grinning demon to dance for eternity was the inspiration to this hoedown fiddle tune.

(Lyrics)

Forty days and forty nights, the Devil was a – dreaming
Around the ark, old Noah's ark, the rain it was a – streaming
The monkey washed the baboon's face, the serpent combed his hair.
And up jumped the Devil with his pitchfork in the air.

. . . . One day the Devil decides to take a nap and he has a dream. At first all is well (or rather, all is Hell), and then he hears someone playing a fiddle. As he listens, more fiddlers join in, and he finds himself smiling and enjoying the music. But, being the Devil, he suddenly realizes that he doesn't like the idea of smiling and enjoying himself, especially to someone else's music. He decides to destroy the melody for the fiddlers by changing the harmony, getting loud and vulgar and just in general raising hell with everything. However, in spite of all the Devil's efforts, the fiddlers hang onto the melody, and in the end, the Devil is forced to dance along with Man in a glorious unison.

The concert begins with the bluegrass fiddler (me) playing "Devil's Dream" in the traditional key and form. As the tune progresses, the orchestra steps into its classical role of painting pictorial tone poems, and both sounds blend to produce Mason's fresh, creative style of music. With that in mind, here is the arrangement we use in the concert. If any of you ever have the opportunity to attend one of Mason's concerts, do so — you'll love it!

"Devil's Dream"

Traditional
Arranged by Mason Williams

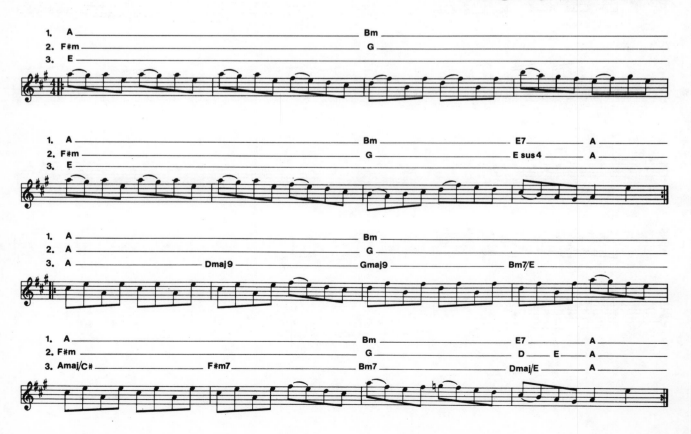

"Huckleberry Hornpipe"

TRAVELING THROUGHOUT THE COUNTRY, I've heard many fiddlers playing "Huckleberry Hornpipe." I'm glad they like it well enough to play it, but many seem to run into difficulty when they reach the third section.

The tune is in *A* and has three parts. The third part begins on the *G* string and advances to the *A* and *E* strings. The long run in the first four measures often stumps even the most accomplished fiddler.

Below is a version of the tune with all three parts. The notes in

brackets in section C are played in the third position on the *A* string. You must play the first note bracketed (*D*) with your first finger. This will automatically put you in the third position.

You can find this tune on Country Gazette's *Don't Give Up Your Day Job* [United Artists, LA090-F], Dan Crary's *Lady's Fancy* [Rounder, 0099], and the Stone Mountain Boys' *Reunion* [Ridge Runner, RR-0015]. The latter album features twin fiddling by Dave Ferguson and me.

"Huckleberry Hornpipe"   **by Byron Berline**

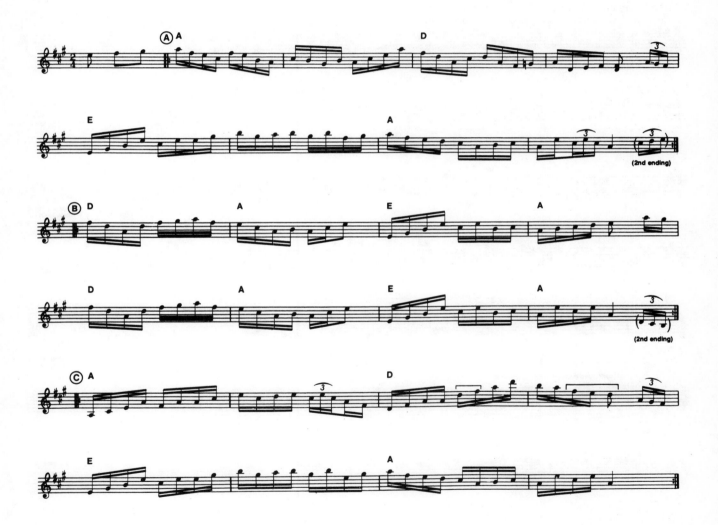

"Limerock"

"LIMEROCK" is one of my favorite fiddle tunes. Years ago, when I began attending fiddle contests with my dad, many of the Texas fiddlers played it. To me, it seemed to reflect a lot of different types of playing; classical, hornpipe, maybe even a little jazz. Whatever it is, it's difficult but fun to play.

"Limerock" has four different sections, in different keys, but there are many variations on each section. I play the sections in the following order: 1-2-1-3-1-4-1. Each time I repeat a section I vary it somewhat.

I have adapted several licks from "Limerock" to other tunes, whether bluegrass or whatever. For instance, I have used the first bar-and-a-half in some other tunes that are in the key of A. Here's the entire tune as I played it on my album *Dad's Favorites* (Rounder, 0100) and on Dan Crary's album *Lady's Fancy* (Rounder, 0099).

"Limerock"

**Traditional
Arranged by Byron Berline**

"Ragtime Annie"

SINCE I BEGAN WRITING a column for *Frets*, I have received letters and calls from folks who tell me how much they enjoy reading through the tunes that I use for musical examples. It's surprising how many fiddlers who read music are hungry for new tunes. Most fiddle players I know (including myelf) play almost completely by ear, and have to learn new tunes by just picking them out or by listening to a tape or a record over and over. Learning new songs is certainly less complicated if you have the ability to read music, no matter how limited that ability might be.

My wife, Bette, helps me out considerably in that department, as she reads music very well. While I play a tune, she transcribes it into musical notation. (I knew she would come in handy someday.) For those of you who don't read music, I suggest that you find someone who does — preferably a piano player or a fiddler who is willing to help. Such helpful musician friends are certainly a blessing to those of us who don't read music, but want to learn. We have all heard the

story about the fiddler who was asked if he could read music, replying, "Well, not enough to hurt my playing." It really isn't that funny anymore. All of us could benefit, even if we could read just a little.

Most fiddlers know "Ragtime Annie," as it is one of the more common fiddle tunes. I think it was the second tune I learned. It may be simple, but I think it has merit; and it is a great old-timey tune. I know for sure that it is a good square dance and clog-dancing number.

Pay special attention to the ending I have added to my arrangement below. That is the way I played the tune on my *Dad's Favorites* album, Rounder, 0100. I wanted to come up with something a little different and John Hartford helped me work the ending out. I think it fits the tune pretty well and adds a little spice. Have a go at "Ragtime Annie," and happy fiddling.

Arranged By Byron Berline

"Ragtime Annie"
Traditional

"Sally Goodin"

IF YOU WANT TO START YOUR day just right, pick up your fiddle and play "Sally Goodin." For me, "Sally Goodin"is the *premier* fiddle tune; every fiddler should know it. If you don't, maybe this will be a helpful introduction.

When played right, "Sally Goodin" has a powerful, building drive to it. I never get tired of playing the tune, and I am sure I do it almost every time I perform. I always knew it was a good fiddle tune, and I had played it for years; but not until I began playing with Bill Monroe did I discover its full power, which is especially apparent within a bluegrass band setting. Of course, the tune can be performed with any combination of instruments and still produce similar results.

"Sally Goodin" has been recorded several times by some great musicians, but my favorite is the recording Eck Robertson did for Victor in the '20s. The recording is a fiddle solo with no backup, which makes it unique in itself. Eck took the tune and really did something with it, adding a variety of parts, including one in the key of F minor. He also retuned his fiddle, raising the D string to E and the G string to A. The result was a cross-key tuning, as is often employed in "Black Mountain Rag." (Several Texas fiddlers still use that tuning for some of the tunes they play in the key of A.)

Eck had a colorful personality, and he often told a great story to introduce "Sally Goodin." I believe it went something like this: "There was a girl named Sally who had two boyfriends. The two boys were both fiddle players, and one of the boys had the last name of 'Goodin.' Sally couldn't decide which to marry, so she thought a fiddle contest between the two would be a good way to make her selection. Of course, the fellow Goodin won the contest, and Sally became Sally Goodin. They were very happy and had a productive life with 14 children, so I'm going to play 'Sally Goodin' 14 different ways."

I am sure that Eck did play it 14 different ways, although I am not going to write out even all the variations I play; but at least you should have a good idea of how the tune goes.

Only the melody is written below, to familiarize you with the tune. I also like to use double-stops here and there, usually on an open string that is adjacent to the string on which I'm playing the melody. Of course, the double-stop note should usually be a harmony that supports the melody note.

"Sally Goodin"

Traditional
Arranged by Byron Berline

ARRANGEMENT © 1980 BYRON BERLINE

"Grey Eagle"

WHILE THERE ARE MANY old-time fiddle tunes around today, it seems that there are only a few that have become popular enough to be played very often. But if you ever attend a fiddle contest where some of the top-notch fiddlers are competing you'll probably hear "Grey Eagle." I first learned the tune from my dad, who had learned it from his friend Frank Mitchell, a fine fiddler from Enid, Oklahoma. I'm not sure where and how the tune originated, but regardless of where it came from, it is a pretty difficult tune to play.

The first recording of "Grey Eagle" that I heard was Howdy Forrester's version from *Fancy Fiddlin' Country Style* (MGM E4035). Howdy called it "Grey Eagle Hornpipe," and his version does sound much like a hornpipe.

Texas fiddlers have a unique way of playing the tune. They play it slower than most other fiddlers, and they utilize the so-called "Texas backup" of accompaniment instruments. "Grey Eagle" can also be played in a straight bluegrass style. I've heard it done every imaginable way, and have personally experimented with most of them. It's a beautiful tune no matter how it's done.

Dan Crary recorded the tune on his album *Lady's Fancy* (Rounder Records 0099), and that has to be the all-time best guitar rendition. Banjoist Larry McNeely did an excellent banjo break to "Grey Eagle" on my album *Dad's Favorites* (Rounder 0100). Larry learned his version from the same Howdy Forrester album that I cited earlier. Howdy is definitely one of the all-time great fiddlers, and I recommend any of his albums as good listening and learning material.

ARRANGEMENT © 1981 BYRON BERLINE

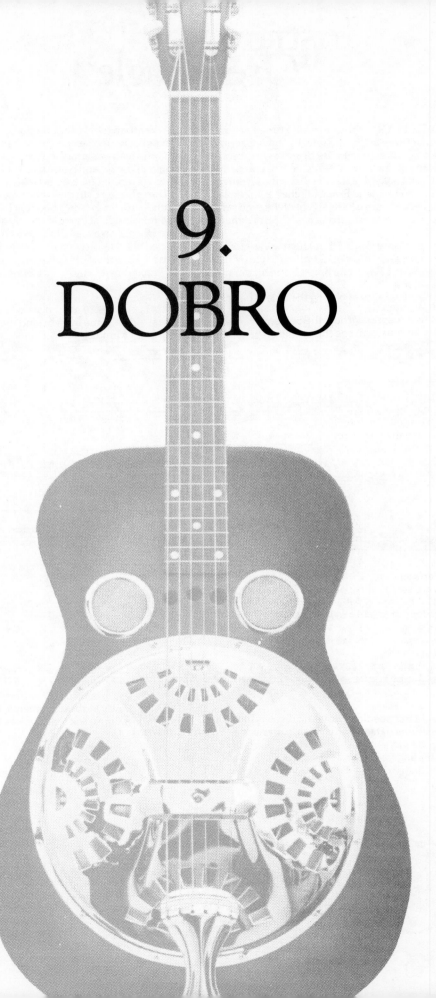

9.
DOBRO

Instructional Tips
MIKE AULDRIDGE
Switching Over

Mike Auldridge has been playing the dobro for over twenty-five years. For the past 12 years he's been a key member of the Washington, D.C.-based bluegrass group, the Seldom Scene. For more detail on this stellar musician see the article on page 80 by Roger Siminoff.

WHEN I FIRST STARTED getting into music, I played flat-picked guitar, then I moved on to fingerpicking guitar, and later I went on to 5-string banjo, which I played for about four or five years, until I really got into playing the dobro.

When switching over to the dobro from guitar or banjo, you can transfer some of your musical skills, particularly fingerpicking skills. But there are some problems you're sure to encounter as you begin to play the dobro. The intonation control with your left hand is very important — learning to play scales and getting all the notes at their proper pitches can be tricky at first. That is part of learning to use the bar, which is the most crucial technique that you must work on to get any satisfaction from your playing.

I'll be honest with you — my learning period was stretched over such a long period of time that I can't really remember how I first caught on to using the bar. Looking back on it now, I can see that the difference between someone who sounds good on the dobro and someone who *doesn't* sound so good is mainly a matter of how much practice time a beginning dobro player (and in fact, all dobroists) devotes to their left-hand barring technique. I can offer some advice to those who want to learn barring technique in a shorter period of time than it took me (which was about eight years!).

Just as with playing the fiddle, there are really no frets — at least none that you can *feel* — to guide you. You have to develop your ear, in conjunction with the more mechanical skills of gripping and moving the bar.

For playing a straight bar position (we won't discuss the more difficult slant-bar positions yet) the grip is fairly standard. Tut Taylor's grip is an exception that comes to mind. Tut holds the bar kind of in the ends of his fingers, rather than laying his fingers out behind the bar and putting his first (index) finger in the groove on the top of the bar.

The "standard" grip is shown in Fig. 1. The fingers are flat behind the bar, in order to kill the string sounds — actual notes or overtones — that come from behind the bar. Muting those sounds is a very basic form of bar "blocking." Notice in Fig. 1 that the back of the bar is lifted to make sure that unwanted notes are muted. To accomplish that, your wrist is constantly moving up and down about 3/4".

Most people who are just getting started with barring have exaggerated wrist movements — be sure you work for economy of motion. The bar really only needs to be a very slight distance off of the unplayed strings — probably not more than 1/64". Remember that your fingers are lying on the strings behind the bar, and they really take care of the muting. However, when you're playing real fast things like bluegrass breakdowns, you don't block at all — all the strings are allowed to ring, similar to a five-string banjo. The muting is more for moderate-paced things, like playing lyrical melodies.

Another important idea to discuss is moving from string to string. Suppose you're doing a lick that goes from the first string down to the third string. As you move from the first string to the second string, you pull the bar back toward you, as in Fig 1. You're no longer barring the first string. Throughout this type of movement, the bar is going back-and-forth perpendicular to the plane of the strings. When you are pulling the bar back toward you, the tip of the bar is never lifted, but the back of the bar is lifted quite a bit.

Now, when you're going the other way — from the low strings to the high strings — you need to dip your wrist downward a little so that the front of the bar clears the strings, as in Fig. 2. So forward runs are more difficult. You have a "blunt" bar that can catch on the strings if you're not careful. Not only must you lift the bar to insure good muting, but you must also dip the bar to get it up over the next strings as you're moving away from you.

Work slowly at these moments, and I guarantee that it will pay off. Set up a simple lick that involves the movements I've described, and strive for a clean sound and economy of motion. And remember, be patient. You can become a much better player by striving to improve your barring technique, no matter how good (or not so good) of a dobro player you are. Don't get discouraged — it takes everyone a long time to master working with the bar.

ILLUSTRATED BY MIKE AULDRIDGE

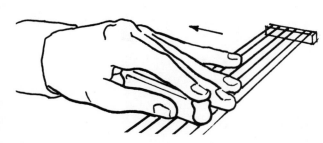

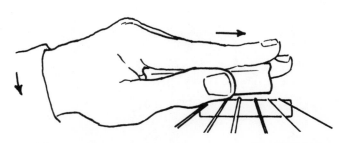

Scale Patterns

AMONG THE MOST IMPORTANT things to know about any instruments are the locations of the various scale patterns. Although it is a basic idea, the study and mastery of scales can take many years. Being able to play in any given key — knowing how to start a lick on a particular step of that key's scale and end the lick on another step —may sound like a simple task at first. But the more you learn about scales, the more you realize how challenging and interesting fretboard scale patterns can be.

Let's start out by keeping things as simple as possible for a while, and talk about finding the C major scale on the third string. First, let's take a look at the formula of whole-steps and half-steps that make up all major scales (see Ex. 1).

Ex. 1

Root	Whole Step	Whole Step	Half Step	Whole Step	Whole Step	Whole Step	Half Step

The key of C major has no sharps or flats, so the formula just goes through the musical alphabet of *natural notes* from C to C, in one octave (eight notes). Keeping in mind that a whole-step is two frets and a half-step is one fret, "walk" up the C major scale on the third string, starting on the 5th fret, as shown in Ex. 2.

Ex. 2

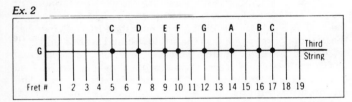

Next, learn that same single-note scale on the first three strings, starting on the third string. One big advantage in crossing over to the other strings when playing the scale is that you don't have to go so far up the neck (see Ex. 3).

Ex. 3

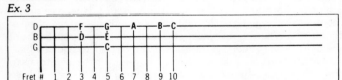

Now, learn that scale one octave lower, using the bottom (lowest-sounding) four strings. Notice how the entire scale can be played within four frets. Start with the C on the sixth (lowest-sounding) string, and play the C major scale shown in Ex. 4.

Ex. 4

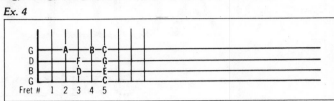

At this point, you can tie together the higher and lower C major scale octaves (Ex. 3 and Ex. 4), and become familiar with the visual pattern of how the scales fall on the fretboard (see Ex. 5).

Ex. 5

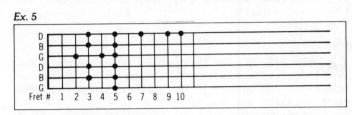

It's very important to memorize the visual patterns for major scales because they are the same — regardless of what key you're playing in. At this point, you really don't have to know what notes you're playing within each pattern, but you should realize that the *root1 or tonic* note (which tells you what key you're playing in) is located on the third string, at the only fret in the pattern that has a scale note on each string. For instance, look back at Ex. 5 and notice that there is a scale note on every string at the 5th fret, so the 5th fret can be considered the "base" fret for that scale pattern. The tonic (root) note for that scale pattern is always on the third string at that base fret. So in this case (third string, 5th fret), the note is C, which means that you're playing a C major scale.

You should practice this scale pattern in a variety of keys; A,C,D,E, and G are good notes to start with. That practice will help you to memorize the visual pattern for major scales, which will eventually enable you to play in any major key.

Fretboard Patterns

MAJOR SCALE PATTERNS were the subject of our last discussion, and we saw how a movable two-octave pattern can be played by crossing over from string to string, thus avoiding unnecessary climbing up the neck. Although we focused on the C major scale, I pointed out that by memorizing the visual pattern, you can play a major scale in any key, depending on what note you begin the scale with. That first pattern is shown in Ex. 1.

Ex. 1

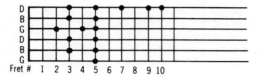

Let's go through a similar process to find another movable pattern for major scales (again the examples will be shown in the key of C). First, let's look at the low octave of the new pattern, starting on the sixth string (see Ex. 2).

Next, learn the high octave of the new pattern, starting on the third string (see Ex. 3).

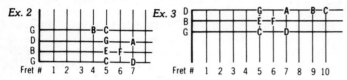

Now combine the two octaves and become familiar with the visual pattern of this new two-octave movable major scale (Ex. 4)

Ex. 4

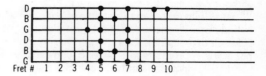

Notice that in the first pattern, most of the notes are *below* the 5th fret, while in the new pattern most of the notes are *above* the 5th fret. Of course all the notes in both patterns are the same; but as with any instrument, it is important to memorize the various scale patterns. That is especially true for dobro players because you're using scales constantly as you play leads and fills.

Choose a simple tune like "Home Sweet Home" or "Auld Lang Syne" and pick out the melody line, using each of the patterns. Then play the same tune in several different keys by moving the patterns up and down the fretboard.

Another way to practice the patterns is to play along with records (slow tunes at first). Figure out what key the song is in and do some backup fills between the vocal phrases, staying within the confines of whichever pattern you choose. Try starting and stopping your fill on different steps of the scale, but never leave the pattern you're working with.

Scale-Based Licks

MANY BACKUP PARTS AND melodies are really nothing more than scales, scale segments, and chords based on scale notes. I think a lot of people use scale-based licks much of the time without realizing that they're doing it.

Basically, you can take two approaches when you look for melody lines or backup fill lines. First, you can play chord-position licks. Chord-position licks are right-hand patterns using a straight bar at the appropriate fret. Second, you can play scale licks. These are usually single-note or two-note lines that use parts of the major scale. These elements are quite versatile, especially when played with rhythmic variations.

Let's talk about a major scale in the key of A. I like to explain it by writing out the alphabet from A to G, adding another A to represent the full octave.

A B C D E F G A

Now let's add the three sharps called for in the key of A major and number the notes for reference purposes.

I	II	III	IV	V	VI	VII	VIII
A	B	C#	D	E	F#	G#	A

In any major key the chords built on the I, III, and VI steps are minor, and the chord built on VII is diminished. For example, in the key of A major, these are the chords that would be properly played in scale sequence:

I	IIm	IIIm	IV	V	VIm	VIIdim	VIII
A	Bm	C#m	D	E	F#m	G#dim	A

In open G tuning (G-B-D-G-B-D), the chord scale looks like this on the dobro neck. (We'll be playing the top two notes of each chord in the notation.)

This is two-note scale played on the first two strings. Notice that the bar must be turned as it goes up the neck. To make the turn I place my index finger on the left side of the bar and push the front edge to the right. At the same time I slide my thumb toward the rear of the bar, which pushes the back edge into the base of my ring finger. There is also a slight wrist movement as I do the turn, but no elbow movement.

Start at the 2nd fret with a straight bar for A (I). Then turn the bar so it contacts the first string at the 4th fret and the 2nd string at the 3rd fret: This is Bm (IIm). Keep the same slant and move the bar up two frets for C#m (IIIm). Next, straighten the bar at the 7th fret for the D (IV). Keep the bar straight and move to the 9th fret for E (V). Slant the bar again to contact the 11th fret on the first string and the 10th fret on the second string: This is F#m (VIm). Straighten the bar at the 12th fret for the G#dim (VIIdim). Finish the scale by playing the octave A with a straight bar at the 14th fret.

All during this bar work, the right hand can be playing thumb and middle finger, alternating them or picking them together. It is very important that you use the thumb and middle finger because it helps to rock the right hand up onto the right edge of the palm to block the notes in what is called right-hand blocking.

When chords have two or more notes in common, they can often be used interchangeably. This is called chord substitution. Look back at the notation and you can see that the Bm (IIm) and D (IV) chords have two common notes (D and F#). These chords are usually interchangeable. The same is true of C#m (IIIm) and E (V), which have the common notes E and G#. The straight bar at the 12th fret is an interesting example too, because it really makes an octave G chord. However, for our purposes, we still play the D and B notes that are also a part of the G#dim chord. It is important to remember that we are thinking and playing in the key of A.

Playing scale-based licks greatly reduces the risk of error as long as you remember the bar positions. Once you learn the scale in A the positions will remain the same in all major keys (starting on different frets), so you don't have to be terribly concerned about memorizing lots of keys. You can start the scale wherever you choose, and end it wherever you choose, within any key you're playing. People always ask me where I find the fill notes. All I do is find the key and work the scale — that's where all the notes are.

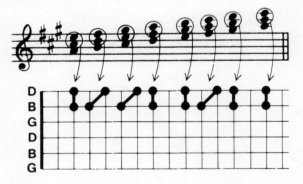

A Straight Substitution

WHEN PLAYING IN A BAND, you have a good deal of latitude in your selection of chord positions and chord substitutions. You can rely on the other members of the group to supply certain notes that you might leave out. One such chord substitution that we'll discuss this month enables you to use a *straight* (major-chord) bar position to play in a minor-chord context.

The common *G* tuning of the dobro (*G-B-D-G-B-D*, low to high) gives you two consecutive *G* major triads (three-note chords). If you hold your bar straight across the 5th fret, you then have two consecutive *C* major triads. If you want to play a *C* minor chord, you have to lower the note on the second and/or fifth string by one fret (more on that in a minute). The important point is that you can't play the *C* minor chord with a straight bar. However, you can get around the problem by playing *E♭* as a substitute chord with a straight bar, and rely on the band to establish a *C* tonality, which combines with your *E♭* triad to create a *Cm7* chord. Let's discuss in more detail how the whole thing works.

First, let's go over the basics of major and minor chord constructions to the notes of the *C* major scale. However, the concepts will apply in any key. A *C* major chord is composed of the first (root), third, and fifth tones of the *C* major scale, as shown in Ex. 1.

Ex. 1

1	2	3	4	5	6	7	8
Ⓒ	D	Ⓔ	F	Ⓖ	A	B	C

Now, let's write a *C* major scale [dorian mode], which basically means that you flat (lower by one half-step) the third and seventh notes of the *C* major scale. The first, third and fifth tones of the *C* minor scale make up the *C* minor chord (see Ex. 2). Adding the seventh note of the *C* minor scale to the *C* minor chord gives you a *Cm7* chord.

Ex. 2

1	2	3	4	5	6	7	8
Ⓒ	D	Ⓔ♭	F	Ⓖ	A	Ⓑ♭	C

Next, let's write a *major* scale, beginning on the third note of the *C* minor scale — an *E♭* major scale, which is shown in Ex. 3.

Ex. 3

1	2	3	4	5	6	7	8
Ⓔ♭	F	G	Ⓐ♭	Ⓑ♭	C	D	E♭

Notice that the first, third, and fifth notes of the *E♭* major scale, (the *E♭* major chord triad) are the same as the third, fifth, and seventh notes of the *C* minor scale. You can play the *E♭* major chord with a straight bar at the 8th fret. With the bass player (and probably other members of the band) supplying the *C* notes, you blend in as part of the *Cm7* chord sound.

Also notice that the *E♭* chord is three frets up from the *C* chord. That relationship applies in any key when you are making the chord substitution we've been discussing. Without stopping to figure out what notes you need to make a straight-bar substitution for a minor chord, just go up three frets from where you would play the major chord that has the same root as the minor minor chord that the band is playing. For example, if the band is playing *A* minor, you would go up to the 5th fret for your straight-bar minor substitution, because your straight-bar *A* major position is at the 2nd fret.

Below is a fretboard diagram showing where you can play the straight-bar substitutions for *Am* and *Cm* (see Ex. 4).

Ex. 4

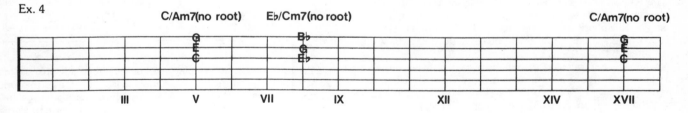

	C/Am7(no root)	E♭/Cm7(no root)				C/Am7(no root)

Two-Fers

PLAYING DOBRO IN A BLUEGRASS band requires not only filling empty spots with scale-derived slides, but also staying up with the driving sound of a 5-string banjo. Banjo players usually have a lot of right-hand pattern licks that utilize the fifth string *G* note, which fits every chord in the key of *G* except the VII diminished. Ignoring the VII diminished for a moment, notice that the *G,A,B,D,* and *E* notes belong to every other relative scale in the key of *G*.

I MAJOR	G	A	B	C	D	E	F♯	G
II MINOR		A	B	C	D	E	F	G	A
III MINOR			B	C♯	D	E	F♯	G	A	B
IV MAJOR				C	D	E	F	G	A	B	C
V MAJOR					D	E	F♯	G	A	B	C♯	D
VI MINOR						E	F♯	G	A	B	C	D	E
VII DIMINISHED							F♯	G♯	A	B	C	D	E♭	F

The *C* in the V scale is flatted to make the dominant seventh chord (*D7*), so the *C* natural note fits everything except the III minor chord. This means that you can play a lick that includes the notes *G, A, B, C, D,* and *E* in every chord (in the key of *G*) except the VII diminished chord and the III minor chord. And even those will work with a slight change, which we will get to in a minute. Just as the banjo player keeps bringing his thumb back to the fifth string *G* to set up his three-finger roll patterns, you can set up hammer-on and pull-off patterns using the notes that are common to the relative scales.

Hammering-on means that you pick an open string and then place the bar over a fret, with the end result of playing two notes while only picking one note with your right hand. Pulling-off is, of course, just the opposite. You pick a barred note and then pull the bar back so that the open string sounds, and again you have two notes for the price of one. Once these techniques are mastered you can play almost twice as fast as you think you can. Almost sounds like magic, doesn't it? Well, it may not be magic, but it's certainly more fun than any magic show, once you get to the point where you can rip through these things by instinct.

You have to start out slowly, thinking of each note as one word, each phrase of notes as a sentence, and each complete lick as a paragraph. With practice you'll be able to fly through whole paragraphs faster than an auctioneer on speed. It is important to go very slowly at first, so that each phrase comes out cleanly. Playing cleanly is a lot more pleasing to the ear than simply playing fast. Your speed will develop naturally, but the clean sound is something you must try to achieve throughout the learning process. Otherwise, you'll end up with some very sloppy habits.

To really get the most out of these techniques, you should develop certain right-hand patterns that allow you to play faster. In the following exercises, your thumb will start on the fourth string and then cross over to the second string.

Ex. 1: Crossover

Ex. 2: Crossover

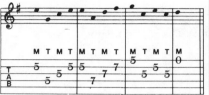

Ex. 3: Hammer and Pull

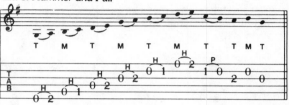

Play this phrase against a *G* chord, making each note equal in time value:

Ex. 4: Hammer and Pull

As you can see, you've played 23 notes but you've only picked 13 of those with your right hand. Almost half of the notes in this type of lick are played with the bar. Also, the whole lick is put together with the six notes (*G, B, C, D,* and *E*) that are common to all the relative scales (with the exceptions that I pointed out earlier).

You could use the same lick while playing through a III minor (*Bm*) change by simply raising the *C* to *C♯* (hammer-on the second string at the 2nd fret instead of the 1st fret). To play through the VII diminished chord (*F♯dim*), just hammer every string at the 1st fret rather than the 2nd fret (I use only the top four strings on this lick).

So, this one lick (interspersed among other licks) could be used several times in a solo, each time with the rhythm instruments playing different chords in progression. It will sound a little different each time.

There are hundreds of variations on licks that use basically the same idea. You generally hammer-on at the 2nd fret — except on the second and fifth strings, which you hammer at the 1st fret. You could fall into a repeating pattern that stays on two strings, just rocking back and forth. Every little change you make in the timing will add something to the feel. It's just a matter of building up a huge bag of tricks and then learning to show them sparingly.

Inventing Licks

INVENTING NEW LICKS is a challenge I have to face most every time I play, whether I'm onstage or in a recording studio. In the studio I try to create fills and solos that will be unique to each particular song. Often onstage I'll try something new, get lost and, in panic, try to find my way back to using certain things that act as pathways to familiar territory. Come to think of it, that happens a lot in the studio too. I might use the same pathway a hundred times and find something new on each trip that will make the licks sound different.

The "feel" of each lick grows out of the tempo of the particular song and what you do within the time you're allotted. I always listen to the lyrics, and I try to say something with the dobro that complements what's being done in the vocals.

You, as an instrumentalist, have the same basic tool that the singer has; the same pathway to weirdness or warmth: the scale. You can use a single-note scale, a harmonizing scale, or a combination of both scales. You can use a sliding-type scale, where you move up and down the neck, rarely varying the strings you're picking with your right hand; or you can run a position scale, where you change strings on almost every other note. The sliding scale should be thought of in terms of running the length of the neck. Position scales run perpendicular to, or across, the neck and fall into patterns spread only a few frets apart.

As an example, here is tablature for the sliding harmonic scale in the key of *C*:

As you can see, one octave stretches 12 frets along the fretboard. Running a sliding scale works best for slow-to-medium-speed songs where you can use the sliding sustains to best advantage. For faster songs, position-based scales work best because you can work out picking patterns that will result in the desired staccato effect.

Below is the single-note position scale of *C*, spanning two octaves in only eight frets:

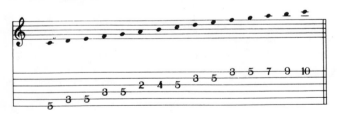

Try this harmonized position scale, which uses three forward slants:

The bar will jump back and forth between the 5th and 3rd fret four times before going up the fretboard in a forward slant.

Now change the feel of that harmonized position scale and add position licks at the *F* and *G* frets and a final *C*-position lick, and you'll have some rough ideas for either a solo or some fill lines within a I-IV-V-I progression in the key of *C*:

F position lick:

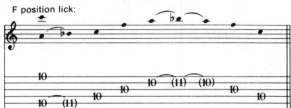

G position lick:

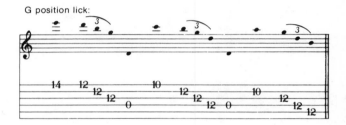

C position lick:

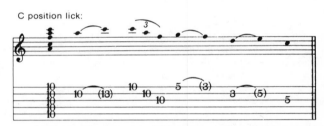

Strum thumb across lower strings and pick 1st string with middle finger in a pinching motion. Quickly lift back of bar to damp all but first string.

C position lick (same harmonized scale positions):

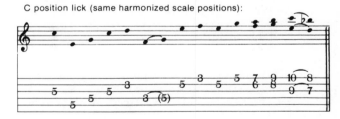

When you're doing these position licks, always pull the bar back towards you to block between each note. To push the bar away from you, toward the first string, just dip your wrist slightly so that the blunt end can slide across the strings.

You should learn both the 12-fret sliding scales (using forward and reverse slants) and the position scales in every key. Be able to go either up or down the scales without thinking any more about it than you would about which foot to move next while walking up or down a staircase. This will leave you free to play around with the time and the "feel" of what you're trying to say. Then you can carry on a good musical conversation with a singer.

Improvisation Tools

WHEN YOU HAVE A BIG enough bag of licks, you can improvise your way through a break on almost any song without even knowing the melody. Of course, the best approach is to learn the melody first, and then throw in a few licks here and there to spice things up a bit.

But let's assume that you're sitting in with a band, and they play a song you've never heard before. Halfway through the tune, they look at you to let you know that your break is coming up. You won't have to pretend that your thumbpick just fell off, or that your resonator just collapsed, if you have a good enough arsenal of licks.

It takes time to master enough licks to feel confident in every key, but let's start with the easiest stuff to work with: the hammer-

on and pull-off licks in the key of *G*.

You should learn each of the licks (Ex. 1-5) separately and really feel comfortable with each one before tackling the next. After you've learned each of the licks individually, string them together in the following order to construct one possible break:

#1 #2 #1 #3 #1 #2 #4 #5

With that combination, you'll be able to fake a ride on about ten songs right off the bat. Next switch the order around and you can add another ten songs to your list.

Ex. 1

Ex. 3

Ex. 2

Ex. 4

Ex. 5

"Pickaway"

EVERY ONCE IN A WHILE A song comes along with some mysterious quality about it that appeals to a lot of people over a long period of time. In the late '60s, banjoist Vic Jordon wrote and recorded an instrumental tune that he called "Pickaway." Vic played banjo with Lester Flatt for a while after the breakup of the Flatt And Scruggs team. Vic has also played with several other top bluegrass acts, and he is now a busy Nashville session artist.

I recorded "Pickaway" as a dobro instrumental on my first solo album, *Mike Auldridge Dobro*, Takoma Records, TAK 7033. I still get more requests for "Pickaway" than for anything else I've recorded. I've also received many requests for the tablature to my solo version.

There are several things that I'd like to call to your attention. The double forward rolls that appear in measures 3 and 11 are played with the bar at the 5th fret, but with first string left open. A similar lick appears in measure 20, but this time the bar is at the 9th fret — again, leaving the first string open. In measure 24, notice the muted thumb stroke.

ARRANGEMENT © 1980 MIKE AULDRIDGE

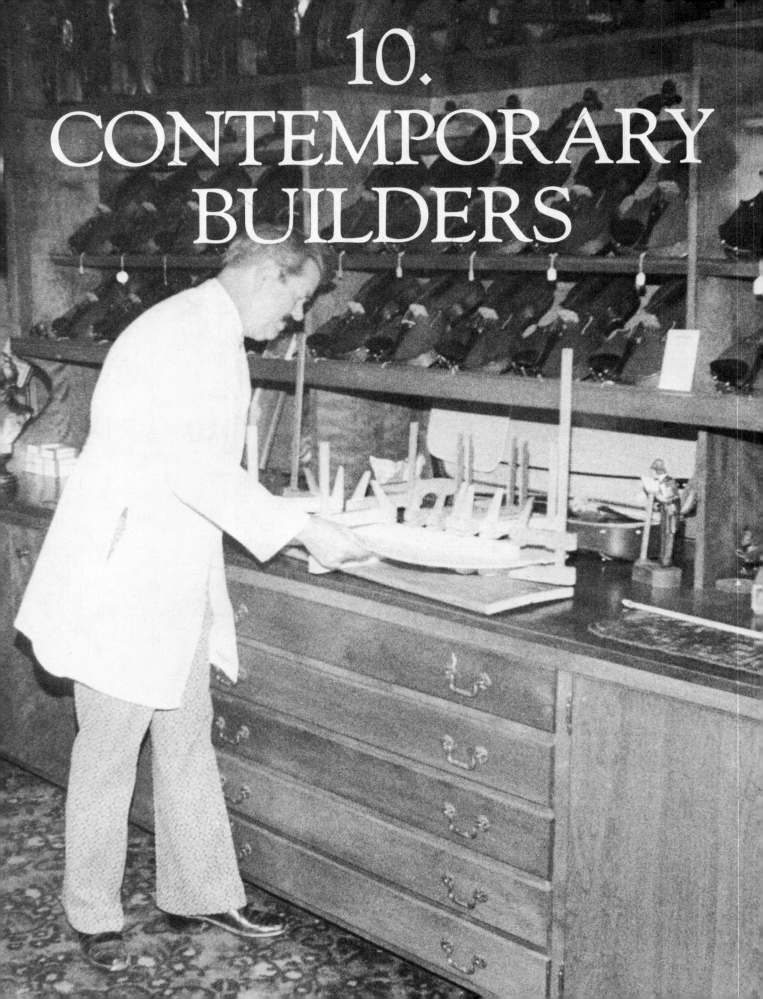

10.
CONTEMPORARY
BUILDERS

Gibson

AIRLINES REFER TO it as AZO, with its modest airport where only a handful of flights go in and out each day. "Downtown" is just a few blocks long, and the city is so spread out that at first glance one might think Kalamazoo was a sleepy little town.

It's far from asleep. Just 50 miles east of Lake Michigan, in the state which bears the name of that lake, little Kalamazoo is a robust center of industrial activity. It piles automotive parts onto one end of Detroit's giant chain of railways. It's the home of UpJohn, one of the nation's largest pharmaceutical companies. It's also the home of a half-dozen colleges, including Western University.

Sometime during the late 1880s, a man named Orville Gibson settled in Kalamazoo and began making musical instruments. By 1902 a company bearing his name was formed, and within two decades the company had become a major force in the manufacturing of stringed musical instruments. The expansion and growth of Gibson paralleled the growing interest in mandolins and guitars during the early 1900s. In 1917, a three-story building was constructed on Parsons Street, in a quiet suburban area about five or six blocks from the center of town. Today, several one-floor additions to the original building spread out over an entire block, and attention is called to its site [225 Parsons St., Kalamazoo, MI 49007] by the huge red chimney proudly emblazoned with the name "Gibson."

For many who work there, the "old building" is a symbol of Gibson's heritage. From time to time, various departments had to be relocated within the entire plant. Several ended up in the old building for short periods, and many employees had the opportunity to share in its warmth. At one time the basement of that building was occupied by the banjo and mandolin departments. Now it is the home of Research and Development, Artist Relations, and Engineering. The second floor houses the employee cafeteria and the parts department. On the floor above are the repair and custom-work departments.

The front entrance of the new building features a small museum, where several of Orville's and the company's earliest instruments are displayed. Business offices are located along the Parsons Street frontage, and behind that is a maze of machinery and instrument makers.

The space closest to the front of the building houses the "mill room," where incoming lumber is stored, sawn, and prepared for body and neck sections. Beyond the next wall the neck blanks are profiled by several automatic carving machines. Necks are run in large batches — several hundred at a time — since the equipment takes some time to set up for each type and style of neck. Those processed blanks needed for current production are sent to the next stage, while the overrun is stacked for future use.

All of the tools and fixtures are stored in secured areas, on shelves reaching up to the ceiling. On some of the highest shelves can be found fixtures for instruments long since departed from Gibson's line of instruments.

The company is highly machine- and fixture-oriented. The elaborate fixturing provides standardization of parts, and assures that each component will be made as designed. Unlike most private luthiers, Gibson has an engineering department that creates mechanical drawings and provides blueprints for everything. An in-house tool and fixture department constructs and repairs all of the fixtures.

Before an instrument goes into production, several dozen samples are made to assure that the entire instrument can go together on a full-scale production basis. This heavy sampling has been one of Gibson's standard procedures since the 1930s, and collectors have come across several

LEFT: *Guitar bodies, stacked in a rack, move in lots from department to department.* **CENTER:** *A large soft buffing wheel is used to put the finishing touches on a rack of completed F-style mandolins.* **RIGHT:** *Excess finish is scraped by hand from the surface of the binding, prior to final finishing.*

instruments that, though not one-of-a-kind creations, have neven been listed in any of Gibson's catalogs.

Wood for carved-top and carved-back instruments is matched and glued and brought into the carving department. Pattern carving machines have follower wheels that work like key-cutters to trace the original pattern's curvatures while a connected cutter head chews its commanded profiles into the new wood.

For several years during the late 1960s and early 1970s, Gibson was using multilaminated rims for its banjo shells. Around 1976, the multi-laminates were abandoned in favor of Gibson's original method of laminating three pieces of steam-bent 1/4" maple into a 3/4"-thick ring. For tube-and-plate rims, a notch is cut into the 3/4" rim and an additional 3/8" maple ring is attached, into which the support lip is cut for the tube.

Sides for acoustic guitars and mandolins are also bent in this department. Mandolin sides are bent using steam as a heating/softening source, and guitar sides are bent on a large, automatic, electrically-heated press. The mandolin sides are placed in metal fixtures that resemble the outer shapes of the instrument. The wood is forced (in one operation) to follow the shape of the fixture, a technique contrasting strongly with the hot-pipe method used by most instrument makers.

Fretboards come from the mill room in the form of planed and sanded blanks. From there they go to "slotting," "binding," and "fretting" departments, with each operation having a specialist whose attention is focused only on that particular procedure. Within each series of departments is a foreman who checks the parts to see that they conform to specifications, before sending them into the next phase.

Finally, all of the components for any given instrument arrive at the assembly point, where tops and backs are glued to their respective sides, and necks are fitted to bodies. According to instrument type, the work is either shared or not shared by the craftsmen. In the mandolin department, for example, one of several craftsmen will do the entire construction: scroll carving, body tuning, neck fitting, and body assembling of an F-5 mandolin, working only on three or four instruments at one time (each in various stages of completion). The necessary hand work dictates this kind of individual craftsmanship, and also means that each instrument will be slightly different and slightly individual.

In other areas, such as banjo construction, where each instrument is "assembled" in the truest sense, one person will do all neck fitting, while another machines rims, or routs for inlays, or binds resonators, or assembles the respective components.

When the instruments are completed and sanded — a stage that Gibson calls "white-wood" — they are taken to "finishing," where a long ceiling-hung conveyor system carries the instruments from staining, to first coat, to binding scraping, and back into the spray room for final coats of finish. After the instruments are sprayed, they are placed back on the continuously moving conveyor belt. By the time the instrument makes its complete cycle out of the spray room and back again, it is ready for more coats of lacquer. The last stop on the conveyor system brings the instruments to "buffing," where they are machine buffed, and placed on movable carts to go to "final assembly."

As the name implies, this is where each instrument receives its tuning machines, bridges, tailpieces, and end pins, strings, and pickguards. Here the nuts are filed, the frets are checked for trueness (and leveled, if necessary), and the instruments are tested and played.

After final assembly, the acoustic instruments join their electric cousins in a sea of pegheads of every shape, size, and color, protruding up from their carrying racks. From there they go into cases and cartons, before leaving Kalamazoo for the shops of waiting music dealers and the hands of waiting musicians.

C.F. Martin Organisation

NAZARETH, Pennsylvania is a small community nestled in the gentle, rolling hills of eastern Pennsylvania. It is a quiet place — only a few miles away from the Delaware River, which separates Pennsylvania from New Jersey. About a mile outside of town, hidden behind some houses, stands a huge, one-story building that is the home of the C.F. Martin Organisation. Established in 1833, Martin is one of the oldest and most respected guitar manufacturers in the world.

The building's reception area contains the 1833 Shop, a store where Martin T-shirts, jackets, accessories, and literature can be found. To the left, in a quiet room, is the Martin museum, which displays examples of the company's finest craftsmanship of the past 167 years. The front portion of the building houses business and executive offices, with the ever-present hum of machinery and workmen in the background.

Behind some swinging doors lies an adventure into another world. The aroma of lacquer and freshly sawn wood permeates the air, and dozens of draftsmen are busy assembling guitars.

Most of the 125 employees live in Nazareth and have woodworking backgrounds. At Martin, they usually are trained for a particular job, such as bracing tops or shaping necks. "We feel we get a higher degree of perfection by having a man specialize," says Mike Longworth, customer relations manager for the company, and author of *Martin Guitars: A History* [available from Martin Guitars, Sycamore St., Nazareth, PA 18064]. "Take some other craftsman who has made 50 complete guitars by himself. That is, he has braced 50 tops, shaped 50 necks, and so on. Compared to him, our man who braces 50 tops a day is going to be better at his specific job than the guy who has done 50 in his lifetime."

To further ensure quality, inspectors carefully check the parts of each instrument every step of the way. First, spruce for soundboards is placed on a high-intensity light box to check for sap pockets, pinholes, or other defects. The "flitches" (stacks of sawn pieces from the same log) of rosewood are examined to assure that backs and sides match in color and grain. Each piece is then numbered with chalk to assure that it will match its corresponding part in a finished instrument. The backs are then glued together in a huge waterwheel-like clamping device. The operator glues one back, clamps it into the wheel, and then rotates the wheel to the next position. He then removes a dried back from the next clamping jig and loads new pieces of wood.

Sides are bent by hand on a hot tube until they have the required shape and curvature. The sides then go to another department to be joined into a full side assembly. From there the assembly is taken to an area where the kerfed (notched) lining is glued and fitted to the top and bottom edges. The glue is applied with a brush, and the lining is held in place with wooden clothespins.

The instruments go from department to department, where the workers perform their special tasks: installing braces, shaping them by hand, fitting tops and backs to the sides, and so on, until the completed bodies and completed necks reach the finishing department. The instruments are given several coats of lacquer, and then dry sanded. The bindings are hand scraped with sharp pieces of flat steel to remove any excess filler or coloring that may have gotten on the binding prior to the first lacquer coats. After the final finishing is done, the necks are attached to their assigned bodies, and bridges and pickguards are installed.

Each step of the way, the guitar is worked on in a manner the Martin company calls "handmade." Although all manufacturers of musical instruments use a great deal of hand work, Martin prides itself in using just a bit more. Other companies carve instrument necks on giant pattern carving machines. Martin shapes them totally by hand. Guitar sides are typically bent by large forming machines, which shape many sides in one operation. Martin shapes the guitar sides by hand. Bracing is machine-shaped and tapered in most other manufacturing situations. Martin carves all of its braces by hand.

To some extent, many guitar makers have copied certain Martin feaures. Guitar X-bracing was invented by Martin around 1850. The dreadnought body shape and the matching of a 14-fret neck to a flat-top guitar were also innovated by Martin. "Virtually every manufacturer in the industry today makes a 14-fret, X-braced, flat-top dreadnought guitar," says Longworth.

Another Martin first was its non-adjustable neck brace design. The solid "T"-shaped bar was introduced in 1934, and was found to be a satisfactory replacement for the ebony center strip widely used at the time. The current brace, which replaced the T-bar in 1967, is a square, hollow, steel tube. Martin feels that this configuration is much stronger than round, adjustable truss rods. If a neck does require strengthening, something other than an adjustable truss rod can be used. Mike points out that "what most people call neck problems aren't really such at all. The top of a guitar, made

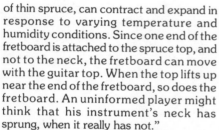

ABOVE: *Rosewood backs are glued and clamped in place.* CENTER: *It takes about 40 hours to hand-fit and glue abalone around the D45.* RIGHT: *Amidst a sea of clamps, a craftsman glues the bracing to the inside of spruce tops.*

of thin spruce, can contract and expand in response to varying temperature and humidity conditions. Since one end of the fretboard is attached to the spruce top, and not to the neck, the fretboard can move with the guitar top. When the top lifts up near the end of the fretboard, so does the fretboard. An uninformed player might think that his instrument's neck has sprung, when it really has not."

Scalloped soundboard bracing was typical of all Martin steel string guitars made until 1944. At that point, heavier-gauge strings became available. "It was noticed that tops were pulling too much, so they decided to eliminate the scalloped bracing in order to strengthen the tops," Mike explains. "But scalloped bracing is being used again with the introduction of the HD-28, M series, and the OM-45, and light-to-medium-gauge strings are recommended on these instruments."

Like other manufacturers, Martin is finding it more difficult to obtain certain woods. It has become harder to procure ebony, for example. Indian rosewood has replaced Brazilian rosewood at the factory, because the Brazilian government terminated all exports of rosewood logs.

To its credit, Martin has been adaptable in its use of woods. In the 1960s, Martin was able to obtain a lot of premium rosewood to be sawn in its own mill. Having its own mill has enabled Martin to procure the best selection of woods from logs that the company purchased specifically for instrument use. Lesser grades of woods that came from some logs were then sold to other instrument manufacturers. Unfortunately, some of those logs did not produce wood wide enough for two-piece dreadnought guitar backs. The larger trees already had been logged out of the readily accessible forests, and Martin had to take the smaller

trees. To make best use of the smaller stock, the three-piece D-35 back was designed. The guitar instantly became one of Martin's most popular styles — eventually overtaking the D-28 in sales.

Although some people say that today's Martin guitars are not as well made as those in years gone by, Longworth says that today's instruments are basically made the same way Martins have always been made. "The truth is," says Longworth, "that the guitar is as well made, if not better, today, due to such factors as better glues and techniques, and a better selection of woods. The problem is that we have not found a way to make a brand new 25-year-old guitar. It must age naturally."

Certain major changes in company policies have occurred throughout the years. Until recently, Martin refused requests for special-order work. Parts would never be switched from one style to another (for example, you couldn't buy an M-38 with a D-45 neck). But in 1979 the company instituted a special-order department, with ground rules that allow the transfer of work from one style to another. To date, quite a few orders have been received. The special-order department is limited by the woods, sizes, and trimmings normally used on production guitars.

C.F. Martin no longer owns the Vega Banjo Company, which was purchased nine years ago from its original owner, William Nelson of Boston. The banjo division was sold to the Galaxy Trading Corporation of Sante Fe Spurs, California, and the last Martin Vegas were shipped from the Nazareth factory in October 1979. Replacing the banjo in the Martin line were three solid-body electric guitars: the E-18 and the EM-18, and an EB-18 bass. These are the first Martin electrics since the old *F* and *GT* series of the '60s.

Another major change at Martin has been the dropping of the "warranty without time limit" in favor of a one-year limited warranty. People used to refer to the Martin guarantee as a "lifetime" guarantee. "There was never a 'lifetime guarantee' on a Martin guitar," says Longworth. "They had been guaranteed to the original owner, without time limit, against defective material and imperfect workmanship. It did not cover accidental damage, normal wear and tear, or negligence. This was voided upon sale to a second owner."

Longworth says that one of the reasons C.F. Martin guitars have maintained their high quality for so long is that there always has been a member of the Martin family associated with th business. Today, C.F. Martin III is chairman of the board, and although he is in his eighties, he can be found at the factory almost every day. His son, Frank, is president and takes an active role in making certain that all aspects of the company run smoothly. Frank's son, Chris (C.F. Martin IV), has served his apprenticeship in the shop and is now preparing for the future, as assistant to the president, in the family tradition.

Ovation Instruments

THERE WAS A TIME when cracks like, "You can't stand it up in the corner," or "It keeps sliding off my lap," got a big laugh in acoustic guitar circles, but the chuckles stopped a long time ago. The whole litany of tongue-in-cheek comments about the roundback, synthetic-body Ovation guitar faded into oblivion as Ovation's unconventional space-age instrument steadily won its way into the hands of leading players around the globe.

It didn't happen overnight. Fifteen years ago, the Ovation guitar was the brainstorm of an aerospace entrepreneur who had visions of combining his huge helicopter and aerospace manufacturing facilities with his hobby — guitars. Charles Kaman, president and founder of Kaman Aerospace, wanted to diversify his operations. His company was building various models of rescue helicopters, with blades made out of fiberglass-covered Sitka spruce. Kaman also happened to be a serious guitarist. To anyone else, there would have been no connection between planes and guitars. But Kaman got the notion that within his manufacturing techniques and advanced materials might lie the germ of a better musical mousetrap. Once the idea had dawned upon him, Kaman didn't stop until he created a fiberglass-back, bowl-shaped guitar body that was married to a traditional Sitka spruce top.

Would his musical idea fly? That part of the story is history now. Thanks to a lot of hard work and a lot of peristence on the part of Kaman and his company, the Ovation guitar weathered snide comments from traditionalists that greeted its debut, and went on to earn international acceptance among both professional and amateur guitarists. Today it is a familiar member of the world's workhorse guitar fraternity.

The first production of the instruments took place in an old building in New Hartford, a quaint New England town in northwestern Connecticut. Since Kaman Aerospace was heavily involved in aircraft manufacturing, the company's tool and machining department was certainly qualified to turn out precision molds and fixtures. But unlike other guitar manufacturers, who made their jigs from hardwood and marine plywood, and high-density particle board, Ovation's engineering staff fabricated fixtures from aluminum and steel, fitting them with special toggle clamps and other trappings of space-age technology.

The Ovation guitars featured a one-piece body of molded fiberglass (the company developed a special formulation, which it called Lyrachord), a wooden head-

block bonded to the inside of the backshell, a spruce top, and a standard wood neck with an adjustable truss rod. Although there were some variations on the traditional X-bracing pattern in the design of the soundboard's reinforcement structure, the main features of the X-brace design were initially retained.

As time went on, and Ovation expanded its line of guitars, there was a need to develop other bracing configurations to achieve the necessary tonal balance with the rounded synthetic backs. Research produced 12 different bracing patterns. The company now assigns these throughout its acoustic guitar line.

Around 1976, as Ovation expanded, the New Hartford facility could no longer house the entire staff and the expanded manufacturing operations. There was some space available at other Kaman Aerospace locations in Connecticut. The engineering, marketing, purchasing, and sales departments were moved to offices near the Kaman corporate headquarters site in Bloomfield (Box 529, Bloomfield, CT 06002). At the same time, more room was needed for the development of the Adamas guitar — a newly introduced instrument that had a composite, laminated soundboard as well as a synthetic body. In the northeastern part of Connecticut, in a small town called Moosup, Kaman had a facility for manufacturing aircraft wing and body parts, but there was some room available for the guitarmaking division.

Today, the 12-string guitars, the Custom Legend, the classical, and the Anniversary models are made in New Hartford, as are all the Ovation solidbody electric instruments (except for the UK-2, which has a synthetic Urelite body). The necks and fretboards for all Ovation guitars also are made in New Hartford on automatic profiling and slotting machines. The body shells, or "bowls," come from Moosup, and necks are shipped in special padded cubbyhole containeers to the Moosup plant for final assembly.

Various bridges, soundboards, and bracings are made in both facilities, according to need and according to the location of special tools. The Moosup plant makes the Matrix guitars (fiberglass bowls, wood-laminate tops, and synthetic necks with rosewood fretboards); Academy guitars (beginners' instruments featuring molded soundboards with integral braces); Applause guitars (beginner/student instruments); Balladeer model Ovations (braced with a modified "A"-bracing, and fitted with wood necks), and Legend model Ovations (standard "A"-braced tops, wood necks,

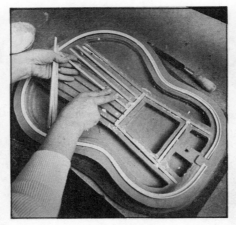

LEFT: *Roundback shells for Ovation's Balladeer model come out of their molds to cool before further processing.* **RIGHT:** *After glue is applied to the braces, they are placed in a rubber mold.*

A finished soundboard is polished against an extra-wide buffing wheel to reduce localized streaks.

and Lyrachord backs). Ovation's premier guitars — the top-of-the-line Adamas series — also are made in Moosup. The Adamas I features an epoxy-graphite soundboard, a solid walnut neck with a carved peghead, a walnut fretboard, and a carved bridge. Ovation's Adamas II features the same graphite soundboard and has a five-piece neck laminated with maple and mahogany; a walnut fretboard; and fancy veneers on the peghead. And the newest addition to the Adamas family is the prototype Adamas cutaway model.

Jim Rickard, Ovation's Engineering and Quality Control Manager, gave us some background on the fiberglass bowl. "Charles H. Kaman set out to build a better guitar by using synthetic materials," Jim recalls. "He had quite a lot of experience working with fiberglass and with spruce. With Charlie's direction, we proceeded to experiment with guitar construction. When we looked at the back, we found that from an acoustic standpoint, the square back was really not the most efficient shape to make. There was no feeling that any real acoustic research had gone into the evolution of the squarish back, and we felt more comfortable with a rounded shape.

"The fiberglass back does give you a change in the sound, and the sound can be modified by changing the bracing on the top. Is wood still a better material? It may be better if you only make a conventional X-braced dreadnought; but if you use some of the special bracing we have designed to go along with the fiberglass back, I do not believe you can say that. 'Better' is a very subjective word. We built a lot of prototypes and we played them all, and then let our ears make the decision. We found that the curved back has a lot of advantages in its reflectance of sound."

Today, the Ovation wood neck block has been replaced by a molded-in-place fiberglass block, and instead of "laying up" two fiberglass sheets to make a molded back, as the company did at first, the backs are molded in a single stage.

The Ovation instrument's round back has been its most striking feature, and

more than a few buyers have made their purchase on looks alone. But, according to Rickard, there is far more to the shape than cosmetics. "One of the keys to the instrument's success is that it has been seen on stage a lot," he explains, "and the one main reason for that is that the guitar proved it could hold up well for traveling. Compared to traditional designs, the guitar is practically indestructible. Players also have seemed to like the way the Ovation acoustic/electric pickup unit handles."

Rather than using conventional nitrocellulose lacquer finishes, Ovation applies a polyester finish to its instruments. The company has found polyester to be more durable, easier to apply, and far more resistant to checking, cracking, and temperature changes than lacquer.

Having pioneered the use of synthetic materials for guitar body parts, Ovation is currently advancing the technology of synthetic soundboards. The laminated Adamas guitar soundboards feature an outer .005″ layer of a graphite/epoxy compound, an .030″ inner-core birch veneer, and an outer .005″ layer of graphite/epoxy. "That produces a top," says Rickard, "of similar overall stiffness to a spruce top that is .100″ thick. It has better resistance to the effects of humidity, and a far more even stiffness [inch for inch] across its entire surface. The characteristic problem with spruce is that in time the spruce has a tendency to arch up or buckle and become less than flat. The graphite tends to remain very flat. Although it will deflect somewhat, it is stable and does not continue to arch more and more."

Today, Larry Coryell and *Frets* Advisory Board member Roy Clark are among the guitarists who perform on Adamas instruments. The detractors who ridiculed Charles Kaman's first roundbacks little imagined that one day they would see the descendants of those guitars on the stages of the *Tonight Show* and Carnegie Hall, but Kaman enjoyed the last laugh. And now all the erstwhile critics can say is, "What will he come up with next!"

— **Roger H. Siminoff**

A special machine automatically cuts, drills, sands, and shapes bridges — from blanks to finished piece.

Guild Musical Instruments

IN A TINY corner of America's smallest state is the manufacturing facility of one of our most prominent guitar makers, Guild.

The Rhode Island company was founded by the late Alfred Dronge, a New York City classical guitarist, teacher, and music store owner. Early in 1952 he learned that some used equipment was available from the Epiphone company, and decided that the time was right to begin production of his own guitar line.

The resultant Guild company was small enough during those first years for Mr. Dronge to oversee every phase of the operation, even taking responsibility for personally checking each instrument before it left the factory.

After four years of expansion, the New York facility became inefficient. There wasn't enough room for desperately needed equipment, and the handling of increasingly large incoming and outgoing lumber shipments became more and more difficult. In 1956 the company was moved to Hoboken, New Jersey, where production capabilities could be more easily expanded as Guild grew. During the years 1968 and 1969, under the leadership of company president Leon Tell, the factory was moved to Westerly, Rhode Island, where it remains today.

The first instruments produced by Guild were large-body acoustic/electric jazz guitars, such as the A500 and CE 100. Then, in the early sixties, the demand for steel-string guitars prompted the company to introduce a series of fixed-bridge, flat-top models, including a 12-string. Today the line boasts more than two dozen steel-string models, an acoustic bass, and four classical styles.

The Westerly plant occupies about 80,000 square feet of production and storage space, and has a staff of 200 workers. Guild's executive offices are in Elizabeth, New Jersey.

One of the first things that impresses the visitor to the Rhode Island facility is that the operation isn't "machine crazy." Equipment is the basic thing one expects to find in a guitar plant, but at Guild the directors prefer to let machines do only what equipment can do best, while allowing people to do what *they* do best. Many of the operations are standard in domestic guitar construction: braces are shaped by hand, the binding is taped on instead of being cloth-wrapped, dovetails are hand-fitted, nuts are filed by hand and necks are sanded by hand. Naturally, many tools and fixtures are employed to assure consistency, and devices such as pattern carvers are used to rough out guitar necks.

Guild technicians keep a watchful eye on the content of their woods, possibly because the plant is located so close to the coastal region (all other major eastern manufacturers are much farther inland). Each guitar is measured and numbered for moisture content. This information is retained for future reference.

Various glues are used on the instruments, according to structural and production requirements. High-frequency (high-speed curing) glues are utilized to hold fretboards to necks, but aliphatic (white) glues are used in all other stages of construction.

The soundboards are Alaskan spruce, selected and graded according to instrument model. Even though the Brazilian rosewood shortage has eased, Guild continues to use East Indian rosewood "because of its stability, not availability," says vice president Neil Lilien.

Craftsmen at Guild are trained for multiple operations and have the opportunity to work at various stations. Certain workers, however, specialize in construction of the company's classical line. All of the workmen at the end of the production line are guitarists capable of checking, playing, and testing instruments as they are completed. Craftsmen throughout other stages have varied experience ranging from woodworking, cabinet making, and guitar building to highly diversified machine operation.

Guild's 6- and 12-string models all use a single "X" bracing pattern with a rosewood bridge plate. Ivory nuts and saddles are used whenever possible (depending on supply), and celluloid is utilized for all bindings.

A lot of attention goes into the last stages of assembly. Neck adjustment is done as a part of the final setup, rather than at some time earlier in production. Instruments hang for seven to ten days after the spraying of the last finish coat, to allow the lacquer to completely set before the final sanding and polishing. Once the instrument has been completely assembled, finished, strung, and tested, it is placed in a large plastic bag and stored. Later it is taken out and once again checked for defects, scratches, loose machines, intonation, neck warp, and other possible flaws.

At various intervals during the production day, instruments are randomly pulled from the final inspection line and thoroughly checked with a Strobo-Tuner to ensure that there have been no production variations in fretting scales, neck-to-body location, bridge position, or saddle placement.

When the instruments finally meet Guild's expectations, they are wiped free of fingerprints, cased, cartoned, and shipped to waiting dealers.

— *Mark Andrews*

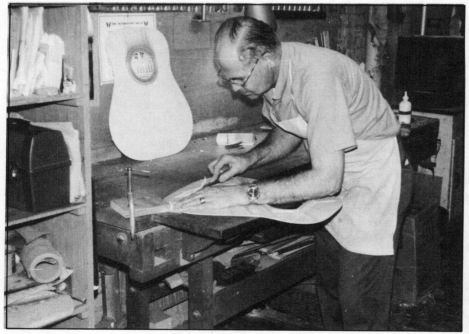

TOP LEFT: *Metal spring clips are used to hold the kerfed lining in position during gluing.* **TOP RIGHT:** *The peghead binding is cut, shaped, and fitted by hand.* **BOTTOM RIGHT:** *Braces are glued on to the tops full size and hand shaped to the correct angle.* **BOTTOM LEFT:** *Binding notches around the body are cut on a table shaper.*

Santa Cruz Guitar Company

SANTA CRUZ IS a small city located about 50 miles south of San Francisco, along the picturesque California coast. It is home to a sizable community of artists and craftsmen, and also is home to a guitar company that bears the city's name.

In 1975, two guitar repairmen, Richard Hoover and William Davis, and college student Bruce Ross felt they "could build a better guitar." Of the three, Ross really was not sure how he could contribute to the actual making of a guitar. Today he says frankly, "I was the only one who never even held a screwdriver. I was going to be a psychologist." But eventually William left, and Ross began practicing his new trade.

The first guitar they built was a dreadnought. Richard remembers, "We wanted to combine our talents and our experiences. We had ideas about bracing and scale lengths, neck shapes, et cetera, and we wanted to put it all together. We were fortunate. Our first guitar was sold before we made it — that was a good feeling."

Bruce adds, "We started at a good time — folks were just starting to come out and say that they were luthiers. It was still novel to have people working out of a garage."

To date, the two sole employees of the Santa Cruz Guitar Company have made more than 140 guitars — including instruments that have gone to such clients as guitarists Tony Rice, Al Orzeck, and Eric Clapton. The current line comprises four basic models: a standard dreadnought; a small-bodied "Nick Lucas-size guitar," called the model H; a special flat-top cutaway with a carved and arched back (the model FTC); and a model F that is "like a [Gibson] J185 body, available with mix-and-match trim, to order." Prices of the company's products range from $1,250.00 to $2,500.00.

The shop is located in a small industrial complex at 328 Ingalls Street (Santa Cruz, CA 95061). The totally dehumidified facility consists of one large room used for sawing, body assembly, and other shaping and fitting operations; a spray room; a staging room, where partially finished components await final assembly; and a buffing and polishing room. A smaller side room is used for storage of fretboard, neck, and bridge blanks.

Like many makers of flat-top steel-strings, Ross and Hoover believe in the standard X-bracing system for soundboards. Hoover speaks for both builders when he says, "We used the X-bracing because it seems to be the most tried and true method to produce what people identify as a *guitar sound*. Also, it has worked for about 100 years. I haven't heard a new bracing system that has produced an appreciably better sound on a guitar. We've experimented quite a lot, but we've still come back to this system."

Pointing to a soundboard in a gluing fixture, Ross says, "Some makers do not believe that there is a treble or bass side of the instrument. We think there is. We attempt to leave the mass of the bracing in the center of the soundboard and relieve it towards the outer edges. We tap on the braces to get a feeling for when the soundboard is most alive. We try to get the top to 'light up.' We don't tune the braces to a note, we just keep removing wood until the soundboard basically comes alive. When we get there, we stop."

Richard added, "We do it to backs, too. That's one reason we've stayed away from a carving machine, because this way we can control the tone and we know when to stop. We've learned to keep some mass near the treble side of the bridge plate and to remove more from the bass side."

"The type of wood you use," Bruce says, "gives the instrument character. We use four woods: German spruce, Sitka spruce, Englemann spruce, and cedar."

Explaining the differences, Richard notes, "German seems to be very hard and very stiff. It gives an especially sharp tone, a bright sound. Sitka is a denser wood, not quite as stiff across the grain, and it gives a good bottom- to-midrange sound. Of course, these are all generalities, because each piece of wood is different. Englemann spruce seems to be extremely light weight, very low in density and almost pithy [soft, porous, like tissue]. It looks like German, but it has a softer, lighter sound. The cedar tends to be extremely fragile across the grain, with very low density, but showing high strength with the grain. Overall, it [cedar] can be a nightmare, because once a crack develops it tends to run and you can't stop it.

"We use Sitka for the braces — vertical grain. We had a lot of material cut up at one time and we kept all the excess." Bruce adds, "On the treble side we will use the higher density wood [for braces], and on the bass side we use the softer wood."

To locate the braces on the soundboard, the makers use plastic templates, drawing the brace positions with pencil. If the braces conform to standard positioning, they are clamped in a specially fabricated fixture. Non-standard bracing configurations are individually C-clamped.

The soundboards go through a drum sander built by Ross and Hoover. The wood is sanded until proper flexibility — determined by hand flexing — is achieved.

Ross and Hoover favor maple for the bridge plates. Richard explains, "Maple seems to be less prone to checking, and it seems to have very good strength. Another

LEFT: *Dick Hoover uses a stationary power buffer to polish the final layer of lacquer on a completed instrument.* **CENTER**: *Bruce Ross indicates the stiffer treble region of a Santa Cruz soundboard, with its slightly heavier bracing.* **RIGHT**: *Hoover and Ross built their own drum sander for thinning soundboards to the point of optimum flexibility.*

important feature is that it is a lighter weight [than the traditional rosewood bridge plate] and is still hard, still strong, with no resins [rosewood is high in resin content, hampering gluing], and it's a lot drier."

In building their guitars, Ross and Hoover use seven different cement types. "Most of the wood-to-wood [joints] gluing uses Titebond, except for neck joints, which use white glue," Bruce says. "It's easy to get out — not that we plan to take it apart; we spend a lot of time fitting our dovetails, and they are true — but someday we might have to get in there [to the neck joint], and white glues are easier to take apart. Celluloid bindings are held on with Duco cement, inlays with epoxy. We also epoxy the truss rods —an unusual assembly where the truss rod nut is located in the very heel of the neck and a hole is drilled through the headblock for access. Fretboard-to-neck bonds are made with Titebond, but the fretboard-to-soundboard junction is made with white glue."

Richard, noting that he and Bruce always strive to purchase the best materials they can find, says, "We don't like to copy other guitars, but we will make a custom guitar on special order. Tony Rice wanted us to copy the general styling and sound of his 1934 [C.F. Martin] D-28. He wanted a

guitar that sounded forty years old. He wanted an old Martin sound. We used a cedar top to get the real old, warm, response. He wanted the bass and said he could [by technique] get his own treble."

When asked how they knew whether they could achieve such a sound, Richard replies, "Just knowing our woods and how we build guitars, and knowing how we achieve different effects — we put all the things together that we knew would give us a really bassy, warm guitar. For instance, the cedar top is a warmer, more open sound, not good for treble. We scalloped the braces, which cuts out the midrange. In fact, since the guitar set up a bit differently once it was strung, we even had to reset the neck the first day it was finished, because the top pulled up more than we anticipated. But we did achieve the effect he wanted. The rosewood back and sides — done at his request — also helped. Usually we don't work with rosewood; we work with maple and mahogany. We use maple on the FTC, and also use German spruce on that model, because we want good projection, a bright sound, and nice separation."

Santa Cruz guitars are finished in a nitrocellulose lacquer made by the Frazie Paint Company in southern California. Bruce explains, "The lacquer is applied in a

light flow coat mixed about 50/50 [half and half, thinner and lacquer]. We do three coats of lacquer, sand it off, do three more, sand it off, do three coats more, sand it off, then do two coats — and we put less lacquer on the top with each process. At each spraying, the top gets one less coat. The top comes out having thinner lacquer than do the back and sides. Then we polish the whole instrument on a buffing machine."

Ebony is used for bridges, fretboards, and peghead veneers. All shaping is done by hand. Richard comments, "So much of our work is custom that we want to do it all by hand. Necks, for example, are all different. We can control the finished product a lot more to our liking."

But Bruce admits that it's tough to make a living when you spend so much time on detail. "Doing this in the twentieth century has to be a lifestyle, because it's definitely not a money-maker project," he says. "It is not feasible to build good guitars fast. If we could, it would not be as fun."

Do Ross and Hoover ever take shortcuts? Ross answers simply, summing up their philosophy: "We will use any tool that does a job better or faster, but we don't compromise on our guitars."

— *Roger H. Siminoff*

John Monteleone

JOHN MONTELEONE's "burning desire to make instruments" led him three years ago to set up his own business in Bayshore, New York (Long Island). In his cozy workshop, he builds more than a half-dozen guitar styles, including a carved-top model. His forte is the mandolin, and he already has made well over 70. Among John's distinguished customers is David Grisman. "I started specializing in the mandolin because I was intrigued to death by it," John says, "and I felt there was a great need for a very good mandolin."

Monteleone's career had a rather unusual and percussive beginning. "You might say everything started off with a bang!" he says. "My mother had a Stadium guitar that wasn't worth too much — it was only good for playing with a bow, the action was so bad. Once, when I was about 13, while playing with it down in the basement, I accidentally wrapped it right around an iron lolly-column and smashed the thing up. What a sound! That kind of introduced me to the inside of an instrument."

John became swept up in the folk boom of the early '60s, and decided he wanted to play guitar. He went from store to store, trying out various instruments. By 14, he had become attuned to their finer aspects and could distinguish between good, bad, and mediocre instruments. He finally bought an inexpensive Harmony 12-string — one of the two or three guitars he ever bought from music stores — and it helped him develop his craft. "It went out of whack," he recalls. "The neck warped and I couldn't play it anymore. There were no repair people that I knew of, so I figured, why not? I can't play it now, I can't lose anything. I put it in a vise and cut the neck off. I had the body of a guitar, and I had to make a neck. So that's what I did. I made a neck, put it on, and it worked real nice. I got to experiment with that guitar quite a bit later on."

Monteleone's father, a talented pattern-maker, trained in sculpture, jewelry, and the arts, strongly influenced his son from the beginning, encouraging him to do fine handwork and to develop a sense of aesthetics, creativity, and proper working habits. When John was 16, he and his father purchased wood from the H.L. Wild instrument supply company, in New York, for John's first guitar. John spent seven years building that instrument in his spare time, while attending college and pursuing other endeavors.

John attended Tarkio College, in Missouri, and graduated in 1970 with a degree in applied music. When he couldn't find a job teaching music, he returned to Long Island to work part-time for his father, and to build guitars for his friends — just for fun.

They bought the materials, and for no charge, John built the instruments.

One night while listening to the radio, John heard some fine mandolin playing. "It was really nice," he recalls. The next day, he called the radio performers. "We started talking about this and that; I told them that I built instruments and they said they were looking for someone who could do some repair work," John recalls. "I went to meet them the next day, and they were impressed with my stuff and said, 'You've got a job if you want it.' I said, 'Sure, love to!'"

From 1973 to 1976, John did repairs, custom inlay, and restoration. He made it a policy to completely inspect and document many of the fine instruments he had access to — especially several Lloyd Loar F-5 mandolins. he also met luthier Jimmy D'Aquisto. "He never formally taught me, but I absorbed a lot of ideas and information from Jimmy," John says.

John never has been interested in mass production. "It has no purpose for me," he says. "It serves a purpose for 'putting a chicken in everybody's pot,' and that's good. But the caliber of instrument that I'm attempting to make is very specialized. It's taken a long time to get to that point."

From the beginning, Monteleone has tried to build a mandolin that reflects his own musical tastes. He likes mandolins with "bottom character" (bass response), so he creates a slightly larger air chamber by elongating the scroll. He uses a shortened, non-bracketed, free-standing finger-rest, lowered 1/8" below the strum line. To allow the mandolin to ring clear, he designed the finger-rest so that it does not obstruct the treble f-hole. The fretboard extension is sectioned and shortened. John also uses his own finely designed solid brass tailpiece.

"In terms of tone," he says, "I think that I've been able to open the instrument up to a broader spectrum of tone — to increase the overall tonal response from the bass to the treble register, and in between. Balance is what I am after. The challenge to me is to get that instrument to be responsive at every level. Physically, I like the idea of form and function."

John's workshop is equipped with a wide array of hand tools, many of which are custom made. He also uses power tools —a band saw, drill press, belt sander, and home-made buffing wheel. He has a separate temperature/humidity controlled area for drying and storage of wood, and a spray-booth. "I generally use about 12 coats of natural lacquer, water-thin, for buildup," he says. "When those are cut down, the finish is about half as thick, leaving a finish that is protective, yet minimal. Then I hand rub it to a high gloss."

John Monteleone has designed an unusually small finger-rest for his F-series mandolins, to avoid obstructing the f-hole.

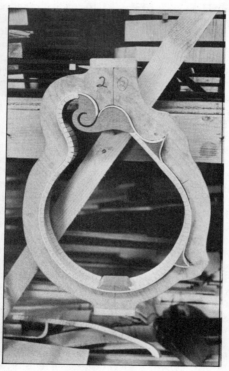

LEFT: *Besides being an excellent craftsman, Monteleone is an innovative and versatile instrument designer.* **RIGHT:** *The complete rim assembly includes head block, tail block, point blocks, and kerfed lining.*

John uses local sources and independent suppliers for his woods and finds "excellent woods at very reasonable prices." He chooses wood by hardness and grain, according to the sound his customer wants. Wide grain is used for more bass, a "chunkier" kind of sound; narrow grain is used for clarity and sweetness of tone.

For his mandolin tops, Monteleone uses German spruce almost exclusively because of its hardness and overall re-

sponse. For the sides and back, he uses Tyrolean maple, which he says lends a subtle softness and flavor to the tone. He finds that Vermont maple, harder than the European variety, works very well for necks. "I think rosewood has its place for certain instruments, too," John explains. "In certain flat-top designs, different varieties of rosewood might be a good relationship for back and sides. I think mahogany flat-tops have been underrated to a large degree. A lot of them sound excellent." Usually, John buys rough logs or planes, which he cuts to size and end-treats to control drying. He then slices the "wedges," stacking them to dry for at least two years.

John uses mother-of-pearl or abalone for delicate inlay decorations. To attach the binding to the routed wooden surface, John makes "glue" by dissolving cellulose nitrate in acetone. Titebond glue is used for all the other construction, but John warns, "You have to experiment with the glue to find out how to use it. For example, putting fretboards on could drive you nuts. The glue is a little thick, and it adds a lot of moisture to the neck. Several times I've put a fretboard on, and it [the glue] has added so much moisture between the joint that the neck has just bent backwards. In those cases, I end up taking the neck apart and straightening it out."

John works strictly on commission, and currently has about an eight-month waiting list for any of his five mandolin models. His instruments range from the very plain "nuts and bolts" two-point (with either oval holes or f-holes) model that sells for $1,200.00, to the F-5 style model and his top-of-the-line "Grand Artist," each of which sells for $2,000.00. "The round or oval hole shapes the tone completely differently," he explains. "It makes a hollower, deeper, more resonant sound. The f-hole has a lot more cutting power; it's a more powerful instrument, and its sound is intended to carry a greater distance."

Though John is in the process of expanding his shop, he is not likely to increase production to more than his current two mandolins per month. "I have had several apprentices, but I continue to work by myself. You might say that I enjoy having total control of the instrument. My concept is a total one. I look at a stack of wood first, and can see it as a finished instrument. The idea of understanding tone, volume, and sound came together after my first guitar. The quest for trying to refine and control tone is always a learning process. I don't think you ever sit on top of the situation completely and say 'This is the answer,' because you're working with different pieces of wood all the time. Each time you pick up wood to make an instrument, you turn the page. You've moved on to a new set of circumstances to deal with, which is good. It's a continuing challenge, which keeps me motivated. I think I'll never stop learning about it."

— *Ira Landgarten*

Stelling Banjo Works

GEOFF STELLING's first banjo "sounded terrible."

"In 1969 I made a Gibson copy, using Gibson parts and making the shell myself," says Stelling, describing the beginning of his career. "I fit it all together the best I could, and it sounded terrible."

It is just as well that Stelling's first effort didn't fulfill his expectations. Frustrated by the banjo's sub-par sound, he kept reworking the instrument until he had developed what is today the patented Stelling wedge-fit tone chamber, a feature that has helped make Stelling Banjo Works in Spring Valley, California one of the most successful young instrument companies in America.

Geoff was still in the Navy back in 1974 when he began getting orders for instruments. What started as a spare-time avocation became a full-time business when he left the Service a little less than two years later. Interestingly, the idea for his tone chamber design came to him from watching Navy engineers solve problems of fitting things together. He devised a tone chamber, wood rim, and flange with respective angular mating surfaces. The more the banjo's head bolts were tightened, the more secure the whole structure became. The compressive force made the rim virtually indestructible, since it compressed the rim inward on itself. That seed grew into a vision of an entire line of banjos featuring the Stelling Pot Assembly, and during the space of two months in the fall of 1975 Geoff left the Navy, sold his house in San Diego, bought a shop in nearby Spring Valley, and with his wife, Gretchen, moved into an adjacent home there.

Geoff turned out his early commercial instruments singlehandly, and soon found that he was selling banjos as fast as he could make them. Even though Gretchen was helping by running the office (which she still does), he needed more help; but the idea of being strapped with a large payroll really didn't appeal to him. Fortunately, there were some craftsmen around who were interested in pooling their talents. A partnership evolved, with each member performing a part of the operation and being responsible for his own workmanship and materials. At that time, production ranged between two and five instruments per month. The partnership arrangement only lasted for a few years, however. As production increased, Geoff found himself at the helm of a growing enterprise, responsible for employees and a payroll in spite of himself.

Today, the Stelling line boasts seven models. They range from instruments with plain wood components, simple inlay patterns, and nickel plating to very elaborately carved, stained, scrimshawn, inlaid, en-

graved, and gold-plated models. Some of the models are the Bellflower, the Golden Cross, the Gospel, the Staghorn, and the Scrimshaw, each reflecting the artistic motif that its model name implies.

Geoff uses walnut, birch, curly maple, and regular maple in making his various banjos. In the past, all Stelling models featured ebony fretboards. A few years ago Geoff switched from ebony to Ebanol, a synthetic plastic-like substance that is as black and dense as ebony and far more stable. "I was having a lot of trouble with the ebony cracking and shrinking," Geoff told us, "and I had bought it from reliable sources, too. If it's not aged sufficiently, it's going to shrink, and then the frets begin to stick out of the side of the binding and after a couple of months everything starts looking sloppy. I want my banjos to last. Ebanol takes inlays better and takes the frets about the same as ebony — and it's jet black." Geoff still buys ebony, using it for his peghead veneers, which he feels is a practical and traditional application. He theorizes that the cracking and checking problem is solved to some extent because of the finish applied to the peghead surface. In addition, he feels that the visible ebony grain is a nice touch on a peghead.

Stelling Banjo Works now employs nine people. Although there is some overlapping of responsibilities, each craftsperson has a particular, preferred specialty. The departments are basically divided into rough sawing, neck making, inlay artistry, rim building, resonator building, finishing and staining, and final assembly. After the instruments are completed, Geoff personally plays and checks out each one. He brings them back to his workbench for any necessary adjustments before signing the Stelling label that is affixed to each rim.

Stelling uses a lacquer, Fuller-Plast, made by Fuller-O'Brien in California. The two-part compound is mixed prior to spraying. Its drying and hardening is accelerated to limit "blushing" and finish checking, and to allow for the application of heavy coats without the finish running. Geoff is currently working on new sources for finishing lacquers, though satisfied with his present supplier. He foresees changes in regulations governing industrial use of such products, or possible shortages. "There are going to be a lot of cutbacks on how many gallons you can use," he says, "and we're getting ready for it."

Stelling models are available with a few different tone chamber designs, but all have the patented Stelling wedge-fit concept. There is one arch-top version and two flat-top versions. The flat-tops basically differ in weight. The rims are constructed of numerous wedge-shaped maple blocks glued in

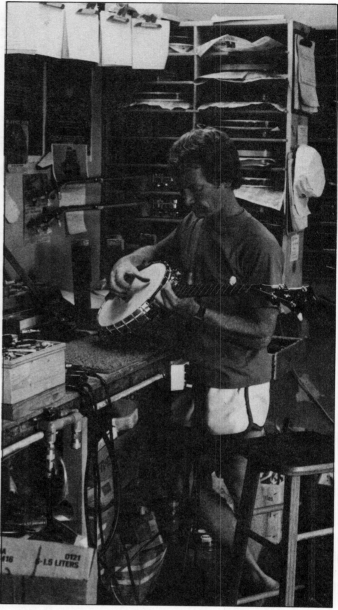

LEFT: *Geoff Stelling has devised a fixture to hold the banjo in an upright position during final assembly.* **RIGHT:** *Jon Wegand is Stelling's scrimshander and also does all of the assembly work. Geoff then checks out the instruments and signs the labels.*

various interlocking-grain orientations. When the wood rim is compressed between the flange and the tone chamber, says Geoff, "nothing can make it delaminate."

Frets visited the Stelling factory on the same day that Dale Reno (banjo player Don Reno's son) came out to evaluate one of the first Stelling mandolins, a unique oval-soundhole design. At that time, three more prototype models were already being made, including a new f-hole model. Geoff prefers to characterize the soundholes of that design as s-shaped.

"I don't want to get locked into making an F-5 [Gibson] copy," he says. "I don't want anybody to think we have anything like that. We want to experiment around with all kinds of dimensions."

Given Geoff Stelling's flair for experimentation, someday his mandolins may be on the "most-imitated" list themselves.
— *Jim Hatlo*

The OME Company

ALTHOUGH THE FIRST production instruments made under the OME Company name came out in 1971, the story doesn't begin there. It really begins ten years earlier, when Colorado craftsman Charlie Ogsbury started producing his aluminum-rim ODE banjos.

Back in the early days of the '60s folk revival there simply weren't any bargain Japanese imports, quality custom makers, or even much in the way of factory instruments to choose from. If you were lucky you might latch onto one of the good instruments. If not, you had to settle for the inexpensive Harmony or Kay banjos.

To fill the void, ODE started marketing its simple, aluminum-rim banjo, an instrument that had quality construction, a minimum of frills, and an attractive price. By the mid '60s, demand for fancier and higher-quality instruments brought about an expansion of the ODE line. Models A through F (with the F model being the fanciest) featured Mastertone-style tone rings, with either mahogany, walnut, or rosewood five-piece laminated necks. Most of all, however, the company offered impeccable workmanship. In 1966 ODE was sold to the Baldwin Piano and Organ Company, and the firm eventually moved to Arkansas.

After the expiration of the five-year "no competition clause" that was part of the purchase agreement with Baldwin, Charlie Ogsbury and some of his former employees formed the OME Banjo Company. With many of the techniques and ideas they had formulated while at ODE, they began producing a new line of banjos. Now, after eight years of production and three relocations, they have come full circle and are back in the old ODE factory outside of Boulder, Colorado. In May of 1979, Charlie became inactive in the day-to-day operations and Jeff Wood was appointed to the position of president.

Initially the OME line featured a simple 5/16" brass rod as the tone ring in the lower-priced models, and a Bacon & Day-type tone chamber on higher-priced models. The rod-type was recently discontinued, but the B&D type is a two-piece tone ring using a 1/4" cold-rolled steel rod with an angular-shaped .060" brass spinning seat over it. Like the old brass rod ring, the B&D-type tone system is supported by a 1/2"-thick laminated maple rim, veneered to match the neck and resonator.

Largely due to the demands of bluegrass players, OME has added what it calls its "chime" tone ring. The "chime" tone chamber, as that on most bluegrass banjos made today, is essentially a Mastertone-style flathead tone chamber of cast-and-

machined brass, fitted to a 3/4" laminated maple rim. Although any OME model now can be ordered with either style of tone ring, the majority of OME's 5-string banjos are made with the cast "chime" tone chamber, while most 4-string models are made with the spun system.

A few years ago, while visiting the OME factory, I had the opportunity to play two banjos, each with a different style of tone ring. My impression was that the spun system exhibited a much fuller sound, with many more overtones, harmonics, or partials than did the cast model. The cast ring produced a crisper, sharper, cleaner note of shorter duration or sustain. Both instruments appeared to have about the same volume, although the spun system seemed to surround the instrument with more music, and the cast system appeared to project the sound forward more.

OME's highest-priced rosewood and maple models feature a resonator back that is carved from a solid piece of wood and is flat on the inside. The major differences between one model and the next involve the type of wood and the degree of frills and ornamentation that is offered. Selections range from the relatively simple mahogany Single X model, at about $800.00, to the fancy carved, inlaid, and gold-plated rosewood Juggernaut III or maple "Big Mogul," at $4,500.00 each.

Over the past five years, OME's tenor and plectrum sales have increased from about five to ten percent of its total output to the current 25 to 30 percent ratio, with the majority of the 4-strings sold being plectrums. Sales of open-back frailing models have dropped off over the last three or four years, although recently there have been some signs of renewed interest.

Banjos, more than most other stringed instruments, seem to lend themselves to assembly-line production because of their bolt-together construction. OME makes various component parts in large runs and then assembles them according to the demand for different models. Ed Woodward, an OME partner and the shop manager, does most of the milling. "We try to make enough parts at one time to last us six months," he says; "by doing things in large batches we save setup time and unnecessary milling operations."

With the exception of bracket hooks, Schaller tuning machines, and Remo heads, OME makes all its own parts. In fact, the company is currently the sole supplier of the L-shaped bracket shoes used by other makers.

Most resonator-type banjos built today use the Gibson-style tube-and-plate system

LEFT: *A row of tenor necks awaits peghead shaping.* **RIGHT:** *Parts for the instruments are constructed in batches.*

as a hook support. OME uses a flange plate to join the rim to the resonator, along with the traditional shoes bolted to the rim (as used on the Fairbanks, Bacon & Day, and Paramount banjos).

The low- to medium-priced OME models all have one-piece mahogany necks. The Juggernaut and Mogul models each feature a laminated, five-piece mahogany, maple, or rosewood neck, reminiscent of the old ODE line. The necks are roughed out on a table shaper to remove excess wood, and final shaping is done by hand.

All models designated triple-X or above have bound ebony fretboards. Five-string banjos come with a standard 26¼″ or long 32¼″ scale. Scales for plectrums and tenors are 26¼″ and 22¾″ respectively. On all models, OME uses the standard dual coordinator rod system for attaching the neck to the pot. The truss rod is adjustable through the heel, requiring that the neck be removed from the pot for adjustments.

Routing for the inlays is done with a pantograph that uses a master template of the peghead and fretboard inlay patterns. This makes for very accurate and consistent cutting of the inlay cavities. Mother-of-pearl and abalone are used for inlays, according to model and instrument grade.

Lacquer is used as a finish medium. Dry sanding is done between each of the six coats and the parts are wheel-buffed after the last coat to bring out the high gloss of the finish.

— *Bob Krueger*

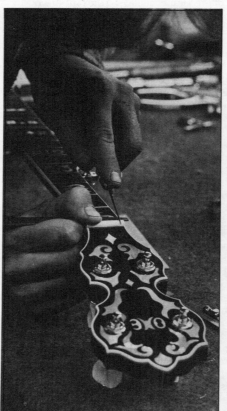

LEFT: *String notches are hand-filed into the nuts.* **RIGHT:** *Assembling all the OME parts into a finished banjo.*

APPENDIX
Recommended Reading

HISTORY

Artis, Bob, *Bluegrass,* Nordon Publications, New York, NY 1975.

Cantwell, Robert, "Believing In Bluegrass," *Atlantic Monthly,* vol. 229, number 3, March 1972, p. 52-54, 58-60.

Cohen, John, "Bluegrass," *Sing Out!, vol. 14, number 3, July 1964, p. 97-103.*

Green, Douglas B., The Origins Of Country Music, Hawthorn Books, New York, NY 1976, p. 115-130.

Hill, Fred, *Grass Roots: An Illustrated History of Bluegrass and Mountain Music,* Academy Books, Rutland, Vermont, 1980.

Lehmann-Haupt, Christopher, "Out Of My Mind On Bluegrass," *New York Times Magazine,* vol. 119, number 41, 140, Sept. 13, 1970.

Lomax, Alan, "Bluegrass Background: Folk Music With Overdrive," *Esquire,* vol. 52, number 4, Oct. 1959, p.108.

Malone, Bill C., *Country Music U.S.A.: A Fifty-Year History,* University of Texas Press, Austin, Texas 1968.

Price, Steven D., *Old As The Hills: The Story Of Bluegrass Music,* Viking Press, New York, NY 1975.

Rinzler, Ralph, "Bill Monroe: 'The Daddy Of Bluegrass Music'" *Sing Out!,* vol. 13, number 1, Feb.-Mar. 1963, page 5-8.

"Bill Monroe—Thirty Years," *Bluegrass Unlimited,* vol. 4, number 4, October 1969, p.2.

Rooney, James, *Bossmen: Bill Monroe & Muddy Waters,* Dial Press, New York, NY 1971.

Rosenberg, Neil V., *Bill Monroe And His Blue Grass Boys: An Illustrated Discography,* Country Music Foundation Press, Nashville, TN 1974.

"From Sound To Style: The Emergence Of Bluegrass," *Journal Of American Folklore,* vol. 80, number 316, Apr.-June 1967, p. 143-150.

Smith, L. Mayne, "An Introduction To Bluegrass," *Journal Of American Folklore,* vol. 78, number 309, July-Sept. 1965, p. 245-256.

BANJO

Davis, Janet, *Backup Banjo,* Mel Bay, 1981.

Dillard, Douglas; Dillard, Kathy Gleason; Knopf, Bill, *Bluegrass Banjo Style Of Douglas Flint Dillard,* Almo (dist. by Columbia Pictures Publications), Hialeah, FL 1980.

Erbsen, Wayne, *Starting Bluegrass Banjo From Scratch,* Pembroke Music Company (Carl Fischer), New York, NY 1978.

Knopf, Bill, *Theory Of Chord Construction For 5-String And Plectrum Banjo,* Ryckman & Beck, 1977.

Hot Licks And Fiddle Tunes For Bluegrass Banjo Players, Chappell, 1976.

Pardee, Pete, *Scales And Arpeggios For 5-String Banjo,* Harbinger Publications, Miwuk Village, CA 95346.

Trischka, Tony, *Melodic Banjo,* Oak, New York, NY 1976.Trischka, Tony and Keith, Bill, *Bill Keith: Banjo,* Oak, New York, NY 1978.

Scruggs, Earl, *Earl Scruggs And The 5-String Banjo,* Peer International, New York, NY 1968.

Weissman, Dick, *5-String Banjo,* Vol. 1-Vol. 3, Big Three, New York, NY.

Bluegrass Songbook, Big Three New York, NY 1976.

Wernick, Peter, *Bluegrass Banjo,* Oak, New York, NY 1974.

MANDOLIN

Grisman, David, Bluegrass Mandolin Solos, available from *Mandolin World News,* Box 2255, San Rafael, CA 94912.

Ten Tunes In Nine Keys, available from *Mandolin World News,* Box 2255, San Rafael, CA 94912.

Statman, Andy, *Jesse McReynolds/Mandolin,* Oak Publications, New York, NY 1979.

Teach Yourself Bluegrass Mandolin, Oak, New York, NY.

Tottle, Jack, *Bluegrass Mandolin,* Oak publications, New York, NY 1974

GUITAR

Barenberg, Russ, Teach Yourself Bluegrass Guitar, AMSCO, New York, NY 1978.

How To Play Bluegrass Guitar, Acorn, 1977.

Flint, Tommy, *Authentic Bluegrass Guitar,* Mel Bay, Pacific, MO 1972.

Silverman, Jerry, *How To Play Bluegrass Guitar,* Saw Mill Music Corp. (160 High St., Hastings On Hudson) New York, NY 1982.

Flatpicker's Guitar Guide, Oak, New York, NY 1966.

Traum, Happy, *Bluegrass Guitar,* Oak, New York, NY 1974.

FiddleBrody, David, Kenny Baker, Oak, New York, NY 1978.

Glaser, Matt, *Vassar Clements,* Music Sales Corp., New York, NY 1978.

Lowinger, Gene, *Bluegrass Fiddler,* Oak, New York, NY 1974; *Bluegrass Fiddling:* Fiddlers & Styles, G. Schirmer, New York, NY 1980.

Phillips, Stacy and Kosek, Kenny, *Bluegrass Fiddle Styles,* Oak, New York, NY 1978.

DOBRO

King, Beverly, *36 Songs For Dobro,* self-published (RR1, Madill, OK 73446), 1974.

Phillips, Stacy, *The Dobro Book,* Oak, New York, NY 1977.

Bluegrass Festival Listing

ALABAMA
May, September
CHATOM, Dixie Bluegrass Festivals
Box 69
St. Stephens, AL 36569
205-246-4553

October
STEELE, Bluegrass and Old-Time Reunion
Rt. 1, Box 379
Steele, AL 35987
205-538-5159

ARIZONA
October
SCOTTSDALE, Annual Bluegrass Sunday
Music Festival
Diamondback Productions, Inc.
Box 27395
Tempe, AZ 85282
602-966-6236
602-276-3242

ARKANSAS
April
MOUNTAIN VIEW, Annual Arkansas
Folk Festival
Ozark Folk Center
Mtn. View, AR 72560
501-269-3851

April
MOUNTAIN VIEW, Southern Regional
Dulcimer Convention
Ozark Folk Center
Mtn. View, AR 72560
501-269-3851

May
MOUNTAIN VIEW, Grandpa Jones
Frailing Banjo Contest
Ozark Folk Center
Mtn. View, AR 72560
501-269-3851

May
MOUNTAIN VIEW, Merle Travis
Finger-style Guitar Contest
Ozark Folk Center
Mtn. View, AR 72560
501-269-3851

June, October
WALDRON, Turkey Track
Bluegrass Music
Box 419
Waldron, AR 72958
501-637-3862

June
VILONIA, Bluegrass Festival
1 Beth Drive
Gravel Ridge, AR 72076
501-835-2451
501-835-0040

August
VILONIA, SPBGMA Anniversary
Arkansas Bluegrass Music Weekend
SPBGMA, Box 95
Lake Ozark, MO 65049
816-65-7172

September
MOUNTAIN VIEW, Arkansas State
Fiddle Championship
Ozark Folk Center
Mtn. View, Ar 75260
501-269-3851

October
MOUNTAIN VIEW, Fiddlers Jamboree
Ozark Folk Center
Mtn. View, AR 75260
501-269-3851

November
MOUNTAIN VIEW, Annual
National Fiddlers Convention
and Championships
SPBGMA, Box 95
Lake Ozark, MO 65049
816-665-7172
501-269-3851

November
LITTLE ROCK, Bluegrass USA
International Convention
1 Beth Drive
Gravel Ridge, AR 72076
501-835-2451
501-835-0040

CALIFORNIA
April, October
NORCO, Golden West Bluegrass Festivals
Box 341
Bonsall, CA 92003
619-726-3498

April
CHINO, Prado Country Family
Festival and RV Show
1830 Commercenter E.
San Bernardino, CA 92408
714-888-6078

June
CHINO, Prado Country Family
Festival and Craft Fair
1830 Commercenter E.
San Bernardino, CA 92408
714-888-6078

June, September
GRASS VALLEY, Grass Valley
Bluegrass Festivals
California Bluegrass Association
Box 11287
San Francisco, CA 94101
415-826-3159

July
WESTWOOD, Topanga Banjo and Fiddle
Contest and Dance Festival
5922 Corbin Avenue
Tarzana, CA 91356
213-345-3795

August, September
CHINO, Prado Country Family Festivals
1830 Commercenter E.
San Bernardino, CA 92408
714-888-6078

September
YOSEMITE, The Strawberry
Bluegrass Festival
Box 210
Modesto, CA 95353
209-571-0254

CANADA
June
CARLISLE, ONT., Bluegrass Canada
Box 120
Carlisle, Ont., Canada LOR 1HO
416-689-4421

June
WOODSTOCK, ONT., The Back 40
Bluegrass Festival and Competition
127 Keats Drive
Woodstock, Ont., Canada N4S 8C1
519-539-5815

June
COLBORNE, ONT., Apple Country
Bluegrass Jamboree
Box 23 Colborne, Ont., Canada KOK 1SO
416-355-3312

June
NEWINGTON, ONT., Annual Oldtime
Country Music Weekend and
Barndance
1421 Gohier Street
St. Laurent, Quebec, Canada H4L 3K2
514-748-7251

July
WINNIPEG, MAN., Winnipeg Folk Festival
8-222 Osborne Street, S.
Winnipeg, Man., Canada R3L 1Z3
204-453-2985

July
RENFREW, ONT., Pinnacle Hill
Bluegrass Festival
Box 356
Renfrew, Ont., Canada K7V 4A4
613-432-4381

July
WATERFORD, ONT., Waterford
Bluegrass and Country Festival
RR 5
Waterford, Ont., Canada N0E 1Y0
519-443-7753

July
VANCOUVER, B.C., Annual Vancouver
Folk Music Festival
3271 Main Street
Vancouver, B.C., Canada V5V 3M6
604-879-2931

July
BOGGY CREEK, MAN., Boggy Creek's
Call of the Wild Mountain Music Festival
Box 117
Benito, Man., Canada R0L 0C0
204-935-2212

July
PALMER RAPIDS, ONT., Annual Palmer
Rapids Bluegrass Festival
RR 2
Palmer Rapids, Ont., Canada K0J 2E0
613-758-2396
416-965-4507

COLORADO
June
NEDERLAND, Annual Colorado
Bluegrass and Mountain Music Festival
Box 5026
Golden, CO 80402

June
TELLURIDE, Annual Telluride Bluegrass
and Country Music Festival
Box 908
Telluride, Co 81435
303-728-4448
303-449-6007

August
HENDERSON, Annual Rocky Mountain
Bluegrass Festival
3100 Jerry Creek South, #1107
Denver, CO 80209
303-777-2736
303-690-6312

DELAWARE
June
FELTON, Eastern Shore Bluegrass
Association's Annual Festival
Box 223
Millington, MD 21651
301-928-3613

September
GLASGOW/BEAR, Annual Delaware
Bluegrass Festival
Box 3504
Greenville, DE 19807
302-475-3454
302-654-3930

FLORIDA
March
KISSIMMEE, Kissimmee Bluegrass Festival
Box 1001
Kissimmee, FL 32741
305-846-2150

March
AUBURNDALE, Florida Bluegrass
Championships
Box 1526
Auburndale, FL 33823
813-293-4921

March, September, November
DUNNELLON, Withlacoochee
Backwater Bluegrass Jamborees
2117 S.E. 16th Lane
Ocala, FL 32671
904-732-7343

April, September
DADE CITY, Sertoma Youth Ranch
Bluegrass Festivals
The Bluegrass Parlor
4810 E. Busch Blvd.
Tampa, FL 33617
813-985-2780

April, October
LAWTEY, Lawtey Florida's Annual
Bluegrass Conventions
Box 56
Olustee, FL 32072
904-752-1563

April, September
MARIANNA, Sand Hills
Bluegrass Festivals
Rt. 4, Box 172
Marianna, FL 32446
904-482-3557
205-343-4510

May, October
TAMPA, Quail Run
Bluegrass Festivals
Box 270666
Tampa, FL 33688
813-949-5539

May, October
LAKE BUTLER, Lake Butler
Berryblossom Bluegrass Festivals
Rt. 3, Box 712
Lake Butler, FL 32054
904-496-2952

GEORGIA
April, September
ST. GEORGE, Boys From Indiana
Okefenokee Bluegrass Festivals
Music City Station
301 Shakespeare Avenue
Madison, TN 37115
615-868-0323

April
DALTON, Raymond Fairchild and
Otis Head Bluegrass Festival
3550 Cleveland Road
Dalton, GA 30720
404-259-9908

May, October
MARIETTA, Georgia's Best
Bluegrass Festivals
3456 Blue Grass Lane
Lithia Springs, GA 30057
404-948-6052

May
HIAWASSEE, Annual Hiawassee
Bluegrass Festival
Box 444
Hiawassee, GA 30546
404-864-7203

June, September
DAHLONEGA, Annual Dahlonega
Bluegrass Festivals
Box 98
Dahlonega, GA 30533
404-864-7201

May, September
ROME, Annual Armuchee
Bluegrass Festivals
2046 Mills Lane SE
Marietta, GA 30060
404-436-2630

December
JEKYLL ISLAND, New Year's
Bluegrass Festival
Box 731
Dahlonega, GA 30533
404-864-2600

IDAHO
June
WEISER, National Old-Time
Fiddlers Contest
8 East Idaho Street
Weiser, ID 83672
208-549-0452

August
HAILEY, Northern Rockies
Folk Festival
Box 656
Sun Valley, ID 83353
208-622-9371

ILLINOIS
May, July
GILSON, Harmony Pines
Bluegrass Festivals
RR 2, Box 151
Gilson, IL 61436
309-876-2381

June
CARTHAGE, Tri-State Bluegrass
Assn. Spring Festival
RR1
Kahoka, MO 63445
314-853-4344

June
MORRISON, Annual Morrison
Bluegrass and Clogger Days
SPBGMA, Box 95
Lake Ozark, MO 65049
816-665-7172

June
LINCOLN, Annual Lincoln Bluegrass
Music Weekend
SPBGMA, Box 95
Lake Ozark, MO 65049
816-665-7172

July
VIOLA, Annual Land of Lincoln
Bluegrass Music Festival
Rt. 1
Viola, IL 61486
309-596-2427

July
DUQOIN, Duqoin State Bluegrass Festival
SPBGMA, Box 95
Lake Ozark, MO 65049
816-665-7172

August
GOODFIELD, Annual Timberline
Bluegrass Music Festival
RR 2, Box 332-B
Effingham, IL 62401
217-868-2964

August
EFFINGHAM, Annual Fall Bluegrass
Festival
RR 2, Box 332-B
Effingham, IL 62401
217-868-2964

INDIANA
May
DERBY, Cedar Valley Spring
Bluegrass Festival
Star Rt. Box 329-A
Derby, IN 47525
812-836-2311

May, September
NOBLESVILLE, Indiana Friends
of Bluegrass Festivals
9310 Shenandoah Court
Indianapolis, IN 46229
317-898-9861

June, September
BEANBLOSSOM, Bill Monroe's
Annual Bluegrass Festivals
Monroe Festival Headquarters
3819 Dickerson Road
Nashville, TN 37207
615-868-3333

August
LEROY/CROWN POINT, Stoney Run
Bluegrass Festival
Lake County Parks and Recreation
2293 N. Main Street
Crown Point, IN 46307
219-769-7275

IOWA
March
CEDAR RAPIDS, Sheraton Inn Early
Spring Bluegrass Festival
SPBGMA, Box 95
Lake Ozark, MO 65049
816-665-7172
319-366-8671

May
SIGOURNEY, Annual Sigourney
Bluegrass Music Festival
SPBGMA, Box 95
Lake Ozark, MO 65049
816-664-7172
515-622-3501

May
COUNCIL BLUFFS, Annual Council
Bluffs Bluegrass Music and
Cloggers Convention
SPBGMA, Box 95
Lake Ozark, MO 65049
816-665-7172
712-545-3375

June
BURLINGTON, Annual Steamboat Days
American Music Festival
807 Jefferson
Burlington, IA 52601
319-752-6365

June
SALEM, Annual Bluegrass Music Festival
RR 4, Box 135
Mt. Pleasant, IA 52641
319-258-7943

July
GUTHRIE CENTER, Annual Guthrie
Center Bluegrass Festival
SPBGMA, Box 95
Lake Ozark, MO 65049
816-665-7172
515-747-3542

August
ALLISON, Annual Butler County
Bluegrass Music Weekend
Rt. 6
Cedar Falls, IA 50613
319-266-4329

August
CENTRAL CITY, Annual Central City
Bluegrass Festival and Fiddlers
Jamboree
SPBGMA, Box 95
Lake Ozark, MO 65049
816-665-7172

September
COUNCIL BLUFFS, Westfair's
Annual Old-Time Country Music
Contest and Pioneer Exposition
8 Gayland Drive
Council Bluffs, IA 51501
712-366-1983

JAPAN
May, August
OHISO, SANDA, Annual Takarazuka
Bluegrass Festivals
B.O.M. Service, LTD.
6-5-18 Kawamo, Takarazuka
Hyogo 665, Japan
0797-87-0561

August
MINAMI-ASHIGARA, Annual Hakone
Bluegrass Festival
Bunny Mtn. Craft Service
2-37-8 Kami-Ikebukuro
Toshimaku 170, Japan
03-916-2027

October
OHISO, SANDA, Annual Red Clay
Bluegrass Festival
B.O.M. Service, LTD.
6-5-18 Kawamo, Takarazuka
Hyogo 665, Japan
0797-87-0561

KANSAS
March
LAWRENCE, Annual Kansas State
Winter Bluegrass Festival
SPBGMA, Box 95
Lake Ozark, MO 65049
816-665-7172

June, September
PAOLA, Annual Bluegrass Music Festivals
SPBGMA, Box 95
Lake Ozark, MO 65049
816-665-7172

September
WINFIELD, National Flatpicking
Championship Festival
Walnut Valley Association
Box 245
Winfield, KS 67156
316-221-3250

KENTUCKY
May, August
VANCEBURG, Annual River Bend
Bluegrass Festivals
Rt. 5
Vanceburg, KY 41179
606-796-3254

May, September
BEAVER DAM/ROSINE,
Bill Monroe's Bluegrass Festivals
Monroe Festival Headquarters
3819 Dickerson Road
Nashville, TN 37207
615-868-3333

June
SLADE, Annual National Mountain-Style
Square Dance Festival
General Delivery
Campton, KY 41301
606-668-6650

July
PRESTONSBURG, Annual Goins
Brothers Bluegrass Festival
Rt. 4, Box 137
Catlettsburg, KY 41129
606-928-2121

July
ELKHORN CITY, Larry Sparks
Bluegrass Festival
Box 23111
Lexington, KY 40523
606-272-2312

August
BEREA, McLain Family Band Festival
CPO 1322
Berea, KY 40404
606-986-8111

September
LOUISVILLE, Annual Kentucky Fried
Chicken Bluegrass Music Festival
KFC Corporation
P.O. Box 32070
Louisville, KY 40232
502-456-8704

LOUISIANA
June
COUSHATTA, Annual Red River
Valley Bluegrass Festival
Rt. 3, Box 264-A
Coushatta, LA 71019
318-932-5651

July
FOLSOM, Luke Thompson
Bluegrass Festival
Box 2063
Baton Rouge, LA 70821
504-775-1743

MAINE
June
CAMBRIDGE, Salty Dog Bluegrass
Music Festival
R.F.D. 1, Box 548
Cambridge, ME 04923
207-277-5624

July
SKOWHEGAN, Skowhegan Bluegrass
Festival
76 West River Road
Waterville, ME 04901
207-872-7082

September
BRUNSWICK, Annual Thomas Point
Beach Bluegrass Festival
Meadow Road
Brunswick, ME 04011
207-725-6009

MARYLAND
May, September
INDIAN SPRINGS/HAGERSTOWN,
Indian Springs Bluegrass Festival
132 School Street

Jerome, PA 15937
814-479-2271
216-641-3118

May, August, September
CONOWINGO, Bluegrass Festivals
Susquehanna Campgrounds
Conowingo, MD 21918
301-378-4294

June
HYATTSTOWN, Annual Bluegrass
Festival
25801 Frederick Road
Clarksburg, MD 20871
301-972-3398
301-253-3332

July
FAIR HILL, Annual Brandywine
Mountain Music Convention
Box 3504
Greenville, DE 19807
302-654-3930
302-475-3454

MASSACHUSETTS
August
HARVARD/LITTLETON, Beaverbrook
Bluegrass Festival
800 Massachusetts Avenue
Boxborough, MA 01719
617-263-3362

MICHIGAN
June
CHARLOTTE, Charlotte
Bluegrass Festival
Box 100
Brighton, MI 48116
313-227-1997

July
NIRVANNA, Whispering Winds
Bluegrass Festival
26104 Groveland
Madison Heights, MI 48071
313-546-7424
313-545-5873

July
WHITMORE LAKE, Annual South
Eastern Michigan Bluegrass Festival
8705 Nollar Road
Whitmore Lake, MI 48189
313-662-0983
313-449-2055

August
FLINT, Annual Flint Bluegrass Festival
400 N. Saginaw Street
Flint, MI 48503
313-232-8900

MINNESOTA
April
COLLEGEVILLE, Annual Swayed Pines
Folk Festival with Fiddle Contest
Box 761
St. Joseph, MN 56374
612-363-8693

August
MINNEAPOLIS, Bluegrass Festival
Minneapolis Bluegrass and Old-Time
Music Association
Box 9782
Minneapolis, MN 55440
612-374-3391

MISSISSIPPI
May
MERIDIAN, Budweiser Country/
Bluegrass Jamboree

Box 4177
Meridian, MS 39301
601-482-6161

June
WIGGINS, Magnolia State
Bluegrass Festival
Box 69
St. Stephens, AL 36569
205-246-4553

June
HOUSTON, Sleepy Hollow Annual
Bluegrass Festival
Box 821
Bruce, MS 38915
601-983-7271

MISSOURI
May
KANSAS CITY, Annual Sunset Arena
Bluegrass Music Weekend
SPBGMA, Box 95
Lake Ozark, MO 65049
816-665-7172
816-734-2929

May, September
DIXON, Bluegrass Pickin' Time
Box 466
Dixon, MO 65459
314-759-7716
314-759-6041

July, September
CHILLICOTHE, McCullough Park Family
Bluegrass Festivals
1560 Calhoun
Chillicothe, MO 64601
816-646-2795
816-646-0117

August
KAHOKA, Kahoka Festival of
Bluegrass Music
RR 1
Kahoka, MO 63445
314-853-4344

August
SILVER LAKE, Don Brown's
Bluegrass Festival
213 Chambers Road
St. Louis, MO 63137
314-868-2052

October
COLUMBIA,
Annual Bluegrass America
SPBGMA, Box 95
Lake Ozark, MO 65049
816-665-7172

December
LAKE OZARK, Anniversary
Bluegrass Music Awards
SPBGMA, Box 95
Lake Ozark, MO 65049
816-665-7172
314-365-3001

NEW JERSEY
July
VERNON, Vernon Valley/Great Gorge
Bluegrass Festival
Rt. 94
Vernon, NJ 07462
201-827-2000

August
STANHOPE, Annual Waterloo
Bluegrass Festival
Waterloo Village
Stanhope, NJ 07874
201-347-4700

NEW YORK
June
HILLSDALE, Sharon Mountain
Bluegrass Festival
Hospital Hill
Sharon, CT 06069
203-364-0270
203-364-5487

July
MONTICELLO, Bluegrass and Old-Timey
Music Weekend
Box 32
Monticello, NY 12701
914-796-1515

July
HILLSDALE/ANCRAM, Berkshire
Mountains Bluegrass Festival
Hazard Productions, Inc.
Box 127
N. Cambridge, MA 02140
617-492-0415

August
GREENWICH, Smokey Greene's
Annual Bluegrass Festival
Box 71
Schuylerville, NY 12871
518-695-3955

August
CORNING, Southern Tier Annual
Bluegrass Festival
R.D. 1, Box 293D
Mansfield, PA 16933
717-724-7572

NORTH CAROLINA
May
CHARLOTTE, Annual Mecklenburg
Bluegrass Fiddlers Convention
2200 N. Brevard Street
Charlotte, NC 28206
704-333-8104

**May, June, July, August,
September, October**
CROSSNORE, Bluegrass, Country,
and Gospel Music Festivals
Box 132
Crossnore, NC 28616
704-733-2807
704-733-0682

June
MOUNT AIRY, Annual Bluegrass and
Old-Time Fiddlers Convention
319 W. Oakdale Street
Mount Airy, NC 27030
919-786-6830

June
CLIFFSIDE, Annual Snuffy Jenkins
Old-Time and Bluegrass Music Festival
Rt. 2, Box 179
Mooresboro, NC 28114
704-657-5411

July
DENTON, The Doyle Lawson and
Quicksilver 3-Day Family Style Festival
25 Braddock Way
Asheville, NC 28803
704-274-5547

August
ASHEVILLE, Annual Mountain Dance and
Folk Festival
Asheville Chamber of Commerce
Box 1011
Asheville, NC 28802
704-258-5200

August
SHELBY, Bill Monroe's Annual Tarheel
Bluegrass Festival
Monroe Festival Headquarters
3819 Dickerson Road
Nashville, TN 37307
615-868-3333

September
CAMP SPRINGS, Annual Original
Bluegrass Music Festival
Rt. 6, Box 243-A
Burlington, NC 27215
919-228-7344
919-229-5767

September
BURLINGTON, Early Autumn Festival
Rt. 6, Box 243-A
Burlington, NC 27215
919-228-7344
919-229-5767

OHIO
April
CINCINNATI, Annual Appalachian
Festival
Box 996
Cincinnati, OH 45201
513-661-2004
513-381-3219

May, September
OTTAWA, Annual Bluegrass Reunions
Box 257
Ottawa, OH 45875
419-523-4433

May
LAURA, O.K.I. Bluegrass Association
Festival
605 Hulman Building
Dayton, OH 45402
513-293-0688

May, September
LUCASVILLE, Annual Scioto Furnace
Bluegrass Festivals
Rt. 4, Box 137
Catlettsburg, KY 41129
606-928-2121

May
CINCINNATI, Timberwolf Bluegrass
530 Probasco
Cincinnati, OH 45220
513-751-4151

June
PIONEER, Funny Farm Campground
Gospel Music Weekend
Rt. 1
Pioneer, OH 43554
419-737-2467

July
MT. GILEAD, Annual Independence Day
Weekend
Box 430
Thornville, OH 43076
419-362-3913

July
DeGRAFF, Bluegrass Festival
445 West Miami
DeGraff, OH 43318
419-523-4433

August
GREENWICH, North Central Ohio
Bluegrass Festival
Rt. 1, Swanger Road
Shilo, OH 44878
419-896-2683

OKLAHOMA
June
DAVIS, Annual Davis Bluegrass Festival
Box 38
Davis, OK 73030
405-369-3368
405-369-3204

August
HUGO, Grant's Annual Bluegrass and
Old-Time Music Festival
Rt. 2, Box 11-K
Hugo, OK 74743
405-326-5598

OREGON
July
HILLSBORO, Hillsboro Bluegrass Festival
Oregon Bluegrass Association
Box 1115
Portland, OR 97207

July
JACKSONVILLE, Peter Britt All Star
Bluegrass and Country Music Festival
Box 1124
Medford, OR 97501
503-779-0847

PENNSYLVANIA
May, September
GETTYSBURG, Semi-Annual Gettysburg
Bluegrass Camporees
3340 Fairfield Road
Gettysburg, PA 17325
717-642-8749
717-334-1731

May
CONESTOGA/LANCASTER, Pell Bros.
Bluegrass and Truth Spring Sing
Box 70
Kirkwood, PA 17536
717-548-3489

June
WIND GAP, Mountain View Park Festival
25 Ironia Road
Flanders, NJ 07836
201-584-2324
215-863-6569

June
ROBESONIA/READING, Annual
Eagles Peak Bluegrass Festival
R.D. 1, Box 247-A
Robesonia, PA 19551
215-589-4800
215-678-0160

July
BATH, Annual Bluegrass Camporee
Box 3
Bath, PA 18014

July
BRODBECKS, Tracy's Family Folk Festival
R.D. 1
Brodbecks, PA 17329
717-235-1837

September
SHARTLESVILLE, Annual Mountain
Springs Bluegrass Festival
Box 365
Shartlesville, PA 19554
215-488-6859

RHODE ISLAND
September
ESCOHEAG, French Cajun and
Bluegrass Music Festival
151 Althea Street
Providence, RI 02907
401-351-6312

SOUTH CAROLINA
November
MYRTLE BEACH, Annual South
Carolina State Bluegrass Festival
105 Lakeview Drive
Chester, SC 29706
803-385-6772

TENNESSEE
May
BRISTOL, Historic Bristol's Bluegrass
and Country Music Festival
New Kingsport Highway
Bristol, TN 37620
615-968-4033

June
KNOXVILLE, Redgate Bluegrass Festival
5802 Kingston Pike
Knoxville, TN 37919
615-588-5361

June
NASHVILLE, International Country
Music Fan Fair
2804 Opryland Drive
Nashville, TN 37214
615-889-7503

June
ELIZABETHTON, Annual Slagles
Pasture Bluegrass Festival
Rt. 3
Elizabethton, TN 37643
615-542-8615

July
MURFREESBORO, Dave Macon Days
1011 Grantland Avenue
Murfreesboro, TN 37130

August
NEW TAZEWELL, Cedar Grove
Campground Bluegrass Jamboree
Box 249
Middlesboro, KY 40965
606-248-3716

August
WARTRACE, Wartrace Pickin' and
Fiddlers Convention
Gallagher Guitar Company
Box 128
Wartrace, TN 37183
615-389-6455

January
NASHVILLE, SPBGMA Anniversary
Bluegrass Music Awards Convention
SPBGMA, Box 95
Lake Ozark, MO 65049
816-665-7172

TEXAS
May, September
BRONSON, Bluegrass and Old-Time
Music Festivals
Box 264
Sulphur, LA 70663

June
PERRIN, Southwest Bluegrass Club
Annual Bluegrass Festival
2222 Greenbrier
Irving, TX 75060
214-253-5620

September
GLEN ROSE, Oakdale Park's
Bluegrass Reunion
Box 548
Glen Rose, TX 76043
817-897-2321

October
EL PASO, Annual Border Folk Festival

Box 722
El Paso, TX 79944
915-541-7780

UTAH
August
ROOSEVELT, Bluegrass Festival
Box 1417
Roosevelt, UT 84066
801-722-4598

VIRGINIA
April
SMITHFIELD, Annual Bluegrass Festival
Rt. 3, Box 92A
Windsor, VA 23487
804-357-7211

May
MINERAL, Bill Harrell Annual Volunteer
Fire Dept. Bluegrass Festival
938 St. Geo Barber Road
Davidsonville, MD 21035
301-261-4110

May
McCLURE/COEBURN, Ralph Stanley's
Memorial Bluegrass Festival
Rt. 4, Box 226-A
Coeburn, VA 24230
703-395-6318

June, September
WAYNESBORO, Annual Bluegrass
Festivals
2487 Calf Mountain Road
Waynesboro, VA 22980
703-942-1068

July
DUBLIN, Pulaski's Old-Time and
Bluegrass Fiddlers Convention
605 First Street SE
Pulaski, VA 24301
703-980-6608

August
GALAX, Annual Old Fiddlers Convention
328A Kenbrook Drive
Galax, VA 24333
703-236-6355

WASHINGTON
May
SEATTLE, Northwest Regional
Folklife Festival
305 Harrison
Seattle, WA 98109
206-625-4410

July
DARRINGTON, Darrington Bluegrass
Festival
Box 249
Darrington, WA 98241
206-436-1006

Artist Index

Watch for these forthcoming titles:

MASTERS OF HEAVY METAL
Edited by Jas Obrecht

Unique musical techniques, personal creative insights and valuable technical detail from the greatest metal artists of hard-core rock and roll. From Jimi Hendrix to the Scorpions, Judas Priest, Def Leppard,and Eddie Van Halen — here is the ultimate documentary of intense, high-energy, guitar-dominated hard rock taken to the full extreme.Profusely illustrated. From the pages of Guitar Player Magazine.

paperback/$8.95 0-688-02937-X

Available in Winter 1984

ROCK KEYBOARD
Edited by Bob Doerschuk
Foreword by Keith Emerson

Fats Domino, Little Richard, Jerry Lee Lewis, Al Kooper, Leon Russell, Booker T. Jones, Elton John, Billy Joel, Michael McDonald, David Paich & Steve Porcaro, Brian Eno, Rick Wakeman, Thomas Dolby, and others — exclusive interviews, true history, astute analysis from the pages of Keyboard Magazine. Photos throughout.

paperback/0-688-02961-2

GUITAR GEAR
Edited by John Brosh

A comprehensive, practical guide to buying, maintaining, repairing, customizing all guitar equipment, accessories, and effects. How gear works and how it's made. Amps, bass guitar, guitar synthesizers, latest developments, information, insight, and inspiration from the pages of Guitar Player Magazine. Illustrated with photos and diagrams throughout.

paperback/0-688-03108-0

THE ART OF ELECTRONIC MUSIC
Edited by Greg Armbruster and Tom Darter
Foreword by Dr. Robert A. Moog

The first definitive book: the creative and technical development of an authentic musical revolution. From the Theremin Electrical Symphony to today's most advanced synthesizers. Scientific origins, the evolution of hardware, the greatest artists — in stories, interviews, illustrations, analysis, and practical musical technique. From the pages of Keyboard Magazine. Completely illustrated.

hardcover/0-688-03105-6
paperback/0-688-03106-4

From your bookstores or directly from the publisher.
Quill
A Division of William Morrow & Company
105 Madison Avenue
New York, NY 10016